THE RIDDLE OF BRONZINO

RICHARD AUTY

UNITED WRITERS
Cornwall

UNITED WRITERS PUBLICATIONS LTD
Ailsa, Castle Gate, Penzance, Cornwall.
www.unitedwriters.co.uk

British Library Cataloguing in Publication Data:
A catalogue record for this book is available from the British Library.

ISBN 9781852001902

Printed and bound in Great Britain by
United Writers Publications Ltd.,
Cornwall.

In memory of

Norman Oakey

(1918–1971)

Contents

	Page
Permissions	8
Plates	9
Acknowledgements	10
Introduction	11
I Bronzino's Life and Times	25
II Bronzino's Art	72
III The *London Allegory*: Why did Bronzino paint it?	89
IV The *London Allegory*: How did Bronzino paint it?	116
V The *London Allegory*: Who is who; what is what?	151
VI *De Morbo Gallico*	189
VII Conclusion: *The London Allegory*: What does it mean?	209
Timeline	241
Notes	244
Bibliography	253
Index	270

Permissions

Grateful acknowledgement is made to the following:

Plates 1, 11, 14 and 15 © The National Gallery, London

Plate 2 Budapest, Szépművészeti Múzeum (Inventory No. 163)

Plate 4 Royal Collection Trust/© Her Majesty Queen Elizabeth II 2018

Plate 5 Dr Peter Gordon

Plates 6 and 10 Galleria degli Uffizi, Florence

Plate 7 Bridgeman Art Library Ltd. and Manchester City Art Gallery, Manchester, UK

Plate 8 Pinacoteca di Brera, Milan

Plate 9 Philadelphia Museum of Art, Gift of Mrs. John Wintersteen, 1950-86-1

Plate 12 ©Edwin Giesbers/naturepl.com

Plate 13 Guillaume Perrin https://www.chambord.org/fr/histoire/le-chateau/les-salles/

Plates 16 and 17 Wellcome Collection

From Cheney I. 'Bronzino's *London Allegory*: Venus, Cupid, Virtue, and Time':

Quoted by permission of The University of Chicago Press

From Gaston RW 'Love's sweet poison: a new reading of Bronzino's *London Allegory*.' : Quoted by permission of *I Tatti Studies in the Italian Renaissance*

From Kandel ER. *The Age of Insight: The quest to understand the unconscious in art, mind, and brain, from Vienna 1900 to the present*: Quoted by permission of Penguin Random House

From Quétel C. *History of Syphilis*: Quoted by permission of Polity Press.

Plates

(As reproduced within this book.)

1 Bronzino: *An Allegory with Venus and Cupid* the '*London Allegory*'

2 Bronzino: *Venus, Cupid and Envy*, the '*Budapest Allegory*'

3 Anonymous, Angelo Bronzino

4 Flemish School: *Emperor Charles V*

5 Notice on a public footpath, Catalonia, Spain

6 Bronzino: *Portrait of Eleonora of Toledo with her Son Giovanni*

7 William Holman Hunt: *The Hireling Shepherd*

8 Bronzino: *Portrait of Admiral Andrea Doria as Neptune*

9 Bronzino: *Portrait of Cosimo I de'Medici as Orpheus*

10 Sandro Botticelli: *The Birth of Venus* (Detail)

11 Bronzino: *An Allegory with Venus and Cupid* (Detail to show Character A)

12 Hermann's tortoise

13 Salamanders

14 Bronzino: *An Allegory with Venus and Cupid* (Detail to show C's sting)

15 Bronzino: *An Allegory with Venus and Cupid* (Detail to show Character K)

16 Woodcut ascribed to Albrecht Durer: *Syphilitic*

17 Philip Galle: *Preparation and Use of Guayaco for Treating Syphilis*

Acknowledgements

Many have contributed to *The Riddle of Bronzino* – no book of this type can be the work of one man. A glance at the Bibliography tells you how indebted I am to the scholarship of many other people. Closer to home, the staff at East Cheshire Libraries have been unfailingly sympathetic and helpful tracking down more obscure texts for me. My wife Moira, Tom Kenny and Jill Turnbull critiqued drafts of the manuscript and made perceptive contributions which have enormously improved the quality and readability of the final product. Emma Kenny helped me to create Figures 1-5. My thanks to all of them.

Malcolm Sheppard at United Writers guided me through the publication process and I thank him for his patience and support.

Moira and my daughters, Kate and Jessica, have encouraged me throughout this project – as they have throughout many others – and they gave me the confidence to venture into print.

Despite all the help that I have received from so many people, I'm sure that the book contains errors, misperceptions and misinterpretations that will be immediately apparent to some readers: these are entirely my responsibility.

Introduction

Natural and man-made riddles, puzzles, codes and the like have fascinated us for millennia; the Sumerians set themselves riddles 4,000 years ago, the Riddle of the Sphinx is 2,500 years old; riddles are found in the Bible, Shakespeare's plays, Jane Austen's novels and the Harry Potter adventures. We can't help but worry away until we have solved them. Some – crossword puzzles, Sudoku, brain-teasers – are relaxing diversions; others – Fermat's Last Theorem – present formidable intellectual challenges; and others – the Enigma Code, the apparently anomalous orbit of Mercury – have more significant implications.

The 'worrying away' at a puzzle is often more entertaining than the sense of triumph we experience when '*Eureka!*' the solution becomes obvious. Possibly this will be the case here as we take faltering steps towards working out what a painting which has been in Britain's National Gallery since 1860 meant to those who first saw it in Florence almost 500 years ago and what it could mean to us today. It is a stunning, rather erotic but very odd painting by a man who was known as 'Bronzino'. No one has been able to decide exactly what it is all about. Love, deceit and disease have all been suggested as solutions to its riddle: none is compelling. Maybe we can do better? This book is an exploration of this painting, an extended meditation on the story behind it. Inevitably, this meandering, discursive book is a reflection of my own ideas, informed by my understanding of what others (and there have been many of them) have had to say about the painting. I hope my thoughts will stimulate you too to think about it, that they will trigger your own stream of ideas and increase the pleasure you get from looking at it – and at other paintings. Let's at least enjoy ourselves in our attempt to unlock its secrets.

Bronzino himself is also something of a riddle: we know very little about his life, and what little is known is somewhat contradictory. He wrote sophisticated lyric poetry and filthy burlesque verses; he created pious religious paintings and staid portraits of the great and the good of Florentine society, but also cheeky portraits full of blatant *double entendres*. And the painting we shall be looking at is a highly emotional and psychologically penetrating representation of lust, anguish, deceit and much more. He has challenged us with his painting – a riddle which 'intentionally … requires ingenuity in ascertaining its answer or meaning' (OED).

We'll begin our quest by going to look at the painting, giving it a title and learning a bit about Bronzino. Then we shall have to think about the circumstances in which it was created, before moving on to examine it in detail and attempting to discover for ourselves what it really means.

The best way for us to get to the painting is to walk in front of the neo-classical facade of the National Gallery in London's Trafalgar Square, through the crowds of tourists and street entertainers, and towards the post-modern Sainsbury Wing on the left-hand (west) side of the building. We'll go into the Gallery through the entrance to the Sainsbury Wing. Before going any further, let's pause to give thanks to the successive British governments which have made access to the country's wonderful galleries and museums free of charge. Then, climbing the wide, stone staircase and turning right at its summit we pass into the West Wing of the old building ('Paintings from 1510 to 1600'), walk through the first (Wohl) room and, steadfastly refusing to be seduced by the marvellous Venetian paintings on display there, we turn right to enter Room 8. There, on the wall in front of us, are three paintings by Bronzino. The largest of them dominates Room 8 (Plate 1). This is the painting which we have come to see. It immediately means something to us: we recognise that there are human figures in it, for example. But our ability to 'read' the painting is an acquired skill, it's the result of past experiences and training, it's an ability which would not necessarily be shared by the proverbial inhabitants of the remote depths of the Amazon rain forest.

Similarly, the text you are reading now comprises an arrangement of marks made in ink on a thin sheet of bleached wood-pulp. To 'understand' the page – to assign meaning to it – we have to follow several conventions. We have to have trained our eyes to follow the ink marks horizontally, from left to right, rather than from right to left or vertically, or even from left to right then from right to left on alternate lines (the boustrophedon or 'ox-ploughing' style). We have to recognise the Roman alphabet and we have to interpret it using the modern English language. So, squiggles making the shape 'dog' convey the idea of a four legged, domesticated mammal rather than the idea of a deity; and 'pan' signifies a receptacle in which to boil an egg rather than signifying a loaf of bread. If we were reading a page written in the sixteenth century we would have to follow somewhat different conventions: for example, the alphabet would be a bit different, 's' would look more like a modern 'f'. After sorting out the alphabet, the language, the grammar and the meaning of individual words, we have to put the words together so that we can assign a meaning to the whole page that takes account of the time and place at which the page was written. Meaning is culturally dependent; it also depends on the interpreter.

Ring-a-ring o' roses,
A pocket full of posies,
A-tishoo! A-tishoo!
We all fall down.

This nursery rhyme has been related to the outbreak of plague in seventeenth century England or even to the Black Death in the Middle Ages. The posies, for example, were the bunches of flowers and fragrant herbs that people would carry in the vain hope that they afforded protection against contracting the disease.[1]

O come, all ye faithful, joyful and triumphant!
O come ye, O come ye to Bethlehem;
Come and behold him . . .

This carol has been interpreted as a covert rallying call to supporters of Bonnie Prince Charlie. According to this reading, the Jacobites are the 'faithful' and they used 'Bethlehem' as code for 'England'. You have to know about the Glorious Revolution and the subsequent Jacobite Rebellion to understand this.[2]

These interpretations of relatively simple, familiar works have become well-known; but each is disputed. They provide good examples of how difficult it is to decide exactly what a text, be it a piece of language or a painting, means or was intended to mean.

The same applies to our painting. At root it is no more than an arrangement of marks made in coloured earth and powdered minerals on plaster-covered wooden planks. We can recognise forms in it and attempt to assign meanings to these forms and to the way in which Bronzino has chosen to assemble them – provided that we are able to follow the relevant conventions. People with no knowledge of western Renaissance art would be unable to understand the marks, just as many people would be unable to understand the marks on this page. And, just as we need some understanding of the contemporary language and culture fully to understand and appreciate the nursery rhyme and the carol, so we need to know about the culture in which Bronzino lived and the conventions of the visual language which he used before we can make a decent stab at working out what his painting might mean.[3]

The painting is extremely beautiful: the colour is opulent, and at first glance it conveys a sense of festivity, of innocent delight. It's fairly big; it's brightly coloured – that's not unusual; the dominant figures are nude – we are used to that. Nonetheless there is something troubling about it: the two principal figures are statuesque in their form and marmoreal in colour; she is a 'full frontal nude', shamelessly exposing herself; the couple are entwined in an overtly sexual embrace, kissing each other on the lips; the male figure is fondling the woman's left breast while squeezing her right breast in the crook of his right arm. At the same time his pert buttocks add a frisson of homoeroticism. To the right-hand side of the painting a chubby nude boy (we'll call him a *putto*) appears to be revelling in the rather dubious conduct of the two principal figures. Their nudity and activities may excite, delight, bore or offend. There are strange and disturbing figures in the background and other things, such as a couple of doves and some masks, none of which make immediate sense. Now the painting becomes intriguing: like it or loath it, you can't miss it and you have to ask yourself what it's all about.

Perhaps the label at the side of the painting will help us to sort out what on earth is going on here? It tells us that this is an oil painting on a wooden panel measuring 146 x 116cm (the material that the paint is applied to, be it wood, canvas or whatever, is called the 'support' and it is conventional to give the height of a painting first, followed by its width). It was painted about 1540-1550 by Bronzino, who lived from 1503 until 1572. It is called *An Allegory with Venus and Cupid*.[4]

Well, that's a bit of help but in many ways it raises more questions than it answers. In particular, we might remember from Classical mythology that Venus (presumably the woman at the centre of the painting and its most prominent figure) is the mother of Cupid who is embracing her in such a frankly erotic manner (at first sight the *putto* might be mistaken for Cupid but in fact Cupid is the boy with wings and a quiver in which to hold his arrows). Should we be adding incest to our catalogue of doubts about this painting? And what about the other figures and objects in the painting? The figure in the top right-hand corner must be Time – an elderly, winged man with an hourglass on his shoulder. And who was Bronzino; why did he paint this strange work; how did he expect it to be interpreted?

As we mull over these and other questions it will be important to remember that it is impossible for us to read Bronzino's mind and extraordinarily difficult really to understand how the work would have been appreciated or interpreted by the few people privileged to see it in the middle of the sixteenth century. This is a truism but pertinent nonetheless and should be regularly recalled throughout this book. LP Hartley was by no means the first to recognise the problem but he expressed it succinctly 'The past is a foreign country: they do things differently there.'[5] Hilary Mantel discussed this subject – and debunked many myths about life in the sixteenth century – in her Reith Lecture 'The Iron Maiden'[6]. She reminded us that 'The first lesson in understanding the past is not to assume anything about ethics, values, tastes.'

William Morris, the doyen of the Arts and Crafts Movement, paraphrased Ruskin, the great Victorian critic and commentator on art, to the effect that studying the Middle Ages teaches that 'the art of any epoch must of necessity be the expression of its social life'.[7] The French philosopher, Michel Foucault, expanded on this basic idea, observing that when people in a particular society at a particular juncture decide that something is true they do so within the context of an agreed set of principles or intellectual rules which make knowledge possible and govern peoples' behaviours, customs, ideas, beliefs and values. These beliefs and values are peculiar to the time and to the society: they determine the codes by which a culture functions; they set the context within which every participant in the culture will live and feel at home.[8] Foucault called each corpus of codes an 'episteme'. For us to understand how Bronzino and his contemporaries interpreted the world in which they found themselves we need to understand their episteme – the system of beliefs and rules which may make no sense to us but which they found utterly convincing and logically coherent. Conversely, ideas which we find convincing and which are fundamental to our understanding of the world would have been not only totally incomprehensible to them but, literally, unthinkable. To take just one facile example, many people in the sixteenth century believed in the power of astrology – we find it virtually impossible to share, empathise with or get to grips with this belief. On the other hand, Robin Fox warns of the dangers of 'Ethnographic Dazzle': the highly visible surface differences between human groups and cultures causing blindness to their underlying similarities.[9] Bronzino was confident that an ancient Greek myth, some two millennia old when he came to use it, could serve as a vehicle for a message that would be relevant to his contemporaries; so, while we are right to be cautious about attributing intentions and interpretations to Bronzino and those who saw his painting, we don't need to discount the suggestion that they had some ideas about it that are similar to our own. Our own episteme gives us different preoccupations and a different vocabulary with which to articulate the meaning that the painting has for us but we share our humanity with Bronzino, with sixteenth century Europeans, and with ancient Greeks.

Foucault found it difficult to understand how one episteme could change to another – how when people are governed by one set of intellectual rules they can break away from these to adopt a radically different set of rules. Whatever the mechanism, he recognised that the transition is likely to be painful and it may be violent – perfectly exemplified by the experience of Bronzino's society in the sixteenth century as it struggled, ultimately without success, to reconcile humanism, heliocentricity, Protestantism and nascent scientific rationalism with the prevalent episteme, which was heavily dependent on dogmatic Christian theology, a deep-seated concern for Salvation and Providence, a geocentric cosmos and a conviction in the influence of the supernatural. We bring contemporary preconceptions to our thinking about Bronzino and his work which are quite unlike those of its sixteenth century audience. We inhabit a different intellectual space to Bronzino and his contemporaries and we cannot escape our own episteme, so his painting will not have the same meaning for us that he intended it to have for his sixteenth century contemporaries. Try as we might, we shall never be able to experience the painting in the same way as they did. The effort to understand what it may have meant for them will nonetheless be a rewarding one and, who knows, we may find that the painting has a meaning for us also, even if that meaning would be incomprehensible to Bronzino.

Spare a moment to think about how we view paintings like this one and the others in the Gallery. And watch how the other people in the room are behaving. Most of us spend at the very most five minutes in front of an individual painting. Sometimes we are able to sit quietly on one of the benches that the Gallery provides and, if we are lucky, this is directly in front of the picture that has caught our attention (not so in the case of the Bronzino we have come to see) but even then it is unlikely that we will devote much time to an individual painting. This is rather strange. Linear works of art such as plays, films or pieces of music demand a much longer attention span than this and we wouldn't dream of spending only five minutes skip-reading a short story that interests us, let alone a novel. Most paintings reward much greater attention than they are usually given; all are to some degree elliptical, allowing both the artist and the viewer to bring creativity to the work – and in this book I'm trying to draw out as many as I can of the rewards that accrue from prolonged musing over Bronzino's very ambiguous painting. Of the many paintings in the Gallery that repay similar scrutiny, *The Ambassadors* painted in 1533 by Hans Holbein the Younger, and hanging in Room 4, has been the subject of an in-depth analysis in John North's book *The Ambassadors' Secret*.[10] The ambassadors are Jean de Dinteville on the left, and his friend Georges de Selve.

They were painted by Holbein while they were in London on a diplomatic mission on behalf of Francis I, King of France, to the court of Henry VIII. We shall meet de Selve again in his capacity as bishop of Lavaur.

Examples of Bronzino's work are to be found in many of the world's major galleries.[11] The National Gallery owns five paintings by Bronzino in addition to *An Allegory with Venus and Cupid*.[12] Not all are on display but before moving out of Room 8 turn to the left of *An Allegory with Venus and Cupid* to look at *Portrait of a Young Man* and *Madonna and Child with Saints* which are more typical of his work: Bronzino was best known as a painter of portraits and of religious works. Other paintings by him that can be seen in the UK are: *Saint Catherine* (Corsham Court); *Lady in Green* (Hampton Court Palace) and *Don Grazia de'Medici* (Ashmolean Museum, Oxford). Bronzino did paint another, more straightforward, allegory featuring Venus and Cupid, *Venus, Cupid and Jealousy* (or Envy) (c.1550) (Plate 2). This is in the collection of the Szépművészeti Múzeum in Budapest.[13] In the academic literature the two are referred to as the *London Allegory* and the *Budapest Allegory*. For simplicity, I'll talk about the *London Allegory* from now on – it's much easier than talking about *An Allegory with Venus and Cupid* and in any case that's not what Bronzino and his contemporaries would have called our painting, it is the title it was given when it entered the National Gallery's collection in the nineteenth century.[14]

The literature about the *London Allegory* and the society in which it was produced is voluminous – I make no claims to offer an exhaustive survey of the opinions and analyses that have been published over many decades: this is not intended to be a 'scholarly' text. In my exploration of the painting I have perforce relied on secondary sources and on synoptic histories of the period; the Bibliography reflects this. Most of the cited books and articles are fairly readily accessible to amateurs like me and my assumed readers with the help of competent booksellers, the local public library and search engines such as Google. When a foray into the academic literature becomes necessary, 'myJSTOR' is invaluable. The Notes and Bibliography sections towards the end of the book provide full citations to my academic sources, together with details of the other sources which have informed my commentary.

So, let's take a last, long, hard look at this remarkable painting. From now on we shall have to rely on reproductions of it – in this book, on postcards and a larger format print or in the *Companion Guide*[4] to the Gallery, all available in the National Gallery shop, and in books about art history – it is a famous and widely illustrated painting. Herein lies a problem: to what extent can a reproduction, no matter how good, convey the essence of a painting?

This question was addressed by Walter Benjamin (1892-1940), a highly influential German, Jewish, Marxist cultural critic and philosopher who made a seminal contribution to the way in which we think about reproductions of works of art. His colourful life ended with his suicide in Portbou, a Catalan village just over the Spanish Mediterranean border with France, while he was trying to escape from the Gestapo in Vichy France.[15] After crossing the Pyrenees on foot, he and his two companions reached Spain, where they thought they would be safe and allowed to move on to Portugal and thence to the USA, where they expected to be reunited with Adorno and other colleagues from the Frankfurt School. Franco's Spanish authorities, however, were dissatisfied with their visas and told them that they would be returned to France the following day. Meanwhile they were held in a hotel under police guard. In despair, Benjamin killed himself. Tragically, he died shortly before the news reached Portbou that the Spanish had had second thoughts – they were going to allow the three refugees to cross Spain and enter Portugal after all. *Passages*, a landscape-art memorial to Benjamin by the Israeli artist Dani Karavan now graces Portbou.[16] A complex man, Benjamin has been described variously as a serial adulterer, compulsive gambler and a user of mescaline and marijuana. He reportedly avoided conscription into the German army in the First World War by drinking large quantities of black coffee in order to simulate heart disease bad enough for him to fail the army medical examination.[17] Anticipating Marshall McLuhan by about 30 years he alerted us to the cultural implications of modern technology. Among his many highly influential papers and books, that which is of particular concern to us is *The Work of Art in the Age of Mechanical Reproduction*, published in 1936.[18] John Berger presented many of the ideas that Benjamin advanced in this book in his highly regarded TV series and book *Ways of*

Seeing. Benjamin focused on the new forms of art, photography and cinema in particular, arguing that their intrinsic reproducibility gives them a unique character. Benjamin's opening remarks are particularly pertinent for us as we study a painting from the middle of the sixteenth century. He begins by noting the difficulty encountered by artists in the past as they tried to copy their own and other's work, contrasting this with the ease of reproducing photographs and films today – and, by extension, the widespread reproduction of paintings in books, on postcards and on posters:

> Around 1900 technical reproduction had reached a standard that not only permitted it to reproduce all transmitted works of art and thus to cause the most profound change in their impact upon the public; it also had captured a place of its own among the artistic processes [i.e. in lithography, photography etc.]…[19]

He compares the modern techniques of mechanical, or process, reproduction (he lumps these together as 'technical' reproduction) with the older techniques such as the production of copies of original works by etchings or engravings (manual reproduction):

> Confronted with its manual reproduction, which was usually branded as a forgery, the original preserved all its authority; not so vis-à-vis technical reproduction… The reason is twofold. First, process reproduction is more independent of the original than manual reproduction... Secondly, *technical reproduction can put the copy of the original into situations which would be out of reach for the original itself.*[19] [My italics]

Benjamin used the word 'aura' to signify the essence of the original in its original context. He asserts that mechanical/ technical reproductions lack the aura of the original, indeed even the original is depreciated because it is no longer unique when reproductions are readily available. Should the reproduction be used in, for example, a greetings card or in an advertisement, its aura – indeed its very meaning – will be changed utterly.

Our experience of many paintings supports what Benjamin was saying. The originals of Monet's *Water Lilies*, Rothko's large colour-field paintings and Jackson Pollock's drip canvases do retain much of their awesome power even though reproductions have made them so familiar – size has a lot to do with this. But although Giotto's frescos remain in the Arena Chapel and so retain some of their aura, this is somewhat depleted by the now virtually secular atmosphere in what used to be a sacred space. And while the Basilica in Assisi is still a sacred space and a place of pilgrimage, the dense crowds there detract from complete engagement with the numinous frescos by Simone Martini, Lorenzetti and Giotto. Nonetheless, the right (albeit not the original) venue can also help a painting to retain an aura, so paintings gain something when seen in an atmospheric gallery such as the Isabella Stewart Gardner Museum in Boston, USA, or the Galleria Doria Pamphilj in Rome. Wherever we are fortunate enough to see an original painting, however, it's as well to remember that any aura that we do sense is unlikely to be the same as it had in its original setting. Specifically, the *London Allegory* now hangs in a large public space where it competes for our brief attention with innumerable other works. Large numbers of us are able to look at the *London Allegory*, whereas it was originally accessible to very few people indeed – and they were almost exclusively male members of the French aristocracy who saw it by invitation. The painting would have been displayed in a palace, probably with few other paintings; given its erotic connotations it may even have been kept in a private apartment to be viewed by an extremely small, privileged group. Our experience of it is unavoidably different from that of its original and intended viewers: further reasons why its impact and meaning for us cannot be exactly what Bronzino intended them to be.

All in all, hanging alongside many other paintings in the busy National Gallery, the *London Allegory* is unlikely to retain much of its original aura. Now consider how much worse our experience of the painting will be after we have left the Gallery – we shall have to rely on our notoriously unreliable memories and on technical reproductions, including those in this book. We shall use copies in which the surface of the work is completely smooth paper or card, all signs of under-painting, of changes of mind and of brush strokes will have been eliminated. Admittedly, in this particular case this may not matter very much because signs of Bronzino's workmanship are few and far between – but think about the difference between, for example, a Van Gogh original and its reproduction. And the colour in the reproductions will rarely match the vibrant colours of the original. Add to that the failure of some reproductions to include the whole of the painting – one, for example, has cropped all four sides of the *London Allegory*, thereby excluding the very important object which the girl is holding in her hand at its right-hand edge,[20] making it impossible fully to appreciate it. To me, in the present context, size is probably the most important issue. For obvious reasons, reproductions in books and on postcards cannot match the dimensions of the original. The *London Allegory* measures 146.1 x 116.2cm; the large copy for sale in the Gallery (Code PF75) 29.2 x 22.9cm and the Gallery's postcard 12.5 x 9.6cm. The impact of these reproductions will be much less than that of the original; our response to the painting will be completely different; its aura will have diminished.

Benjamin and his fellow critics and commentators on art wield enormous power: they influence what we see, what galleries choose to display and the opinions we hold about individual works, schools and artists. Ruskin defended Turner for his 'truth to nature' in the face of bewilderment, or in some cases derision, and promoted the Pre-Raphaelite Brotherhood. But he didn't get everything right – a salutary reminder not to take critical opinion as gospel truth: writing about Whistler's *Nocturne in Black and Gold: The Falling Rocket* (Detroit Institute of Arts, Detroit) Ruskin libelled the artist by saying that he was a 'coxcomb [for asking] two hundred guineas for flinging a pot of paint in the public's face.'[21] He had to pay Whistler a derisory one farthing in compensation, but no costs, leaving Whistler bankrupt and the reputations of both men severely damaged – Whistler got the last laugh by his reply to the defence counsel's question whether he thought the two day's work he had put into the painting was worth 200 guineas: 'No, I ask it for the knowledge of a lifetime'. This reply drew applause in court and has been used ever since by professionals of all types when challenged to justify their fees.

This was James Abbott McNeill Whistler (1834-1903), the American dandy who spent most of his adult life in Europe, particularly London, where he died. Now highly regarded, he was a leading member of the Aesthetic movement which comprised artists who used harmonies of colour and composition to convey the mood rather than the content of a painting (he gave some of his works musical titles such as 'symphonies' or 'nocturnes'). He is not to be confused with the now sadly overlooked Rex Whistler (1905-44).[22] As a student at the Royal Academy this Whistler was expelled for 'incompetence' so he moved to the Slade, where his talent was recognised by Henry Tonks (1862-1937)[23] who was instrumental in getting him his first commission – a mural which is still in the restaurant at Tate Britain.[24] Tonks was a surgeon and artist famed for his before-and-after pastel drawings of the results of plastic surgery performed by Sir Harold Gillies on the faces of soldiers mutilated in the Great War,[25] and for his tutoring at the Slade of Stanley Spencer, Paul Nash, David Bomberg, Percy Wyndham Lewis, William Orpen, Spencer Gore, and other luminaries.[26] He features in Pat Barker's novels *Life Class* and *Toby's Room*.[27] In the 1930s, by now a successful painter, illustrator and stage designer, Rex Whistler was a regular visitor to Plas Newydd, home of the Paget family, the Marquises of Anglesey (now a National Trust property) where in 1936-8 he created the largest canvas painting in the UK (17.7 x 3.7 m [58 x 12 feet]). It is a *trompe-l'oeil* seascape painting that fills a whole wall of the dining room with an imaginary vista of Italianate churches, castles, Snowdonian mountains and a complete harbour wall, with tricks of perspective that make the scenes appear to change when the mural is viewed from different parts of the room.[28]

Amazing though the mural is, the highlight for me of a visit to Plas Newydd is the artificial leg displayed there. It was made for Henry Paget, Lord Uxbridge, who commanded the British cavalry at the Battle of Waterloo. He was hit by a canister shot which had just missed Wellington's horse, Copenhagen. The thing I like about it, along with the fact that Paget survived the above-knee amputation, is the reported exchange between him and Wellington who was just next to him: Paget – 'By God, sir, I've lost my leg!' Wellington – 'By God, Sir, so you have!'[29] *Sang froid*, a stiff upper lip, and no post-traumatic-stress counselling for him – a different episteme.

Whatever the deficiencies of the reproductions that are available to us; regardless of the weakening of the aura of the original and recognising that our perceptions of the painting are unavoidably different to those of its original audience – 'we are where we are'. We should move ahead, try to answer some key questions about the *London Allegory* for ourselves and hope that by doing so we can enhance our enjoyment of this remarkable work:

> Our response to art stems from an irrepressible urge to recreate in our own brains the creative process – cognitive, emotional and empathic through which the artist produced the work … art is an inherently pleasurable and instructive attempt by the artist and the beholder to communicate and share with each other the creative process that characterizes every human brain – a process that leads to an Aha! Moment, the sudden recognition that we have seen into another person's mind, and that allows us to see the truth underlying both the beauty and the ugliness depicted by the artist.[30]

Let's begin by asking 'Who was Bronzino?' and setting the *London Allegory* into its artistic, social, historical and intellectual context before wrestling with its elusive meaning.

I

Bronzino's Life and Times

History: An account mostly false, of events mostly unimportant, which are brought about by rulers mostly knaves, and soldiers mostly fools.
(Ambrose Bierce, *The Devil's Dictionary*, 1911)

Bronzino (Plate 3) was born in Monticelli, a suburb of Florence in 1503; he died in Florence in 1572. So far, so good but there is not much else that we can say with confidence about his life – he is something of an enigma.[1] We owe much of our knowledge of Bronzino's life and work to Giorgio Vasari (1511-74), an artist who lived in Florence for much of his life and who wrote a massive tome *Lives of the Most Excellent Architects, Painters and Sculptors* (1550; 2nd Edn, 1568). We shall return repeatedly to Vasari. Vasari had little to say about Bronzino's early years[2], most of what we do know comes from a collection of some twenty recently recovered archival documents.[3] Bronzino's background was modest, he was the son of a butcher, but how his talent was recognised and then developed by established masters in Florence isn't known. According to Vasari, his first master was an unnamed hack painter, and he was later, briefly, a pupil of Raffaellino del Garbo; then at the age of about eleven or twelve, he entered the studio of Jacopo Pontormo (Jacopo Carrucci, from the village of Pontormo near Florence, 1494-1557), one of Florence's leading painters, where he remained until in his mid-twenties being trained by Pontormo in fresco and panel painting. There has been some confusion about Bronzino's real name, suggestions were made that his surname was Allori or Tori, but it is now thought that he was baptised Agnolo di Cosimo di

Mariano di Agnolo di Antonio di Agnolo di Toro,[4] reflecting the practice at the time which was to identify people by the names of their male forebears, rather than by a family name.[5] He acquired the nickname Bronzino in the 1530s – perhaps he had a rather bronzed complexion or hair, or the name refers to the sculpted feel of his figures; alternatively the name might refer to his rumoured homosexuality (known generically as 'sodomy' in those days) – copper and tin were code for the anus in contemporary burlesque poetry and bronze is an amalgam of these two metals.[6] Vasari alternates between referring to him as Bronzino and as Angelo. The practice of referring to eminent artists by nicknames looks odd to us but it was commonplace in Renaissance Italy, though rare in Northern Europe and more recently – we wouldn't think of calling David Hockney 'Bradford' or Grayson Perry 'The Dress'. So, the notoriously stubborn Cenni di Pepi (1240-1302) was named 'Cimabue' ('Ox Head'); Jacopo Robusti (1518-94) is known as Tintoretto because he was the son of a dyer (*tintore* in Italian); Paolo di Dono (1397-1475) was nicknamed 'Uccello' (bird) because of his many paintings of birds. Even 'Botticelli', which means 'little barrel' in Italian is a nickname, it was given to the corpulent Florentine civil servant who was the artist Alessandro di Mariano di Vanni Filipepi's brother.[7] The Sienese painter Giovanbattista Bazzi (1477-1549) was known as 'Sodoma' – you may be able to guess why; a poet friend of Bronzino was called 'Il Lasca' (the cockroach).

In 1522, when Bronzino was nineteen years old, the plague broke out in Florence so he and Pontormo left the centre of the city to avoid the Black Death and stayed three miles away at Certosa di Galuzzo, a cloistered Carthusian monastery.[8] Bronzino spent the remainder of his life in Florence, with the exception of a formative couple of years (1530-2) in Pesaro on the Adriatic working with Raffaellino del Colle on frescos for Guidobaldo, Duke of Urbino, and studying works by Parmigianino; he was in Rome in 1546 and 1548, and later in Pisa at the behest of Cosimo I de'Medici (Duke, and later Grand Duke of Tuscany), the ruler of Florence, for whom he worked as a court painter from 1539.[1]

As far as we know, Bronzino never married, never had a sustained relationship with a partner of either sex and never fathered a child. His deepest emotional relationships in adult life were with his master and friend Pontormo and with Cristofano Allori, an armourer whom he met some time before 1528. He ended up living in Allori's house in the Corso Adimari near to the Duomo (now renamed the Via Calzaiuoli) and after Allori's death, probably in 1541, he took on responsibility for the Allori household of five people, together with his own mother and his niece. His close association with the Alloris may account for the mistaken idea that his own family name was 'Allori'.[4] Cristofano's son, Alessandro Allori (1535-1607) became Bronzino's ward (possibly his adopted son), his pupil and his only real artistic follower;[9] he adopted Bronzino's name, as did his own son, the painter Cristofano Allori (1577–1621). Through his relationships with Pontormo and the Alloris Bronzino created a family for himself without which life would have been very difficult for them all, because in Renaissance Florence the family, reinforced by the guild and confraternity, provided the status, support and validation in both private and public life that was vital for self-defence and survival in periods of danger and hardship.[10] The family imposed order and maintained stability in society, so the life and structure of the family were important. The husband was indisputably the head of the family unit; he ruled over his wife, and the children were subordinate to their parents. The fundamental importance of the family unit as the lynch-pin of the society and the family hierarchy itself were both strengthened by making female sexuality acceptable only within the context of a monogamous marriage and by the idea that promiscuous women caused a deadly disease.[11] Bronzino's support of the Allori household and of his own mother and niece gave him security and a position in society but it came at significant expense to him – at a time when the average craftsman could expect to earn about 40 ducats a year he was spending 62 ducats a year just to feed his household, an indication of how successful his painting business was.[12] When he died Bronzino left all his pictures, drawings and materials to Alessandro, a gesture that was practical – he knew that they would be put to good use – generous and a response to Bronzino's own disappointment at Pontormo's failure to bequeath him his painting materials.

Alessandro, like Bronzino, became a court painter for the Medici; he painted portraits very similar in style to those of

Bronzino, to such an extent that some portraits that had once been attributed to Bronzino were later correctly accredited to Allori, who turned out to be one of the last Mannerist painters.

Elizabeth Pilliod's examination of the recently discovered documents has increased our previously sketchy knowledge of Bronzino's life and work[3] which had relied almost exclusively on the biography of him, published while he was still alive, by his fellow Florentine painter, and architect, Giorgio Vasari. Vasari was taught how to draw by his cousin the painter Luca Signorelli and, aged thirteen, he moved to Florence as the pupil of the painter Andrea del Sarto and the sculptor Baccio Bandinelli. When his patron, Alessandro de'Medici, with whom he had been educated, was murdered in 1537 he left Florence and wandered round Italy. When he returned to the city he joined the stable of painters in the court of Alessandro's successor, Duke Cosimo I. There Vasari was successful as a painter of historical frescos, as a designer of festivals (an important part of the work of a court painter) and as the architect of the Uffizi. He was knighted by the pope in 1571 and was recognised throughout Italy as the authority on art. His influence has extended well beyond the confines of Italy in the sixteenth century. He is now credited with initiating the modern discipline of Art History through his book *Lives of the Most Excellent Architects, Painters and Sculptors* published in 1550; the biographies of more painters, including Bronzino, were added for the Second Edition, 1568. Vasari's thesis was that the arts had reached a pinnacle of perfection in Classical Greece and Rome, that they had declined thereafter in what became known as the Dark Ages and that in Italy since about 1300 there had been 'the restoration or rather the renaissance' of the arts. Working his way through prominent and now less familiar Italian painters from Giotto, Masaccio, Leonardo da Vinci and Raphael, Vasari reached Michelangelo, painter, architect and sculptor, who was his hero, the *non plus ultra*, after whom all would be mere dwarfs.

A meander: *non plus ultra* (*ne plus ultra* is an accepted alternative) comes from the Latin *nec plus ultra* ('nothing farther beyond'), said to have been inscribed on the Pillars which, according to Greek mythology, were built by Hercules near the Straits of Gibraltar to mark the edge of the then known world. The inscription warned sailors and navigators to go no farther. It is thought that Giorlamo Fracastoro, personal physician to the young Holy Roman Emperor Charles V and another amazing inhabitant of this remarkably small world whom we shall encounter again,[13] suggested *Plus Oultre* as an appropriate imperial motto, signifying Charles's intention to ignore the ancient warning, take risks, surpass himself and go 'farther beyond', especially over the ocean to the Americas. It then became the motto of Habsburg Spain and featured on the Spanish dollar as well as on Habsburg propaganda in Europe.[14] Today the inscription, along with the Pillars of Hercules, is featured on both the national flag and the emblem of modern Spain – ironically so in light of Spain's loss of its empire across the ocean.

The title of Vasari's great work *Lives of the Most Excellent Architects, Painters and Sculptors* is a bit of a mouthful, so it's often referred to simply as *Lives of the Artists*. This is misleading – in Vasari's day there were no 'artists' as we know them. Instead painters, sculptors, architects, goldsmiths, glassblowers, ceramicists and other craftsmen were *artifice*, artisans: no European language had a word for 'artist' or differentiated 'artists' from 'craftsmen'.[15] The status of painters was the same as that of all *artifice*, they were not yet freighted with our romanticised idea of the artist as an independent, bohemian, iconoclastic, free-spirited genius – that wouldn't come to fruition until the nineteenth century. And they were more versatile than they became in later centuries – Michelangelo was a painter, a sculptor, a poet, a musician and a designer of fortifications. In keeping with this view of 'art', great importance was attached to the excellence of the craftsmanship which went into making the *artifice*'s products – and their paintings and sculptures were seen very much as 'products' which had to display the immaculate application of all the *artifice*'s skills. Works of art were functional and skilfully fashioned objects, made on commission for profit, they were not primarily personal expressions.[16] Those *artifice*, like Bronzino and Vasari, who were employed by the Renaissance princes did manage to establish a higher status for themselves within the hierarchy of court staff and some, like Velazquez in the next century, were ennobled. The very greatest of them dressed as courtiers and accepted 'honoraria' for their work so that they could mix with nobles whose rank prevented them from working for pay. Most court *artifice*, though, received a salary and board and lodging in return for painting portraits, decorating rooms, painting furniture, designing tapestries and, importantly, designing the sets and costumes for the frequent festivals, carnivals, celebrations and weddings that were such a feature of courtly life. Vasari earned enough to be able to afford to build himself an imposing house, making a public display of the status that he thought he deserved. Bronzino, as we have seen, was able to support a large household.

Today we love to visit Florence and the other northern Italian Renaissance towns to feast our eyes and minds on the spectacular art and revolutionary architecture that abound there. The Duomo in Florence, the Baptistery in Pisa and Raphael's Stanza in Rome – all make these places unique. But our experience today gives a very partial idea of what these cities were like when this marvellous art was being created. For sure, these were vibrant, bustling cities in the fifteenth and sixteenth centuries but they were also violent, edgy places in which all but the most privileged struggled to eek out a precarious existence.

John Julius Norwich says that 'The beginning of the sixteenth century was an exciting time to be alive'.[17] That might possibly have been true if you were one of Europe's rulers, though they had to worry about succession, rebellion, assassination, shortage of money, religious schism and the territorial ambitions of their rivals, but for lesser mortals life could be a gruelling and seemingly arbitrary succession of disease, siege, repression, exploitation and famine. Bronzino was not exactly a lesser mortal but nor was he an aristocrat; life was hard for him, he had to compete for work with the many other talented *artifice* active in Florence at the time and, of course, he had to remain healthy.

Florence was past its republican best by the first half of the sixteenth century and it was not at ease with itself.[19] Its intellectual dominance of the Italian peninsula was being eclipsed, first from about 1498 onwards, by Rome, and after 1527, by Venice. The city-state comprised the walled town itself together with the surrounding countryside, called the *contado*, and the towns and villages within it. The population, about 70,000 people in 1520, fell to about 50,000 during Bronzino's lifetime and only rose to 70,000 again in 1650. Inside the city walls there were some 180 churches, 270 woollen-goods shops (much of Florence's wealth came from the wool trade), 66 apothecaries' shops, 44 goldsmiths and jewellers, 54 sculptors and stonemasons and 33 banks. The Medici family, who came to dominate Florence in the fifteenth century, had made their money as wool merchants and bankers.[19]

Like everyone else in Europe, the Florentines in the sixteenth century had to contend with risks that they were virtually powerless to mitigate. There were the endemic risks of famine and natural disasters and of diseases such as tuberculosis and malaria. Epidemic disease was a constant threat, plague in particular, but also scarlet fever, typhus, cholera, smallpox, the sweating sickness and many others, none of which was well understood. Plague was terrifying. At the beginning of the centuries-long Second Pandemic (which hit England in 1348: the Black Death, which killed about 60% of the inhabitants of London in the space of nine months), plague reduced the population of Florence from 115,000 in 1338 to 50,000 by 1351. The pandemic dragged on in Florence with minor outbreaks every few years until in 1630-3 the last major epidemic killed about 10% (7,000) of the population.[20] (This epidemic struck England in 1665 as the Great Plague; it was chronicled by Daniel Defoe and Samuel Pepys, killed at least 15% of the population and caused Newton to flee Cambridge). Bronzino and his contemporaries were not to know that their city would be relatively plague-free until 1630: they lived with the knowledge that any of the many relatively small outbreaks of the disease could quickly explode into one that would leave a random one-in-three of them dead by the end of the week. During Bronzino's life-time there were minor epidemics in 1505, 1509 and 1522 and a more serious one in 1527-31.[21] We choose to forget how vulnerable we still are to some viral epidemics and how we may soon once again be defenceless against bacterial epidemics, of which plague could be one, if antibiotic resistance really takes hold. Our complacency would surely have exasperated our ancestors. The influenza epidemic that killed more people than the First World War is now less than a distant memory and bird-flu never came to very much; the Ebola outbreaks have been far away and relatively quickly contained by good public health measures. We have been incredibly fortunate that HIV-AIDS is so difficult to transmit – even so it was bad enough in Europe and the USA in the 1980s, and it's still a disaster in the developing world; but imagine what would have happened when it first broke out and before there were effective counter-measures had it been transmissible by droplets in coughs and sneezes (like pneumonic plague). One wonders how Bronzino and his contemporaries coped with this threat of a rapid and painful death hanging over them. And how they dealt with the more mundane problems of toothache, hernias, broken bones, stomach ulcers and the like for which they had no effective pain relief other than alcohol (stupefying) and opium (addictive), no recourse to surgery and little prospect of a cure for most diseases. We should empathise with Cardinal Giovanni de'Medici rushing to attend the conclave that convened after the death of Pope Julius II in 1513. Despite the access which Giovanni's position and wealth gave him to the best that medicine could offer, agonising pain from his anal fistula exacerbated by his gross obesity and his stomach ulcer prevented him riding a horse, so he had to be carried over atrocious roads in a litter all the way from Florence to Rome.[22] Bad enough: the ravages of syphilis were worse (Chapter VI).

Religion attributed the suffering that was an inescapable part of life to God's divine plan. Prayer, piety, religious ceremonies, fasting and moral rectitude were believed to prevent or ameliorate the impact of malign providence, so they played an important part in any regime intended to relieve suffering. No doubt they were valuable sources of consolation. Unfortunately, however, even the certainties of religion were beginning to look increasingly insecure. The authority of the Catholic Church was being challenged as never before; the ability of the saints to intercede on a petitioner's behalf was denied. Bronzino's contemporaries did have access to Italian translations of the Bible – Nicolò Malermi's *Malermi Bible* in 1471; Fra Zaccaria of Florence published a translation of the New Testament in 1542 and Santi Marmochino the Old and New Testaments in 1543. They had taken what they read in the Bible at face value – or they had been content to accept their Church's exegesis of it. But suddenly they found themselves on shaky ground. Luther published his ninety-five theses in 1517, attacking the profane issue of the sale of indulgences and opening a fierce debate on fundamental precepts of belief such as the Real Presence at the Mass (transubstantiation), the existence of purgatory and the moral authority of individual conscience as opposed to the teaching and practice of the Church. His challenges added to those which were already stimulating debate about the legitimacy of some of the other traditionally held beliefs and assumptions that underpinned European society and culture.[23] And now that printed works were more readily available these challenges became widely known and debated – a dramatic change from the days of Luther's intellectual forebears, Wycliffe in fourteenth-century England and Hus in fifteenth-century Bohemia.

Moves to reform the Catholic Church and to stop some of the worst excesses of the clergy and the Curia had begun in the previous century. In particular the Conciliar Movement had tried to give Councils of the church authority over the pope but it had fizzled out, unable to overcome the power of the Vatican and of other vested interests.[24] Luther and his followers then initiated the devastating reform which became Protestantism, prompting the Catholic Church's response formulated at the Council of Trent (1545-63): rejecting rapprochement and launching the Counter-Reformation. In the second two thirds of the sixteenth century, the blood-soaked popular uprisings and wars of religion which followed the Reformation and which continued well into the seventeenth century tore Christendom apart and much of, effectively co-terminus, mainland Europe with it. In Italy Protestants found some early adherents to their cause, notably amongst a group of senior clerics – called the *Spirituali* because they believed that the Holy Spirit was the force by which God sent grace through faith. An attempt was made, by Duke Cosimo amongst others, to reconcile traditional Catholic beliefs and practices with the Protestant challenges at a colloquy in Regensburg in 1541 but this was abortive, the *Spirituali* and others fled Italy to join their Protestant friends in Switzerland[25] and Italy, including Florence, pretty well remained loyal to the Roman Church thereafter.[26] So the peninsula escaped the worst of the cataclysm that soon engulfed Europe north of the Alps, sparing us the need to get into the tortuous detail of the Reformation in northern Europe.

Isabella, Queen of Castile (the 'Extirpator of the Muhammadan Heresy' according to her tomb in Granada, 1504) sponsored Columbus's 1492 voyage to the West, in the expectation that he would discover a new route to the Orient which, as well as providing trade and gold, could be used to attack Islam from the rear and open a new route to the Holy Land. Columbus failed to help with the extirpation of Islam but he gave Spain plenty of gold and even more silver. He gave Europe plenty else besides plunder: potatoes, tobacco, maize, a profound change in how the world was perceived, and disease. And the transfer, good and bad was a two-way one which is known as the 'Columbian Exchange'.

Columbus's expansion of the known world to the West was but the most dramatic of the many consequences of the European voyages of discovery. The Portuguese, capitalising on Vasco da Gama's discovery of the sea route from Europe to India in 1498, overthrew the powerful Muslim kingdom based on the town of Malacca (in modern Malaysia) in 1511. This enabled the Portuguese to dominate the Strait of Malacca – valuable then and now as the world's most important route from the Indian to the Pacific oceans: a third of the world's traded goods pass this way every year en-route between Europe and the Middle East (oil) and China, Japan, Indonesia and the other countries of East Asia, giving it frightening strategic significance as the USA and China jostle for dominance in the region. Muscovy was expanding eastwards: over the course of the century its population doubled and by 1600 its eastern border extended from Archangel on the White Sea to Astrakhan on the Caspian.

There was exploration of the cosmos, too. Copernicus published *De revolutionibus orbium coelestium* in 1543 – posthumously for fear of the reaction that it would provoke. Less well known is the fact that he wrote an outline of his ideas 30 years before. The *Commentariolus* (1514) was not published in his lifetime, but it was circulated quite widely, to such an extent that in 1533 Pope Clement VII and several of his cardinals attended lectures in Rome at which the pope's secretary, Johann Albrecht Widmannstetter, explained the ideas presented in the *Commentariolus*.[27] Copernicus proposed seven cosmological postulates, amongst them: the centre of the earth is not the centre of the universe; the stars are immovable, their apparent daily motion is caused by the daily rotation of the Earth; the Earth is moved in a sphere around the Sun, causing the apparent annual migration of the Sun; all the spheres revolve about the sun as their mid-point, and therefore the sun is the centre of the universe; 'what appear to us as motions of the sun arise not from its motion but from the motion of the earth'.[28] The pope found the lectures interesting and he was sympathetic to Copernicus's ideas; he may well have discussed them with his Medici relatives. Over the coming years Copernicus expanded on his ideas, modified some of them and presented observational evidence and calculations in support of them in *De Revolutionibus*, a difficult, technical work. One way or another, heliocentricity must have been a topic of discussion in the Medici palace in Florence long before 1543.

To add to the risks of famine and pestilence which beset all the peoples of Europe and their worries about the validity of their fundamental beliefs, the Florentines in the sixteenth century, Bronzino amongst them, had to contend with immediate and interdependent threats of war, political instability, corruption and extortion. The economic environment was fragile too; invasions and changes of regime led to uncertainty at best, theft of a state's treasury and destruction of its infrastructure at worst. The sudden influx of vast quantities of gold and silver from the Americas began to lead to damaging inflation in the latter half of the century.

Every individual was subject to the whim of an often volatile and capricious superior in a rigid hierarchical society and if your city was overrun by enemy troops you could expect rape, pillage and slaughter. Some 25,000 people, 85% of the population, died in the fire that ended the siege of Magdeburg in Saxony in 1551[29] and 13,000 died in the sack of Rome in 1527. If you were too closely identified with the wrong (i.e. losing) faction torture, mutilation, incarceration, exile or execution could follow – and not an easy execution by firing squad but public evisceration, botched beheading or immolation. Civil unrest and popular protest readily led to bloody and destructive violence, usually provoking an equally violent response and savage reprisals. 100,000 died in the Peasants' War in central Europe (1524-5). In England the Prayer Book Rebellion of 1549 resulted in over 5,500 deaths.[29] Bronzino died three months after the start of the St Bartholomew's Day Massacre during the first 24 hours of which French Catholics, probably instigated by Catherina de'Medici, slaughtered between 5,000 and 10,000 Protestants – more Christians died at the hands of other Christians in the massacre than were martyred by the Roman Empire in its entire existence. Pope Gregory XIII was so thrilled when he was told of the massacre that he declared a Jubilee Day of public festivities in Rome and celebrated a High Mass with tremendous pomp and ceremony. He also commissioned two frescos for the Vatican by Vasari, one depicting the Battle of Lepanto and the other, to hang alongside it, the wondrous Massacre.[30]

For Bronzino, living in Florence may have been a bit like living in Kabul, Baghdad or some parts of Mexico City today – never too sure whom to trust, never too sure who will be in power and seeking vengeance tomorrow, never confident that one's business, savings, property, person or family are safe. One quarter of babies born in sixteenth century Florence would die before their first birthday; half before their 10th; life expectancy at birth was 25 years and someone who reached adulthood could expect to die in round-about their 55th year.[31] So Bronzino, who died in 1572 aged 69, had a long life. He was fortunate enough, or canny enough, to enjoy the patronage of the rich and powerful, giving him a relatively comfortable standard of living and of hygiene, both of which will have contributed to his longevity and that of other Renaissance *artifice*; popes lived for even longer;[32] the Medici didn't do so well.

Many Europeans interpreted the precariousness of their lives and the disjointedness of their world as unequivocal signs that the world was about to come to an end. Their belief in the Last Days stemmed from interpretations of scripture giving the earth a life-span of six thousand years, more than five thousand of which had already elapsed. The risk of being conquered by the Ottoman adherents of another religion (which forecast the end of the world in the Hijara year of 1000, 1592 in the Christian calendar), caused panic in Europe.[33] The Fifth Lateran Council of 1512 tried to calm nerves by forbidding preaching on the Last Days but the almost hysterical reaction to the perceived threat contributed to the febrile political and theological climate for much of the fifteenth and early sixteenth centuries. Lest we begin to feel too superior it's worth remembering the equally deluded and horrendously expensive panic over the 'millennium-bug' (Y2K) issue created by the Information Technology community in our lifetime. The corollary to the belief that the world was about to end was an added sense of urgency about mankind's obligation to make the world as close as possible to how God wanted it to be – to create God's kingdom on earth. God's wrath should He find the earth to be in a poor state when He brought it to an end would be only too imaginably bad. Clearly, there was a long way to go; immediate, fundamental reform was needed in every facet of life,[34] including, unfortunately, reform of the Catholic Church, just at the time when the Church should have been in the vanguard of efforts to deal with fear about the millennium. If the Church wouldn't reform itself, external forces were gathering to do the job for it.

The actions of the papacy affected the simplest domestic decisions and the most complex issues of diplomacy, economics, politics and war. The Church was a super-state, a rapacious raiser of taxes, a juggernaut which acted as king-maker, power-broker, and intellectual bully. It united the peoples of Europe, gave them a sense of community and provided meaning to life in a frightening world. Growing up in a secular society it is difficult for us to understand what a profoundly unsettling experience the challenge to the Church's authority must have been in an era when religion was an integral part of everyday life. The Reformation was an existential threat to everyone, whether they favoured Reformation or were opposed to it – consequently, the response on both sides was visceral and savage. The Church's default reaction to criticism was to cry 'heresy', excommunicate the offender and invoke the formidable powers of the inquisition. Rome's bungled reaction to Luther's legitimate concerns about the administration of the Church and his critique of dogmatic theology polarised the debate and led to Reformation where compromise might have been sufficient.[35]

The peninsula in which Bronzino lived was home to city-states (Venice, Florence, Sienna, Padua, Urbino etc. – many of which made substantial contributions to the Renaissance), predominantly Florence, in the north; Venice to the East; the Papal States in the middle of the country and the kingdoms of Naples and Sicily in the south. It would not become the politically unified state of 'Italy' for another 350 years (Garibaldi), just as the plethora of powerful and not-so-powerful Germanic states in the Holy Roman Empire of Bronzino's time would not become 'Germany' until the middle of the nineteenth century (Bismark). The Italian language in various dialects was essentially common throughout the peninsula, and there were tentative moves towards Italian unification; although none of the component states was powerful enough to impose it, several were strong enough to prevent it –

stalemate. As well as being very jealous of their independence, fiercely competitive and ready to go to war with each other at the slightest provocation, the various polities were constantly threatened by the expansionist ambitions of at least four regional hegemons: the Popes who wanted to increase their writ on earth; the Holy Roman Emperor; the King of France and the Ottoman Sultan.

During the fifteenth century wealthy Florence, nominally a republic but largely in the hands of the Medici family, had been at the forefront of the intellectual and artistic revolution which was later known as the Renaissance. A small group of, almost exclusively, men, notably Erasmus of Rotterdam (1466-1536), amalgamated Christian and classical Greek and Roman learning to change the medieval, essentially religious, approach to life and its meaning to one in which man and human nature were considered to merit study in their own right. The Christian Humanists[36] came to consider that the purpose of a man's life was to strive to extend his intellectual powers in order to enhance his awareness of God; they would have been distressed to know that in time their learned pursuits would become ends in themselves. Their philosophy provided the intellectual fuel for the Renaissance, and like any revolution it provoked a reaction. In Florence Savonarola used his oratorical skills to vilify the new ideas and foment disaffection in the Florentine people, who were already restless because of a coincidental invasion of Italy by the French, their traditional allies, who were *en route* to the Kingdom of Naples. Savonarola incited the Florentines to replace Medician rule with a republic – which then proceeded to burn him. The Spanish restored the Medici to power in 1512.

In 1494 Charles VIII, King of France ('a young and licentious hunchback of doubtful sanity'[37]) had led a 25,000-strong army into the peninsula, starting what turned out to be a seven decades long series of invasions by one regional power or another. The immediate *causus belli* was Naples, which was in Spanish hands. It was contested by France supported by Cardinal Giuliano della Rovere, and Spain supported by the Borgia Pope Alexander VI. The French were welcomed by the inhabitants of Milan, Lucca and Pisa. Florence had fought a long, debilitating war with Pisa, which had served as its port since the Florentines had occupied the city in 1406. In the following decades the port began to silt up, restricting access to the sea and when France invaded northern Italy in 1494, Pisa took the opportunity to reclaim its independence. Fifteen years of inconclusive battles and sieges followed. The war was prosecuted so incompetently that the Florentines arrested, tortured and beheaded their own military commander. However, the war of attrition eventually so depleted the resources of Pisa that the city had to be sold, first to the Visconti family from Milan and then, in 1509, back to Florence again.

The French were also welcomed by the Florentines; enthused by Savonarola's eschatology, they were delighted to see the French depose the ruling Medici and send Piero de'Medici, 'The Unfortunate', and his brother, Cardinal Giovanni, into exile in 1494. The French went on to occupy Rome and to reach an accommodation with the pope, but their brief occupation of the city was brutal. Then they marched to Naples where they were welcomed and, shortly thereafter, resented. Meanwhile, rival powers had been getting themselves organised. Ferdinand and Isabella, dual monarchs of Spain, were not willing to see their Neapolitan dependency fall into French hands; the Holy Roman Emperor Maximilian didn't want French power to grow and the pope had his own designs on Naples. Milan, frightened by the success of its French allies, changed sides. The Spanish regained Naples quite quickly and in concert with the other powers formed a Holy League (the League of Venice, 1495) which drove the French out of Italy for the time being, setting the scene for years of invasions, sieges, battles and mayhem.

In the first third of the century the Italian peninsular ('Italy') was riven by this series of conflicts which are known as the 'Italian Wars'.[38] These were struggles for power and land between the French monarchy, the papacy and the Holy Roman Emperor, who by this time was always a member of the Habsburg dynasty. The three parties came together and split apart in various permutations of alliances, Leagues and enmities and secured the help of other players from time to time, all vying for power, land and status. None turned out to be sufficiently strong decisively to defeat the others.

Florence's situation in the sixteenth century, therefore, was complex. Savonarola had exposed the internal weaknesses of Florentine governance and the French exposed the military vulnerability of the state. So, by the time Bronzino was born (1503), Florence had declined and Rome had gained ascendancy to become the intellectual and political leader of Italy. In its turn Rome would be sacked by the Holy Roman Emperor in 1527 to be eclipsed by Venice, so that towards the middle of the sixteenth century many of the composers, writers and artists who had been working in Rome moved to Venice, quickly adding lustre to that city. Charles V's preference for the Venetian painter, Titian, rather than any one of the *artifice* then working in Florence or Rome reflects this change in status for a city which had been out of favour for many years. Previously, Venice had angered Pope Julius II by seizing cities in the Romagna which had traditionally been his. Julius II, of the della Rovere family was elected pope in 1503 in succession to Alexander VI, of the rival Borgia family.[40]

The papacy was found to be in a mess when Julius took over. Key papal cities had been lost, Bologna and Perugia to rebellion, Faenza and Rimini had been grabbed by the Venetians. And the French were determined to compensate for their loss of the Kingdom of Naples to the Spanish by controlling as much of northern Italy as they could. They still ran Milan, controlled the Florentine Republic and had allied themselves with Mantua (supposedly within the Emperor's sphere of influence) and with Ferrara (a papal dependency). Reported to have ordered Michelangelo, who was carving a statue of him: 'I am no schoolman. Put a sword in my hand, not a book.'[41] Julius began by trying to take back the papal cities. Leading his troops in person Julius recovered Perugia and Bologna, both without a fight. Then, diplomacy having failed to persuade the Venetians to yield Faenza and Rimini, he managed to cobble together the League of Cambrai, allying the French, the Spanish and the Empire with the papacy to strip the Venetian Republic of all its mainland possessions. The Battle of Agnadello (1509) left the republic with only the island city itself. It was widely believed that this was God's punishment for Venice's sins – sodomy, ostentatious dress, nunneries turned into brothels. The Doge introduced a rigorous austerity programme and preparations were made to withstand a siege. In the event, the Venetians managed to avert the danger and to rebuild their state through a mixture of good fortune, skilful diplomacy and some military might, aided by the defection of many of the lost cities away from the League and back to Venice. The pope did a deal with the Venetians, angering his French allies who were thereby denied some of the expected spoils of the war and then he made matters worse by trying to turn the Emperor against them as well. By 1517 Venice had recovered most of the land lost ten years before. Thereafter a policy of cautious neutrality kept most of the Republic secure for the next three hundred years. Such studied neutrality was not a straightforward option for the Florentines, whose ruling elite was intimately linked to the papacy and, through marriage, to both the Emperor and the King of France.

After his victory at Agnadello Julius wanted to rid himself of his French and Spanish allies for whom he felt he had no further use. He demanded that the other Italian states, including Venice, join him in another Holy League to drive out the 'foreign barbarians'. The city-state of Florence refused to join but one of its prominent citizens came to play a key part in subsequent events, for the pope chose Cardinal Giovanni di Lorenzo de'Medici (Giovanni, 1475-1521) to lead the Holy League in the field. This intelligent but fat, idle man was the second of the three sons of Giovanni Lorenzo de'Medici, 'Lorenzo the Magnificent' (1449-92), and the one who had been ear-marked by his father as the family's candidate for high ecclesiastical office: he had been made a Cardinal at the uniquely early age of thirteen. After increasingly senior Church appointments while exiled from the Republic of Florence he was now the head of the Medici family.

The Florentines' refusal to join his latest League infuriated the pope. They had no quarrel with Spain and preferred not to antagonise the French, for even though the French had supported the Pisan rebellion, they had also briefly occupied Florence in 1494 and liberated it from the Medici's 'tyrannical' rule and supported the popular republican government – which is how Giovanni and other members of the family came to be exiled. Nonetheless, Julius did manage to ally with the Venetians and the Swiss (who wanted to install their own candidate as Duke of Milan) to attack Ferrara, winning the Battle of Mirandola in January 1511. To Florence's delight, the pope's army was then itself slaughtered by the French at the River Ronco in April 1512 (Battle of Ravenna). Giovanni was captured and held in a pigeon loft to be ransomed but he escaped in a basket. Despite their victory the French then withdrew from Italy without putting up much more of a fight – strategically they had to turn their attention to burgeoning threats from England and from Spain. Seeing on which side their bread was buttered, Parma and Piacenza, two important cities previously in the hands of the French, promptly declared their allegiance to the pope.

With France out of the way the pope turned his attention to the punishment of Florence for its perceived disloyalty to him. Julius allowed Giovanni, now back from his brief spell in captivity, to lead an assault on Florence, promising to let him reclaim his family's fortune and authority there should the campaign succeed. The Holy League's forces surrounded Florence and captured Prato, 10 miles north-west of the city. Despite Giovanni's pleas for restraint, the troops pillaged Prato in an 'appalling spectacle of horrors' that ended with the deaths of some 4,000 of the town's defenceless inhabitants. 'The nuns of the invaded convents were forced to submit to the unnatural as well as the natural lusts of the soldiers. In the streets, mothers threw their daughters into wells and jumped in after them'.[41] Determined to avoid the same fate, the citizens of Florence deposed the republican government and handed control of the city back to the Medici.

As if this wasn't bad enough, in the background there was the menacing presence of the Ottoman Empire. Having destroyed Byzantium in 1453 the Ottomans now threatened the Empire, besieging Vienna in 1529, taking large parts of Hungary (Battle of Mohács, 1526) and holding Greece and the Balkans. The major European powers, distracted by their internecine struggles and by the Reformation, found it very difficult to mount a coherent and effective response, so the Ottomans remained a threat looming over the continent throughout the period, ameliorated somewhat, but not eliminated, by the European's victory at the sea battle of Lepanto in 1571.

As with the day to day problems of life in the city, all these traumas added to the psychological stress of life at the time. Bronzino didn't know that in the event Florence would not suffer in the Reformation; he could not know that the Ottomans would fail to seize Vienna, sweep up the Danube valley and into Germany nor cross northern Italy and march into Florence. Just as we lived through the Cold War not knowing that none of the protagonists would initiate a nuclear exchange and just as today we do not know what the impact of the erosion of the Post-War Settlement, of Islamic militancy or of Russian revanchism will be on our liberal, democratic, post-Enlightenment lives, Bronzino and his contemporaries lived in a state of profound uncertainty about their physical and confessional future.

The effect on Bronzino of the constant uncertainty is detectable in many of his less formal paintings, less so in those commissioned to provide reassuringly optimistic propaganda. The official portraits tend to show staring, affectless men and women – cold or intensely introspective, guarded and keeping their thoughts strictly to themselves in these dangerous times, they maintain an unbridgeable distance between themselves, as representatives of the ruling elite, and their subjects. On the other hand, Bronzino's poetry, written for private circulation, is more suggestive: in some of it he directly addresses subjects such as Need and Fear.

Cardinal Giovanni and his illegitimate cousin, close friend and confidant Giulio di Giuliano de'Medici (Giulio, 1478-1534) entered Florence to re-establish Medician control of the city on 1 September 1512; the family would remain in power for most of the rest of Bronzino's life. Giovanni himself ruled Florence for a few months, then he handed over to his younger brother Giuliano di Lorenzo de'Medici, Duke of Nemours (Giuliano, 1479-1516). In February 1513 a plot to assassinate Giuliano was uncovered.[42] Forty-four year old Machiavelli was implicated but cleared after four drops on the *strappado*; despite this atrocious experience (or maybe because of it) he wrote approvingly one of the lines for which he is infamous: a prince 'must be held in constant fear, owing to the punishment he may inflict.' Giuliano died three years later to be succeeded by his nephew Lorenzo di Piero de'Medici, Duke of Urbino (Lorenzo II, 1492-1519), son of his elder brother, Piero.

Giovanni, by now an ailing and grossly overweight man, was elected pope in 1513, taking the name Leo X ('God has given us the papacy – let us enjoy it,'[43]) thereby bringing Lorenzo the Magnificent's plan for him, and for the family, to fruition.[44,45] Despite having been a cardinal for thirty-eight years he was still in minor orders: he was ordained priest four days after his election. Born in 1475, Giovanni di Lorenzo de'Medici was the cleverest of Lorenzo de'Medici's three sons. Contented, generous though indecisive (his immediate predecessor, Julius II called him 'Your Circumspection'[45]), he was intelligent, lazy, an expert theologian and possibly agnostic but he was chaste and serious about his calling, taking as his motto 'Happy are those who are irreproachable in their life, who walk in the way of the Lord' (Psalm 119).[45] He aspired to make Rome a great city once more, the centre of Christian humanism, learning, literature and the arts. In order to do this he had to maintain the peace secured by Julius II but in the end events, his personality and his rivals conspired against him. The French, now ruled by Francis I (1515-47), crossed the Alps again in 1515 with designs on Milan, which they seized. The election of Charles V as Holy Roman Emperor in 1519 gave him control of both German and Spanish wealth and resources; he too had ambitions in Italy. Leo was able to play the two parties off against each other, getting Charles to drive Francis out of Milan and buying French loyalty to Rome for the next 300 years by ceding some control of the church in France to him in a Concordat with the French throne.[46]

In the early 1500s Rome was an inhumane and blood-soaked place. It had a population of some 50,000, about the same as Florence; there were about 100 murders a week.[47] These data give a vivid indication of the lawless nature of the place but they deserve to be taken with a pinch of salt, and other sources put the murder rate in Rome at about thirty-five a year (still three to five times that of New York today).[48] One hundred murders a week amounts to some 5,000 a year, that's a horrendous 10% of the population. We can reasonably suppose that at that time about 20,000 of the people living in Rome would have been young, less than, say, 15 years old – and so relatively unlikely to be murdered. Excluding the children brings the risk to an adult of being murdered to an improbable 16%. There must be something wrong here. Either there were fewer than 100 murders a week – perhaps 100 was the rate achieved in one extraordinary week, the average rate being much less, or maybe many unexpected deaths were incorrectly identified as 'murders'. Alternatively, perhaps there were some 50,000 people in Rome at any one time, with the resident population being substantially increased (and the murder rate per head being correspondingly decreased) by the pilgrims, clergy, delegates and other visitors to the city, many of the more senior of whom would have been accompanied by an entourage of acolytes, servants, secretaries and hangers-on. This teeming mass of people enjoyed the services of 7,000 prostitutes working in bordellos which paid a licence fee that eventually reached the Vatican treasury.

Leo wanted to clean Rome up, a project that had begun during the reign of the previous two popes. The objective was to return the city to its former glory, to make it worthy of its position at the centre of Christianity. Leo began to spend lavishly; he was a generous man with ambitions which far exceeded his own means or those of the papacy. He reopened and expanded the university in Rome; he invited poets and artists to Rome, notably Raphael, most of who were heavily subsidised by the Vatican; he hunted and drank with great enthusiasm and above all, he continued a huge building project initiated by Julius II: the construction of the new basilica dedicated to St Peter. All this gave Rome a febrile and louche atmosphere. And it required money: lots of it. On behalf of the Church, Leo borrowed heavily; he taxed the faithful; he sponsored pervasive simony and he allowed the sale of 'indulgences'. Julius II had started the latter practice – granting Catholics remission of punishment due for past (or even future) sins, provided that they went to confession and contributed financially according to their means to the fund for the building of the new basilica. Although Leo did try to administer the system honestly, it was quickly and massively abused, giving Luther and fellow reformers a potent weapon, though by no means the only or most theologically persuasive one, with which to attack the Church and the papacy – 'the scarlet whore of Babylon' in Luther's eyes.

The part played by the issue of indulgences as a populist slogan is analogous with that of 'free movement of people [within the European Union]' in the debate about whether or not the United Kingdom should remain a member of the EU. There are many sound political, historical, economic, psychological and social arguments on both sides of each argument – but 'the sale of indulgences', like 'free movement', became a totemic and emotive theme round which popular opinion was mobilised, with profound consequences.

When he took office Leo tried to tackle several strategically important issues. Putting personal interest before public duty he gave the future of the Medici family the highest priority. His objective was to establish a Medici principality in central Italy. In this he was only partially successful. He did restore the Medici to power in Florence. One of Leo's first actions as pope was to start a process which would result in his cousin Giulio being declared legitimate – enabling him to give Giulio a cardinal's hat, thereby positioning him to win the papal tiara, ideally in immediate succession to himself. He excommunicated Francesco della Rovere, Duke of Urbino, nephew of Julius II, who had rebelled against Leo in 1516, tortured the envoy sent to Rome to appeal against this high-handed revenge and installed his own nephew Lorenzo de'Medici as the Duke in Francesco's stead – provoking yet another small but ruinously expensive war. Securing the integrity of the Papal States came next. Here he had some success, limited by the intrinsic weakness of his position vis-á-vis the regional powers, France and the Empire. He continued the revival of the city of Rome begun by his predecessors in the fifteenth century and by Julius II. Here, after a good start, he failed, sowing the seeds for the ruin of the city after his death and his attempts to defray the vast cost of the project handed the Protestant movement an easy target.

Finally, having taken over leadership of the Fifth Lateran Council from Julius II he had the opportunity to address the issues raised by Luther and his immediate followers, who were looking for reform within the Church rather than for a complete break from it. He might have been able to build a reformed but united, 'universal' Christendom if he had been prepared to accept some of their proposals, while rejecting others and compromising in some disputed areas. Instead he dug his heels in, missed this early opportunity to avert the threat of revolution, asserted papal as opposed to conciliar authority, left the Protestant movement to develop along more radical lines and failed to prevent the cataclysmic events of the Reformation and its aftermath.

When he assumed the papacy, Leo left Florence in the hands of, first his brother Giuliano, then of his nephew Lorenzo II. The Florentines very soon got fed up with Lorenzo. He was autocratic; he wouldn't accept advice from better-informed civil servants; he adopted a quasi-regal personal and administrative style. He soon obliged the Florentines by dying of TB and syphilis at the age of 25, shortly after his marriage to a cousin of Francis I, King of France, which had been arranged by Leo and

Francis. Lorenzo left a daughter, Catherine, who would become queen of France through her marriage (arranged by Guilio de'Medici, Pope Clement VII) to Henri, second son of Francis I.[49] When Henri died of an infected wound sustained in a jousting accident, Catherine acted as Regent for her young sons; she was unable to cope with the religious crisis that faced France and watched helplessly as it plunged into a vicious civil war between Catholics and Protestants that would last for forty years. From the perspective of the Medici's 'selfish gene', however, the marriage was phenomenally successful: Medici DNA entered the Valois, Bourbon, Habsburg and Stuart genomes and was spread throughout the leading families of Europe. Amongst Catherine and Henri's children were three future Kings of France and Marguerite (Reine Margot), who married Henry of Bourbon (King of Navarre, Henry IV of France), initiating the Bourbon dynasty. Marguerite's daughter Henrietta Maria married Charles I of England and her sister, Elizabeth of Valois, married the Habsburg Philip II of Spain.

Catherine's glittering progeny were a long time coming: the first wasn't born until ten years after her marriage. Even though Catherine was only fourteen years old when she married, her failure to produce a child for so long raised questions about her own and Henri's fertility, though not about the consummation of the marriage – which Francis witnessed on the night of their wedding to prevent the possibility of a later annulment of the marriage. A year after their wedding, Henri began a long affair with the beautiful Diane de Poitiers, who remained a dominant force in his life for the next 25 years; Henri much preferred her to his rather plain, 'slovenly' wife who was obliged to live in a bizarre *ménage à trois* until Henri died, at which point she wasted no time in banishing Diane. The issue of Catherine's childlessness became even more serious when Henri became the heir to the throne on his brother's sudden death in 1536. She tried all sorts of remedies for her 'infertility', including alchemy, divination, potions made from the urine of pregnant animals, the powdered sexual organs of stags, boars and cats and so on. Catherine also consulted doctors, of course. Two doctors, Nicolas Venette and Jean Fernel, found that she had an inverted uterus; more significantly, they also examined Henri and found that he had a penile abnormality (hypospadias and chordee) which was probably the explanation for the couple's failure to conceive – despite receiving advice and practical help about the techniques of sexual intercourse from none other than Diane de Poitiers.[51] Fernel then took charge, suggesting various coital positions to minimise the effects of Henri's hypospadias and prescribing pills of myrrh for Catherine.[52] When she did finally conceive (1543) Fernel was rewarded with a pension for life and the queen's position was secured. Eventually seven children survived from Catherine's ten pregnancies.

Jean Francois Fernel (1497-1558)[53] was another remarkable Renaissance polymath, one of the key figures in sixteenth century science and medicine. He came to medicine late, after first studying and making important contributions to philosophy, mathematics and astronomy; one of the lunar craters is named Fernalius in his honour and he calculated the circumference of the earth to within 1% of its true value. When he turned to medicine he began to promote clinical science, as opposed to the role of magic and astrology in health, believing that 'the whole book of healing was nothing other than a copy of inviolable laws observable in Nature.' He published studies on the physiology (he invented the word) of the gut, the heart and the nervous system.[54] He too will crop up again.

Back now to Florence, where Lorenzo's death in 1519 caused a succession crisis. The Medici had such a firm grip on power at this point that the choice of a successor to Lorenzo was, effectively, in their hands. The only male heirs with a good claim to lead the city were both still children: Pope Leo's other nephew Ippolito (his brother Giuliano's illegitimate son) and Alessandro (perhaps the natural son of the pope's cousin Giulio, either by a Moorish slave from Naples or by a peasant woman from the Campagne – if he wasn't the son of Lorenzo, Duke of Urbino).[55] Rather than establishing a strictly hereditary line which would have placed Catherine, still an infant and, even worse, a female, at the head of the family, Leo decided to put Giulio, Archbishop of the city, in nominal charge while retaining a firm grip on Florence himself throughout his pontificate, Giulio being in effect his Viceroy.

Giulio brought the finances under much tighter control, so the state began to flourish once more. But when Leo X died in December 1521, Giulio rushed off to Rome hoping to take his turn on the throne of St Peter. Tactical blunders within the conclave made him unsuccessful on this occasion. A Dutchman, Adriaan Floriszoon Boeyens, former head of the Spanish Inquisition and tutor to the Holy Roman Emperor Charles V, was elected as Adrian VI. Another contender for the papacy this time round was Cardinal Wolsey – he lacked support but how would history have played out should he have won? Giulio turned his attention to cultivating Charles V, from whom he secured a generous pension and the archbishopric of Toledo. Adrian, an aspiring but unsuccessful reformer, survived for less than two years. His death was attributed to poison but he was in ill-health anyway so this may have been no more than sensationalist conspiracy theorising; this was becoming a habit: poison had been similarly implicated in the deaths of the five preceding popes. With the backing of the French, the Emperor and of Henry VIII, Giulio finally won the tiara, as Clement VII, in 1523 after a conclave that lasted 60 days, the longest in history. He turned his attention to the Church and to international affairs, foolishly entrusting Florence to the teenaged Ippolito and Alessandro and then compounding his mistake by imposing a trio of poorly qualified and resented advisors on them. This blunder was typical of his papacy. He was vacillating, irresolute and reputed to be afraid of making a decision. Though pious and hard-working he was described as 'somewhat morose and disagreeable, far from trustworthy and naturally disinclined to kindness.'[56]

Clement made ineffectual attempts to placate both the French and the Emperor. When Francis I invaded Milan in 1523 Clement made a secret pact with him to defeat the Emperor but the Battle of Pavia in 1525 was a disaster for him, Francis was captured and released only after ceding Burgundy to the Emperor and renouncing his claims to Naples and Milan. Recognising the threat posed by the newly enlarged Empire (and conscious too of the implications of the defeat of the Hungarians at the hands of the Ottomans at Belgrade in 1521 and then at Mohács in 1526), Clement constructed the League of Cognac, uniting France, the Papal States, Venice, Florence and Milan against the Empire. Charles was furious and determined to 'teach the Pope a lesson he will never forget'.[57] He assembled armies to move south over the Alps and north from Naples to trap Clement in a pincer movement. Clement assembled an Italian-Swiss force in northern

Italy and might have defeated the Emperor's army had he not dithered, called a truce and then insulted Charles still further by calling him 'the pope's vassal'.

The Emperor's northern forces included many Protestants from Germany bent on deposing 'the anti-Christ' in the Vatican and stealing his possessions. The imperial troops were fed-up with the delays caused by Clement's vacillations, and Charles had been unable to pay them for months – their commanders began to lose control of them and they marched south looking for loot. Initially they had designs on Florence but heavy snow made it difficult for them to approach the city, which they by-passed in return for a huge bribe – a lucky escape for Bronzino and his fellow citizens. The marauding army made for Rome, where some 27,000 of them arrived in May 1527. Despite the significant improvements made by Julius and Leo, the city was still a mess: weak, demoralised and in a bad state of repair. The ancient Roman buildings had been demolished piece-meal over the centuries, the stones being used to build modest houses for the inhabitants of the now much smaller town. Farm animals grazed in the streets, weeds sprang up amongst the paving stones and malaria was endemic. The attack in thick fog on the 6th May easily overwhelmed Rome's feeble defences and the streets began to run with blood, its inhabitants brutalised, mutilated and murdered. Some 8,000 died on the first day, another 5,000 over the next six days as the city was devastated. Led by the Germans, the troops desecrated churches and monasteries, sold nuns for a pittance, extorted great wealth in exchange for the lives of prominent citizens, abused leading *artifice* and vandalised great works of art. Bronzino would have been horrified to hear about the events in Rome: the painters Perino del Vaga, Marcantonio Raimondi and Gulio Clovio were tortured and impoverished; the architect in charge of the building of St Peter's was mistaken for a rich prelate, captured and released only after he had established his real identity by drawing the corpse of the imperial commander who had been killed in the assault on the city.

Rome's misery continued for the rest of the year, with hunger, plague and the further depredations of the occupying army reducing the place to abject poverty. Pope Clement, trapped in the Castel Sant'Angelo and then freed by Charles in exchange for a 'king's ransom', escaped to the bishop of Orvieto's miserable, tumble-down palace, penniless and disguised as a peddler. The sack destroyed not only the city of Rome but also, and for ever, the temporal power of the papacy, the claim of the Roman Church to be the inheritor of classical civilisation, and the hope that 'Italy' comprising a number of small, independent states could resist subjugation by one or other of the larger states to its north. It also exposed Clement's weakness – which Henry VIII noticed and promptly exploited, at the expense of his queen, Catherine of Aragon.

Instead of empathising with the Romans and thanking their lucky stars that they had escaped the same fate, the Florentines rejoiced that a Medici Pope had been humiliated. Delirious crowds, Bronzino amongst them perhaps, marched through the streets of Florence shouting anti-Medici slogans and ripping apart an effigy of the pope. Ippolito, Alessandro and their entourage of advisors and sycophants fled; an anti-Medici, republican administration was installed again, this time with the help of the Emperor. Friends of the Medici were terrorised; all signs of the Medici were effaced from buildings; Catherine de'Medici, now eight years old, was seized and confined to a convent. A resurgence of the religious enthusiasm experienced in the days of Savonarola led to the proclamation that Jesus Christ was King of Florence and the declaration of a 'Republic of Christ'. The worst excesses of Savonarola's time were avoided, but strenuous efforts were made to obliterate all remnants of the Medici's rule; strict sumptuary laws were introduced and gambling, carnivals and other public entertainments were banned.

The pope, humiliated by the sack of Rome crept back from Orvieto to the Vatican. He was desperate to preserve the Medici's fortune and influence, and to achieve this he had first to restore their rule in Florence. He could not look to the French for help – they had invaded Italy yet again in 1529, reaching Naples before plague and over-extended supply lines forced them to withdraw. With nowhere else to turn he had to bow to Charles V's growing power. He agreed to recognise imperial authority in Italy and to crown Charles V. Charles had been crowned by the Electors at Aachen in 1520 but that had made him only Emperor elect – *Romanorum rex semper Augustus* – pending his highly symbolic papal coronation, which would signify the unity of the Empire and the Papacy, the twin pillars of Christendom. It transpired that his papal coronation, in Bologna in 1530, would be the last of the line that stretched back to Charlemagne's coronation on Christmas Day 800 A.D. In return Charles agreed to betroth his seven year old natural daughter, Margaret, to Alessandro and to return the Medici family to power in Florence – using force if he had to.

The Florentines had other ideas. They determined to resist, mobilised their militia and appointed Michelangelo to supervise the reinforcement of the city's defences. He ran away, taking a lot of money with him, and had to be lured back to complete the work, which was almost done by the time some 40,000 imperial forces arrived in Tuscany and invested the city in early Autumn 1529. *En route* to Florence itself they had employed the 'devastators' in their ranks to raze the surrounding villages and to destroy the region's agricultural economy – a scorched-earth policy, which gave those barricaded behind the city walls a good idea of what to expect.

The people of Florence defied the siege through the winter of 1529-30 and then through the following spring and summer, but months of starvation and the outbreak of plague finally sapped their morale. They are reported to have been 'reduced to eating mice', which commanded prohibitively high prices in the city's markets. The word 'reduced' implies great reluctance, indicative of the dire straits they found themselves in – they certainly were in dire straits, but the eating of mice is not necessarily a sign of desperation. Diet is one of those highly contingent cultural phenomena, like religion, which depend on where and when you were born, who your parents were, how you were educated, and by whom. Cows, horses, snakes, snails and the witchety grub all find their way onto menus somewhere, why not mice? Mice were luxury items in first century Rome: Robert Harris describes a dinner party hosted by the millionaire Numeris Popidius Ampliatus on the eve of the destruction of Pompeii in AD 79. The menu included oysters, lobster, sea urchins, mice rolled in honey and poppy seeds, sow's udder stuffed with kidneys, sow's vulva and the tongues of storks. Seneca said 'eat to vomit: vomit to eat' – which calls to mind today's young people who consider a night getting hopelessly drunk a great night out. Lucius Popidius, a guest at Ampliatus's party was disgusted by the sensation of crunching on the tiny bones of the mouse which good manners obliged him to eat.[58] This is fiction, of course, albeit well-researched fiction but it is as well to remember that here Harris is projecting feelings appropriate to his twentieth century western readers on to a character who lived 2000 years ago and with whom he is intending that we should identify to some degree. A reminder that the same caution should apply to our attempts to understand the interior make-up of Bronzino and his contemporaries. Writing about historical fiction, Suzannah Lipscomb quotes Robertson Davies to good effect: 'we all belong to our own time, and there is nothing whatever that we can do to escape from it. Whatever we write will be contemporary even if we attempt a novel set in a past age.' She goes on to say that much the same applies to history itself: 'This is not the past, it just looks like it.'[59] Mice were probably a delicacy in many parts of the world in the sixteenth century; they certainly are so today. I once bought grilled mice from a roadside stall in East Africa – though I must confess that I was unable to bring myself to eat them, which says more about me than about the mice or about those who enjoy eating them.

So, after a year of privation, popular opinion in Florence began to favour a negotiated return of the Medici if this would guarantee a benign end to the siege: 'Give us the Medici, who can give us bread'.[60] Terms were agreed with the Emperor; Medici rule was re-established in the person of Alessandro. Ippolito, now a Cardinal, bitterly resented Alessandro's appointment to a position which he had thought would be his. He died in 1535 *en route* to Tunis where he hoped to persuade Charles V, there to fight the Ottomans, to depose Alessandro in his favour. Predictably enough, Ippolito's death has been attributed to poison given to him by an agent of Alessandro. The return of the Medici to Florence was supposed not to be accompanied by the usual reprisals but, for many, it was far from benign. Several leaders of the anti-papal group were tortured and exiled; others were imprisoned or banished for life; Florence was bankrupt, the city had been wrecked and many houses in the *contado* had been demolished. Alessandro became tyrannical once Pope Clement VII's restraining influence was removed by his death in 1534. Charles V supported Alessandro, ignoring representations from the people and from Ippolito to depose him and went ahead with his plan to marry his daughter Margaret to Alessandro.

Alessandro was close to his jealous and dissolute cousin, Lorenzino de'Medici, with whom he would party, whore and, rumour had it, share a bed. In January 1537 Lorenzino hired an assassin, the condottiere Michele Tavolaccino (who rejoiced in the nickname of Scoronconcolo), – as you do – and with his help he very messily murdered Alessandro. It is not clear what Lorenzino's motives were for the crime – he tended to support the republican cause in opposition to the Medici – but immediately after killing Alessandro he fled to Venice instead of taking advantage of the murder. If he was expecting to be called back to assume the leadership of Florence he was to be sadly disappointed.[61]

Hiring an assassin seems to have been a straightforward business, though it didn't necessarily work out well – Lorenzino failed to capitalise on the murder of his cousin. In Verdi's dramatisation of the squalid goings-on in the Italian courts of the sixteenth-century his eponymous 'hero' Rigoletto (a hunchback, so one of the curiosities that the rich and powerful liked to have in their households) hires the assassin Sparafucile to murder the notoriously predatory Duke of Mantua. The duke's courtiers abduct Rigoletto's daughter Gilda for the duke's amusement, the duke duly has his evil way with her but she believes his protestations of true love and hero-worships him. Accordingly, she foils Rigoletto's plot, substituting herself for the assassin's intended victim. Strangely enough from our perspective, Verdi took his plot from Victor Hugo's tragedy *Le roi s'amuse*, transposing the action to Mantua from France in the 1520s, where Hugo's villain was none other than Francis I. Burkhardt says that paid assassination was common, being most frequent in Naples and rarest in Florence, although even here it appears to have increased rapidly during the turbulent start to the sixteenth century; only with the accession of Cosimo I was it brought under control again.[62] Throughout the period murder was common, and commonly used as an instrument of policy; poisoning and stabbing were popular means of dispatching a rival or an enemy and of avenging a perceived wrong or pursuing a vendetta. The first handbook on poisons was published by the Florentine Cardinal Ferdinando Ponzetti in 1521. Most prominent people, the pope included, had a taster to sample their food for poison, so other means were sought for delivering the poison to the victim.

In 1517 several cardinals were alleged to have bribed Leo X's surgeon, Vercelli, to inject his patient with poison while he operated on his anal fistula; an alternative version of the story has it that the salve for the pope's anal fistula was laced with poison. Murder was so common that the sudden death of a prominent person was immediately assumed to have been unnatural, no matter how improbable a dispassionate assessment might make that seem – making it very difficult for us to determine how many deaths really were unnatural.

When Alessandro's body was discovered, Medici supporters led by Francesco Guicciarini, the head of the civil service, were afraid not only that an anti-Medici faction might grab the reins of government but also that the Spanish might seize this opportunity to impose a severe colonial regime, as they had done in southern Italy. The Medici faction rallied quickly, suppressed news of the assassination and took control of the government of Florence before opposing forces could organise themselves. Bribing the Captain of the Guard, who could otherwise have used his soldiers to frustrate them, they chose as their leader Cosimo de'Medici (1519-74, Cosimo the Great), an intelligent but inexperienced seventeen-year-old with a patrician pedigree. He became Cosimo I, Duke of Tuscany, subsequently elevated to Grand Duke by Pope Pius V in 1569 (this title was not recognised by the Habsburgs nor by the other Italian duchies). Despite their wealth, arrogance and power, up until now the Medici family had been pretty hopeless as leaders of Florence and of the Church. But Cosimo's accession ushered in a period of stability and public decorum for Florence which would last for the rest of Bronzino's life.

Clement VII died in 1534. Of the seven popes who succeeded him during Bronzino's lifetime only one, Pius IV, was a member of the Medici family. None of the seven had the time and still less the inclination for close involvement in Florentine affairs.[63] A familiar mix of the pious, the venal and the sadistic, each pope had to maintain the uneasy balance of power between France and the Empire, respond to the threat posed by Protestantism and, in some cases, feather his own nest. Fortunately for Italy, the attention of the great powers was directed elsewhere in the latter part of the sixteenth century. The papacy was not so fortunate when it came to dealing with Protestantism: Europe has been living with their collective failures ever since. Many of these popes made serious attempts to reform the Church in response to the challenge – sadly, however, some wanted to reform it in one direction and some in another and all had to deal with powerful vested interests. Pope Paul III (1534-49), a shameless promoter of his own, Farnese, family's interests and fortune, was nonetheless one of the more determined reformers. The leaked report of an independent enquiry which he had commissioned exposed a shocking catalogue of abuses within the Church, opening the way for him to summon a General Council of the Church which convened in the imperial city of Trent and included Lutherans amongst its delegates. The Council began its deliberations at the end of 1545 after each of the several interested factions had done its best to delay or even abort it. In defiance of the Emperor the Council of Trent set out determined to resolve fundamental doctrinal issues: justification by faith, transubstantiation and purgatory. Only sporadically attended by senior clerics other than the Italians, the Council dragged on for years (it was suspended for a time by the ultra-conservative pope Paul IV). Finally, in 1563, it rejected an accommodation with Protestantism and instead launched the Counter-Reformation.[64] Its conclusions were more to do with the administration of the Church than with doctrine, which it tried to dodge or to leave ambiguous. But it did confirm that only the Church could interpret the scriptures and that religious truth derived from Church teaching as well as from the Bible. It confirmed traditional views of original sin, and merit; it confirmed the Real Presence during the Mass. The doctrines of purgatory, the efficacy of intercession by saints and of the veneration of relics were reasserted; indulgences were declared to be effective but their sale was banned. It rejected the Protestant claim that salvation was to be achieved through faith, rather than through observance of the sacraments of the Church. On the organisational side, the Council reformed the monastic orders, defined the process for the appointment of bishops, and improved the training of priests, in which it favoured scholasticism and St Thomas Aquinas in particular, rather than study of the scriptures. Most significantly it strengthened the authority of the pope, making everyone in the Church subordinate to him – and liable to punishment for disobedience – and declared that henceforth marriage would be valid only when the wedding took place before a priest and two witnesses. Rather vague statements were made about religious images, stressing their importance as vehicles for teaching the, largely illiterate, laity: these had a huge effect on the development of Roman Catholic art.

Pope Pius V (1556-62), brutal, conservative, ex-Inquisitor set himself the task of keeping Protestantism out of Italy, which along with Spain was the only large territory still free of the heresy by this time. His draconian measures were successful – and by cleaving to the Roman Church most of the Italian states avoided the large-scale bloodshed which accompanied the Reformation in northern Europe. But they did suffer the excesses of the Counter-Reformation and they denied themselves the benefits of Protestantism. Though Florence under Cosimo I was less turbulent and relatively untouched by the Reformation it couldn't avoid the other profound physical, psychological, political and intellectual events which were beginning to shake the very foundations of European society.

The leader of the Holy Roman Empire was 'elected' by a select sub-group of seven of the rulers (unimaginatively given the titles of 'Elector') of the plethora of small and large Germanic states, including places that are not obviously 'German', to act as the primus-inter-pares of the lot of them. The Emperor was required to summon a Diet, or assembly of the representatives of the members of the Empire (roughly: seventy-two dynastic titles twenty-five major secular principalities, ninety archbishoprics, bishoprics and abbeys, sixty-five imperial cities and the imperial knights[65]) to discuss imperial policy and to agree legislation. The various meetings of the Diet were named from their venue – hence the delightfully named Diet of Worms, held in Worms in 1521 at which Charles V denounced Martin Luther. Though they acknowledged their allegiance to the Emperor the individual states retained a substantial degree of autonomy, meaning that they might choose to defy him, in matters of religion for example: the Elector of Saxony gave Luther sanctuary and many states adopted Protestantism and forced the Emperor Ferdinand to conclude the Peace of Augsburg in 1555, despite his father Charles V having vowed to extirpate this heresy. While, in theory any suitably qualified statesman might be elected, by Bronzino's time and until Emperor Francis II brought an end to the ramshackle system rather than allowing Napoleon to take it over, the Holy Roman Emperor was always a member of the Habsburg (often anglicised to Hapsburg) family.[66] Complicating matters still further, the Habsburgs were hereditary rulers in their own right of the 'Crown Lands' – essentially greater Austria with varying swathes of contiguous territory in the Balkans, Moldova, Bohemia, Ruthenia, Transylvania and Hungary that were won and lost as the fortunes of war, military competence, and the wealth and ambitions of the Habsburgs and their neighbours waxed and waned.

For most of Bronzino's adult life the Emperor was Charles V, one of the most powerful and intelligent of a very mixed bunch. His power and influence were such that his decisions had repercussions throughout Europe, indeed throughout much of the known world, and couldn't help but have an impact, even if an indirect one, on Bronzino's life.[67] He was the grandson of the Emperor Maximillian and of Ferdinand and Isabella; as the only living heir to the Burgundian, Habsburg, Aragonese and Castillian lines[68] he inherited, first the Kingdom of Burgundy, then the Kingdom of Spain (which brought with it southern Italy, the Spanish possessions in the Americas and immense wealth). Pope Leo X gave the 15 year-old Charles a rose made of wrought gold 'because he is soon to be the most important man in the whole of Europe'.[68] By the age of 25 he had inherited claims to seventy-two separate dynastic titles, twenty-seven kingdoms, thirteen duchies, and twenty-two countries. The blend of different states, countries, continents and, ultimately, religious affiliations was a weak and fractious one. As early as 1521 Charles transferred responsibility for Austria to his younger brother Ferdinand, who became King of Bohemia and then of Habsburg Hungary after the Battle of Mohács in 1526 which left the Kingdom of Hungary partitioned between the Habsburgs, the Ottomans and the Principality of Transylvania. Charles never attempted to unify his several remaining fissiparous dominions and by the end of his life the Habsburg patrimony was in pieces.

Maximilian I, the previous Habsburg Holy Roman Emperor, had died in 1519. His son, Philip the Handsome, married a Castilian, Joanna (Juana) the Mad, and had six children, who would become two emperors and four queens, but Philip predeceased his father – leaving Maximilian's grandson Charles of Ghent (1500-58) to inherit the Crown Lands and access to the funds he needed to bribe his way to the imperial title. He secured this in 1519 in a competition with his younger brother, Archduke Ferdinand, with Francis I, Valois King of France and, improbably, with Henry VIII of England. Pope Leo was vociferous in his support of Francis but the German electors were united in opposition to the Frenchman. Leo withdrew his support for Francis and, with the aid of enormous bribes totalling 852,000 guilders, of which 544,000 guilders were provided by the Fugger family,[69] Charles was elected. The longstanding antagonism between the Valois and Habsburg houses was not helped by this, particularly as France now found herself squeezed between Habsburg-ruled territories to the north, south and east. For the remainder of their lives Francis and Charles were locked in a bitter struggle for the dominance of Europe. Charles was determined to retain his Italian possessions, which meant that he had to keep the French out of the peninsula. Francis, for his part, saw strategic advantages to a presence in northern Italy through which he could threaten Naples, Sicily and Sardinia and disrupt communication between Spain and the Habsburg heartlands in the east. This power struggle soon flared up into open warfare over the issue of who controlled Milan, easy marching distance from Florence; Charles won the Battle of Pavia (February 1525), captured Francis and, briefly, held him hostage in Madrid. Charles promptly sent some of his victorious army north to crush the revolting peasants – the massacre of Frankenhausen (May 1525), the final act of the German Peasants' War, leaving 3,000 to 10,000 peasants and only a handful of imperial troops dead.[70]

Incidentally, and only peripherally to do with Bronzino, musing about the tortuous dynastic affairs of Spain provides none-the-less entertaining and not completely irrelevant background. The revered Catholic Monarchs (*Los Reyes Catolicos*) – Ferdinand (of Aragon) and his first cousin Isabella (of Castile) – completed the *Reconquista* when Granada fell to their army in 1492. Aragon had traditionally looked on the Mediterranean as its preferred sphere of influence and in pursuit of this policy it had annexed Sicily and Sardinia in the fourteenth century. This limited French influence in the Mediterranean so the French tried to redress the balance by invading Naples. But in 1504 Naples was added to Sicily and Sardinia as a Spanish possession, reinforcing the antagonism between Spain and France which would persist for centuries. The more powerful Castile left the Mediterranean to Aragon and concentrated instead on trade with countries to the north, particularly trade in wool.

Dynastic marriages were central to the Catholic Monarchs' foreign policy, as they were to that of all royal houses at the time. Ferdinand and Isabella had seven children; Juan, the Spanish heir was married to the Habsburg princess Margaret; his sister Juana was married to Margaret's brother, Archduke Phillip of Burgundy, the Habsburg heir, Charles V's father. Another daughter was Catherine of Aragon, Henry VIII's first wife. Following a catalogue of accidents, the Catholic Monarchs were left with no children to inherit their own throne. Juan died before his parents and Juana was driven mad, reputedly by the sexual excesses of her husband, Philip.

Isabella died in 1504, leaving Castile to her deranged daughter and her libertine son-in-law. Phillip died shortly thereafter, leaving his and Juana's son, Charles of Ghent, as his heir. Meanwhile, Ferdinand, who was still alive, retained the crown of Aragon and was appointed Regent for his daughter Juana, who was unfit to rule over Castile or anywhere else. She had collapsed when Phillip died and spent the next few months carting his body round Spain by night in a hearse drawn by eight black horses, accompanied by her retinue and torch bearers. She opened the coffin from time to time just to check on the state of the decomposing corpse, having been told by a monk that Phillip would revive. Eventually despairing of this wondrous event she retired to a nearby palace where she remained, as Queen of Castile, until her death 46 years later.

Ferdinand ruled as Regent in her stead and became, it is said, the model for Machiavelli's Prince, published in Florence in 1513. Ferdinand died in 1516; despite his best efforts he didn't leave a son to succeed him, so the throne passed to his grandson, Charles of Ghent, the heir to both Isabella and Ferdinand, though he was allowed only to be co-ruler with his deranged mother, still vegetating in her palace. And so we come full circle, to the Emperor Charles V, Holy Roman Emperor, King of Spain (confusingly, although rejoicing in the appellation of King Carlos I, he was strictly speaking King only of Aragon and joint ruler with his mother of Castile, and not King of the whole of the

Spanish peninsular), head of the Burgundian and Habsburg houses and a louring influence on Bronzino's home city-state.

Charles V married Isabel, daughter of the King of Portugal. He had three children with her and an affair with an inn-keeper's daughter led to him fathering Don Juan of Austria, the victor of the Battle of Lepanto in 1571. Charles married his son Philip (later to become Felipe II of Spain – of Armada fame) first to his first-cousin a Princess of Portugal, then to his maternal first-cousin, Mary I (Tudor) of England, the daughter of Catherine of Aragon and Henry VIII, with the intention of bringing England into the Habsburg constellation. Mary's childless early death thwarted him – thank goodness. Keeping it in the family, Philip's third wife was his distant relation Elisabeth of Valois, the eldest daughter of Henry II of France and Catherine de' Medici (Francis I's granddaughter). Finally Philip married his niece – Anne of Austria.

More pertinent to our story, as Holy Roman Emperor and ruler of the Habsburg Crown Lands, Charles had to contend with two superpower rivals: the French to the West and the Ottomans to the East, as well as with the destabilising effect of Protestantism. After listening to Luther and rejecting his arguments at the Diet of Worms in 1521, Charles cast himself as the champion of the Catholic Church against both the Protestants and the Muslims. Luther had to place himself under the protection of the Elector of Saxony and his followers were subjected to years of vicious persecution, culminating in their overwhelming defeat by Charles at the Battle of Mühlberg 1547. Following this event a Diet was summoned to be held in Augsburg. Here it was agreed that the ruler of each state within the Empire had the right to choose between Lutheranism and Catholicism on behalf of all his subjects. This concession, enshrined in the Peace of Augsburg, was signed by the next Emperor, Charles's brother Ferdinand.

French resistance to the Holy Roman Empire was both political and visceral. The French considered their royal family to have been founded by a saint (St Denis) who had met Christ – an infinitely superior heritage, in their eyes, to the Holy Roman Emperor's supposed continuity with the pagan rulers of ancient Rome. The French claimed to be prudent, law-giving, pious, committed to reform of the Church and to peace in Christendom; they concentrated on diplomacy and on forming an anti-imperial axis. Henri II (1547-59), the son of Francis I, took 'Until it fills the whole universe' as his personal slogan, in conscious opposition to Charles V's '*Plus ultra*'. In reality, power, wealth and security fuelled their mutual antagonism at least as much as such febrile appeals to national characteristics.

From 1520 to 1566 the Muslim Ottoman Turks were ruled by Suleiman, a charismatic character who well deserved his sobriquet 'the Magnificent'. At Mohács in 1526 he seized most of modern-day Hungary and clearly intended to move further westward. Charles and his heirs led the defence of Christian Europe, relying on Austrian money (the Crown Lands), mercenary troops, largely from the Empire, and Polish allies. In defiance of Charles, Suleiman led his armies through the Balkans to the gates of Vienna (1529) – the capital of Charles's family lands and a seismic event for the whole of Europe. The Ottoman incursion was repelled, but it was a frightening and close-run thing. Meanwhile, the Turks had joined forces with Barbarossa, a pirate chieftain who was terrorising the coast of North Africa. He was one of the long line of Barbarossas (Red Beards) who crop up in history because hirsutism (red hair in particular) was seen as evidence of power – it all began with Esau, a red-haired, hirsute man. Friedrich I Barbarossa was a great twelfth century Emperor after whom Hitler named the Nazi invasion of Russia that turned out to be his nemesis (who says history doesn't repeat itself: think of Napoleon, think of Afghanistan?). Hitler had a thing about medieval German history, his First Reich was the Ottonian empire, his second Bismark's and his Third Reich was his own: intended to last for a thousand years it was destined to be even more ephemeral than its imagined predecessors. Barbarossa the pirate seized Algiers in 1529 and Tunis in 1534. Spain was threatened with Muslim resurgence and Europe with Muslim invasion from the south-west, mirroring the Ottoman threat from the east. In 1535 Charles V assembled a fleet of 400 ships and 30,000 troops from all round the Mediterranean to attack Tunis. Barbarossa fled and thousands of Christian slaves were liberated after enduring years of gruelling labour as galley slaves. Charles's fortunes were reversed six years later when he made a disastrous attempt to retake Algiers. Then Tunis itself was lost in 1560. In 1565 the Ottomans threatened Malta, successfully defended by the Knights of St John. But Suleiman then died, leaving the Ottomans in some disarray and the Papal States, Venice and Spain allied to capitalise on their enemy's weakness. Don Juan of Austria led a fleet which roundly defeated the Turks at the Battle of Lepanto – 7 October 1571.[71] More than two hundred Ottoman vessels were captured or sunk against only thirteen losses on the victorious side; 15,000 Christian galley slaves were freed in this the last battle to have been fought between oared vessels. Vasari commemorated the event in a mural in the Sala Regia in the Vatican, the companion piece to his celebration of the St. Bartholomew's Day Massacre. Cervantes fought at Lepanto and wrote about it. He was wounded three times and permanently lost the use of an arm in the battle: 'On that day the insolent pride of the Ottomans was broken forever. It was the greatest occasion the centuries had ever seen'.[72] Cervantes was letting his imagination as a novelist run away with itself – Lepanto was far from the end of the Ottoman menace. Subsequent Emperors regularly dealt with Ottoman raids into the rump of the Hungarian lands that remained in Habsburg hands and into the land just east of Vienna. Thousands of imperial subjects continued to be captured and enslaved. The threat to the Empire was real – the capture of Vienna would have opened the Danube valley and provided the enemy with an invasion route right into the centre of Bavaria and greater Germany – and the menace persisted right through to the great siege of Vienna in 1683, which did turn out to be the Ottoman's final and unsuccessful throw of that particular dice. The apogee of Ottoman power in the sixteenth century still resonates: speaking to expatriot Turks living in Europe in 2008, Recep Tayyip Erdoğan, Prime Minister (now President) of Turkey railed against assimilation as 'a crime against humanity' and urged his audience to wield 'a constitutional element' instead of just being 'guests' in the countries to which they had migrated.[73] The following year Ahmet Davutoglu, Turkey's foreign minister, gave a speech in Sarajevo in which he said: 'As in the sixteenth century, which saw the Ottoman Balkans as the centre of world politics, we will make the Balkans, the Caucasus and the Middle East, the centre of world politics in the future'.[74]

By the time of Lepanto, Charles was dead. His deranged mother, Juana, lived until 1555 so Charles didn't formally become King of Castile until then, by which time he was tired and prematurely old. He promptly abdicated, passing the imperial crown to his brother Ferdinand (who had been elected King of the Romans in 1531) in time for him to sign the Treaty of Augsburg. The Low Countries and Spain with all its overseas possessions went to his son Philip in 1556, thereby splitting the Habsburg possessions for ever and paving the way for the war of The Spanish Succession at the beginning of the eighteenth century. Charles retained the title of Emperor until just before his death but he retired with his cat, a parrot and a household staff of 150, to a monastery where he passed his time in comfortable apartments enjoying his art collection, trying to synchronise his huge collection of clocks and gorging on anchovies and beer (and, we hope, also in prayer). Two years later he insisted on attending a rehearsal for his own funeral, caught malaria and died. Ferdinand inherited the Empire along with the Habsburg Crown Lands.[75] Based in Vienna, he focussed on resisting the Ottoman threat while his nephew, Philip, based in Spain, concentrated on the Mediterranean and the Americas, on suppressing revolt in the Spanish Netherlands and on fighting the French.

Although as an adult he had a regal figure, the young Charles who ascended the thrones of Europe was an unprepossessing character – not the charismatic presence that his status might lead one to expect, particularly in an era when physical presence still counted for a lot. He was clumsy and his huge 'Habsburg Jaw' forced his mouth to hang open – making him look stupid. The Habsburg jaw is thought to have originated in a Polish royal family, the first Habsburg to have displayed it was Maximilian I, Emperor from 1486 to 1519. As well as having a jutting lower jaw the Habsburgs often had an abnormally thick lower lip, sometimes an abnormally large tongue, unusually-shaped heads, a droop to their lower eyelids, flattened facial features, and a distinctive shape to their nose. Maximilian's grandson, Charles V is shown in Plate 4, painted before he became Emperor. One cannot but feel sorry for him and be surprised that the unknown artist doesn't appear to have made much effort to flatter his sitter. The Habsburg Jaw has been held up as a good illustration of the perils of the transmission of recessive genes through the consanguineous mating that results from marriage between close relatives. In fact it is now thought that the famous deformities are transmitted by autosomal dominant genes – so only one parent has to display Habsburg facial characteristics for their children to have a fifty-fifty chance of displaying the same characteristics; in-breeding may just have exaggerated the effect. That's not to say that the Habsburgs escaped the genetic consequences of their predilection for furthering their dynastic and political ambitions by arranging marriages between cousins, nieces, uncles and the like. The extent of their inbreeding increased over the reigns of the Habsburgs so that when the end of the Spanish Habsburg line was reached in the physically and mentally disabled Charles II who died aged 38, without issue in 1700, Juana of Castile (the Mad), appeared in his family tree no less than fourteen times because of first and second cousin unions: he was more inbred than he would have been had his parents been brother and sister. Charles II suffered from an extreme version of the Habsburg Jaw, he had difficulty speaking and he drooled because his tongue was far too big for his mouth. He also suffered with intestinal upsets, convulsions and premature ejaculation or impotence. He was unable to speak until the age of four and couldn't walk until the age of eight. He was short, weak and quite thin; whether or not the jaw can be attributed to in-breeding, two other conditions thought to have affected Charles II, pituitary hormone deficiency (which can result in infertility) and distal renal tubular acidosis, a cause of kidney failure, are both caused by recessive mutations in different genes: they would have been made more common by in-breeding. The Spanish and Austrian Habsburg lines were equally in-bred; so the extinction of the former but survival of the latter is most likely due to the differing impact of environmental and political events on the two branches of the family: the contingencies of Nurture having a bigger effect than those of Nature.[76]

The risks of consanguinity have not gone away – how could they have done? There is still a high incidence of inherited conditions in some northern and midland cities in England where a large Muslim population of Pakistani origin keeps up a tradition of first-cousin marriages. In one of these cities, Bradford in West Yorkshire, the incidence of abnormal babies is about 300 per 10,000 – roughly double the rate for the UK as a whole. Pakistani women are at increased risk of having an affected baby and most of this is due to consanguinity. The risk is relatively small, however, first cousin marriages produce only a 3.6% increase in abnormal babies over the population base-rate and about 93% of these parents' children appear to be healthy. The Habsburgs made things much worse for themselves, of course, by repeating the consanguineous matings for generation after generation.[77]

Bronzino would have known about all the turmoil in his world – intellectual, theological, military and dynastic. Although he was spared the cacophony of information thrust in front of us in newspapers, television, the internet and all the rest, he did move in court circles in Florence where he would have met or listened to ambassadors, courtiers and other well-informed people. He may not have been on first-name terms with them but he would at least have picked up gossip in the servants' quarters. And he spent many hours painting the portraits of members of the Medici court; what did they talk about, either to Bronzino or to other courtiers in the room, while they sat for him? In the streets, shops and markets of Florence he would have encountered itinerant merchants, craftsmen, priests, and also mercenary soldiers looking for the next war. People were constantly on the move round Europe, earning a living, making a pilgrimage, carrying messages. News travelled by word of mouth and also in the extensive correspondence between the developing networks of courts, academics, bankers, humanists and natural philosophers. At this time, too, printed books, pamphlets and religious and political tracts, and engraved, etched or wood-cut illustrations were becoming more numerous, much cheaper, more readily accessible and disseminated more widely, aided by developing postal services.[78] What Bronzino learnt about developments in the world beyond Florence must have made him feel excited and anxious.

The very foundations of Bronzino's static, geocentric, divinely ordained world were being shaken. Maybe folk just got on with life, which their environment made tough enough anyway without getting too preoccupied with existential angst: *que sera sera*. That seems improbable, however. How could they not be troubled by the fundamental challenges to their understanding of the universe and their place in it?

Can we find a modern analogy? Is this how people today remain sane while living in the shadow of an active volcano or on a geologically active major fault-line? Was the realisation that the earth is but one of many planets, rotating on its axis and moving round the sun, liberating or as profoundly disturbing as we would find the realisation that the *Matrix* films present the world as it really is? Do our worries about Brexit, Islamic extremism, President Trump's White House, Putin's ambitions, North Korea's unpredictability and so on come close to equating to Bronzino's worries about disease, siege and the destiny of his immortal soul? Probably not. One thing we can be sure of: we cannot get inside Bronzino's head. If he did believe in the literal truth of the Bible (Psalm 93: 'Thou hast fixed the earth immovable and firm, thy throne firm from of old.') he would also have accepted the biblical justifications for slavery, as did the overwhelming majority of his contemporaries, who used slaves as domestic servants and who were inured to the use of their (non-Christian) prisoners-of-war as galley slaves. It is impossible for us to identify with that belief and very difficult for most of us to accept the literal truth of other Biblical pronouncements – although modern creationists still do manage to do so. We should acknowledge that our understanding of Bronzino's world-view is as fragmentary as our understanding of the world-view of adherents of IS/Daesh. In both cases we are dealing with an episteme alien to our own and therefore extraordinarily difficult, or perhaps even impossible, for us fully to comprehend. Luther, incidentally, dismissed Copernicus, though never by name, as a fool because he held opinions at variance with the Bible: 'People give ear to an upstart astrologer who strove to show that the earth revolves, not the heavens or the firmament, the Sun and the Moon … So it goes now. Whoever wants to be clever … must do something of his own. This is what that fellow does who wishes to turn the whole of astronomy upside down. . . . However, as Holy Scripture tells us, so did Joshua bid the sun to stand still and not the earth.'[79] Calvin apparently never directly attacked Copernicus – the quotation so often attributed to him is spurious: 'Who will venture to place the authority of Copernicus above that of the Holy Spirit?' but he did attack the heliocentric theory: 'We will see some who are so deranged, not only in religion but who in all things reveal their monstrous nature, that they will say that the sun does not move, and that it is the earth which shifts and turns. When we see such minds we must indeed confess that the devil possess them.'[80] And the Church's reaction to Galileo's discoveries is well known.[81] What was Bronzino to think?

The exchange of ideas and information throughout Europe was facilitated by the fact that educated people had access to a common language: Latin. This had begun in the Catholic Church, which had used a comprehensive system of information exchange for centuries. Pope Leo X loved classical Latin and spoke the language fluently. He wanted to make it the universal language of educated people, to improve their mutual understanding and to foster civilisation and peace.[82] In the Vatican he encouraged the use of Latin in correspondence, in formal meetings and at meal times and he sponsored poets and prose writers to produce works in the language. For a time enthusiasm for producing literary works in Latin spread across Europe and the humanists shared their ideas through books and an extensive network of correspondents using Latin, albeit a 'humanist' Latin more relaxed in vocabulary and syntax than the language used in theological texts. Erasmus's *Colloquies* (1518) was a Latin primer designed to help with conversational Latin; thirty reprints had appeared by 1522 and it remained a 'set text' for years to come.[83] Erasmus's vision of a community of humanists able to share ideas with each other in a common language (*res publica literaria*) was a reality in the first part of the sixteenth century. The disadvantage of writing in the vernacular is well illustrated by *Tratado sobre las pestiferas Bubas* (1498),[84] one of the best early books about syphilis, a new disease which was reaching epidemic proportions in Europe at the time. Its author, Francisco de Villalobos who later became court physician to Charles V, chose to publish his book in his native Spanish, so it was not widely read – to the detriment of the author, of ignorant medical attendants, of physicians wrestling to deal with the new disease and of its victims.[85]

However, the vernacular triumphed in the end.[86] There was a spell when French approached the status of a universal language for Europe and for the Tsar's court. Now English can claim to have reached this position for the world. But we find ourselves in the situation illustrated in Plate 5. This is a photograph of a notice prominently displayed on a coastal path in north-eastern Spain. The path is a well-developed one, frequented by the Dutch, English, French, German, Russian, Spanish and other tourists whose presence and goodwill are vital to the region's economy. The language is Catalan – impenetrable to most of the tourists, who will be able do little more than guess that it is warning them that they risk a fine (*sancio*?) of up to €300 if they do (or, maybe, fail to do?) something. But what is prohibited? The little picture is no help. Catalan is the official language of the region, in which the campaign for independence has caused such trouble of late. The assertive use of Catalan and the refusal to use Spanish in notices such as these is therefore understandable – but the refusal to make any concessions to those who cannot speak this minority language is arrogant and indefensible. Use two languages, at least one of which is likely to make sense to most of those who are meant to comply with the instruction or to benefit from the information.

Dante, who wrote *The Divine Comedy* (1320) in the vernacular, began the assault on Latin (a battle joined by Chaucer (c.1343-1400) and Langland (c.1332-c.1386) in England). Bombastus von Holenheim (1493-1541), who styled himself Paracelsus (meaning 'surpassing Celsus', a renowned ancient Roman physician) rejected the use of Latin, choosing to give his lectures on medicine in Basel in Swiss-German. Paracelsus was enlightened in many ways, rejecting the Galenic system for example, and he made an important advance in the relief of pain by inventing *laudanum* (ironically, the word is derived from the Latin meaning 'something to be praised') a solution of opium in brandy with added crushed pearls, henbane and frog-spawn and a good dose of alchemical rationalisation – he boasted that he possessed '. . .a secret remedy which I call laudanum and which is superior to all other heroic remedies' but alongside this achievement he also sold dubious medical remedies and told fortunes, proclaiming that he was imbued with magical power. Despite his sceptical approach to traditional medicine and to those who practised it he was a great believer in astrology (this was the age of Nostradamus [1503-66]) as well as in alchemy, as were so many of his contemporaries, including Cosimo de'Medici and his grandmother – other areas in which we struggle to come to terms with the mind-set of these people who had what appeared to them to be rational arguments to justify their beliefs. In fact, to say that people believed in astrology, alchemy and so on fails to get to grips with their psychology; rather, we should recognise that they didn't just believe these things, they <u>knew</u>, for example that the heavenly bodies had a direct effect on the course of their lives, that the earth was at the centre of the universe and that the Philosopher's Stone was there to be found.[87]

One of the great missed opportunities for the European Union, surely, has been its failure to promote the adoption of an equivalent 'common language'. One of the EU's initiatives could have been to require each member state to publish all widely accessible informative documents (e.g. government information sheets, letters, notices and forms, restaurant menus) in the appropriate local language plus another language 'X'. 'X' would be common throughout Europe, so that in Germany, for example, notices would be printed in German and in 'X', in France they would be in French and in 'X'. In Catalonia the notice that I am complaining about would still be in Catalan but it would be repeated in 'X'. That way European citizens need learn only their own local language and 'X' to be confident of understanding and being understood, at least at a basic level, throughout the EU. This would be cumbersome but perfectly feasible – it already works in Canada, where the two languages are English and French. The problem, obviously, lies in the choice of language 'X'. English would be the most logical today and from an international business perspective (it would also be the most convenient for me) but the members of the EU are unlikely to go along with that, particularly if the UK is no longer a member of the Union. French and German are probably mutually unacceptable. Spanish is very widely spoken in the world at large so it is a real possibility. But what about a neutral choice? How about realising Leo's ambition and using Latin? A few neologisms would be needed to cope with modern vocabulary but much of our modern vocabulary already has classical roots (quiet, temptation, popular, umbrella, document) so the problem would not be insurmountable. It was a spoken language in the Vatican – still is in Derek Jarman's film *Sebastiane* (1976), not a film I'd recommend if you find the *London Allegory* too *risqué*.

Such were the turbulent and precarious times in which Bronzino lived. There is a rich fund of information about day-to-day life in Renaissance Florence and about the political and religious situation in sixteenth century Europe. But we have very little information about the life of Bronzino himself, about the trials, tribulations and triumphs of his personal life, about how he passed his days in the streets, workshops, houses and palaces of the city in which he spent most of his life. We do, however, have his art – written and painted – and it's to his painting in particular that we shall turn next.

II

Bronzino's Art

In art, immorality cannot exist. Art is always sacred even when it takes for a subject the worst excesses of desire; since it has in view only the sincerity of observation, it cannot debase itself. A true work of art is always noble, even when it translates the stirrings of the brute, for at that moment, the artist who has produced it had as his only objective, the most conscientious rendering possible of the impression he has felt.

(Auguste Rodin[1])

An erudite and accomplished lyric and burlesque poet as well as a painter, Bronzino probably felt that his poetry, particularly his lyric work, was at least as important as his painting. His poetry is less familiar to us than his paintings: it was handwritten for private circulation amongst a small circle of aficionados and wasn't published until long after his death. The poetry, like the painting, draws on Bronzino's many great Florentine predecessors; and in particular on Petrarch and Michelangelo. He also enjoyed a long-lasting friendship with the poet Benedetto Varchi who wrote and lectured about love in all its aspects; the two exchanged sonnets each praising the other's merits.[2] Both were members of Cosimo's court and of the Accademia Fiorentina. Bronzino defended Varchi against attacks by literary critics and against accusations of immorality. The *London Allegory* may have been a response to one of Varchi's poems.[3] Bronzino's frequent and direct allusions to love between men in his burlesque poems have led to the suggestion that Bronzino was gay but this may be to read too much into them. This sort of poetry – and Bronzino was by no means the only one writing allusive or overtly erotic verse[4] – was intended to be subversive, shock, to break taboos, to cock a snook at officially sanctioned mores; lewd references to every type of sexuality were expected, and particularly to sexual practices that were officially frowned upon (sodomy, for example, though common in sixteenth century Florence, was a capital offence). Similarly, although some of his paintings have frankly homoerotic components – and the *London Allegory* is a prime example – they also feature plenty of sexually alluring women.[5] His risqué poetry eventually did him some harm: tastes changed, Savonarola had condemned burlesque poems and consigned them to his Bonfire of the Vanities (1497) and doubts about the genre persisted. So in 1547 as the Counter-Reformation gained traction, leaders of the Accademia Fiorentina declared that burlesque work was 'deceitful and wicked' and expelled Bronzino from their number (he was readmitted twenty years later, helped no doubt by his presentation of distinctly non-burlesque poems in praise of the Medici). He also suffered the humiliation of public censorship, one of a group of painters and writers accused of immoral art and improper sexual behaviour, and turned to writing respectable lyric verse in the Petrarchian mode championed by the Accademia, and to less controversial painting.[6]

Bronzino's painting master was Pontormo, to whom he was apprenticed in about 1514 and with whom he collaborated until Pontormo's death in 1557. The 'strange and shy' Pontormo, trained by Andrea del Sarto, was the leading painter in mid-sixteenth century Florence and one of the pioneers of the style which became known as Mannerism. He was a disturbed, probably tormented, man. Vasari, who admired Pontormo says that his father died when he was five years old, his mother when he was ten and his grandfather two years later – 'he was so afraid of death that he would not even hear it spoken of and avoided having to meet dead bodies.'[7] He was generally thought to be a rather prickly character; a loner who lived in an attic which could be reached only by a ladder that he pulled up after him; secretive and difficult for patrons to work with – which may help to explain why he was never appointed a court painter to the Medici family, unlike both Bronzino and Vasari. He was a bit of a hypochondriac, keeping a record of his ailments: kidney disorders, erratic bowel movements, itches, minor injuries and living in constant fear of the plague. His extreme reluctance to engage with other people ('He never went to festivals or to any public gathering, so as not to be caught in the press.') extended to an aversion to using live models – one story claims that he got round the problem by using corpses which he kept in a large tub in his studio, to the distress of his neighbours. But this doesn't tally with Vasari's account of his aversion to dead bodies. He was also less attuned to the propagandist style of portraiture that the Medici were looking for – preferring religious subjects and marvellous figure studies in chalk. Bill Viola has taken Pontormo's *The Visitation* (c.1528-9) as the inspiration for *The Greeting* (1995), one of his thought-provoking works of video art,[8] a film which demands at least ten minutes close attention, this being the duration of the complete work. Bronzino must have been one of very few people who could relate to Pontormo, to whom he became very attached; he worked hard to care for him in his old-age, incorporating his likeness in some of his frescos, completing some of his unfinished works, regularly entertaining him to meals in the Bronzino-Allori household and writing nineteen sonnets lamenting Pontormo's death.[9]

The prolonged apprenticeship that they served with a master trained painters to carry out all the steps that lay between having the initial idea for a painting and delivering the final immaculate, durable product. There were practical guides to help them, notably *Il libro dell'arte* (c.1400)[10] by yet another Florentine, the painter Cennino d'Andrea Cennini (c.1360 – before 1427). This is a 'workshop manual' for late Medieval and early Renaissance painters in which Cennini provides information on pigments, brushes, drawing, panel painting and casting, amongst other techniques and tricks-of-the-trade. Cennini mentions oil painting briefly, which argues against the popular belief that oil painting was invented by Jan van Eyck (1390-1441). In the next generation the Florentine architect Leon Battista Alberti (1404-72) wrote *On Painting* (1435), a more theoretical account of perspective, light, colour, composition, style and narrative. Books were no substitute for practical experience, however, and with so much to learn apprenticeships usually lasted at least six years, after which the successful painter could become a journeyman, and eventually a master himself.

Pontormo and his pupil are categorised by art historians as

Mannerist painters, though these are retrospective judgments which neither would have understood.[11] The term has had various meanings over the years, so it's not particularly helpful. It is derived from the Italian *maniera*, a term originally applied to literature to signify elegance of deportment, grace, ease of manner, virtuosity, fluency and refinement. These traits were esteemed in the sixteenth century for distinguishing the period from earlier, coarser patterns of behaviour. Vasari attributed *maniera* to the works of art which he most admired: those by Leonardo da Vinci (1452-1519), Michelangelo (1475-1564) and Raphael (1483-1520). In his definition of *maniera* he included 'abundant invention continued in the smallest things' and 'grace exceeding the measure'.

Vasari was a far from impartial biographer: he was a polemicist for the art of his native city in general and that of Michelangelo in particular and what he wrote was often coloured by his personal relationships with the artists whose work he was describing, some of whom were a threat to his professional standing. Nonetheless, he is still a valuable source of information about Italian Renaissance *artifice* and their work.[12] He plays a very important part in the story of the *London Allegory*. Vasari got on to Bronzino in the 10th and last volume of *Lives of the Artists*. The extracts from the book in the Penguin Classics series do not include the section on Bronzino – a measure of his importance today (nor, incidentally, does the standard undergraduate Art History text mention him[13]). Vasari appears not to have liked Bronzino.[6] His biography relegates Bronzino to the second rank on account both of his technique and of his neglect of history painting, which was held to be the most elevated genre and of which Vasari himself was a leading practitioner. Vasari says that Bronzino's best work comprises 'diligent' portraits and 'bizarre and capricious' burlesque poetry. In this context 'diligence' means highly finished, achieved as the result of painstaking labour and if pushed to the limit might be taken to imply that Bronzino's paintings are overworked and fussy. Vasari describes a *Nativity* by Bronzino as 'of such beauty that it has no equal' and writing of the portraits 'These portraits of the illustrious men of the House of Medici are all natural and vivacious, and most faithful likenesses'. Conspicuous by its absence amongst these apparently complimentary remarks is any comment about

Bronzino's facility in *disegno*. *Disegno* is a somewhat ambiguous term, the meaning of which changed during the course of the Renaissance. By Vasari's time it signified the principle at the heart of painting, sculpture and architecture; it encompassed the ideas of rule, order, variety, invention, judgment and, above all, the intellectual component of the visual arts, crucial in the ongoing debate about the painters' status relative to other *artifice*. This quality assumed particular importance in 16th century criticism and Vasari is lavish in his praise of the *disegno* evident in the work of his hero, Michelangelo.[14] So Vasari is damning Bronzino with faint praise by failing to comment on *disegno* displayed in his paintings. Bronzino got his own back: he fails to mention Vasari in any of his poems, many of which honour his literary and artistic friends and colleagues.

While painters were expected to pay homage to their illustrious predecessors, the deliberate mimicking of another's style was disapproved of, it was condemned as 'mannered', which engendered the use of 'Mannerist' as a derogatory term, used by seventeenth century critics to describe mid- and late-sixteenth-century works which they held to be derivative, contrived or excessively refined, with over-bright colours and distorted figures. Modern definitions of Mannerism emphasise the refinement and sophistication which are displayed in these elegant, highly finished works of art that are beautiful and which treat pleasing subjects: 'polished, rarefied and idealised away from the natural: hot-house plants, cultured most carefully. Mannerism is a 'stylish style'.[15] Nowadays Mannerism is accepted as a poorly defined style adopted by some of the painters in the period that followed the High Renaissance. But it is interesting how terms of critical abuse get neutralised and adopted as mainstream signifiers – 'Mannerism' joining 'Gothic' 'Impressionist' and 'Cubism', though it still carries a whiff of the trivial.

Some see Mannerism as a reaction against the elevated High Renaissance concept of art as a vigorous but controlled expression of classical balance; others see it as a development from the High Renaissance, an expression of the spiritual crises of the time, or as pure art for art's sake.[16] Michelangelo was the immediate inspiration for Mannerist art, which tended to exaggerate many of the qualities found in his work. Scenes in

Mannerist paintings are confused, the rules of perspective are not applied rigorously, there are often lots of figures and many extraneous details, making it difficult to identify the key protagonists and even the story or event that the picture is intended to portray, reducing its emotional impact. Many of the figures have their backs turned to the viewer, something that was particularly offensive to Ruskin, doyen of Victorian critics, champion of the Pre-Raphaelites and of Turner, who loathed Bronzino and his work which was:

> vile … in colour, vacant in invention, void in light and shade, a heap of cumbrous nothingness, and sickening offensivenesses, is of all its voids most void in this, that the academy models therein huddled together at the bottom … turn their backs upon him [God], to show their unagitated faces to the spectator.[17]

Elsewhere Ruskin wrote:

> It is very difficult … to divest ourselves of the prejudices which have been forced upon us by the base grotesque of men like Bronzino, who, having no true imagination, are apt, more than others, to try by startling realism to enforce the monstrosity that has no terror in itself.[18]

Mannerist colours are usually vivid, somewhat metallic but cold, adding to the viewer's lack of engagement with the work. Murray is writing about Pontormo's *Joseph with Jacob in Egypt* (1518; Room 8 in The National Gallery) when he says that the artist is obliged only to create an interesting design for which he may borrow from many sources without paying too much attention to how they relate one to another; most of his comments are equally applicable to the *London Allegory*.[19]

As well as teaching him the basic skills he needed as a painter, Pontormo instilled in Bronzino a great respect for Michelangelo and an appreciation of the Mannerist style, which he was to make his own. Pontormo's work is idiosyncratic, often an expression of his fear-ridden, misanthropic character: staring eyes in cold, blank faces that fail to engage; twisted hands; distorted, writhing nudes; figures often shown from the back and faces, when they are shown at all, depicted summarily with scant attempt at characterisation. But he pays great attention to details such as draperies, utensils, architecture (sometimes northern European) and, in

Joseph with Jacob in Egypt a remarkable spiral staircase, which seems to be suspended weightlessly and to be going nowhere. In his discussion of this painting, Vasari says that the boy sitting at the foot of the steps just to the left of the spiral stairs, wearing a dark cloak and brown tunic and holding a shopping bag, is the young Bronzino 'a figure so alive and beautiful it is a marvel'.[20] Pontormo uses glorious colour, flowing rhythms and beautiful designs but he doesn't manage, or doesn't want, to convey emotion: there is no suffering, no real grief, no depth of feeling. In this Pontormo is far from unique – after the High Renaissance mastery of the psychological portrait, painting was becoming a more intellectual exercise, an expression of literary symbolism, allegories and the like which could be 'read' or deciphered like a text. Vasari and his contemporaries chose to attempt the personification of abstract ideas rather than the representation of character through expression and gesture.

When he had completed his training and achieved the status of Master, Bronzino established his own workshop in Florence. There he in turn trained Allori who began his career by designing acres of flower and plant fantasies for the tapestries of *Stories of Joseph* (1549) which Bronzino was working on while continuing his thriving portraiture practice. Also in the workshop were Flemish artists, retained to paint the draperies and jewellery which were important features of the portraits.[21]

Bronzino had more success conveying character than Pontormo had done and he made a successful career as a portraitist, best known for his penetrating and imaginative portraits of poets, musicians and of other friends and admirers from amongst the elite in Florentine society and, in particular, of members of the Medici family. He often included portraits and portrait-like figures in his religious works, attracting unwelcome attention from the custodians of the Counter-Reformation. Bronzino's Medici portraits fulfil their predominantly propaganda purpose of expressing the family's God-given right to rule. They are minutely detailed, highly finished and above all 'elegant'. Detailed props such as books and statues often appear in his portraits to help to define the subject. The *Portrait of a Young Man* (National Gallery, Room 8) shows us an assured person, interrupted in his reading. There is a sculpture of Bacchus in the background.

Bronzino's service in the court of Cosimo I de'Medici began in 1539 by which time he had developed his own style, harder, more defined and with a smoother finish than Pontormo's. He stayed in the duke's service, and consequently a prominent figure in Florentine artistic circles until his death, although he was overshadowed by Vasari after 1555. His first task as a court *artifice* was to help to create the elaborate decorations for the events held to celebrate Cosimo's marriage to Eleonora of Toledo. Then he started work on his masterpiece, a chapel for the new Duchess in the Palazzo Vecchio, (completed 1564). He decorated the chapel with frescos that display all the hallmarks of Mannerism: fantastic colour, foreshortened, muscular nudes, contorted figures, exaggerated musculature and cold expressionless women.

Cosimo regularly commissioned portraits of himself, his family and his court – many of these were copied several times. These were often timed to commemorate notable events in the life of the court or of Florence; some were gifts designed to propitiate potential aggressors or to smooth the path of difficult negotiations; many were for propaganda purposes, hence their frequent reproduction to help 'spread the message', proclaim legitimacy and assert authority, just like the photographs of the state president that are displayed in shops, hotels and government offices in developing countries today. Cosimo attached great importance to the state portraits – more than he attached to Bronzino's other work for him. Now, although the portraits are admired, they are of less interest than the allegories and the decorations in Eleonora's chapel. The official portraits are beautiful in their detail, their finish and their design but they are cold, the faces haughty, studiously detached and affectless. Maybe they are intended to maintain the psychological distance between the aristocratic sitter and the plebeian masses. Alternatively, they have been said to 'betray the watchful repression of emotion and the deadened sensibility resulting from life under a violent and capricious tyrant'.[22] One portrait is still particularly highly regarded: the *Portrait of Eleonora of Toledo with her Son Giovanni*, now in the Uffizi Gallery, Florence, probably painted around 1545 (Plate 6). Eleonora was the sixth child and second daughter of Don Pedro di Alvarez di Toledo, Marquis of Francavilla and brother of the powerful Duke of Alba.

He was Charles V's most senior lieutenant and his ruthless but effective Viceroy in Naples from 1532 until his sudden death aged 68, in Florence, in 1553. Eleonora married Cosimo I in 1539 and had eleven children with him, seven of who survived. Cosimo commissioned several portraits of her, in this one she is accompanied by Giovanni, her fourth child, aged two at the time. The portrait is a propaganda piece all about the Medici dynasty. Eleonora was never painted with her daughters (and there were plenty to choose from) but she was painted by Bronzino with her eldest son, Francesco, a decade or so after this double portrait. Why not paint the eldest son – the heir – first and leave this double portrait to follow? The answer could be that this sequence is a reflection of the strategy devised by Cosimo's maternal great-grandfather, Lorenzo the Magnificent, for the family to control both Florence and Rome. He had planned for his eldest son, Piero, to succeed him in Florence, his fourth child, Giovanni, being intended for holy orders and the papacy. The plan worked in so far as Giovanni was elected Pope Leo X in 1513 but Piero ruled for only two years (1492-4) before being exiled, with the consequences discussed, in you may think tedious detail, above. Despite this set-back Cosimo obviously thought that his great-grandfather's strategy had much to commend it – in particular, power. He aspired to copy it and got off to a good start, interpretable by all who cared to think about it, by naming his own fourth child Giovanni. These children, male and female, of the rich and powerful were just pawns in an international dynastic game of musical chairs – or, worse still, pass the parcel: epitomised by Elizabeth Valois, daughter of Henri II of France and granddaughter of Francis I, who was married to Felipe II, King of Spain, son of Emperor Charles V, rather than to Felipe's son to whom she had been betrothed, and with whom, in Verdi's opera *Don Carlos* at least, she was in love. Giovanni only partially fulfilled Cosimo's expectations; he was made a Cardinal at the age of seventeen but died of malaria two years later, only a few days before both Eleonora and Giovanni's younger brother, Garzia, died of the same disease.

Eleonora sat for Bronzino wearing a brocade dress which is Spanish rather than Florentine, indicating her Spanish ancestry; it is painted in meticulous detail, occupies much of the picture space and, being stiff with embroidery and gold thread, it hides the shape of her body.[23] David Hockney suggests that Bronzino used a *camera lucida* device to help him capture the fine detail on the dress.[24] And the fine detail is important: Bronzino included several luxurious and fashionable adornments to her costume; the design on the breast of her dress is a pomegranate, a symbol of fertility, lauding her fecundity and defining her role in Cosimo's court; the jewels include Medici devices and emblems, probably made by Benvenuto Cellini. The long pearl necklace may have been Eleonora's wedding gift; it included fifty enormous pearls acquired from Venice by Eleonora's mother-in-law Maria Salviati. Eleonora and Giovanni adopt rigid postures; there is minimal bodily contact and no psychological contact between them. She is reputed to have been pious and haughty which may account for the fact that her face is impassive and delineated less sensitively than her dress but the close attention to detail and realistic presentation, blank facial expressions implying a detached arrogance, and overpowering costumes that almost smother the sitter are typical of Mannerism. Eleonora's portrait is pure propaganda, far from a cosy family portrait that captures the intimacy and tenderness that we now expect to find in an encounter between a mother and her young child and which we are assumed to appreciate in our politicians' saccharine 'Season's Greeting' cards. The point of the painting is not to give us any insights into the character of the duchess, nor to show us what sort of relationship she had with her son, though perhaps it does achieve this unintentionally, nor even to tell us what she really looked like. No, it is all about projecting an image, a rank, and a dynasty that has staying power.[25] With the exception of the last point, the same can be said of the portraits of Elizabeth I Queen of England that are so familiar to us: mask like facies, elaborate costumes, multiple copies and, in her case, sometimes the accoutrements of her regal status such as sceptres or sea battles in the background.[26] There are obvious similarities between these portraits and the, very familiar, contemporaneous portraits of Henry VIII by Holbein which are also highly detailed, smoothly finished works with a propaganda purpose.

Amongst the portraits painted by Bronzino is a group known as the 'Allegorical Portraits'. An allegory is 'a story, poem or picture which can be interpreted to reveal a hidden meaning, typically a moral or political one: *Pilgrim's Progress* is an allegory of the spiritual journey' (OED); the less familiar *Theban Tablet of Cebes* is an allegory which presents the whole of human life with its dangers and temptations.[27] Allegorical paintings are common throughout the history of European art.[28] Some identify a mundane sitter with a mythological or religious figure; others, including the *London Allegory*, have a more complex agenda. Because they use symbols to represent an idea or concept (a dove to represent peace or the Holy Spirit, for example) allegories are culturally specific – making many of them difficult for us to understand.

The Pre-Raphaelites were particularly keen on allegories and we can turn to one of their familiar paintings to exemplify the type and to show why some of these paintings can be hard to interpret. *The Hireling Shepherd* (1851) by William Holman Hunt (Plate 7) – intended as 'a rebuke to the sectarian vanities and vital negligences of the day' – appears at first glance to be a painting about a young shepherd enjoying a bucolic dalliance with his girlfriend instead of doing his work of guarding the sheep. As sheep are wont to do, the flock has strayed, one lamb is taking a green apple from the girl's lap, which may be tasty but which will certainly be indigestible, another is about to damage a field of ripe corn. To modern eyes the painting is grotesquely romantic – the colours vivid, the countryside immaculate; the weather perfect. The shepherd is well-fed, clean and in rude health – he is not one of the rural poor who populate paintings of the Barbizon School or Thomas Hardy's novels, more likely he's a prosperous yeoman farmer. The buxom wench might be the Squire's daughter dressing-down to join in a village pageant. The scene could be one from a Disney cartoon – with the exception that the characters' eyes are of normal size, they have not been infantilised in the way that cartoon characters' eyes are nowadays.[30] But these characteristics were all part of the Pre-Raphaelite search for visual realism and the true colour of sunlit shadows – and their response to Ruskin's exhortation to painters to fight the conventional, the blind, and the wicked. The moral of the painting, on first reading, is obvious – and valid: do not allow sex to lead you to neglect your responsibilities, dire consequences are sure to follow. This is a very complex painting, however, full of allusions to Shakespeare, Milton, Ruskin and the gospels and it is an allegory, so some background knowledge is needed in order to read it in the way the artist intended.[31] Most of us don't have the necessary background at our fingertips, any more than we have the background knowledge needed to read the *London Allegory* without first doing some homework. *The Hireling Shepherd* was painted 300 years after the *London Allegory* when the Oxford Movement was at its controversial height, exacerbated by Pope Pius IX's decision to re-establish the Roman Catholic hierarchy in England in 1850 which prompted many Protestants to fear for the English Church. This was the debate, most intense in the University of Oxford but engaging the whole country, about the relationship between the English and Roman Catholic Churches. Roughly speaking the highly charged arguments were about how far Church of England doctrine (transubstantiation – yes or no?) and practice (candles and incense – yes or no?) could move in the direction of Roman Catholicism without falling over a precipice and surrendering itself into the clutches of Rome? Manning and Newman had already made the move to Rome and Keble was struggling manfully, and successfully, to remain true to the English Church. The whole thing was very emotional; entertainingly, if not necessarily particularly rigorously described by Lytton Strachey in his pioneering biography of Cardinal Manning, and more soberly by MacCulloch (2010).[32] In Holman Hunt's painting, the honest, straightforward, upright, simple, innocent shepherd may be taken to represent the Church of England or its clergy; the voluptuous, seductive, flashy, sluttish girl, the Church of Rome or, less provocatively, the Anglican clergy's self-indulgent entanglement in the distractions of the arguments of the Oxford Movement; the sheep are the people of England, simple honest folk who need firm guidance if they are not 'like sheep to go astray'. Sheep are a quintessentially English species of domesticated animal, their habits are very familiar and Christ was the 'Good Shepherd'. There is no need to labour the point – the allegory is obvious once the context is understood. Hunt himself provided some commentary on a few of the details in the painting – the sheep who will die from eating grain and the lamb fed sour apples symbolise the effects of neglect and the death's-head moth signifies human mortality – the dire consequence of the failure to do one's duty.

Some allegorical paintings are relatively easy to read, even today; others demand some familiarity with Classical and Renaissance literature and mores. Bronzino's *Allegory of Admiral Andrea Doria as Neptune* is one such (Plate 8). Here is a distinguished man, a Genoese *condottiero* and admiral. At various times he had served both the French King and the Emperor in their wars against each other, and the Pope and Emperor in theirs against the Ottomans. Bronzino has portrayed him, nude except for a loin cloth, as Neptune the Greek god of the sea. To understand the painting we need to be familiar with the Greek pantheon. We also have to know how to identify the various gods in paintings, to distinguish Neptune from St Jerome, for example; this requires us to know what 'attributes' the various gods and other figures have with or close by them to enable us to recognise who they are. Neptune will have a trident, St Jerome a lion, St Catherine a wheel, and so on. Those of Bronzino's contemporaries who were privileged to see his paintings were steeped in Classical literature – that's what the Renaissance was all about – so they would have had no trouble recognising Neptune – whether or not they could recognise Andrea Doria in this pose is another matter. They might have been more interested in the suggestive way in which the shadowy form of his penis is just visible behind the cloth that drapes his pelvis and in the thick, phallic shafts of his trident and of the massive ship's mast in the background. But what an interesting way to celebrate a local hero. Imagine a similar nude portrait of Andrea Doria's contemporary, Frances Drake, or of Nelson; or perhaps Vladimir Putin would be a modern alternative, he likes striking macho, bare-chested poses.

There were also less highbrow references in works of art at that time, interpretation depending more on awareness of local slang than on knowledge of classical mythology. So, in one of his poems, *La padella*, Bronzino tells how decapitated eels can be revived in a frying pan; eels symbolised the penis and the frying pan the buttocks, so the poem is about sodomy.[33] In Caravaggio's painting *The boy bitten by a lizard* (1594-5) in the National Gallery an androgynous youth recoils as a lizard, hidden amongst some cherries, bites his finger. Understanding that the lizard symbolised the penis and cherries symbolised sexual lust leads to a possible interpretation of the painting as an allegory pointing to the fact that love can have painful consequences.

Not so easy to read and far removed from his formal state portraits is a strange depiction by Bronzino of his master, *Cosimo I, as Orpheus*, the mythical musician and passionate husband (Plate 9), which may have been commissioned as a wedding present for the Duchess Eleonora. Many painters of the time made changes to their works (known as *pentimenti*) as they went along, or even after the work had apparently been finished. Bronzino was no exception – in fact he was prone to make a lot of these changes to his pictures. He made substantial changes to this portrait of Cosimo, removing drapery, repositioning the bow and changing the shape of the viol's peg board, all to increase the erotic charge of the work. Cosimo is shown from the back but twisting round to look over his left shoulder. This representation of a figure from multiple aspects was a contemporary fashion by which painting competed with sculpture, the latter claiming to be the superior art because it could represent figures in three dimensions.[34]

The Medici court dwarf Braccio di Bartoli, called 'Morgante' after a gentle giant in a poem by Luigi Pulci, was the subject of an unusual and rather cruel allegorical painting by Bronzino that is in tune with his burlesque poetry. Dwarfs and deformed or disfigured people were victims of the Renaissance (and later) passion for collecting the strange, the novel and the exotic. In part the collections were records of the archaeological, scientific and geographical discoveries of the age: they demonstrated how *au fait* the rich collector was with the latest discoveries. But they also harked back to a medieval belief that ostentatious displays of power and wealth make Heaven jealous and provoke malign demons, both being assuaged by the sight of the disabled or abnormal who served as counters to the sins of pride and vanity.[35] At court dwarfs were also thought to add a festive atmosphere, they provided entertainment and companionship for children and they worked as jesters. Dwarfs make frequent appearances in portraits, usually as extras to emphasise the sitter's perfection rather than being there as individuals in their own right.[36] There are engravings of Cosimo's coronation which show that several dwarfs were present at the ceremony.[37] Many Renaissance rulers counted dwarfs among their possessions, a fashion that lasted from the Middle Ages all the way through to the late eighteenth century; the Emperor Rudolf II (1552-1612) kept a regiment of dwarfs and Peter the Great (1672-1725) a large troupe of them.

'Abnormal' people were collected and displayed as a sign of wealth and power because of their rarity and 'monstrosity' and they were bought and sold throughout Europe.[35] The three Gonzales sisters, their father and their brothers were of normal stature but they were all covered in a thick pelt of body hair. They spent their lives in the courts of sixteenth century Europe, where they were welcomed and well cared for, cherished as captivating animal-human hybrids, and as reminders of St Wilgefortis who miraculously grew a beard to deter the pagan king who was expected to marry her and of Mary Magdalene, who was covered by her long hair.[38]

Standards were different in those days, so Nano [dwarf] Morgante was often humiliated – he even had to fight, naked, with a monkey. Despite this, to our eyes, abuse, and unlike dwarfs in some courts who were treated as mere chattels, Morgante was an honoured member of Cosimo I's court.[39] He was paid a retainer, granted land and allowed to marry, even though he remained the property of the duke, who commissioned many paintings of him and a sculpture by Valerio Cigoli which is still in the Boboli Gardens in Florence. The sculpture is called 'Bacchus' but comparison with Bronzino's portrait makes the subject unmistakable. Morgante is riding a tortoise, making a mockery of the familiar equestrian statue and alluding to Cosimo I's motto '*festina lente*' (hasten slowly) which had also been the motto of the Roman emperors Augustus and Titus. Cosimo chose a tortoise with a wind-filled sail on his back as his personal symbol, connoting his ambition to achieve a perfect balance between speed and patience in his life and rule. Tortoises abound in the decoration of Cosimo's Palazzo Vecchio adding another layer of meaning to Cigoli's sculpture of Morgante.

It was common practice for Renaissance princes to adopt symbols for personal or family use, in addition to their more formal heraldic devices. In the case of the Medici family the formal device was a gold shield on which were arranged five red balls (*palle*) and one blue ball in which were three gold *fleurs-de-lis* – indicating the family's long-standing relationship with the kings of France, which began with Louis XI who negotiated a reduction in his kingdom's debts to the Medicis in exchange for allowing the Medici bank to use the *fleur-de-lys* as a marketing device, akin to the grant of the Royal Warrant to businesses in the UK today.[40] In addition to his personal tortoise Cosimo made use of the laurel branch that had been associated with the Medici family since the time of Lorenzo 'The Magnificent'. It appears, for example, in Botticelli's *Primavera* and in many other paintings and medals, including some versions of Bronzino's *Portrait of Cosimo I de'Medici in Armour* (c.1546) and his *Portrait of Eleonora of Toledo with her Son Giovanni* (Plate 6), in which Eleonora's pendant includes the laurel. The plant usually appeared as cut branches with sprouting leaves: the *broncone*. The Medici used the evergreen laurel and the *broncone* to symbolise the re-growth of Florence following the family's return to power. Cosimo saw the characteristics of the laurel as a reflection of himself, a new branch of the family growing back with renewed vigour after Alessandro's assassination had left the Medici without an immediate heir.[41]

Bronzino depicted Morgante nude, front and back on the face and obverse of a single piece of canvas. On the front, with his genitalia hidden by a butterfly, he is preparing to go off to catch birds; he is holding an owl which had been trained to catch small birds. The painting on the back shows him returning from his expedition, carrying his catch. Compared with Bronzino's other extant work this appears to be crudely finished, though its poor condition may be partly to blame for this. Morgante is lumpen, fat and bow-legged in striking contrast with either Andrea Doria or Cosimo. Nude bodies were meant to be idealised, regardless of reality – that was the point: they were representations of Classical beauty. Similarly, Morgante's face is ugly and contorted. No flattery here, instead a refusal to abide by the conventions of either straightforward or allegorical portraiture: it is not exalting virtue or celebrating great achievements, it is not conferring additional status on its subject. By parodying the artistic conventions of the day Bronzino has taken on himself one of the accepted roles of the court dwarf or jester, which was to present a satirical image of the ruler and his court. At the same time Bronzino has again provided his answer to the age-old question which was exercising Florence's cultural community at the time: which is the superior art-form, sculpture or painting? Painting, of course, Bronzino replies: not only can it represent a subject from all angles, as he had done some ten years earlier in the *Portrait of Cosimo I de' Medici as Orpheus*, but it can also show the passage of time.

The theme of the *Budapest Allegory* (Plate 2) is similar to that of the *London Allegory* but the composition is less complicated and the probable meaning of the painting more obvious. Venus is leaning on a vase of roses, holding an arrow which points downwards to the dubious pleasures of carnal love. Cupid holds an arrow pointing upwards, towards the delights of heavenly love. The figure in the background with snakes in its hair may represent jealousy or envy, while the kneeling child crowning another child with flowers may represent innocence. Similar figures occur in the *London Allegory* so a detailed discussion of their possible meanings can wait for now. A technical analysis of the *Budapest Allegory* has shown that Bronzino changed his mind about it a few times: there are several over-paintings and other revisions (*pentimenti*) in it. For example, there used to be a satyr in the lower right-hand corner where the two children are now playing with their garland of flowers.[42] This painting probably dates from about 1550, later or roughly contemporaneous with the *London Allegory*, making it unlikely that someone saw the *Budapest Allegory* and asked Bronzino either to repeat it or to make a new, rather more complicated, version of it.

III

The London Allegory: Why did Bronzino paint it?

Now that we have studied Bronzino's life and the episteme in which he lived, we can turn our attention to the *London Allegory*. We shall begin by asking why Bronzino should stray from his path as an established painter of religious subjects and official portraits to produce this strange work. Once again, we encounter a riddle for it is by no means certain for whom or for what purpose the painting was created.

Substantial works of art like the *London Allegory* demanded the time, money, intellect and hard physical labour of an established master *artifice*, his apprentices and his studio assistants; they were not produced 'on spec' as they might be today. Bronzino would not have started work until he was sure that he had a client who would cover the cost of the work and leave him with a profit. In return for his money the patron would have demanded an input into the painting – its size, the quality of materials that Bronzino would use and, of course, its subject matter.

Presumably, Bronzino painted the *London Allegory* in response to a commission from a wealthy Florentine client, but we are not sure who the client was. The most straightforward assumption is that it was Cosimo I. After all, Bronzino was a citizen of Florence, of which Cosimo was the ruler, and Bronzino was one of Cosimo's court *artifice*. So, Cosimo commanded and Bronzino obeyed. Vasari's biography of Bronzino supports but does not confirm this assumption:

> Wherefore the Duke, having recognised the ability of this man [Bronzino], caused him to set his hand to adorning a chapel of no great size in the Ducal Palace for the said Lady Duchess... The Lord Duke, having seen from these and other works the excellence of this painter, and that it was his particular and peculiar field to portray from life with the greatest diligence that could be imagined, caused him to paint a portrait of himself, at that time a young man... About the same time, also, he executed in the Palace for the Carnival, two years in succession, two scenic settings and prospect-views for comedies, which were held to be very beautiful. And he painted a picture of singular beauty that was sent to King Francis in France, wherein was a nude Venus, with a Cupid who was kissing her, and Pleasure on one side with Play and other Loves, and on the other side Fraud and Jealousy and other passions of love. The Lord Duke had caused to be begun by Pontormo the cartoons of the tapestries... he gave orders that Bronzino should do the rest.[1]

I have quoted Vasari at length to include the bracketing statements which set his remarks about the *London Allegory* in context. We'll return to this passage in a moment. Meanwhile just note that although the context implies that Cosimo commissioned the *London Allegory*, Vasari does not specifically say that he did, making it possible that Cosimo first came across the painting after Bronzino had started work on it on behalf of a different client (Bartholomeo Bettini, perhaps[2]). Cosimo liked it and hijacked the commission only to find that the 'completed' painting was too sexually explicit, which prompted him to give it away to the less straight-laced Francis as soon as he could.[3] My opinion is that Cosimo commissioned the work but in a relatively anodyne form; then before it was completed he decided to give it to Francis and, on that account, asked Bronzino to make changes to the painting which substantially increased its erotic charge and increased its relevance to the king.[4]

Vasari (above) does not tell us who sent the picture to King Francis, and there is no evidence of its presence in France in the sixteenth century.[5] Nor does Vasari say when the *London Allegory* was created. The other works that he mentions can be dated to the early 1540s and if he meant that the *London Allegory* was sent to Francis I it must have been completed before the king's death in

1547, so a date of about 1545 is assumed for the painting – but it is only an assumption. Finally, if Vasari is writing about the painting that we call the *London Allegory*, his description is not very good – he doesn't mention the prominent figure of Time, and he gets muddled about which side the various figures are on. Vasari's biography of Bronzino was included in the second edition of his *Lives*, published in 1568, long after we think the *London Allegory* was painted and sent to France, so Vasari could have forgotten about the details of the painting if he saw it in the mid-1540s, and he had no opportunity to look at the work again to refresh his memory. He may have seen what is now the *Budapest Allegory*, which he does not mention in his book, soon after it was painted in about 1550 and could very well have confused the two paintings.[4]

We can be confident that the *London Allegory* was sent to a French king and it will be easiest for us, I think, to move forward on the generally accepted assumptions that Cosimo commissioned it and that he sent it to Francis I. In Chapter V we shall look briefly at a suggestion that it was sent to a different French king – and do not find it to be compelling. If we are wrong about Cosimo's initial role but correct to think that he became involved at some stage, some minor aspects of our interpretation may prove to be ill-founded but our most important conclusions should remain valid – I hope. Certainly we should be on safe ground when we attribute the leading roles in our story to Cosimo and Francis I, plus Bronzino, of course.

Cosimo de'Medici, was chosen to rule Florence in 1537 in succession to Alessandro, after he had been assassinated by Lorenzino de'Medici.[6] Cosimo was the great-great-grandson of Lorenzo, Brother of Cosimo (1389-1464), the Medici *Pater Patriae*; his mother, Maria Salviati, was a grand-daughter of Lorenzo the Magnificent. Cosimo's new fiefdom was in decline, impoverished and demoralised by years of unstable government, corruption and warfare in which it had been little more than a pawn in the power games played by the popes, the emperors and the kings of France.

Cosimo was well educated, although he was young and inexperienced he was determined to be his own man. He would have looked back on Italy's recent history with fear and revulsion and vowed to do all in his power to prevent Florence becoming embroiled in the continuing struggle between the rival powers. The cabal which chose him expected him to be a relatively passive figurehead who would do the bidding of a team of 'magnificent counsellors' appointed by them. He would also be constrained by the fact that the formidable Fortezza da Basso, which dominated the town, was occupied by Spanish troops loyal to the emperor. They were commanded by Alessandro Vitelli who held Alessandro de'Medici's wife and illegitimate son as hostages in the Fortezza, along with Cardinal Cibó and most of the Medici's treasure. Before indulging his taste for hunting, hawking and fishing and his ambition to restore the fortunes and image of Florence, Cosimo had to assert his authority on the government of the city. He was austere, secretive, suspicious to the point of appearing paranoid at times – but recent Florentine history justified his doubts about those around him. Though he listened to his counsellors, Francesco Guicciardini and Francesco Vettori, to his secretary, Francesco Campana, and especially to his mother, he reserved decision-making to himself.

Disaffected Florentine citizens, led by Filippo Strozzi, soon played into Cosimo's hands by raising an army and attempting a coup. They were decisively defeated by Cosimo's forces, led by the military commander, Vitelli, at a battle near Prato in 1537. Cosimo promptly consolidated his hold on the city by executing the rebel leaders, many of them scions of Florence's most prominent families; sixteen were publicly beheaded, many others died in prison or were murdered in the cities in which they had taken refuge. Some years later Lorenzino de'Medici, responsible for Alessandro's assassination and the only remaining Medici with a good rival claim to the leadership of Florence, was done to death in Venice: he was stabbed with a poisoned dagger, probably at Cosimo's behest. Cosimo secured his position as the undisputed ruler of the city and began to flex his muscles. Vitelli was dismissed and sent off to Rome; Vettori was sidelined; Guicciardini retired (and in retirement wrote a celebrated history of Italy to which we owe much of our knowledge of the period); Cibó was sent back to Rome after alleging that Cosimo had tried to poison Alessandro's son, Giulio.

Tyrannical but hard-working and effective Cosimo restored the fortunes of Florence, put the finances on a sound footing, established a stable, just government and an efficient bureaucracy, safeguarded the interests of the working people, improved the infrastructure of the city and the *contado*, improved the productivity of Tuscan agriculture, expanded the area under Florentine control and built a fleet which later played a creditable part in the Battle of Lepanto. He also strove to distance himself and his regime from the loose morals of Alessandro's court; he was chaste and faithful to his wife, he re-introduced sumptuary laws and clamped down on public displays of immorality, violence and gambling. He reorganised the system of magistracies in the state. All within the sixteenth century context of self-interest – Cosimo took full advantage of his position to enrich the Medici family.

Prostitution was rife in Florence when Cosimo came to power; Aquinas had said that it served a public good – like sewers – drawing on Aristotle to argue that it is preferable to sodomy. It was tolerated, taxed and regulated by the Onestà (Office of Decency), whence the income went into Cosimo's treasury but from there it was disbursed to support the Convent of the Converterite (which received the money directly from the registered prostitutes from 1559 until the eighteenth century).[7] Cosimo reinstated laws which obliged prostitutes to wear a red, green or yellow veil when they appeared in public, clamped down on corruption in the Onestà and created official residential streets for prostitutes.[8]

'Sodomy' (homosexuality) is also said to have been very common in Renaissance Florence. Possibly this was because the city's men got married at the unusually late average age of roughly 30 to 31, and because of the large number of men who remained lifelong bachelors – approximately 12 percent of the male population. This left a large population of young, frustrated males in a city where many women were sheltered by their families or were otherwise inaccessible. Donatello, Poliziano, Michelangelo and other *artifice*, including Pontormo and Bronzino, of course, were probably homosexual; Leonardo was charged with sodomy, but the case never came to court; in 1556 Benvenuto Cellini was sentenced to four years in prison; Lorenzo 'The Magnificent' was probably bi-sexual. To judge by court records, sodomy was a routine part of the drinking, gambling and open sexuality of the single male culture. On August 31, 1512, thirty young aristocrats, the father of Cosimo I amongst them, broke into the Palazzo della Signoria demanding that the council revoke the sentences of all those who had been exiled or deprived of office for sodomy. Their action helped to overthrow the republican government; Guilio and Guiliano de'Medici acceded to their demands when they seized power two weeks later.[9] There were further relaxations of the law and moderation of sentences over the next couple of decades. All this changed with the advent of Cosimo. He was temperamentally puritanical, at least by the standards of the day, and both he and his subjects were scared by an earthquake and by thunderbolts which damaged the Duomo which they interpreted as portents of worse punishments to come should they fail to improve moral standards within the State. Duke Cosimo, greatly frightened, put himself in God's hands and, supported by the clergy, created two very severe laws, one against blasphemy and the other against sodomy, imposing harsh penalties on delinquents, even death.[10] The clamp-down on sodomy had an immediate effect – there were a lot of convictions in the 1540s, but many fewer subsequently, either because the laws had had the intended deterrent effect or, more likely, because the authorities ceased to enforce them so diligently.[11]

Cosimo's campaign to tighten the governance of the city-state and improve public morality came at a personal and a public cost. At first he was supported by the workers of Florence and by some of the leading families of the city. But his high-handed decision-making style and his withdrawn, unfriendly personality gradually alienated his citizens. Florentines, 'as persons who were always insatiable,' began to hope and agitate for 'some kind of ruin against the Duke, who was gradually becoming more strict with his subjects.'[12] They acknowledged Cosimo's achievements and were grateful for his sponsorship of their pageants and feasts but they didn't warm to him and rarely offered him much in the way of overt support. For his part Cosimo grew increasingly morose and cannot have been cheered by living under the constant threat of assassination. Several attempts were made to murder him – despite the ghastly punishments inflicted on those would-be assassins who were unfortunate or incompetent enough to be caught. To move around his own city he had to go well-armed, wear chain mail and be accompanied by a bodyguard.

His foreign policy was determined by the weak position of Florence in a world dominated by the two regional powers,

France and the Holy Roman Empire. When Cosimo came to power in Florence, Charles V and Francis I were well entrenched as rulers of the Holy Roman Empire and of France respectively. Their mutual antipathy was as toxic as ever and crystallised over the issue of ownership of Milan. The Church, so important to Florence in the previous hundred years, was of less immediate significance to Cosimo. The papacy had been severely weakened by the wars which culminated in the sack of Rome; only one of the popes during Cosimo's rule was a member of the Medici family, so they had less personal interest in his fortune or that of Florence. The accession of Pius IV to the papacy in 1559 did strengthen Cosimo's position somewhat because Pius was a Medici of Milan and well-disposed to the Florentine Medici.[13] He gave a cardinal's hat to Cosimo's son Giovanni in 1560 and, after Giovanni's death, one to another son, Ferdinando, in 1563. In reality, the popes were forced to devote most of their attention, and to use what political capital they did have, to countering the Protestant threat outside Italy. Florence was never seen as a hotbed of Protestantism and after the flight of the *Spirituali* following the Regensburg colloquy in 1541[14] the popes felt secure enough to leave the city alone. France and the Empire were a different matter; they continued to have designs on the Italian states as pawns in their struggles with each other for dominance in Europe. Only too well aware of the potentially dire consequences of Florence's relatively weak position, Cosimo had to be appropriately subservient to the dominant power of the day without alienating the other power – the weaker of the two today but potentially the more powerful tomorrow, contingent on the outcome of future events elsewhere. Ideally, Cosimo wanted both powers to treat his domain with benign indifference. His situation was not unlike that of Ukraine and the Baltic States today – caught between the EU and Russia they are paying a heavy price for appearing to favour their neighbours to the west.

When he came to power in 1537 Cosimo had to accept that Florence was a vassal of the emperor, Charles V, who could call on the Spanish troops garrisoned in the Fortezza da Basso to bring the Florentines to heel should they become disaffected and agitate for greater autonomy. Cosimo attempted to cement his relationship with Charles V by arranging to marry his daughter Margaret (Alessandro's widow). Charles, however, preferred to secure the pope's loyalty so he sponsored Margaret's marriage to Pope Paul III's grandson. Cosimo next approached Don Pedro of Toledo, Charles's trusted viceroy in Naples. Don Pedro agreed to the marriage of Cosimo with his only daughter Eleonora – immensely rich but as demanding, volatile, arrogant and extravagant as the best of the Medici (Plate 6). Their marriage, in 1539, was a success and it was only in the company of his wife and his daughters that Cosimo seems to have been really at ease. She was in poor health for the last few years of her life and died, probably of malaria, in Cosimo's arms in 1562. Her death was closely followed by those of their two young sons and of Cosimo's favourite daughter – leaving him inconsolable. He tried to assuage his grief by hunting more fanatically than ever, by eating enormous meals and by taking first a young mistress and then a young wife, whom he quickly came to loathe.[15] Cosimo died, exhausted, in1574 at the age of fifty-five.

By the time of his death only four of his and Eleonora's eleven children survived: Francesco, who succeeded him as Grand Duke of Tuscany, Ferdinando, who succeeded Francesco, Isabella and Pietro. And this was not to be the end of the family's tragedies. In 1553, eleven-year-old Isabella had been betrothed to twelve-year-old Paolo Giordano Orsini, a liaison her father thought necessary to secure Florence's southern border and to cement his relationship with the ancient Roman Orsini family. On 16 July 1576 Isabella died unexpectedly during a hunting holiday. According to her brother this occurred 'while she was washing her hair in the morning' but more credence is given to the report of the ambassador from Ferrara that she was strangled at midday by her husband in the presence of several named servants. Orsini probably killed Isabella because she had been carrying on a love affair with his cousin Troilo Orsini. 1576 was a bad year for sudden deaths in the Medici family. Isabella's cousin, Leonora, had died of a similar 'accident' only a few days before her. And her younger brother Pietro de' Medici accused his wife of adultery and strangled her with a dog lead. He had her supposed lover Bernardino Antinori imprisoned and killed. Joanna of Austria, Francesco's wife, died in 1578 aged 31, possibly having been pushed down a flight of stairs but more likely of a ruptured uterus.

Let's turn now to King Francis, likely recipient of the *London*

Allegory. After the death without surviving issue of Louis XII the French crown had passed to his cousin Francis (1494-1547), from the Angoulême branch of Louis's Valois family. Francis and his sister, Marguerite (1492-1549), were raised by his widowed mother Louise (1476-1531), whom he held in awe, kneeling whenever he spoke to her. Louis XII had not trusted his heir-presumptive so he hadn't bothered to train him in state-craft. Instead he sent him to join the army at Guienne at the age of eighteen. There Francis learned something about warfare and a lot about the licentiousness of camp life, which he found very much to his liking. Betrothed at fourteen, Francis married Louis XII's frail, gentle and pious fourteen-year-old daughter Claude when he was twenty. She bore Francis a child each year to a total of seven pregnancies before her death in 1524. In 1515, at the age of 20, Francis became king of France as Francis I (1515-47).

Francis was an intelligent man but inexperienced, not very well educated ('he had small Latin and less Greek'), frivolous, self-indulgent and lacking well-informed, genuinely impartial advisors. Because he was outgoing, credulous, inconsistent and incapable of dissembling he was politically inept. He allowed himself to be dominated by favourites whom he promoted and dismissed capriciously. Ambassadors to his court reported on his negligence and his ministers were driven to distraction by it. He relied heavily on the wise counsel of his mother and sister but after his mother's death of plague in 1531, by which time his sister was living far away with her husband the King of Navarre, he was on his own. His mother and sister were powerful influences over him throughout their lives; they indulged Francis and forgave, if not actively encouraged, his excesses. Later in life his mistresses, particularly his 'official mistresses' Francoise de Chateaubriant and Anne de Pisseleu (Duchess of Etampes, whose advice was prejudiced by her antipathy towards Charles V) significantly influenced his policies and actions.[16]

Francis's great ambition was for France to achieve supremacy over the emperor, a struggle which eventually bankrupted the kingdom and left the country no larger and no more secure than it had been under Louis XII. At first, though, he had a glorious success leading his army in a bold trans-alpine march, capturing Milan and leading the French cavalry in person to defeat the formidable mercenaries of Duke Sforza and Pope Leo X at the

e

Battle of Marignano (1515). The supposedly chastened pope, who needed French help in his disputes with the empire and with England, propitiated Francis with concerts, banquets and stage shows, offered him a *Madonna* by Raphael and negotiated the Concordat of Bologna that returned the benefices of the wealthy Church in France to the pope in exchange for granting the king the authority to appoint bishops in France.[17] Francis gave Sforza a pension, signed a perpetual peace treaty with the Swiss and bought Tournai back from Henry VIII of England. To pledge his 'unalterable friendship' he betrothed his first-born child, Princess Louise, to the Habsburg prince Charles of Austria, who was already King of Spain and was soon to become Holy Roman Emperor (Charles V); Louise died in childhood, as did her sister Charlotte who was also betrothed to Charles.

Then things began to go wrong; ambition triumphed over common-sense; Francis made a bid for the imperial crown when Maximilian I died in 1519, infuriating Charles and reigniting the bitter feud between the two kingdoms. The series of wars between France and the Habsburgs which followed lasted until 1756. Francis found himself surrounded by the sea to his west and by Charles's territories to the south, east and north-east. He tried to form an alliance with Henry VIII of England whom he met at 'The Field of the Cloth of Gold' (1520) but Henry preferred an alliance with Charles, though he would prove to be a fickle ally to both countries throughout his life. Four of the Italian Franco-Imperial wars occurred during Francis's reign. The first culminated in the defeat of Francis I at Pavia (1525) and his captivity in a grim fortress in Madrid. After muttering about abdication and blustering, 'I am resolved to endure prison for as long as God wills rather than accept terms injurious to my kingdom!' he ratified the brutal Treaty of Madrid (1526), and was released. Under the terms of the treaty he had to surrender Burgundy and leave his two eldest sons as hostages. Francis, the Dauphin (1518-36, aged eight) and Henri (1519-59, six years old) were just recovering from measles and they were kept in such bad conditions that the experience left them permanently psychologically damaged and Francis infected with the tuberculosis that would eventually kill him. The king, who had suffered a life-threatening illness himself while in captivity, felt he had no alternative but to sign the treaty; he did so with his fingers crossed, declaring privately that the word and signature of an imprisoned knight were valueless and also that it was not within his power to dismember his kingdom. Francis's wife, Claude, had died in 1524 which left him free to accept another of the treaty's terms – his betrothal to Eleanor of Portugal, sister of Charles V as an earnest of the reconciliation between the two houses. They were married in 1530. Everything was then thrown into confusion when provinces which Francis has been forced to cede to the empire refused to be handed over. Exasperated, Charles kept the children for another four years; his army ravaged Italy and captured Pope Clement VII. Francis could not openly defy the emperor so he diverted himself with hunting trips, with travelling around the country, building elaborate castles, enhancing his collections of paintings and sculpture and with founding the Collège de France – anything rather than make a serious effort to resolve the international situation.

The second Italian war, in which France was allied with Italian princes including Pope Clement VII (League of Cognac, 1526), led to further humiliation for Francis and to the sack of Rome (1527).

Eventually, Francis's mother and Charles's aunt worked together to negotiate a relaxation in the terms of the Treaty of Madrid (Treaty of Cambrai, 1529 – the *Paix des Dames*) so that Francis could get the boys back, though to do so he had to renounce his claims in Italy and pay a ransom of two million gold crowns (four and a half tons of gold). In the 1530s genuine but ultimately unavailing attempts were made to settle the differences between France and the empire but just as Cosimo came to power in Florence the fraught relationship between these two great powers broke down again. Francis, who had been busily building a standing army, chose to start the third war in 1536 when Charles was chastened by the failure of his recent expedition against Tunis. French troops marched into Piedmont and Savoy, and those of Charles V into Provence. The Dauphin died that year – inevitably there were rumours that he had been poisoned by Charles V but it is more likely that it was the conditions under which the emperor had held the boy in Madrid that killed him; his brother, Henri, became Francis's heir. Pope Paul III led the negotiations which brought this third Italian war to an end with the Treaty of Aigues-Mortes, supposedly heralding a ten-year truce (1538). The emperor visited France, where he was lavishly entertained. The rapprochement was short-lived.

So, the Franco-Imperial wars were well under way in 1539 and Cosimo had to support his suzerain, Charles V. The emperor was short of money to pay his army so Cosimo plundered Eleonora's dowry to help him and in return Charles withdrew his garrisons from the Fortezza da Basso, Livorno and Pisa. These towns were promptly brought back under Cosimo's control. A decade later Cosimo helped Charles's Spanish troops with their attack on Siena, a longstanding enemy of Florence defended by Filippo Strozzi's son, Piero. The French moved to relieve Siena. It took the combined Florentine and imperial forces three years (1553-5) and a siege to defeat the Sienese and their French allies, led by this time by Francis's successor, Henri – leaving the population of the town reduced from 16,000 to 6,000 and the countryside devastated.

At Siena and throughout his reign Cosimo's allegiance to the emperor was obvious for all, including the French, to see. The allegiance brought with it the risk that the French would turn on Florence, should they ever be strong enough to do so – either because of the city-state's strategic importance to the empire, or as a way to divert imperial forces to its defence, or to wound the emperor and add to Francis's possessions. Just in case there was a shift in the balance of power, Cosimo had to maintain friendly relations with the French, so that in the event that they did gain the upper hand, they would not wreak revenge on Florence. Cosimo may have seen the truce brokered between Francis and Charles at Aigues-Mortes as his licence to establish cordial relations with the French king. However, the rapid collapse of the truce must have made the early 1540s a particularly difficult time for him: Charles and Francis continued to quarrel about Milan; Francis was building an anti-Habsburg coalition, predominantly with northern European states, with which he planned to strike when the time was ripe. Charles was looking vulnerable; he was distracted by the rise of Protestantism in his northern territories and by Turkish aggression in the east. In 1540 a Habsburg fleet destroyed an Ottoman fleet off Alborán Island in the Mediterranean but the following year the imperial campaign in Algeria failed; and the Ottoman leader, Suleiman the Magnificent, took Buda. The next year the emperor mounted an abortive military campaign in Algeria. Two French diplomats were murdered by imperial troops in 1541, giving Francis (urged on by the Duchess of Etampes) an excuse to take advantage of Charles's difficulties: war erupted in Italy again in 1542. In this latest round of fighting Francis allied himself with James V of Scotland and with Suleiman, against the emperor, who was allied with Henry VIII of England. There was vicious fighting in Italy, France, and the Low Countries, and attempted invasions of both Spain and England. Fortunes swung this way and that as the various parties tried to take as much territory for themselves as they could. Nice (an imperial possession) was taken by combined Ottoman and French forces and Suleiman took the Hungarian (Habsburg) cities of Esztergom and Székesfehérvárin in 1543. The latter would remain in Ottoman hands for the next 145 years. In 1544 the French defeated forces of the Holy Roman Empire in the Battle of Ceresole near Turin. It must have looked to Cosimo as though Francis was in the ascendant – and like the weakling trying to appease the playground bully he may have felt he had to try to protect Florence by sending Francis a gift. The pendulum then swung against the king; Charles invaded eastern France; King Henry VIII besieged and captured Boulogne and by the autumn of that year Charles and Francis agreed to cease hostilities (Peace of Crépy); Francis still had to prosecute his war with England while Charles had to deal with the Protestants and with Ottoman incursions in the East; neither had designs on Florence. Cosimo could relax. It was during a naval engagement with French galleys in the Solent to repulse Francis's attempt to invade England via the Isle of Wight in 1545 that Henry's ship Mary Rose sank after thirty-four years' service.

The death of his old ally Pope Clement and the election of the Farnese Pope Paul III were bitter blows which forced Francis to refocus his relationship with Rome, just as he was confronted by the posting of vituperative anti-Catholic placards in Paris and several other cities in his kingdom: *l'affaire des placards*.[18] Francis reacted savagely to what must have appeared to him to be a much more dangerous challenge to his authority and to that of the Church than it really was: he instituted a reign of terror and persecution of Protestants which lasted for decades, merging imperceptibly into the wars of religion which raged throughout France for a century. In the early 1540s, just as Bronzino was painting the *London Allegory*, booksellers were being burnt at the stake in Paris and the Sorbonne was drawing up the first index of forbidden books.[19] In 1540 Francis officially declared Protestantism to be 'high treason against God and mankind' which warranted the most brutal suppression. Countless acts of dispossession, torture and judicial killing followed; worst of the many atrocities was the annihilation of the town of Mérindol and many surrounding villages in 1545, with the slaughter of thousands and the enslavement of hundreds in the French fleet of galley-ships.[20] We can imagine that Francis must have welcomed the refined distraction provided by the *London Allegory* with its reassurance that he was a cultured man at the head of a sophisticated court, able to rise above the brutal repression that he had chosen to inflict on his subjects.

Reasonably friendly links had been built between the Valois and Medici families over the previous few decades and these gave Cosimo a base on which to build his relationship with Francis. First, Louis XI allowed the family to use the *fleur-de-lys*; then, albeit sporadically, the French had been allied with the Medici popes, Leo X and Clement VII, in some of their Leagues against the Holy Roman Empire and the Ottoman Turks. Then Francis had spent time soliciting Leo's and Clement's help in his efforts to regain Milan. Back in 1517 he had congratulated Leo's nephew Lorenzo de'Medici when he became head of the Florentine government – 'I intend to help you with all my power. I also wish to marry you off to some beautiful and good lady of noble birth and my kin so that the love I bear you may grow and be strengthened'. True to his word, Francis arranged for Lorenzo to marry the royal princess Madeleine de La Tour d'Auvergne. Madeleine and Lorenzo both died soon afterwards but not before they had had a daughter – none other than Catherine de'Medici. Clement VII brokered her marriage to Henri de Valois, heir to the French throne. Catherine was a formidable woman, destined to become a force in European power politics. Francis became close to his daughter-in-law whose intellect and ideas about the role of the monarchy he respected. Together they encouraged an 'Italianisation' of the French court, introducing Italian cuisine, music and art which opened an avenue through which Cosimo could ingratiate himself with the French. He allowed Cellini to visit Paris in 1537 and to return there for four years in 1540.

The Italianisation of his court helped Francis to join Cosimo and many of their fellow European monarchs in a competitive effort to create sumptuous courts through which they could display their taste and wealth. Humanists and poets, such as Vincenzo Borghini, and the historians Scipione Ammirato and Benedetto Varchi enjoyed Cosimo's patronage. And Bronzino, poet as well as painter, wrote sycophantic Petrarchan sonnets extolling the Medici; in 1551 he reported from Pisa where he was painting the duke's children: 'I am continually with these most saintly sovereigns, and I rejoice in the blessed sweetness of so good and benign a prince.'[21] Cosimo encouraged the formation of a small private Academy in Florence and soon gave it official status as the Accademia degli Umidi, which was converted into the Accademia Fiorentina in 1547 – this is the organisation that expelled Bronzino because it judged his burlesque poetry to be 'deceitful and wicked'.

Cosimo's determination to modernise the Florentine civil service led him to house all the various offices and committees in a single building. This was the Uffizi ('Offices'), designed and built by Vasari, his superintendent of buildings, and first used as an art gallery by Cosimo's son Francesco. Cosimo restored the plundered Palazzo Medici, and completed the Biblioteca Laurenziana, commissioned by Clement VII in 1523 but not completed until 1571. Cosimo moved his official seat from the Palazzo Medici to the Palazzo della Signoria in 1540, signalling the security of the Medici's position in Florence. Eleonora disliked the Palazzo della Signoria and bought the Palazzo Pitti in 1549; she and Cosimo moved there the following year, renaming the Palazzo della Signoria the Palazzo Vecchio, the 'Old Palace', and leaving behind the frescos in the private Chapel of Eleonora on the second floor of the palace on which Bronzino continued sporadically to work until at least 1565.[22] These religious works in the chapel are famous for epitomising the highly-stylised, impersonal, affectless elegance of Florentine Mannerism.

As a patron of music, Cosimo merged the cathedral and baptistery chapel choirs and personally chose the master responsible for the cathedral choir of about thirty singers. He also maintained a brass ensemble which usually played at military functions and state processions and a wind band which performed at public and religious ceremonies, at mealtimes and at official receptions in the Palazzo Vecchio. His court composers wrote madrigals, a popular genre which was stimulated by Pietro Bembo's 1501 edition of poems by Dante and Petrarch (the Canzoniere, 'Songbook'). Bembo (1470-1547) was a Venetian, a self-appointed champion of the Tuscan language.[23] Bronzino looked on him as a model when he abandoned the burlesque in favour of more refined poetry. Madrigals strike modern listeners as quite refined works but some were almost bawdy – *Per Dio, Tu Sei Cortese* (1540-6) for example describing the symptoms and signs of syphilis – The Pox.[24]

However genuine their sympathy with the arts might have been, the sixteenth century monarchs' magnificent buildings and collections of the works of the very best *artifice* were instruments of policy, designed for their self-aggrandisement and to display the munificence of their past and present patronage. Nonetheless, we can but admire their taste and discernment and be grateful that much of the glory of these courts remains for us to enjoy.

Both Francis and Cosimo took a personal interest in their collections and in the *artifice* whom they sponsored – for them it was much more than a matter of sending agents out to build up a collection with which they could overawe their rivals. Life at court must nonetheless have been tense and stultifyingly dull – governed by a rigid protocol that reinforced a jealously guarded hierarchy and always at the whim of a capricious despot. There can have been few genuinely relaxed moments; otherwise there would have been no need to employ characters like Morgante to provide light relief. Diversions such as complicated, painted allegories would have been very welcome.

Cosimo encouraged the traditional demotic entertainments in Florence – feasts, pageants, horse-racing, football and chariot races; he demanded refinement in personal and public behaviour and dress and he pandered to the popular craving for fancy titles by creating his Order of St Stephen into which he inducted as knights 'young people who now despise trade and commerce'.[25] He also shared the patrician interest in music, science, horticulture, archaeology – in which he was a pioneer – and botany. He was a knowledgeable collector of medals and Etruscan artefacts – and claimed descent from the first Etruscan settlers in Tuscany and the title *Ducatus Etruriae*. Cosimo visited the workshops of Florentine painters and sculptors to inspect their work and called on writers and scholars to remind them of his continuing interest in what they were doing. He tried to lure Titian from Venice and Michelangelo to return to Florence (both without success, though he did manage to get hold of Michelangelo's body for burial in Florence in 1564). He commissioned work by Pontormo and, of course by Bronzino, by Cellini, when he returned from Paris in 1545, and later by the Mannerist sculptor Giambologna, who settled in Florence in 1557. In his cadre of court artists Cosimo boasted Bronzino, Ammanati, Cellini, Giambologna and Vasari.

Assuming that Cosimo did commission the *London Allegory* in the 1540s, he had a galaxy of talented painters on hand from which to choose one to create the painting for him. Why did he choose Bronzino? Well – Pontormo was probably too old, too wedded to religious painting and too obstreperous to be considered; Cellini, more a sculptor than a painter, was in France; Vasari was younger, not yet as well established as Bronzino and he liked to think of himself as a member of a better class of more serious painters because he worked in the more elevated genre of 'history painting' – he did eventually displace Bronzino in the court pecking-order but not until a few years later; Ammanati and Giambologna came to prominence only in the 1560s. Bronzino was already a Medici favourite, having painted so many family portraits, and he was engaged on the decoration of Eleonora's chapel at the time. On top of that, if Cosimo wanted a subtle allegorical painting, who better to turn to than the painter who had already given him the allegorical portraits of Andrea Doria (Plate 8) and of Cosimo himself (Plate 9) and who was also the author of allegorical burlesque poetry? Bronzino didn't work exclusively for Cosimo; amongst his other patrons was Bartolomeo Panciatichi, a French-born Italian diplomat and poet who developed Protestant sympathies while at the court of Francis I. He returned to Florence in 1539 but regularly visited France – he may have recommended Bronzino and brokered the deal which took the *London Allegory* to France. And Bernado de'Medici, Cosimo's ambassador to the court at Fontainebleau was in France between December 1544 and July 1545 – perhaps that is when the painting was delivered.

The *London Allegory* wasn't the only significant painting by Bronzino that Cosimo gave to those on whose good-will Florence depended. The *Deposition* from behind the altar in Eleonora's chapel, completed in the middle of 1545, was given to Nicolas Perrenot de Granvelle, Charles V's first minister. Vasari: '….it was removed from there by Duke Cosimo for sending as a present, as a very rare work, to Granvelle, who was once the greatest man about the person of the Emperor Charles V'. Granvelle had been instrumental in the negotiations which led to Charles returning the fortresses in Florence and Livorno to Cosimo. The Farnese family – rivals of the Medici – had already given him a large, valuable sculpture of Jupiter so Cosimo had to match that, or better still, trump it.[29]

Francis I was six feet tall; despite a large nose and thin legs he was considered to be handsome; his nickname was *Le Roi Grand Nez*. The many portraits of him emphasise, perhaps even exaggerate, his physical attractiveness and display his elaborate wardrobe; they were deliberately created pieces of propaganda intended to make his subjects familiar with his image and to improve his standing in foreign courts where he was thought to be weak and inconsistent.[30] Francis was the epitome of a Renaissance monarch: well-built and physically brave, with a refined deportment, affable, quick-witted and blessed with an amazing memory, courteous, a brilliant talker and a sincere lover of literature, the arts and architecture.[31] He grew up to love chivalrous romances, songs, hunting, tennis and violent exercise so he was the darling of the young bucks and rakes who hung around the French court. His relentless pursuit of women, which continued throughout his life, was part and parcel of his hedonistic life-style; he had several acknowledged mistresses and many other liaisons; it was said that 'He loved greatly and too much; for being young and free, he embraced now one, now another, with indifference' – just one of the many contemporary gossipy reports that helped to spread his reputation throughout Europe as an inveterate libertine.[32]

The French court was an extravagant institution: Francis had a staff of over 500, the queen had her own household, as did the queen-mother, and the royal children had about 240 attendants of their own. Over 700 soldiers guarded the royal household and there were always court followers, including semi-official *filles de joie* in addition to the king's acknowledged mistresses.[33] Like all monarchs of the time, Francis maintained the practice of Royal

Progresses, regularly moving his entire court round his kingdom and seldom staying in one place for very long. This carefully planned circuit of his kingdom enabled him to show himself to his subjects – to project his power – and also to dump some of the costs of the court on to the unfortunate nobility or towns on which the court chose to quarter itself. The moves were a huge undertaking. The court moved its people, furniture, tapestries, plate and documents: when the court descended on Bordeaux in 1526 stabling and fodder had to be provided for, a barely credible, 22,500 horses and mules.[34] The bishop of Saluzzo described the court to Cosimo: 'This court is like no other. Here we are completely cut off from business, and if by chance there is any, no hour, no day or month is set aside for anyone to deal with it. Here one thinks of nothing but hunting, women, banquets and moving house…'[35] It was even worse, but less futile, than the modern nonsensical migration of the European Parliament from Strasbourg to Brussels and back again every month. Francis liked to make less traditional excursions too, wandering the streets of Paris at night in search of bawdy houses where he could enjoy the services of common prostitutes.[36]

At home Francis I was a (poor) poet, a champion of the new humanism and, like so many of his fellow rulers, he took a keen interest in the arts. He owes much of his surviving reputation to the *artifice* and literati who competed for his patronage; as one of the most generous patrons of the arts of his day he tried to create a centre of learning and art in France, modelled on Rome and Florence. He was reasonably tolerant (until *l'affaire des placards*), an epicurean, an admirer of Erasmus, a reader of the Protestant Melanchthon and a patron of Rabelais – whose stories, like the burlesque poetry of Bronzino, were full of fantasy, satire, the grotesque, bawdy jokes and sexual *double-entendres*. Francis built one of the great libraries of Europe and made university education free to all who could benefit from it. He rebuilt the Louvre Palace in Paris and built or remodelled most of the chateaux along the River Loire. Many of his buildings, including chateaux and the reconstruction of the Cathedral of Notre Dame at Senlis and much of the furniture within them were adorned with carvings of salamanders (some of them crowned), as was the livery of the king's guard – Francis had adopted the animal as his personal emblem. From medieval times the salamander had been feared because it was supposed to be poisonous and for its reputed ability to survive all types of fire. It symbolised the man who had overcome great tribulation and survived the fires of passion, the man who, having retained the peace of his soul and his confidence in God, epitomised chastity, virginity and loyalty – so Francis's adoption of it was a bit tongue-in-cheek, perhaps. The salamander also featured in alchemical lore – and we know that Francis was interested in alchemy and supported a group of mystics and cabalists at his court.[37]

Francis recruited poets, painters and scholars to his court and appointed the ageing Leonardo da Vinci as the 'First Painter, Engineer and Architect to the King' in 1516. Leonardo brought the *Mona Lisa* with him to France, where he lived until his death in 1519. Florence briefly fell from Francis's favour because of the behaviour of Pontormo's teacher, Andrea del Sarto. The king had attracted the great Florentine painter to France by offering him the money he needed to pay off the debts of his extravagant wife. Del Sarto worked diligently on religious paintings and on a portrait of Francis's infant son but begged the king's permission to return briefly to Florence. The king allowed him to make a short return visit to Tuscany and gave him money with which to buy works of art for the royal collection while he was there. Del Sarto squandered the money and reneged on his sworn promise to return to France. He stayed in Florence, safe from the wrath of Francis but not from the plague, which killed him in 1530.

Francis's agents hunted for Italian paintings, sculptures, precious stones, enamels, books and rare manuscripts to ornament the French court. Lorenzo de'Medici, acting as agent for Leo X commissioned Raphael to paint *The Holy Family of Francis I* (Musée de Louvre, Paris) for Francis and Claude in 1516-7. A fallow period for the arts followed in the 1520s because the French treasury had been depleted by another round in the wars with the empire. When he was free to do so again Francis began to enlarge his favourite chateau – Fontainebleau – to which he attracted the painter Giovanni Battista Rosso (1495-1540), a Florentine who had learnt from Del Sarto and from Pontormo but who was working in Rome at the time. Rosso arrived in 1531 and spent the rest of his life in France as Francis's 'Director of stuccos and paintings'. He had been a pioneer of Mannerism in Italy and in France; along with Giulio Romano (c.1499-1546, brought from

Mantua) and Francesco Primaticcio (1504-70, from Bologna), he created a distinctive French style of Mannerism. The king liked overtly erotic works of art: he enjoyed female nudes in 'fine art' representations of mythological stories, and in more secular images of the emasculating 'woman on top' and of lesbian couplings. He built a private gallery for himself decorated by Rosso and Primaticcio with paintings of pagan gods and satyrs – just the sort of gallery in which to hang the *London Allegory* when it came to France.[38] The English ambassador to the court was given a tour of the gallery by the king himself in 1540, followed by a visit to the bathhouse on the storey below, where he saw the king's mistress and other nude ladies.[39]

The result of Francis's imaginative patronage was the 'School of Fontainebleau' centred on a palace that was famous throughout Europe and the envy of many of his fellow monarchs – bursting with art and artefacts of the very highest quality and refinement, where scholars, poets and musicians rubbed shoulders with the rude provincials more usually found in the courts of Europe at the time. And he wanted beautiful women round him all the time, saying, 'A court without women is a year without spring and a spring without roses.' As well as continuing to collect the very best Italian art Francis recruited a formidable cadre of French painters, sculptors, architects, printmakers, tapestry makers and craftsmen to succeed the Italian immigrants. Cosimo could be confident that Francis would appreciate his present of a masterpiece of Florentine painting and he could hope that it would encourage him to treat the little city-state gently.

For all the trappings of regal power and the glory of his court, Francis's life was frequently restricted by recurrent bouts of illness. Much has been written about his health but it is impossible to know with any certainty exactly what afflicted him. Medicine at the time worked with a different theory of disease and with a different vocabulary to those with which we are familiar and some of the accounts of his condition were malicious. Similarly, the treatments favoured in Francis's time often mystify us: Francis is known, for example, to have carried 'Mummy balm' or 'Egyptian Salve' with him in case of a sudden illness or accident. This medicine concocted from the corpses disinterred from Egyptian tombs was reputed to cure stomach pains and bruises. However, there are some reliable accounts of

Francis's several illnesses – it's their interpretation that is problematic. It is often said that the king had been treated for syphilis. The disease was common and his sexual adventures must have exposed him to it; his doctors believed he had it and it has an important part to play in the interpretation of the *London Allegory*, so I have devoted Chapter VI to syphilis as it existed in the sixteenth century. Let's concentrate here on the contemporary accounts of Francis's illnesses and their treatment.

Francis's philandering began when he was about fifteen years old and by 1512, when he was eighteen, his mother was reporting that he was being treated for a disease of 'his secret parts'.[40] He was said to have recovered but his subsequent history of chronic abscesses casts doubt on this. In 1524 he was sick 'of his own French disease'[41] and in September 1525, while miserably incarcerated in Madrid, Francis suffered from migraines, pain in old wounds and he developed a fever which was to last for three weeks. Very soon his condition was so bad that his doctors expected him to die. The emperor – his captor – and his sister Marguerite hurried to Madrid to be with him. The Archbishop of Embrun said a Mass at his bedside, in the presence of Marguerite.[42] An abscess was detected in (on?) the king's head which either ruptured spontaneously or was lanced, and he began immediately to improve. Georges De Selve, Bishop of Lavaur, whom we have met before (he is the man in black on the right in *The Ambassadors*), reported the king's recovery following his heroic efforts to swallow the Host presented to him by the archbishop.[43]

Francis's mother described her son's recovery as almost miraculous. Miraculous or not, his recovery was not complete, he suffered a relapse which left him weakened and susceptible to recurrent illness for the rest of his life, with a changed personality, subject to sudden reversals of mood, excesses of severity and clemency, inconsistencies in his statesmanship and in his personal behaviour: his mind sometimes wandered.

Francis was ill again with a tertian fever (which sounds like malaria) some nine months later and Cardinal Wolsey found him 'lying on a couch with a white sheet made for the easement of his leg, which was so swelled he could not stand.' In 1535 he was so ill that he had to delay his invasion of Savoy until the beginning of 1536. And then in 1539 he had a serious relapse, 'with an abscess which was below his stomach and from which he was in great danger'. In 1544, with the emperor's troops about to invest Paris, Francis was ill again. Cellini thought that the emperor could easily have taken the city and Francis despaired for his health and for the military situation. Paris was saved by Henry VIII's decision to march on Boulogne rather than give his ally, Charles, the help he needed to take the city.

By January 1545 the king was seriously ill, suffering with an intermittent fever, fainting fits and an excruciatingly painful abscess 'in his lower parts'.[44] The abscess was cauterised and a large volume of pus was drained from it. Syphilis and an ulcerated bladder were suspected. After a month he had recovered sufficiently to leave Fontainebleau in a litter though 'dead in respect of the ladies' but a few weeks later the abscess had to be drained again and some of his doctors, despairing of his life, began to talk about his insides being rotten. In July he recovered after bleeding copiously from a ruptured blood vessel in his groin and at the beginning of 1546 his abscess burst spontaneously, to his great relief. He was able to go hunting again with much of his old vigour restored. A contemporary first-hand report described him as 'completely regal';[45] no hint here of the ravages of advanced syphilis. Francis's personality changed after his illness in Madrid in 1525 but not in a way that could convincingly be likened to the mental disorders which we now know to be caused by tertiary syphilis – but how would delusions of grandeur be recognisable in an absolute monarch?

Other accounts were less favourable. Francis was said to be suffering from attacks of lethargy and depression – his mental state can't have been helped following the death of plague in 1545 of Charles of Angoulème, his third and favourite son. He was even more restless in his travels than before; his face had become full and heavy; he was losing his teeth and hair. Whatever the cause of his decline – syphilis, tuberculosis, chronic gonorrhoea, the cumulative effect of old injuries, something else or a mixture of many things, the verdict that 'ladies more than years caused his death' is likely to be correct.[46]

He continued to function as head-of-state and to enjoy life in his hedonistic court – but it was obvious that his days were numbered so there was much behind-the-scenes jockeying for position in anticipation of the power struggle that would follow his death. Francis was delighted when the news of Henry VIII's death on January 28th 1547, aged fifty-five, reached France: 'he laughed loudly and joked with his ladies'. But this reminder of the mortality of kings soon made him more thoughtful and subdued and by March 1547 he was acknowledging that his own death was imminent. He began to put his temporal and spiritual affairs in order and died on the 31st of March, aged fifty-two, with extensive organ failure, lesions on the lungs, throat, stomach and urethra and wasting of his kidneys. The cause of his death remains hotly disputed, specifically: did he or did he not die of syphilis? From our perspective it doesn't really matter; what is clear is that his doctors believed that he had contracted the disease and they did treat him for it. At the time almost any genital or peri-genital lesion might have been attributed to syphilis. In particular chancroid and lymphogranuloma venereum, which cause suppurating swellings (bubos) in the groin, were not distinguished from syphilis until the late nineteenth century. Gonorrhoea is another alternative, it could well have caused a urethral stricture and, ultimately kidney failure, fistulae and abscesses (resulting in the condition graphically but accurately known as 'watering-can perineum'). Or the abscess may have been tubercular – again, wrongly, attributed to a venereal infection; we just can't be sure.[47]

Would Cosimo or Bronzino, or Francis himself have believed that the king had syphilis? There are many reasons to think that they would have done. Life was much more public in the sixteenth century than it is today, there was very little privacy as we would understand it, even the rich lived cheek-by-jowl with their domestic staff. Bodily functions, disease and deformity were such commonplace sights that they hardly registered – although people with overt skin diseases, often lumped together as 'lepers,' were ostracised. Gossip pervaded everyday life and since people lived in such close proximity with one-another there was plenty of material to gossip about. Gossip became a powerful means of social control – both informally and appearing in the formal records of the court.[48] Every aspect of the royal family's behaviour was scrutinised – eating, sleeping, washing, dressing, excreting, procreating. There was concern at the French court about the ability, or willingness, of the king's son Henri to consummate his marriage with Catherine de'Medici, so the king watched them in bed with each other, reporting: I 'wished to watch them jousting and each of them jousted valiantly.'[49] Francis's many sexual encounters with women of all classes were well known as were the risks of disease to which these encounters exposed him. Ambassadors reported Francis's several illnesses to their masters and, in any case, it would have been impossible to prevent gossip about every aspect of Francis's life leaking from his court of over a thousand people. More concretely, we know that Bartolomeo Panciatichi was moving regularly between the courts of Cosimo and Francis: gossip would have travelled with him and his entourage. Cosimo and Bronzino must have heard about Francis's illness and its likely cause.

The first report of Francis having a venereal disease described as 'his own French disease' (so possibly syphilis) was in 1524, before his captivity in Madrid and a year after the death of Claude. It used to be said that he had caught the disease from La Belle Ferronière, one of his mistresses. She in turn had caught the disease from her husband who had deliberately infected himself in a brothel in order to revenge himself on the king who had cuckolded him. According to this account, the king then passed the disease on to Claude, who died from it.[50] The lack both of evidence that Claude had the disease and of any hint of congenital syphilis amongst her many children both argue against Francis having had syphilis before Claude's death in 1523; and the story about La Belle Ferronière and her husband is now discredited.[51]

Some of his doctors evidently thought that the king had syphilis – Jean Fernel refused to treat him with mercury, on account of its toxicity, preferring a decoction of his own, about which he later wrote a book. But the fact that Fernel was considering the use of the metal, which was the established treatment at the time, implies that he thought the king did have syphilis – although mercury was used for many skin diseases, notably leprosy, so it is possible that Fernel had other diagnoses than syphilis in mind. Incidentally, don't many of Francis's reported symptoms and signs sound like those of mercury poisoning? The reports of the king's illnesses are partial and hard to interpret now, and both syphilis and mercury poisoning can produce a whole range of effects. Without actually seeing, questioning and examining the patient ourselves it is impossible for us to decide what was really wrong with him. Back to the point that what matters is what his contemporaries thought was wrong with him.

So: Cosimo decided to give Francis a present – an allegorical, erotic painting by Bronzino on the theme of Venus and Cupid. A careful reading of Vasari leaves us uncertain whether Cosimo commissioned the painting with Francis in mind (as many authorities say that he did) or whether, like the altarpiece from Eleonora's chapel, he decided to give the painting away only after he had taken delivery of it from Bronzino. If the latter, it is conceivable that he hadn't been all that closely involved in its conception and that he didn't appreciate all the possible interpretations of the riddle contained within it. Alternatively, Cosimo may have decided to give the painting to Francis only after seeing a partially completed version of it – this decision about its ultimate destination may then have prompted Bronzino to make very substantial revisions to it, most of which increased its eroticism, which would have suited Francis's tastes though not necessarily those of Cosimo. It's unlikely that Cosimo would have allowed so significant a work by one of his acknowledged painters to be gifted to Francis without his approval – the potential diplomatic ramifications of the transaction would have been too important for him to ignore.

If Cosimo sent the *London Allegory* to France in the mid-1540s as Vasari implies, Francis will have had very little time in which to enjoy it, let alone puzzle about its meaning. Terminally ill, he spent much of 1546 wandering disconsolately round the eastern provinces of his kingdom. He never made it back to Fontainebleau, dying at Rambouillet in 1547, aged fifty-two.

The frank eroticism of the painting meant that the *London Allegory* had to be kept hidden from public view – it is not even mentioned in the official catalogue of Francis's collection – it was reserved for private contemplation and discussion by Francis himself and his immediate circle. The painting's provenance is patchy; it doesn't feature in the catalogues of paintings in the French royal collection even in the seventeenth century. It may have been in Lord Spencer's (Diana, Princess of Wales's forefather) collection at Althorp in the mid-eighteenth century, having reached England with Henrietta Maria when she came over to marry Charles I; by that time a thin veil had been painted over Venus's mons veneris and a sprig of myrtle had been added to hide Cupid's natal cleft. The painting resurfaced (discreetly hidden behind a curtain) in Paris in the collection of Edouard Beaucousin from which the National Gallery bought it in 1860. The National Gallery's first director, Charles Eastlake, thought the picture perfectly moral, and not the most provocative of those he had acquired from Beaucousin, but knowing that 'clergymen & others' would find it offensive ('voluptuous') he ordered the gallery's restorer to hide Venus's tongue and the nipple being fondled by Cupid. Eastlake didn't realise that the picture had already been censored. All these additions were removed in a restoration carried out in 1958.[52] In a further effort to avoid controversy Eastlake gave the work the bland title similar to that by which we know it today: *Venus, Cupid and Time – an Allegory*.

IV

The London Allegory: How did Bronzino paint it?

Stranger, pause and ask thyself the question,
Canst thou do likewise?
If not, with a blush retire.
(The Mystery of Edwin Drood, Charles Dickens Ch. 4 [1870])

So, we are not sure who commissioned Bronzino to paint the *London Allegory*. Vasari implies that the painting was commissioned by Cosimo, who then gave it to the king of France. But it may be that someone else asked Bronzino to paint it, leaving Cosimo to commandeer it while Bronzino was working on it. Let's leave the question open for the time being and consider the relationship between the painting's first (male) sponsor and the painter. When this sponsor instructed Bronzino to paint the *London Allegory* he presumably told him how much he was prepared to pay for it, how large the work should be, what the subject matter should be, what pigments should be used (or at least how much expensive lapis lazuli and gold leaf should be used) and he would have given him a dead-line by which time the painting had to be finished. If Cosimo was the sponsor and if he had already decided that he was going to give the painting to the king he may have told Bronzino that this was his intention. Implicit in the commission would have been the requirement that the new painting be well conceived, well made and durable; its superb craftsmanship was going to be part of its appeal – everything from the carpentry of the support and of the frame to the quality of the pigments, the application of the paint and the subtlety of the image must shout 'quality'; it had to display *disegno* and *maniera* of the highest order.

Although we can be confident that the sponsor was familiar with Ovid's *Metamorphoses* and with some of the many paintings based on stories from those poems,[1] it is impossible now to know exactly where he got the idea for the *London Allegory* from or just how detailed were the instructions he gave about the identity and disposition of the principal and the supporting characters that were to be included in the painting. No doubt he did tell Bronzino that he wanted the painting to be intriguing, difficult to interpret and, possibly, erotic – a riddle that would entertain the viewer while flattering his erudition. There was a respectable intellectual justification for works which had hidden meanings and for painters to create 'fantasies' in which familiar, and purely imaginary, forms were combined with novel, allegorical intent.[2] Erasmus (writing about 'emblems', i.e. mottoes or epigrams) approved the art of suggesting a thought by withholding it.[3]

In the West the history of erotic art extends at least as far back as pharaonic Egypt and archaic Greek vase paintings from the fifth century BCE. The genre has continued without interruption, so that plenty of examples of paintings with overt or hidden erotic meanings can be found in the work of both Italian and Northern European Renaissance sixteenth-century artists.[4] Nudity on its own may have been introduced into paintings and sculptures for erotic purposes, excused by the supposedly uplifting overt meaning of mythological subjects. And even pious Botticelli added erotic symbolism to his otherwise chaste nudes to signify their fertility – his *Venus and Mars* (c.1485 National Gallery, London, Room 58) shows Mars's genitalia discreetly hidden by drapery but his fingers mimic a limp penis and a scrotum; Venus's left-hand thumb and first finger clasp a fold of her gown to make a vulval shape.[5] Even less ambiguous is the same painter's famous and very familiar *Birth of Venus* (1482-5, Uffizi Gallery, Florence). Venus is not embarrassed by her nudity, though she's using her long hair to hide her pubis and she's covering her right breast with her wrist – but she's beautiful in face and figure and her left breast is exposed: this is an erotic painting. And, remembering Botticelli's trick with Venus's left hand in *Venus and Mars*, look carefully at Venus's handmaid in *Birth of Venus* (Plate 10). She's approaching her mistress in order to conceal her nudity with a large gown but her raised right hand holds the edge of that gown to make an unmistakably vulval shape which encloses a leaf to symbolise new growth.[6] Now, as a clear indication that Cosimo would have known what he could expect from Bronzino, turn back to Plate 9 the *Portrait of Cosimo I de' Medici as Orpheus* – what does the peg box on the viol resemble? And what is Cosimo holding in his right hand? Yes, it's the bow for his viol, but the *double entendre* is unmistakable. The dog is Cerberus, guardian of the underworld, which Orpheus charmed with his singing – what part of the underworld is he looking at so fiercely? Or Cosimo had only to look at the fresco that Bronzino had just completed on the ceiling of Eleonora's chapel in the Palazzo Vecchio: the quadrant in which he depicts St Michael the Archangel is flanked by a *putto* who sports a large courgette between his thighs.[7] All this sexual imagery was intended to celebrate fecundity as well as to titivate.

Bronzino and his patron may have enjoyed working out the way in which their painting's real meaning was to be hidden and they probably discussed the revisions which Bronzino made as his work progressed. Maybe they were helped by some of the many humanist scholars living in Florence at the time, though it's obvious from his poetry, in which he names many of the leading classical authors (who were available in vernacular translations) that Bronzino himself was a very well-read man, able to devise an infuriatingly abstruse puzzle unaided. Many authors have identified texts which may have contributed to Bronzino's construction of his riddle – often these have been compromised by the author's preconceived ideas, by confusion about whether the supposedly influential texts were published before or after the presumed date of the painting (about 1545) and by lack of confidence in Bronzino's facility with Latin. The poet Benedetto Varchi (1502-65) translated some Ovid for him, so he may not have been very confident in that language.[8] Bronzino's own poetry, his reading, his conversations with Varchi and his assumed discussions with the similarly widely read Cosimo will all have informed his design of the painting. And Robert Gaston goes so far as to suggest that the purpose of the *London Allegory* might have been to represent human erotic love and its consequences more alluringly than poetry could do (there was a spirited discussion at the time about the relative merits of painting and poetry, akin to that about painting and sculpture). If this is so, when we attempt to interpret the painting we should look at the poetry familiar to Bronzino and his contemporaries (Chapter V). Gaston has used the evidence of Bronzino's poetry and other contemporary sources to compile an impressive list of the authors whom Bronzino had read, amongst them Aristotle, Homer, Horace, Livy, Ovid and Vitruvius (all almost certainly in translation) together with Varchi, Ariosto, Berni, Boccaccio, Petrarch and Michelangelo. Varchi said that Bronzino knew all of Dante and most of Petrarch by heart.[8] Plenty of material there for him to turn to if he needed inspiration or precedent.

In his fanciful account of the creation of the *London Allegory*, Alan Fisk – who tells his story through Guiseppe, Bronzino's supposed apprentice, catamite and model for Cupid – says that Cosimo gives only the vaguest instructions to the painter. This seems inherently improbable for such a substantial work, commissioned by a discerning patron. Whoever the patron was he would not have allowed Bronzino free rein, for the very idea that a work was the personal expression of the *artifice* would have been alien to him. It is equally unlikely that Bronzino would have dared to hide a subversive message in the painting, hoping to evade detection by Cosimo. Why would he do such a thing? There is no record of him trying to do so in his other paintings (the burlesque poetry is a different matter). Cosimo is known to have made regular visits to his artists to check on work-in-progress – if he already had it in mind to give the *London Allegory* to Francis I it is inconceivable that he would not have supervised its production, at least in its final stages. He must have discussed and approved the several possible interpretations of its hidden meanings with the painter, particularly as Bronzino was making changes to the painting as he went along – many of them increasing its eroticism. One suggestion, however, is that the painting turned out to be a bit too *risqué* for Cosimo's taste and that's why he gave it away.[9]

When he had decided or been told what was expected of him Bronzino faced the challenge of translating his brief into a real painting. We can imagine him staring at, literally, a blank sheet of paper and wondering where to begin. Unlike painters of earlier epochs, he would have started with some rough sketches which would then be incorporated into a cartoon for transfer to the painting panel.[10] But sketches of what? He had been asked to draw Venus, Cupid and assorted other figures and from the outset, perhaps, to give the painting an unmistakably erotic charge and to challenge the viewer to solve a riddle. Beyond that he was on his own.

So Bronzino followed his normal practice, which he applied to his poetry as well as to his painting, of looking for precedents which could inform his work. Where did he look? In particular, he would have been inspired by his reverence for Michelangelo, his close relationship with Pontormo and his nostalgia for the glories of fifteenth-century Florence. Today such homage to illustrious predecessors might lead a painting to be condemned as 'derivative' – one of the most pejorative critical terms in the modern lexicon. But it was the approved practice in the Renaissance and for long afterwards – apprentice painters were trained to copy the works of their most eminent, respected and admired predecessors: to emulate the style of the masters was laudable.[11] Change did occur but it usually took the form of slow, incremental improvements within an established convention, revolutionaries were rare – Giotto, Titian, Caravaggio spring to mind. Mannerism evolved from the High Renaissance, it was not revolutionary. Bronzino knew that his subject matter was not novel – his aim, while working within accepted conventions, was to come up with a novel treatment of it, 'an *invenzione* with echoes, conscious echoes of the great Florentine tradition… behind the [*London Allegory*] there is patently present the active genius of Michelangelo.'[12]

Many references to the greatest Renaissance masters can be discerned in the *London Allegory*.[13] Kenneth Clark (he of *Civilisation* fame) likened Venus's zig-zag pose to that of Christ's body in Michelangelo's *Pieta*, which Bronzino would have seen in the Duomo in Florence.[14] Similarly, much has been made of the similarity of Venus's pose in Bronzino's painting and that of the Virgin in Michelangelo's *Doni Tondo* (Uffizi Gallery, Florence); even though the *Doni Tondo* is a religious painting (a Holy Family group) both principal figures have twisting poses and are touching each other (in most Holy Family groups the infant Jesus is held by his Mother but is not touching her or at least not in such an affectionate way).[15] Time in the *London Allegory* may be derived from Joseph in the Doni Tondo.[16] Bronzino would also

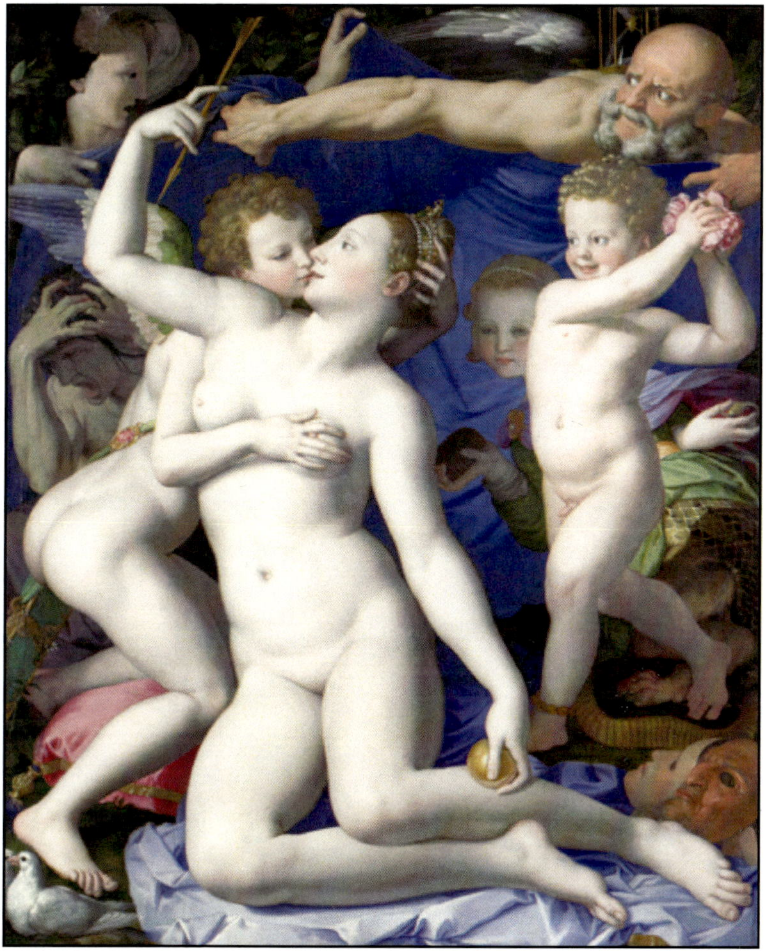

Plate 1
Bronzino: *An Allegory with Venus and Cupid*, the *'London Allegory'*.
[c.1545, Oil on panel, 146.1 x 116.2cm]

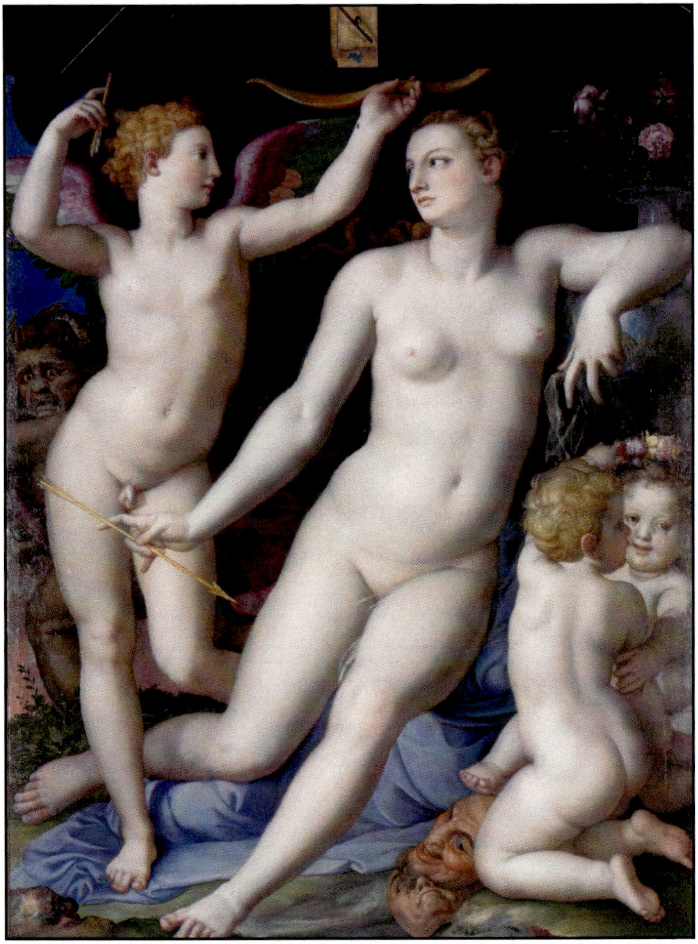

Plate 2

Bronzino: *Venus, Cupid and Envy,*
the *'Budapest Allegory'.*

[1548-50, Oil on poplar 192 x 142cm]

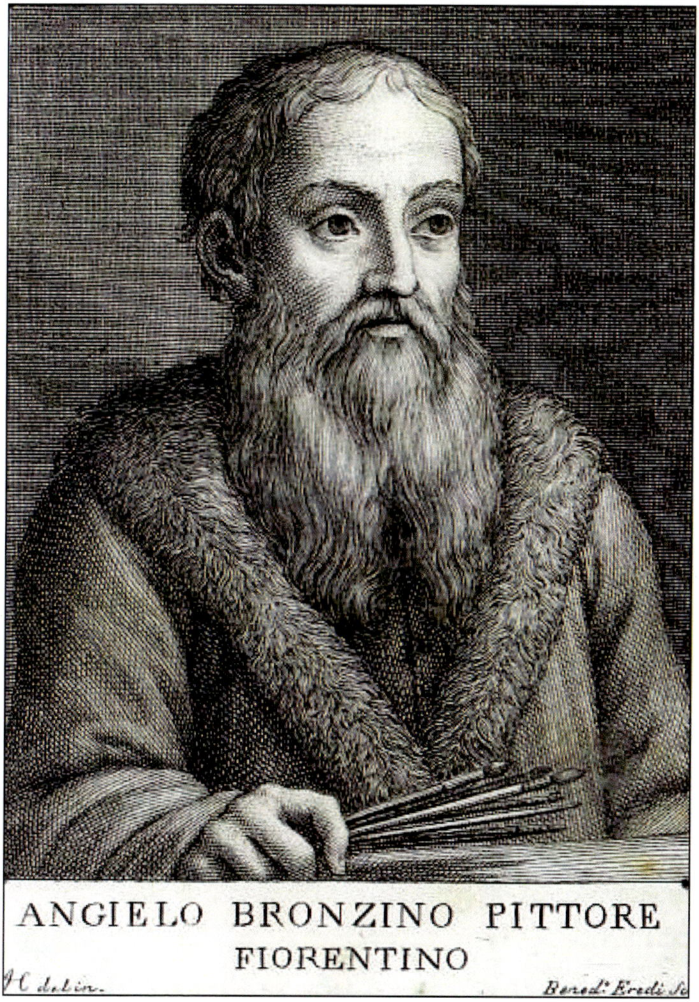

Plate 3

Anonymous, Angelo Bronzino.

Rau AF, Rastrelli M. Degli uomini illustri nella pintura, scultura, e architetura con loro elogi, e ritratti, Florence 1763-76 Vol. 6, p114.

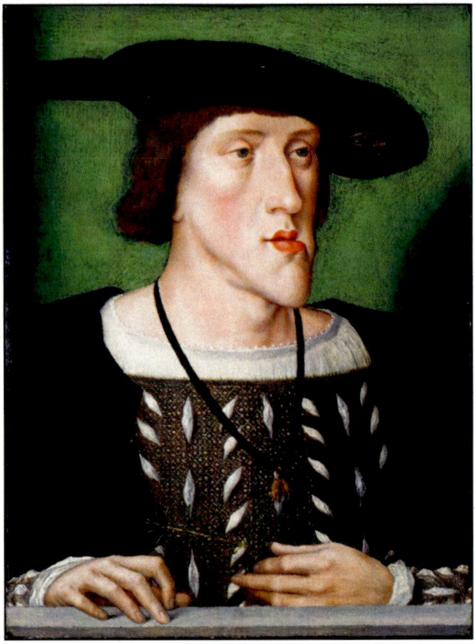

Plate 4

Flemish School: *Emperor Charles V*.

[1515, Oil on panel 43.8 x 32.2]

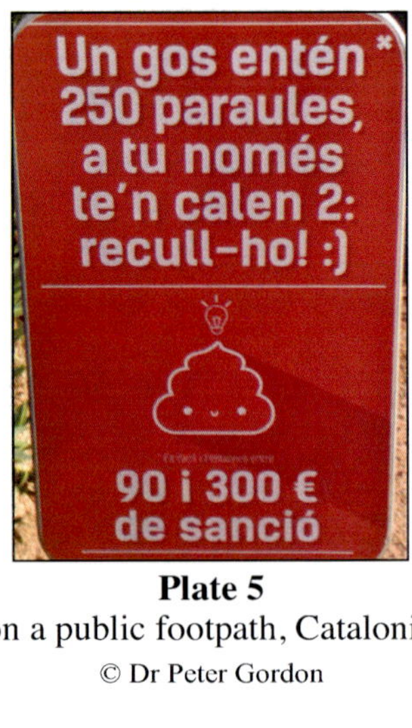

Plate 5

Notice on a public footpath, Catalonia, Spain.

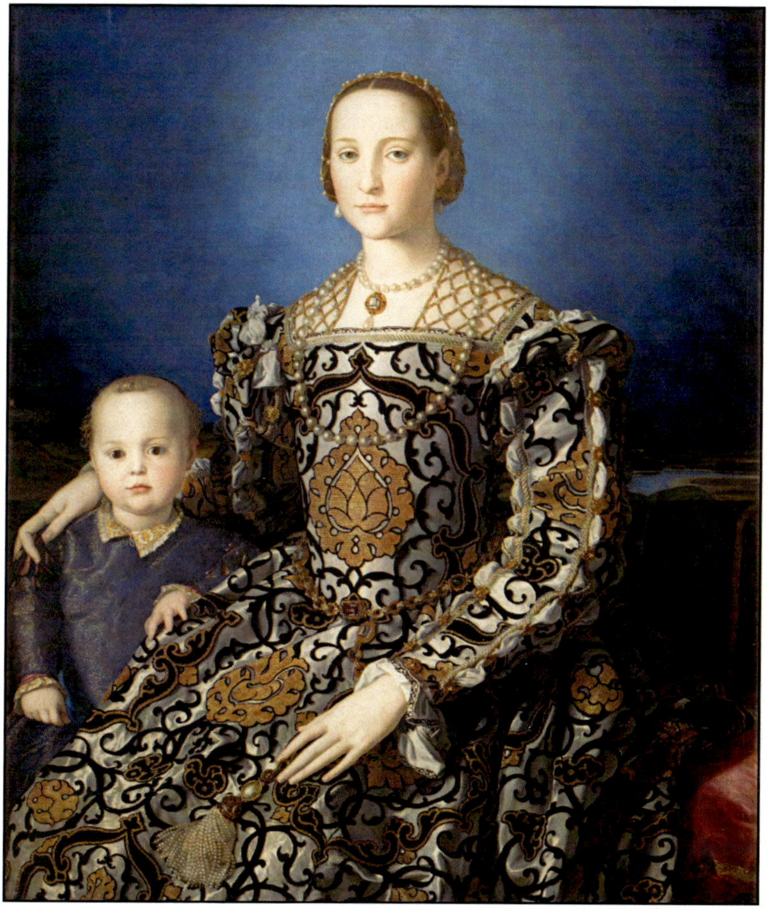

Plate 6

Bronzino: *Portrait of Eleonora of Toledo with her Son Giovanni.*

[1544-45, Oil on panel 115 x 96cm]

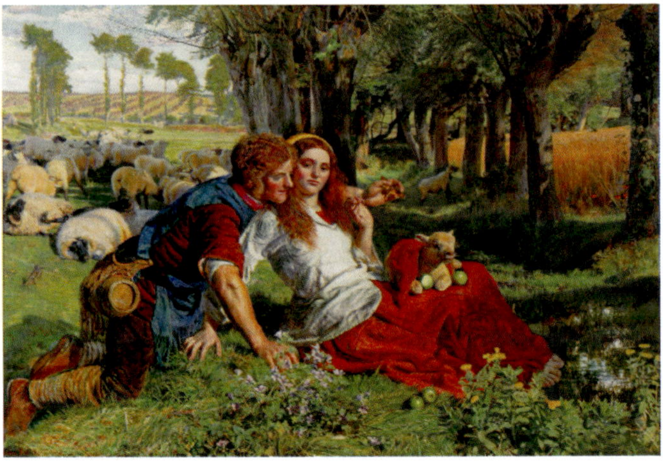

Plate 7

William Holman Hunt: *The Hireling Shepherd*.

[1851, Oil on Canvas 76.4 x 109.5cm]

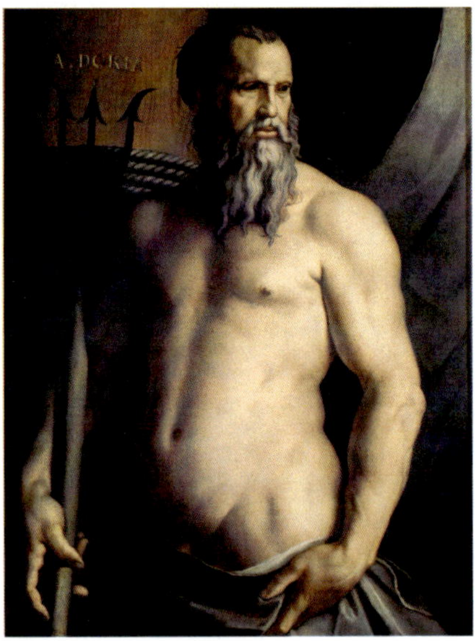

Plate 8

Bronzino: *Portrait of Admiral Andrea Doria as Neptune*.

[c.1540, Oil on canvas 115 x 53cm]

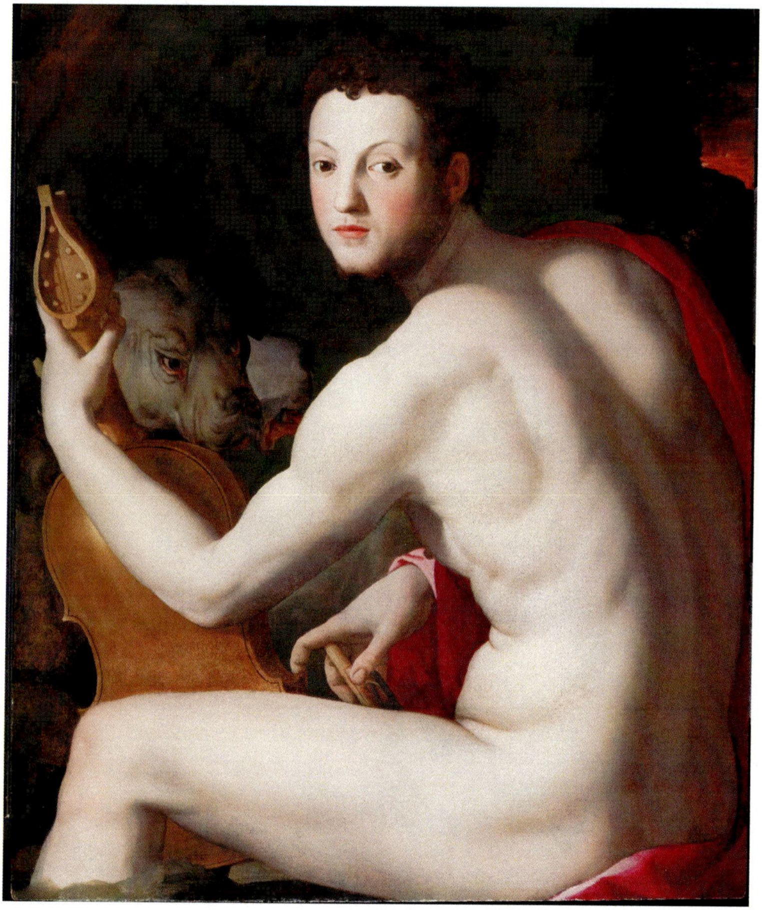

Plate 9

Bronzino: *Portrait of Cosimo I de'Medici as Orpheus.*

[c.1537-1539, Oil on panel 93.7 x 76.4 cm]

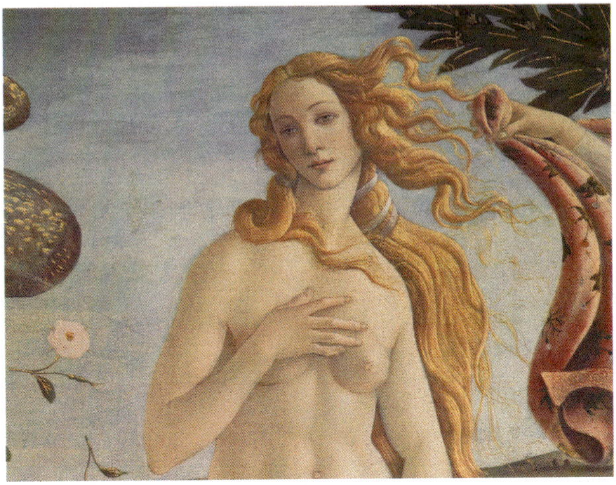

Plate 10

Sandro Botticelli: *The Birth of Venus* (Detail).

[c.1486, Tempera on canvas. 172.5 × 278.9 cm]

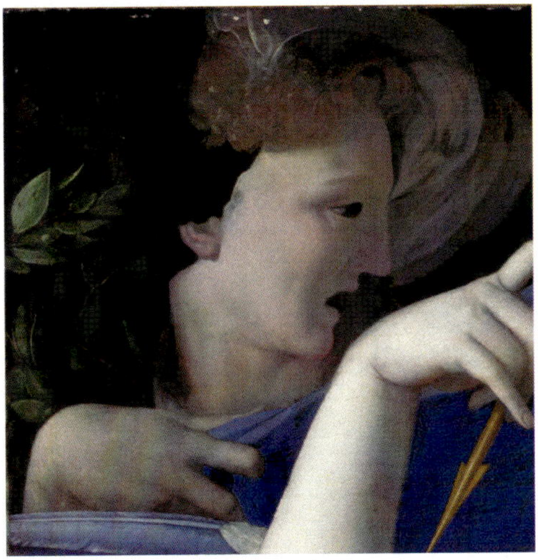

Plate 11

Bronzino: *An Allegory with Venus and Cupid*

(Detail to show Character A)

[see Plate 1 for full painting]

Plate 12
Hermann's Tortoise
(Testudo hermanni).
©Edwin Giesbers
/naturepl.com

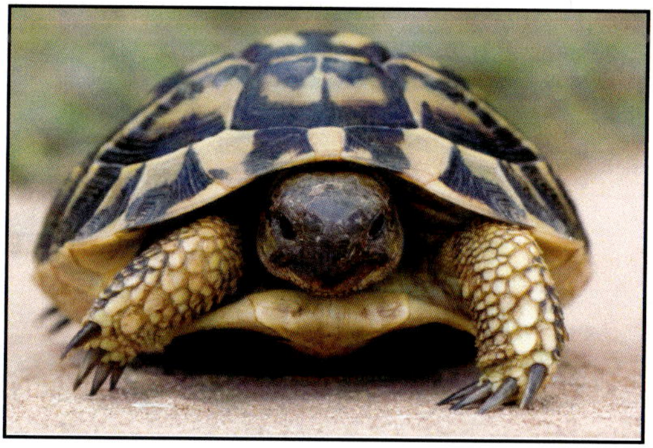

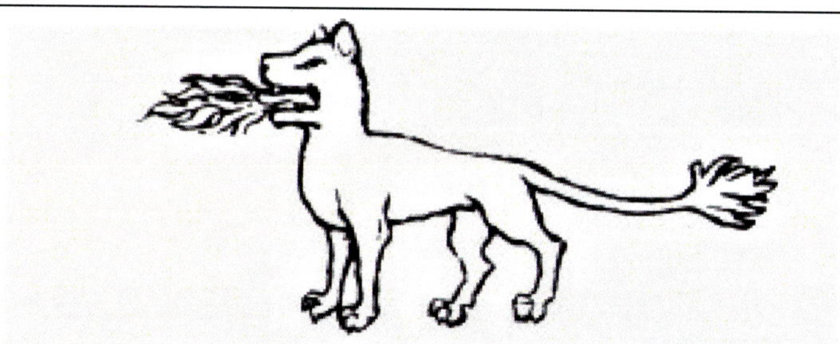

Salamander crest of James, Earl of Douglas. From garter-plate.

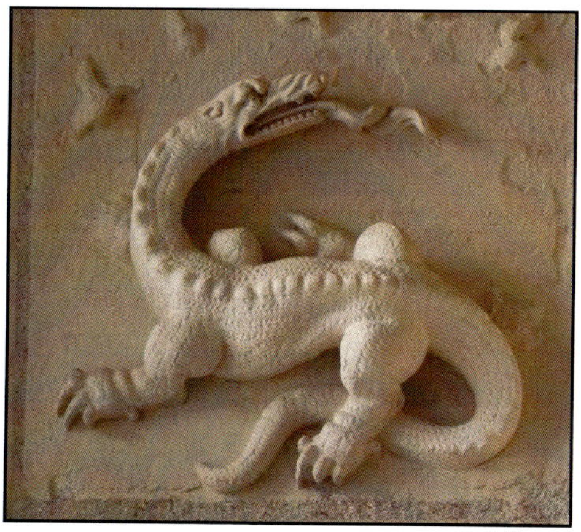

Plate 13
Salamanders
Above:
A heraldic representation of the animal
Fictitious and Symbolic Creatures in Art, by John Vinycomb, [1909]
Left:
Carved in the interior stonework at King Francis I's 'hunting lodge', the Château de Chambord, Loire Valley, France.
©Guillaume Perrin

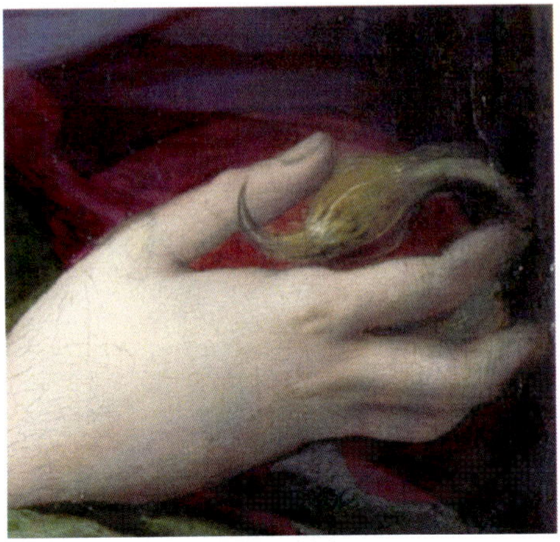

Plate 14
Bronzino: *An Allegory with Venus and Cupid*
(Detail to show C's sting)
[see Plate 1 for full painting]

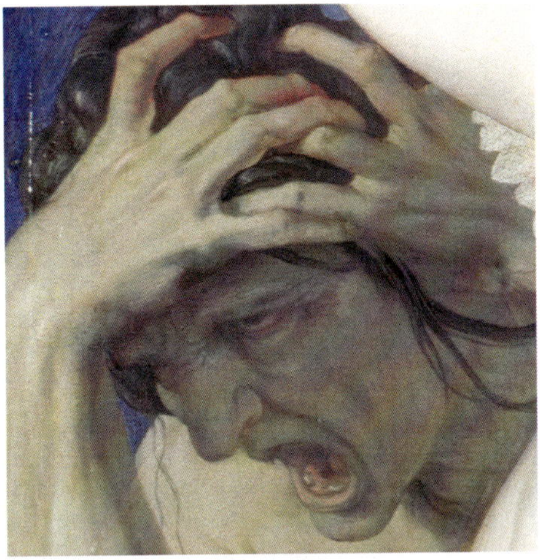

Plate 15
Bronzino: *An Allegory with Venus and Cupid*
(Detail to show Character K)
[see Plate 1 for full painting]

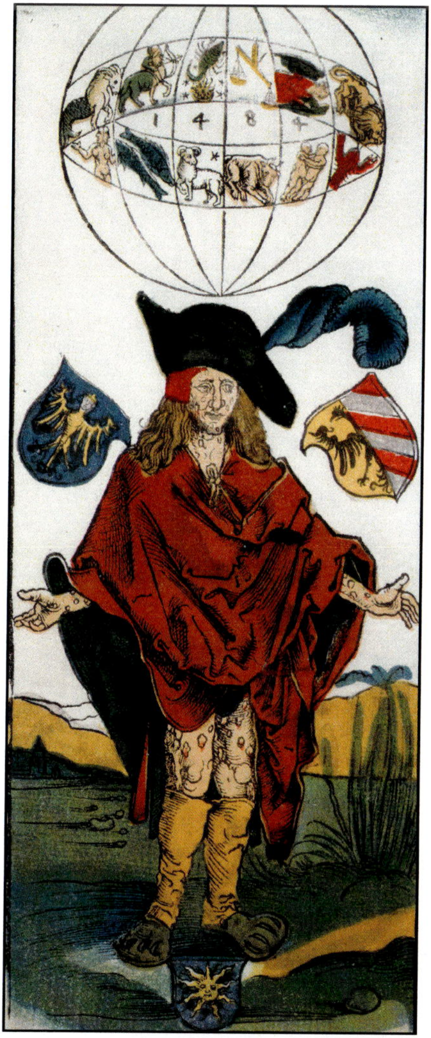

Plate 16

Woodcut ascribed to Albrecht Durer: *Syphilitic*

1496 Broadsheet, text by Ulsenius

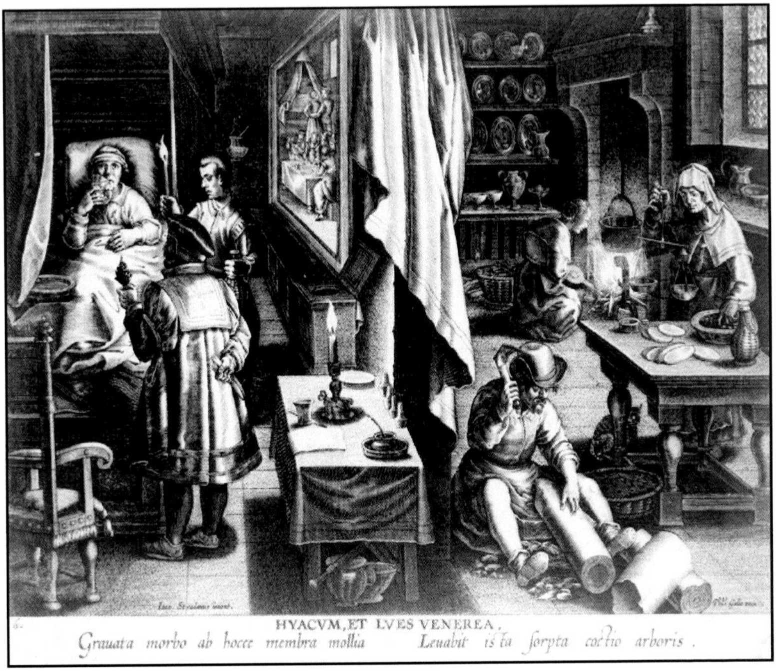

Plate 17

Philip Galle: *A man in bed suffering from syphilis, amidst a busy domestic scene.*

c.1570 Line engraving after Jan van der Straet (Joannes Stradanus).

Preparation and use of Guayaco for Treating Syphilis

Archives d'Ordre National des Pharmaciens, Paris, France

have seen an oil painting of *Venus and Cupid* painted in 1532 by Pontormo after a design by Michelangelo. This had been intended for a room in the house of Bartolomeo Bettini, a Florentine banker – in the event it went first to Alessandro and then to Cosimo de'Medici. Bronzino painted portraits of Dante, Petrarch and Boccaccio for the same room and would have seen Pontormo's painting either there or in Cosimo's palace.[17] Pontormo's barely adolescent Cupid sits on Venus's voluptuous body, leaning forward to kiss her; she is kissing him while looking towards his quiver. Venus is nude, fully exposed, lying on blue drapery and pulling one of Cupid's arrows from its quiver with her right hand. There are two masks (probably Virtue and Vice) on the left-hand side of the painting, tied to Cupid's bow by a pink ribbon, roses (an attribute of Venus) in a vase above and the statuette of a young man, either dead or in pain as a result of love, below them.[18] Venus's fingers are elegantly elongated in the typically Mannerist style – she can hardly be said to be grasping the arrow with the serious intent of dragging it from Cupid's hand. The parallels between this painting and the *London Allegory* are too obvious, and too many, to dismiss.

Where else might Bronzino have gained inspiration? The orientation and musculature of the arm of Time stretched along the upper border of the *London Allegory* are very reminiscent of the arm of God at the centre of Michelangelo's fresco on the ceiling of the Sistine Chapel. Indeed the bearded face of Time is not dissimilar to that of Michelangelo's God, stretching out to animate Adam. The fresco was painted between 1508 and 1512; Bronzino could have seen it on one of his visits to Rome in 1546 or 1548 (about or shortly after the time he was painting the *London Allegory*), or drawings of it may have made their way to Florence earlier in the century. Pontormo had visited Rome in 1511 and had been allowed to climb the scaffolding to study the fresco while Michelangelo was working on it. It had a profound effect on his own work (Vasari said that Pontormo never managed to liberate himself from Michelangelo's influence) and he must have discussed the Sistine Chapel frescos with his pupil many times over the coming years. Michelangelo hid in the Chapel of San Lorenzo in Florence for three months in 1530 to evade the pope. While he was there he covered the walls of the Chapel with drawings and sketches of Christ and with some sketches which may be reproductions of images from the Sistine ceiling.[19] So, Bronzino had no need to leave Florence to get a good idea of what Michelangelo had created in Rome.

Pontormo drew many androgynous figures, notably a hermaphrodite (Galleria degli Uffizi, Florence) whose curly hair and pronounced buttocks look very like those of Cupid in the *London Allegory*. And Bronzino certainly liked curly hair – compare the hair of Cupid and the *putto* in the *London Allegory* with that of the Christ-child and of the young man in the paintings by Bronzino that hang alongside the *London Allegory*. The head of the figure on the far left in the *London Allegory* strongly resembles one in a sketch of warriors' heads which Leonardo da Vinci made for one of the figures to be included in his *The Battle of Anghiari* (which is now lost). Another possible influence on Bronzino was Pontormo's Deposition (1525-8) in the Capponi Chapel, Santa Felicita, Florence, which is unusual for the empty space in the centre of the picture. All the figures in this painting seem to recoil from this void, perhaps to signify the Virgin's desolation at the death of her son. Finally, the *London Allegory* looks a bit like a parody of Raphael's *Holy Family of Francis I* (The Louvre, Paris), which had been a gift from Pope Leo X to Claude, the wife of the French king. This places the Virgin and Child in the centre with the attendant figures in the background defining a rectangular frame-within-the-frame.

Contemporary taste and his own experience will also have influenced Bronzino. The figure of Cupid is shown from both the front and the back – just as Cosimo was in Bronzino's *Portrait of Cosimo I de' Medici as Orpheus* (Plate 9), contributing once again to the debate about the relative merits of painting and sculpture. He may also have been alluding to a classical sculpture of Venus chiding Cupid which is now lost, though a nineteenth century copy by Gibson is in the Usher Art Gallery, Lincoln, UK.[20]

Whatever their antecedents, the *London Allegory*'s shallow picture space, the highly finished surface, muscular arm, elegantly sinuous bodies, languorous limbs and elongated, stylishly posed hands, fingers, feet and toes all proclaim Bronzino's *maniera*.

Having crystallised his initial ideas about the painting Bronzino would have begun the daunting task of turning these into a quality product acceptable to his demanding patron: into a gift fit for a king.[21] The finished painting would be the result of a collaborative effort between Bronzino himself, independent 'sub-contractors' and the apprentices working under Bronzino's tutelage in his workshop. Allori is unlikely to have been one of those apprentices; he was less than ten years old when Bronzino's workshop was engaged on the *London Allegory*. First of all, Bronzino had to decide on the support he was going to use. Occasionally he painted on a canvas or on a copper plate[22]; overwhelmingly, however, he favoured the traditional support of wooden panels. The idea of using stretched linen or cotton canvas was a relatively new one that was gaining in popularity, particularly in Venice where there were many workshops producing sailcloth which could be used by painters as well as by seamen. Canvas wouldn't overtake wood as the preferred support for another hundred years or so, but Botticelli had painted his *Birth of Venus* (c.1486) in tempera on canvas and some of Bronzino's famous contemporaries (for example the great Venetian painter, Titian (1490-1576)) were already using it, attracted by its lower cost, lighter weight, simpler preparation and, because it could be rolled-up, greater portability than wood. On the other hand, canvas was relatively untested at this stage and Bronzino may have been worried about its ability to withstand the rigours of transportation, of time and of atmospheric pollution. And maybe he didn't really know how to prepare and use a canvas support; certainly the double portrait *Nano Morgante*, one of his ventures onto canvas, has not survived well, although the *Portrait of Admiral Andrea Doria as Neptune* is in better condition. Perhaps snobbery came into it too – canvas could have been perceived as the cheap or lazy option and a bit insulting to the recipient of a gift.

The preparation of the wooden panel would have been a prolonged, laborious and painstaking process. Knowing the time that the work was going to take, painters began to prepare panels well in advance of receiving the commissions for which they would eventually be used. The panel would be made by a carpenter using a radial-cut piece of wood from one of a large variety of species of locally grown trees. In Italy it was usually seasoned white poplar, willow or cypress; in northern Europe, oak, pine, beech or ash were preferred. Skill and experience were needed to select the wood. As today's brewers, vintners or owners of tea estates and the makers of herbal medicines and similar products know (or should know), the qualities and chemical composition of plants, including trees, vary considerably even within a species, depending on the age of the plant, the nature of the soil in which it is growing, the season at which it is harvested and on the part of the plant, or tree, from which it is cut. For Bronzino's purposes the wood would have been taken from the heart of a dormant tree – sap-wood or wood taken from a tree cut when the sap was rising would contain too much water and would shrink and warp when dried. Seasoning for at least one or two years after felling was required to remove the resin, which would also cause the panel to split or warp if it was used prematurely; some workshops would soak their smaller panels in boiling water to get rid of the resin more quickly and completely, though the wood had to be dried out very thoroughly after that, because wet wood also warps. The chosen piece would be planed and sanded and if necessary it would be joined with other pieces to make a panel of the desired size and shape. Reinforcing strips applied to the back of the panel reduced the risk of warping but they had to accommodate movements caused by expansion and contraction, so they were glued into grooves cut into the panel, rather than being nailed or screwed together. The finished panel could be as much as 10cm thick.

In the case of the *London Allegory* three unequal sized planks of wood were aligned vertically and held together by butterfly shaped hardwood splines set into blind mortices. Wooden dowels were knocked through the planks from the front to hold the splines in position; the ends of some of them are detectable in the surface of the painting. At some stage, well after the painting was started, another 2.7cm wide strip of wood was added to the left-hand side of the support, without splines and dowels. This was to provide room for some of the *pentimenti* that Bronzino decided upon after he began to paint.[23]

These wooden supports are substantial objects with their own vulnerabilities. Wood, even very old, thoroughly seasoned wood, expands in damp air and shrinks if it dries out in a warm environment, but old, dried oil paint can't keep pace with these movements and may crack, break away from the surface and flake off the painting. Recent conservation work on the *Budapest*

Allegory has highlighted some of the problems that can arise with these wooden panels. It revealed that Bronzino enlarged this painting by adding two planks to the panel, which was later enlarged again on three sides to make the composition less cramped. But the new planks were cut against the grain of the original panel, creating additional stresses which could lead to the paint layers breaking away from the support.[24] And, like any painting, whatever the support, wooden panels are vulnerable to physical assault, be it natural (fire, flood) or malicious: in 2003 a visitor punched the *London Allegory*, possibly weakening the joints between its panels and making it unfit to move for exhibition outside the National Gallery.[25].

That was the support. On top of it came the 'ground' – the surface to which the paint was going to be applied. Preparing this was another laborious process contracted-out to specialists or delegated to workshop assistants.[26] The wooden panel would be coated with a mixture of animal-skin glues and resin and perhaps covered with linen. Once this had dried a mixture of finely-powdered gypsum and glue called *gesso* would have been applied, dried and sanded smooth before another layer of it was added. Up to fifteen layers of *gesso* might be applied, the last one being sanded and then burnished to give a smooth, hard surface. The preparation of the ground was a tricky business too – careless mixing or application could leave tiny bubbles of air in the *gesso*; the surface would crack if the mix contained too much glue and the layers might separate from one another if the strength of the mixture varied from layer to layer. For the *London Allegory* Bronzino also added a layer of animal-glue on top of the *gesso* ground so that it would absorb less of the paint. Finally a thin, translucent layer of honey-coloured *imprimatura* was applied.[27]

After preparing his ground and tracing the cartoon for his painting onto it, Bronzino would have turned his attention to the palaver of making his paints. Before the advent of the industrial manufacture of artists' materials in the nineteenth century (including the invention of the collapsible paint-tube in 1841 which liberated the artist from the workshop and initiated *plein aire* oil painting), painters used to make their own paints or buy a few of them from specialist dealers. Apothecaries often sold the raw materials or they might offer fully prepared paints, although many of the latter were made from second-class materials, were adulterated or were not even what they purported to be – Cennini warned painters about vermillion mixed with brick dust. Some colours (pigments) could be stored for a while in leather or bladder pouches but most had to be made afresh each day; if the same colour was needed over many days or weeks in a painting it was vitally important, but not easy, to maintain its consistency from one day to the next. Making the paints was another critical task which was delegated to assistants and to the apprentices who had to learn all about making and mixing paint. Every painter had to have a thorough understanding of the characteristics of the materials he worked with (and it was almost always a man). In the sixteenth century most pigments came from locally occurring minerals, from plants or from animals. Of the more exotic pigments 'red lac' or 'carmine' came from the cochineal insect found in India or, later, in Mexico. Carmine was so esteemed that it quickly became the third greatest import from the 'New World' (after gold and silver). The very expensive 'Indian yellow' came from the urine of cows fed on mango leaves. The most expensive pigments of all were gold, silver and ultramarine – so expensive that patrons specified the quantity and quality of these materials that they wanted to be used in the work they commissioned. Gold and silver, so much a feature of medieval and early Renaissance painting, were not used very much in the sixteenth century but ultramarine was still popular and because of its cost it was an important indicator of the status of subjects within a painting, of the painting itself and, by association, of the owner of the painting.

Ultramarine is an intense velvety blue hue, familiar to us in the cloak worn by many a Renaissance Virgin Mary and prominent in the backdrop of the *London Allegory*. It comes from lapis lazuli, a very hard, sodium-calcium-aluminium silicate sulphate, the most complex of the mineral pigments and extremely difficult to grind. It got its name 'beyond the sea' from its source, far away from Italy, in mines in the valley of Kokcha in the mountains of Afghanistan. It came in various grades and cheap alternatives were available. Because it was so extraordinarily expensive it was normally used only as a thin glaze over a light base and sometimes as a tempera (pigment bound with egg-yolk instead of oil), even in an oil painting, to avoid the possibility of it picking up a yellow tint from the oil medium. Cennini described how ultramarine was made. Finely ground lapis lazuli was soaked several times to draw off the first and best, rich violet-blue solution. The remaining powder was mixed with melted wax, resins, and oils, wrapped in a cloth and kneaded in a dilute lye solution to squeeze out more of the blue colour. This process was repeated at least three times, with each successive extraction generating a lower quality material.

More prosaically, many 'earth' colours came from rocks found locally – the red-brown colours Raw Sienna and Burnt Sienna came from a rock found in Tuscany – but the more distant Hartz mountains were the source of particularly highly esteemed earth pigments, so there was a brisk, specialist international trade in these materials.

Even the grinding of a pigment required skill because the particles had to be fine and of regular size, and a few pigments can be damaged by incorrect grinding – the poisonous chrome red (basic lead chromate) exemplifies the care needed to get the pigment just right: when heated it turns reddish brown; when mixed with acetic acid it turns yellow; if ground for too long it becomes lighter and assumes a more yellowish-red hue. Every pigment had its own properties of hue, permanence, and compatibility with other pigments. Many of the materials used were poisonous and, since they were being ground into a powder, they were easily inhaled or absorbed through the skin; only rudimentary precautions would have been taken. The mineral cinnabar for example, which made the colour vermillion, is mercury sulphide. Ingested or inhaled it produces any of the many horrible acute or chronic effects of mercury poisoning, including: nerve damage, kidney failure, bladder infections, swollen gums, loss of teeth, severe mouth ulcers, emotional lability, depression, arthritis, repeated infections, and so on and so on – the adverse effects of mercury are protean.

After grinding, the pigments were bound with a wide variety of different oils (media) each of which had its own character that could affect the behaviour of the pigments themselves. The painter had to know what binder-to-pigment proportions to use and the range was considerable: from 10% (e.g. vermillion, cinnabar) or less, to as high as 180% (e.g. Burnt Sienna, iron and manganese oxides). All sorts of other things were added to the paints, including 'siccatives' to hasten drying and extenders to make them go further. Many painters experimented with the recipes for their paints but this could be risky, their mistakes might become obvious only years later. Sir Joshua Reynolds (1723-92) is notorious for his pretty haphazard use of unconventional media and pigments, which he used in untested proportions and combinations. He tried to give a natural-looking pink tinge to his flesh tones by using carmine instead of the traditional vermillion but he didn't realise that carmine fades over time when it is mixed with white. Trying to achieve the same results as the Italian Renaissance masters but without having to wait ages for his media to dry in the cold, damp English climate, he added wax to his media – melted beeswax mixed with turpentine made a paste that he added to his oil-pigment mixtures. He would then use this and other glazes and varnishes one on top of the other, despite the fact that they dried at different rates. Even more catastrophic was his failure to allow his white ground to dry properly before applying his colours. When this happened, the paint didn't stick to the ground, so the picture blistered and cracked. All was made much worse by his fondness for bitumen, which darkens in a horrible, ugly way. The upshot of his experimentation was that many of his later works had to be returned to his studio for remedial work; many others are now discoloured and their surfaces are a disaster.

Some colours had to be manufactured rather than extracted from naturally occurring materials. The green verdigris (copper acetate) was made either by hanging copper plates over hot vinegar in a sealed pot until a green crust formed on them or by attaching copper strips to a wooden block with acetic acid, then burying the sealed block in dung. A few weeks later the pot was dug up and the verdigris scraped off. The old masters used verdigris for want of anything better; they knew that it would blacken over time if mixed with other colours so they isolated it by placing it between layers of varnish. There were several ways to make white lead (lead carbonate, very poisonous), one was first described in c.300BC. In it strips of lead were rolled into spirals and placed in an earthenware jar containing vinegar. The open pots were buried under tanner's bark or dung which fermented, generating heat and releasing carbon dioxide; the acetic acid vapour and carbon dioxide reacted with the lead to form lead carbonate and the heat accelerated the process, which nonetheless could take six to fourteen weeks. Minium (red lead oxide, so called because it was first mined by the Romans from the River Minius in NW Spain) could also be made by the hazardous process of heating the white lead in air. The temperature had to be carefully regulated: too hot and the colour changed to a light violet, becoming a yellowish-red on cooling; not hot enough and a red-yellow colour was produced that was not permanent enough ('fugitive') but which could be removed by washing with sugar-water.[28]

We can see from these few examples how complex and labour-intensive the most basic tasks involved in producing a late-Renaissance painting were – and consequently how multi-talented the great masters had to be. And on top of having the artistic and technical skills, they had to have the management skills needed to run a small business: project-manage the activities of a busy workshop, delegate tasks, order materials, train apprentices, secure new commissions and make a profit.

The recipes for red lead, verdigris and other manufactured colours show that the *artifice* and the apothecaries or their suppliers were practising chemistry – though of an unsystematic kind with only a very limited theoretical understanding. The transformation of painters' materials was often understood in alchemical terms. Cennino Cennini's 14th-century treatise on painting described six colours on his palette as 'made by alchemy.' The very idea of 'chemistry' didn't exist in Bronzino's day but the production of coloured materials had a key place in the practice of alchemy, that curious mix of technique, magic, astrology, psychology and wishful thinking, which was widely followed. Led by Bronzino's contemporary Paracelsus, alchemy was beginning to transmute into an embryonic science that we might recognise.[29] Though the occult, the search for the Philosopher's Stone and the conversion of base metal into gold would continue to occupy some alchemists for another century or so, many would follow Paracelsus's lead into a more rational discipline based on observation and experiment. The alchemists heated, calcined, sublimed and distilled substances while closely observing the transformations that were taking place within their vessels. They thought of these transformations as bridges between the spiritual and the material realms; spirit was believed to rise up, separating from the substance at the bottom of the vessel and descending again to spiritualise the material into an essence or tincture. Animal symbols were used to represent key alchemical processes, so a black toad was an image for the seething black mass of amorphous substance being processed in a flask at the beginning of an alchemical experiment, while a white eagle represented the white steam or fumes which rose up into the neck of the flask as a mixture was heated. The alchemists thought that Nature is perfectible and that it is continually improving itself, that metals tend, or 'wish', to become gold and that left to themselves for centuries they will in fact do this. They thought that a knowledgeable and reverent man who accepted that matter is an expression of divinity could intervene to accelerate this natural process of growth. By, as they saw it, delving deep into the heart of Nature the alchemists tried to reveal the secrets of Creation and to achieve immortality – this search and its completion constituted their 'Great Work'. Not surprisingly there were many ideas about how to do all this and, despite many alchemists keeping the details of their practices a closely guarded secret, a voluminous literature developed to guide the practitioner. They believed that an alchemical process occurred through a cycle of colour changes, from an initial blackness to 'the perfection of the quintessence'. The alchemist envisaged each stage of the process being heralded by a colour change and by a meeting with certain animals.[30]

Believing that colours are an expression of fundamental stages of nature the alchemists gave them a central position in their doctrine. The western alchemical tradition described four critical, sequential states (reduced to three in some later versions) which the alchemist tried to instantiate by the judicious timing of his work, his manipulation of chemicals and his incantations.[31] The first state was called *nigredo* (black). Here a starting material was dissolved; it was a destructive, sorrowful state symbolised by the Black Crow, the Raven or the Toad. This was followed by an intermediate state, the 'Peacock's Tail,' characterised by an explosion of colours in the reaction vessel. This stage was associated with the goddess Venus and the peacock. Some alchemists, particularly those who worked primarily with vegetable matter and processes, instead of with minerals, interpolated another (or alternative) stage here: the Green Lion, representing the green raw energy of nature. The vivid colours of the Peacock's Tail would overcome the blackness of the first state and leave a whiteness called albedo, the next state, usually represented by a white Virgin, a White Eagle, a Dove or a Swan and associated with the female, silver, and the moon. This was a moment of rejoicing, of hope; it was a proof that darkness would not last forever.[30] The next state was *citrinitas* (yellowing), a stage often abandoned after the fifteenth century or incorporated in the final state. *Citrinitas* represented the male or the sun. Blending the *albedo* (female) state with the *citrinitas* (male) state was believed to be particularly important; it constituted the 'chemical wedding' from which the hermaphroditic offspring – Mercury – would be born. Finally, the successful alchemist would take his material through to *rubedo* (redness), the final state, the triumph of the Great Work. This was the creation of the Philosopher's Stone, a transparent red stone, often portrayed as a Phoenix, supposed to transmute base metal into gold, perfect anything from metals to human beings and give long life or immortality.[32]

To us this all sounds weird and wonderful – if not barking mad. In Bronzino's time, however, alchemy retained much of the intellectual respectability and rigour that had attended it in the medieval period. Many eminent people took a serious interest in it, believing that the occult provided an understanding of the forces controlling the universe. The Medici family were enthusiastic supporters of alchemical experimentation. Cosimo I inherited his interest in alchemy from his grandmother Caterina Sforza (1463-1509), who had been a devotee of alchemy. She collected over four hundred alchemical, medicinal, and cosmetic recipes, and wrote extensively to fellow alchemists about materials and laboratory techniques. Cosimo in turn wrote alchemical recipes in his own hand and passed his enthusiasm on to his son and successor, Francesco, who was fascinated by chemistry and alchemy, devoting time and money to his laboratory, the Studiolo in the Palazzo Vecchio (where there is a portrait of Cosimo I and his wife Eleonora by Bronzino and a series of scenes by Vasari depicting alchemical experiments). Francesco performed chemical and alchemical experiments himself and, while he did not manage to complete the Great Work, he did make the first successful imitation in Europe of Chinese porcelain. Alchemically based workshops were also set up for the production of medicines and for glasswork. Two

Scottish physicians trained in the enlightened alchemical methods of Paracelsus were brought to Tuscany by Duke Cosimo: Jacopo Macolo, reader in medicine and prefect of the Pisa Botanical Gardens, who may also have been the Duke's personal physician; and Giovanni Macolo, professor of chemistry at the laboratory annexed to the botanical gardens.

In France, Francis I was also interested in astrology, alchemy and the Cabala and there were plenty of savants, mystics and cabalists in his court.[33] Interest in alchemy has persisted, surviving the scientific revolution and the Enlightenment. Even Newton took some aspects of it seriously. Carl Jung's thoughts about the Collective Unconscious were triggered by his realisation that different alchemists over the centuries had independently assigned very similar symbols to the various alchemical ideas and practices. He went on to apply his analytical psychology to the esoteric component of alchemical practice, seeing in it an encoding of critical psychic processes. He interpreted the Great Work as a metaphor for the process of individuation (akin in this respect to the classical myths and to the plots of many of the great novels).[34]

Even though every serious alchemist failed to achieve the final *rubedo* state or to complete the Great Work, alchemists did make an important contribution to the improvement of life in early-modern Europe. As well as giving painters a host of attractive colours, they purified salts, made medicines and contributed to the glass, ceramic, cosmetic and other trades. Paracelsus turned to the alchemists when he wanted to look for and test alternative and new cures for diseases. And the alchemists developed techniques and experimental practice (distillation being a particularly important contribution) and formulated various theories about the properties and interactions of minerals and metals – though usually mistaken the refinement of these theories provided a starting point for the science of chemistry.

During the Middle Ages and the Renaissance not only alchemists but also theologians, astrologers, mystics, physicians and others assigned symbolic meanings to colours, to trees and flowers and to groups of twelve, seven, three or even one; in fact to almost anything that might appear in a painting, and many of these things could have several meanings.[35] The theological colour code was fairly stable: white symbolised purity; red, charity; yellow-gold, dignity; black humanity; green, new life; blue, linked to the divine, could also stand for the unusual and potentially dangerous; white, green and red together represented the three cardinal virtues of faith, hope and charity. Colour might also reflect the dominant of the four humours in a person's make-up: yellow, choleric: black, melancholic; red, sanguine; white, phlegmatic. The trouble is that apart from these very broad generalisations, the codes differed over time and depended also on local culture and geographic area. Mutually contradictory systems of colour symbolism could be in use at the same time. Much the same applies today. Colour still has strong associations: the 'Orange Revolution' in Ukraine, 'feeling blue', 'rolling out the red carpet'. Red is the colour of socialist or communist political movements in Europe, blue the colour of the Conservative Party in the UK; but in the USA the opposite applies, states held by the right-wing Republican Party are 'red' and those held by the left-wing Democratic Party are 'blue'. Cardinals in the Roman Catholic Church wear red; we dress our guardsmen in red tunics.[36] Red is but a 'grown-up' version of pink, and only a century ago it was 'blue for a girl, pink for a boy': in 1918 a trade magazine *Earnshaw's Infants' Department*, published in Chicago, replied to a reader's question: 'The generally accepted rule is pink for the boys, and blue for the girls. The reason is that pink, being a more decided and stronger colour, is more suitable for the boy, while blue, which is more delicate and dainty, is prettier for the girl.' The 'generally accepted rule' was not reversed until the 1940s.[37]

In the face of such inconsistency it becomes extremely difficult confidently to assign a 'meaning' to any particular hue in a specific painting. Conversely you can read whatsoever you wish into the colours in a painting by deciphering the code to suit your preconceived ideas. Writing in *Painting and Experience in Fifteenth Century Italy*' Michael Baxandall is adamant: 'There are no secret codes worth knowing about in the painters' colour'[38] and elsewhere he reminds us that 'In systems like classical mythology and Christian theology, matured and elaborated over centuries, almost anything can signify something … many things can signify various things'.[39] Best we avoid any but the most straightforward interpretations of colour in Bronzino's *London Allegory*.

It is nonetheless worth thinking about the colours that Bronzino chose for his painting, without yet trying to assign 'meanings' to them. Obviously, sixteenth-century painters had a good understanding of colour; of the behaviour of their pigments when laid alongside one another; the effects which could be produced by mixing pigments and, as oil painting developed, the effects of laying a glaze of one pigment over another. But they lacked any theoretical basis for their use of colours. Red, yellow and blue were recognised to be special in some way, but there was only the most rudimentary understanding of, and no language for, 'primary' colours (red, yellow, blue, which cannot be made from a mixture of any other colours), 'secondary' colours (orange, green, violet, each being a mixture of two primaries), 'tertiary' colours (green-yellow, yellow-orange, orange-red, red-violet, violet-blue and blue-green) and 'complimentary' colours (a primary is complimented by the secondary colour derived by mixing the other two primaries; so red and green are complimentary). Alberti (c.1435) and Leonardo da Vinci (c.1495) were the first to try to come up with some rational principles to describe the nature of colour but the painter's colour wheel with which we are familiar derives from one published by Newton in his *Opticks* of 1704, where it was designed to help with the mathematical analysis of colour mixing. The concept of primary, secondary, tertiary and complimentary colours wasn't established until the nineteenth century.

Although the *London Allegory* is striking for its vivid hues, relatively few have been used. The pale flesh tones and the expanse of rich blue curtain in the background dominate the painting. An acid green, a rich rose-pink and a pale lilac are also present and that's about it, and the colours at the periphery are muted. Blue and green lie alongside each other on the colour wheel, which means that the red has all the more impact. The choice and distribution of colours owe much to Bronzino's High Renaissance heritage. Intense shading, dark shadowing and rosy cheeks were characteristics of High Renaissance painting that were exaggerated in Mannerism and the bright colours in the foreground focus attention on the principal characters.

Bronzino applied his freshly prepared colours using a brush which had most likely been made in his workshop from either soft hairs or bristles held in quills or bound to sticks with thread or wire; Cennini had told painters how to do this in *Il libro dell'arte*. Because of the way in which they were made the brushes had to be round – the metal ferrule which made flat and filbert shapes possible wasn't invented until the eighteenth century.

He would have started by applying a layer of earth-coloured paint to his *gesso* ground. This would have been allowed to dry before further layers of paint and then glazes were applied, each layer being allowed to dry before the next was added. The under-painting, some of which is still visible in small areas,[27] was there to help to define the colour values of the upper layers of paint by blending with them optically but not physically, reducing the risk of them becoming muddy. Today's practice is usually more immediate – painters work *alla prima*, applying their paint directly to a primed, white canvas, working wet-into-wet and doing most of their colour mixing on the canvas rather than on the palette.

Before going any further let's make life a bit easier for ourselves by labelling the figures and objects that we are going to be discussing as we examine the painting (Figure 1). Some of the figures and many of the objects are a bit problematic so at this stage we'll avoid committing ourselves about what these figures and objects are. They have been designated by letters for the time being. We don't know what title Bronzino gave to his work but Vasari describes it: '…wherein was a nude Venus, with a Cupid who was kissing her, and Pleasure on one side with Play and other Loves [*altre passioni d'Amore*], and on the other side Fraud and Jealousy and other passions of love'.[40] so it is reasonable to identify two of the principal characters as Venus and Cupid. Vasari, writing over twenty years after Bronzino is thought to have painted the work, failed to mention Time, who is readily and unambiguously identifiable by his wing and his attribute – an Hourglass. Vasari's '*altre passioni d'Amore*' also cause trouble. If translated as 'other Cupids' they don't exist. If he simply meant 'other representations of romantic passion' we might conclude that he was referring to the figures in the background on one side of the painting or the other. But the capitalised '*Amore*' argues for him meaning 'Cupids'. This partial description of the painting suggests that Vasari may not have seen the *London Allegory*; he may even have got muddled up about which figures appear in the *London Allegory* and which in the *Budapest Allegory*. Alternatively, rather than trying to give a detailed, figure by figure, description of the painting he may have been attempting an overall interpretation of it, highlighting the contrast between the representation of pleasure one side and pain on the other.[2]

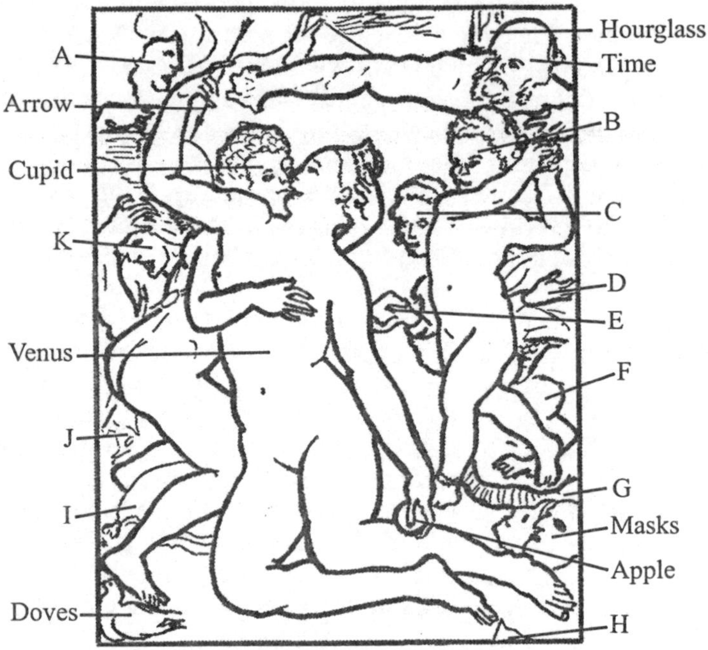

Figure 1
The *London Allegory*: Key figures and objects.

At first sight most of the figures and objects in the painting are unrelated to each other and many defy definitive identification. How was Bronzino to dispose his cast of characters on the flat surface of his support in such a way that the painting didn't become a chaotic mess? According to Renaissance practice Venus and Cupid, the principal players in his drama would be placed prominently and, most likely, centrally. They might also be expected to be, if not the largest of the figures, then at least not significantly smaller than those of the supporting cast. Bronzino followed these conventions; even though he is classed as a Mannerist painter he didn't hide his principals in a crowd of similarly sized and dressed lesser characters in the way that, for example, Pontormo had done in *Joseph in Egypt*. In size, form and colour, Venus and Cupid dominate the *London Allegory*, providing the emotional and compositional stability to which the viewer can return should the other compositional devices discussed below fail to prevent it collapsing into incoherence. Exactly where on the support should he place Venus, Cupid and the others? Did he rely on his experience, his respect for his predecessors' work and on intuition to order a meaningful and satisfying arrangement, or did he have a more calculated schema in mind? Most likely all of these, and there is plenty of evidence in the painting itself that he changed his mind about the details many times as his work took shape. But the broad outline of the composition seems to have been fixed from the outset, as were the identity and position of the seven figures and their physical and psychological relationships one to another.

It is relatively easy to see that some paintings have an underlying geometric structure – the figures in many Holy Family paintings are disposed to form a pyramid, for example, and Mondrian's paintings are obviously geometric. As with the interpretation of colour, however, the urge to rationalise and, in this case, the lure of numerology, make it all too easy to take this sort of analysis of a painting to extreme lengths. In 1963 Charles Bouleau published a lengthy book entitled *The Painter's Secret Geometry* in which he examined dozens of paintings from Classical to modern times, finding within them all sorts of elaborate geometric or arithmetic schemes. Described by Dover Publications as a cult classic, it was republished in 2014. Perspectival constructions can readily be checked for accuracy but otherwise modern scholarship is sceptical about this sort of mathematically-based pictorial analysis unless it is supported by internal evidence – such as construction lines still detectable in the painting's under-drawing – or by documentary evidence. One objection is that because it is impossible to measure all the features within a painting with absolute precision it is also impossible to discern the painter's decisions about relationships within and between the features. This is taking healthy scepticism too far – surely it was sufficient for a painter to decide that, for example, his horizon-line should lie roughly on the mid-horizontal of his ground rather than, say, a quarter of the way down from the top, he didn't need to measure the mid-point to the nearest millimetre? Similarly, it is suggested that since it is possible to conjure up innumerable composition lines on a painting, none can be accepted. This argument too throws the baby out with the bath water – Bouleau may have taken the exercise to an extreme but it isn't unreasonable to suppose that painters had, and have, a compositional scaffold or armature in mind, nor that in some cases (particularly in the medieval and early-Renaissance periods) they were mathematically rigorous, based on a pentagram or on musical intervals, perhaps.[41] Identifying these structures post-hoc is risky – it is all too easy to find what you want to find. But provided it isn't carried too far it can help us to understand why and how a painting 'works', why it is more than a jumble of marks on a flat surface and how the eye is led round the painting in much the same way as the ear can appreciate the rhythm underlying a piece of music.

Piero della Francesca (1415/20-1492) has the dubious honour of being the painter whose work has been subjected to the most relentless of these analyses.[42] Piero was a competent mathematician who had a thorough understanding of the classical geometry of Archimedes, Plato and Euclid; in his turn he published two textbooks of mathematics. It is not surprising therefore that his paintings have been scrutinised for evidence of an underlying mathematically determined structure, nor that his *Baptism of Christ* (1440-50, National Gallery, Room 54), is claimed to show many of these expected structural features, in particular division into thirds horizontally and quarters vertically. Some take this type of analysis further, suggesting that the geometrical (or mathematical) structure not only orders the image but also symbolises something else – a three-fold division or a triangle, for example, might symbolise the Holy Trinity.

If we are going to look for compositional lines within the *London Allegory* we should work with the original (impractical) or with a good reproduction of it. Bronzino's painting in the National Gallery measures 146.1 x 116.2cm a H:W ratio of 1.26:1. The painting is reproduced all over the place but rarely with dimensions that accurately reflect the original: the image in the large format reproduction sold by the National Gallery has a ratio of 1.27:1; in the National Gallery's postcard it is way out at 1.30:1; elsewhere ratios of 1.28:1, 1.29:1 are easy to find. Bouleau's small reproduction comes in at 1.26:1 as does the larger one in Susan Woodford's short guide, so it's the latter that I have used here.[43] All this serves as a reminder of Benjamin's exposé of the consequences of the ready availability of reproductions and our dependence on them. If the reproductions that we rely upon for our knowledge of the great works of western art are not even in the right proportions, let alone in the right size, the right colours or the right location it is hardly surprising that our experience of them (and of the originals should we ever be fortunate enough to encounter them) will be aberrant. While thinking about the misleading scale of the readily available reproductions of the *London Allegory* it's worth pointing out the variability in the reproductions of the colours in the painting – most commonly the loss of brilliance in the reproductions – and not only of this painting; I am very often struck by the brilliance of an original that has become familiar from dull reproductions in books.

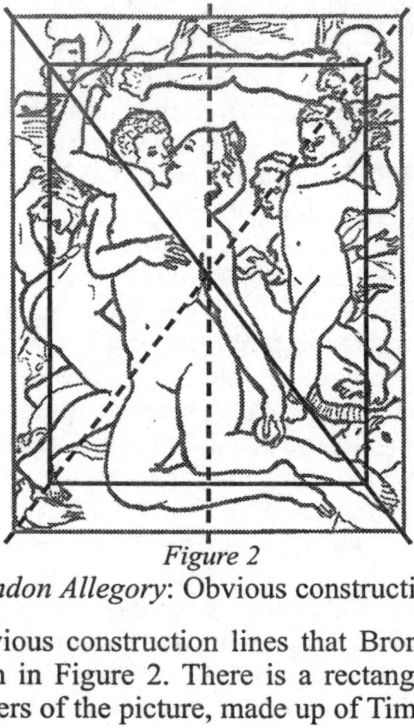

Figure 2
The *London Allegory*: Obvious construction lines.

Some very obvious construction lines that Bronzino may have used are shown in Figure 2. There is a rectangular framework within the borders of the picture, made up of Time's outstretched arm, Venus's raised forearm and right lower-leg and figure B's torso and left forearm. Muted tones are used in those parts of the painting which lie outside this rectangle, making the objects and characters there particularly difficult to see, let alone interpret (and virtually impossible to see in most reproductions, where the reduced scale adds to the problem). Bronzino was not afraid to use much lighter tones within the rectangle, so the obscurity of the periphery must be deliberate – he wanted the viewer to come close to the picture, to peer into the shadows, to struggle to see and work out what's going on there.

Figure A, Venus's right shoulder, her left arm and her left ankle and foot lie on the upper-left to lower-right diagonal. Time's head is inclined along the opposite, top-right to bottom-left diagonal, which also catches the faces of figures B and C, Cupid's right knee and toe and the doves. Venus's left thigh lies along the vertical line which bisects the picture – interesting that the bulk of the two principal figures, Venus and Cupid, fall almost entirely within the left-hand side of the painting, balanced by the three prominent figures on the right-hand side. There is a void between Venus and C, occupied only by E. Other diagonal relationships can be identified – for example B's right-forearm is in line with C's hand (E) and with Cupid's right lower-leg. H, Venus's right foot, Cupid's right elbow, the jewel on the strap of Cupid's quiver and the front of K's face lie on another diagonal. Will Fisher, who focuses on the homoerotic and bisexual elements in the *London Allegory*, draws attention to the diagonal lines which link Venus's left foot, her apple and Cupid's buttocks, and B's rose petals and forearm with Venus's left nipple and Cupid's buttocks.[44]

So, there does seem to be a well-defined scaffold that anchors the principal figures and which, in some cases, may reinforce a message buried within the painting. Some more vertical relationships can also be identified very readily – it's always possible to draw a straight line between two points, of course. And we could go on for some time, finding several lines which link more or less important elements of the painting but this wouldn't necessarily be a very useful exercise and we'd be none the wiser about whether or not Bronzino himself made use of them or was even aware of them. The very idea of a scaffold suggests stasis but while these lines do indeed provide some logic to the composition they also, paradoxically, introduce some fluidity – for they help to lead the viewer's eye round it. So if, for example, we first notice the kiss, the lines that we have identified then carry us up to A and across to Time; or down to the masks, across to the doves and up to Cupid's bottom. The scaffold is not the only thing that keeps the eye moving, but it makes an important contribution to the dynamism of the painting.

Other lines within the painting play off one-another in an exciting way: Venus's curved right arm is echoed by the arm of K and by Cupid's right arm and right leg; Cupid's right foot is parallel with both of Venus's feet; B's left thigh and right calf form a right angle that's mirrored by Cupid's right leg; and look at the pose of B's torso – it's almost exactly the same as Venus's and the position of B's left arm is very similar to that of Venus's right arm.

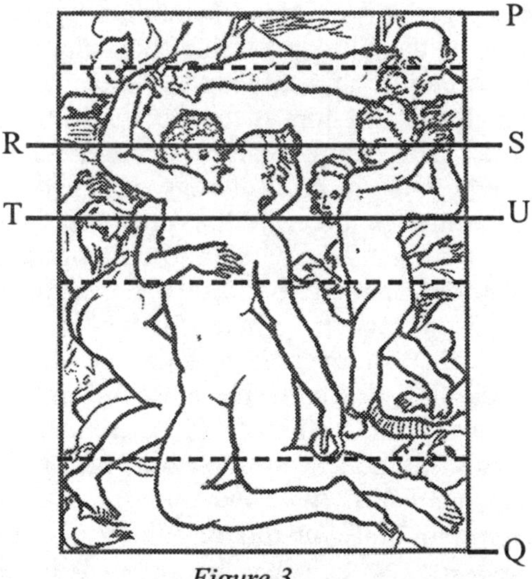

Figure 3

The *London Allegory*: possible horizontal relationships.

We should explore some horizontal relationships as well, though this will be a more contentious, speculative exercise (Figure 3). The broken lines suggest what some of these relationships might be. None is particularly exciting – the broken, bisecting line, for example, links the elbows of character K and of Cupid with one hand of C (E) – and the faces of all the characters lie above it. The lower broken line links three potentially important features in the painting – the tassel on the cushion, Venus's apple and the masks; a bit more scaffolding, perhaps but, so what? Potentially more interesting are the lines T-U and R-S, particularly the latter. Now for a brief diversion to explain why this is so.

In 600 BCE Euclid and Pythagoras explored the properties of a straight line (X-Y, below) divided into two unequal parts X-Z and Z-Y. They found one position of Z, such that the ratio of the length of the shorter segment (Z-Y) to the longer (X-Z) is the same as that of the longer segment (X-Z) to the whole (X-Y).

$$i.e \quad \frac{\text{Z-Y}}{\text{X-Z}} = \frac{\text{X-Z}}{\text{X-Y}}$$

This unique proportion (given the symbol φ by the mathematicians) is known as the Golden Section (or Golden Mean); it can be applied to rectangles and to pairs of rectangles in which the ratio of the lengths of the sides is the Golden Ratio, φ, as well as to straight lines.[46] The Greeks realised that there is a particularly pleasing aesthetic balance to buildings designed using Golden Section proportions. In the Middle Ages the Golden Section acquired a mystical aura; it was held to be a perfect, God-given ratio which enabled painters to divide a flat picture in the most beautiful way possible. It gained further lustre during the Renaissance because it appeared to combine the knowledge of antiquity with the Christian faith. The most eminent mathematician of his day, Luca Pacioli ('Father of Accountancy and Book-keeping' and the first person to publish a work on double-entry book-keeping), published his *Divina Proportione* in 1509. He was a close friend of Leonardo da Vinci and of Piero della Francesca and his book was illustrated with drawings by Leonardo. In it the Golden Section is described as the 'divine proportion' because it is beyond definition and in this respect is like God and, in its three-in-one proportion, symbolic of the Holy Trinity. Fascination with the Golden Section has persisted to this day – to such an extent that in 2017 *National Geographic* magazine chose this ratio as the topic for the first volume in its series devoted to mathematics; the magazine's owners saw that there was profit to be made from a book about a mathematical relationship that 'has fascinated more brilliant minds than π or e put together'.[47] Fascination with the ratio does not in itself mean that its supposed aesthetic properties are real – there is a school of contrary opinion.[48] On the other hand, some psychological experiments (and there have been many on the composition and aesthetics of paintings) do appear to show that people may prefer proportions close to the Golden Section, that they find it to be aesthetically more satisfying than all other proportions. If this is so, it is likely that artists will intuitively default to approximately Golden Section proportions which art historians armed with tape-measures and calculators may then retrospectively, and erroneously, attribute to careful calculation.

Nonetheless, Piero della Francesca (in the *Baptism of Christ* and elsewhere), Leonardo da Vinci, Durer, Claude Lorraine and many other artists throughout the ages, including the twentieth century artists and architects Graham Sutherland, Le Corbusier, Mondrian and Dalí have used the Golden Section and Golden Rectangle. Golden Section relationships can also be found in plants and animals, poetry, music, the dimensions of a credit card, of a four-biscuit Kit-Kat bar, in fact all over the place – calculation, intuition or coincidence?[49]

The true value of φ is irrational – which means that, like π, it never repeats itself no matter to how many decimal places you express it and its calculation is mathematically demanding; the ratio can also be derived geometrically using a ruler and compasses but that's complicated too. Fortunately, others have done the work for us: we know that the value of φ is about 1.618, its reciprocal is 0.618. So, we can use this number to search for Golden Section features in the *London Allegory*. Bronzino lived at a time when the Golden Section was still exerting a powerful effect, so we might expect him to have used it to structure his painting. On the other hand, there are so many figures and objects in the painting that we could probably find a Golden Section relationship between three or more of them quite by chance if we were to search hard enough: finding the ratio will not necessarily mean that Bronzino put it there. Line T-U in Figure 3 lies at the Golden Section on the line P-Q. It is moderately interesting, linking the face of character K with the left-upper arm of B and the chin or mouth of C. Line R-S lies on the Golden Section for P-U; it links Venus's right elbow, Cupid's eyes and wing, Venus's eyes, the eyes of figure B and the rose petals held by B. This is a bit more interesting. I can't make a convincing case for anything of significance lying on a vertical Golden Section line – the apple and E are close to one, and Venus's left nipple is almost on one – but a miss is as good as a mile. H does lie at a Golden Section point but may not be a significant feature. Even a direct hit would be far from proof that Bronzino used the Golden Ratio to construct his painting. Much more likely he anchored his composition on a horizontal (Figure 3) and diagonal scaffold (Figure 2), using a straight-edge together with good doses of experience and intuition but without the aid of compasses or an abacus.

Powerful centrifugal forces are in play, leaving the void in the centre of the painting, behind Venus's left shoulder. Cupid's arrow points, as arrows do, directly to character K at the left-hand edge of the painting. K and the more visible of the two doves is looking to the left; Cupid's right lower-leg and Venus's right upper-arm are leading the eye out to the left; Cupid's buttocks and his bent right arm similarly point to the left. The left arm of character A and Venus's right forearm point upwards. Character B's arms and character C's hand D point to the right. Venus's left arm, her thighs and her feet point downwards. The very act of trying to see what's going on at the edges of the painting and in the four corners pulls the eye and mind away from the encounter between Venus and Cupid.

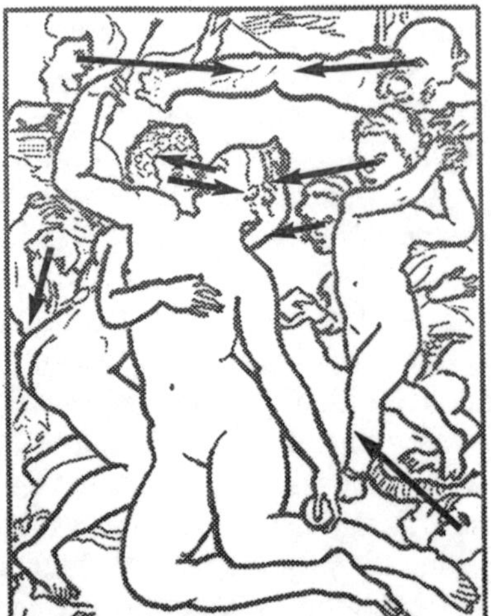

Figure 4
The *London Allegory*: who is looking at whom?

An analysis of the sight-lines of the characters in the painting will help us to understand how these centrifugal forces are neutralised and it provides an opportunity to introduce the modern concept of 'the gaze'. Recognising that in the past the typical viewer of a painting was male – and this was certainly true of the *London Allegory* – modern art historians have drawn on psychoanalytic and feminist theory to identify the sexual objectification of women in paintings (and other media, film in particular). Most depictions of women in paintings have been commissioned and painted by men for the enjoyment of men, who subject them to their 'male gaze', empowering the men and negating the feelings, thoughts and sexual drives of the woman. The fact that the women are very often depicted nude and/or in situations in which they are dominated by men supports the contention that these paintings are designed to satisfy the male's deep-seated drive for the sexual pleasure to be gained from looking: scoptophilia. The voyeuristic pleasure they derive from looking at these women while not themselves being seen adds a further negative connotation, verging on the sadistic.[50] Figure 4 shows us that while we stare at the characters in the painting most of them are looking towards the centre of the panel, creating a dynamic that counteracts the centrifugal forces and the static structure of the scaffold to pull our eyes back to the interaction between the dominant figures of Venus and Cupid. Where are the various characters looking? Only one discomforts me by staring directly at me. Venus and Cupid are not looking at the secondary characters – of course not, these are allegorical, they do not exist in the same physical space as Venus or Cupid. Nor are they looking at me, the viewer of the painting: so I can gaze on them, be a peeping-tom, without the risk of being caught out, without feeling threatened or excited by a knowing return of my gaze – be it homosexual or heterosexual. The masks and B seem to be looking at the sexualised kiss exchanged between Venus and Cupid. Time and A are looking at each other (or is A looking at C?[51]); K is looking away from the scene of the action. C is the only character who comes close to looking at me, the viewer (originally, at the owner of the painting) and her expression is pensive – is C trying to tell me something? Is she telling me that there is a message here that applies to me – one about which I too should be pensive? Is she alerting us to the fact that this is more than just a decorative, diverting painting? And if C is looking at me, what am I looking at? Well, obviously I am gazing at a naked woman and adolescent boy mutually engaged in a sexually charged activity of some sort; perhaps I am satisfying my scoptophilic drive? More prosaically, though no more palatably, rather than wanting to dominate women in an unequal power relationship, perhaps I am just responding to an evolutionarily determined instinct to enjoy looking at nubile women who will make good 'breeding stock'. The male gaze may be the product of evolution, expressed in a way which depends on the cultural and social context. The more patriarchal a culture is, the more men will feel justified in openly treating women as sex objects; and it would be hard to find more patriarchal cultures than those of the Renaissance courts.[52]

The sheer physicality of the principal characters, particularly Venus and Cupid, grab and hold the viewer's attention, pulling it back to the centre, where it can dwell with approval, envy or disgust on what they are doing to each other. The animated expression on the face of B and the self-absorption of Venus and Cupid place the action at the centre of the work but the intriguing figures and objects disposed round the perimeter are distracting. They intrigue because, in most cases, they are hard to identify and in all cases their meaning is obscure or ambiguous. The fact that many of them are difficult to see and to understand cannot be accidental – Bronzino could have made them more clearly visible without making them easier to interpret. Why he chose not to do so will be explored in Chapter V. As we peer into the shadows at the periphery of the painting we begin to notice tiny details – Bronzino considered these important enough to spend time and effort on them, so we in turn should ask ourselves what they might mean. Character K, for example has no teeth; there are two doves, not one or three or more; there is foliage behind the head of character A and behind the hourglass and some tiny white flowers on top of J – these have been identified as *Verbena officinalis*.[53] Something is propping-up the masks – perhaps there are three of them, not just the obvious two. Then, lest we become fixated by the periphery, we notice similar details at the centre and our attention is pulled back there. The cheerful character B doesn't appear to be in any pain but he is standing on a thorn (impossible to see in most reproductions). The strap of Cupid's quiver (J) has a red and gold clasp. Venus is naked except for an elaborate pearl and gold headdress, on which is perched a tiny golden figure – of a nude woman posed in almost exactly the same way as Venus herself. Could this be another dig by Bronzino at the inferiority of sculpture, unable to compete with the versatility of painting?

Although the figures are fairly static, they do direct the eye round the scene. So, starting with the dominant figure, Venus, the viewer's eye moves down her left arm to the apple, up the trunk of B to Time's head, along Time's arm to the arrow, which then leads on to K.

Peering at these details, particularly Venus' head-dress, as we must do if we are to identify the characters and smaller objects, we find ourselves invading the personal spaces of a nude woman and a nude youth; our engagement with them which was voyeuristic when we first approached the painting now begins to feel horribly like an assault. Recoiling from this disconcerting self-awareness, we are forced to distance ourselves from the central motif and examine our own response to the whole scene; we step back, try to comprehend it in its entirety and to examine its meaning both as an intriguing intellectual riddle and as a challenge to our own psyche. As we step back, we engage again with C, who is still looking knowingly at us. But now we can't see the details – once more we are forced to approach the scene more closely and to recognise that 'reading' the painting properly will demand an intimate and discomforting engagement with it: we begin to suspect that the meaning of the painting will be rather dark.

Venus and Cupid – the obvious centres of attraction – appeal to the scoptophilic delight we derive from looking at a voluptuous, nude woman and a nude adolescent boy caressing each other – playing to our heterosexual and homosexual desires and fantasies (overt or covert, accepted or repressed) and to our feelings about incest, whatever they may be. If we are disturbed by our own modern, 'Western liberal' reaction to the painting, this is unlikely to be the reaction that the work was intended to evoke in the powerful, sixteenth century and – most importantly – male viewer for whom it was created. The painting is unashamedly erotic, kept in a private apartment it would have been seen and appreciated by a small, select circle of men.

Just as there are centrifugal and centripetal physical forces that hold our eyes within the confines of the painting while guiding them round it, so there are psychological forces in play as our attention shifts from the clearly visible principal characters to the obscure peripheral ones and from the large forms to the smallest details. As we move backwards and forwards the better to see the whole scene and then the fine details and as our eyes move around it, the conscious and unconscious parts of our psyche are being activated: we move from conscious ideas about its meaning to unconscious associations, fears and fantasies. We need to explore the meanings of the various characters and symbols before we can fully appreciate the range of emotions and ideas evoked by the painting (Chapters V and VII).

So the *London Allegory* is packed full of stresses which would tear it apart were it not for the dominant figures of Venus and Cupid, the centripetal gaze of most of the characters and the scaffold of straight lines which stabilises it, preventing our visual and mental attention from flying off in all directions, never to return to the central focal point of the painting. But the scaffold isn't allowed to make the painting arid and boring. Quite the contrary – the content of the painting and other internal features make it an exciting, even discomforting, work.

Lest we get too confident in our ideas about how the picture was composed and congratulate ourselves on our perceptive analysis, let's remind ourselves that it was Bronzino's practice to make many *pentimenti* as he worked: that may undermine some of the discussion above. A substantial restoration of the *London Allegory* was carried out in 1958 and a more limited scientific examination of the painting in 1998. These allowed a detailed examination of the fabric of the painting[54] and the removal of some over-painting which had been added, probably during the reign of Louis XIV to tone down its eroticism.[55] This included a veil covering Venus's pubis and a myrtle branch covering Cupid's buttocks. The overpainting ordered by Eastlake when the painting was first exhibited in the National Gallery was also removed, revealing Venus's tongue and her erect left nipple between the first and second fingers of Cupid's right hand. Cupid's arrow was shown to have been one of the *pentimenti* and Time's right hand may originally have clasped Venus's right hand. Time's hand was then changed to a clenched fist, which left Venus's hand up in the air with nothing to do – so she was given the arrow to hold.[56] The restoration, coupled with inspection of a couple of copies of the *London Allegory* made in the latter half of the sixteenth century, showed that at some time after the copies were made, and for an unknown reason, some 5cm had been cut off the lower border of the panel. Because of this, Venus now looks more squeezed into the picture than was the case originally – her toes are closer to the lower border than Bronzino had intended them to be. And, perhaps the small object H would have been interpretable had an extra 5cm of it been visible.

The scientific examination of the painting in 1998 revealed several other changes. Most substantial, and significant, was a radical reorientation of Cupid who had originally been seen front-on with most of his torso hidden behind Venus. Bronzino repainted him in his current mannered pose, twisted round to make his buttocks more prominent and showing him from two angles – in fact his pose is now so contorted that it parodies the established Mannerist style. He gave Cupid a cushion to kneel on, made him obviously an adolescent rather than a child and added his quiver (J); later still he painted the flower on top of the quiver. The additional 2.7cm-wide wooden strip had to be added to the left-hand side of the panel to accommodate the revised pose – a major undertaking as the painting was already quite advanced and a clear indication of how important Bronzino believed the revised pose to be. The extra space on the left of the support allowed Bronzino to depict the forearm of K more completely than before and to give Cupid a bigger wing. But that left less room than originally intended for K, who is now squashed into the small area between Cupid's back and Venus's right upper-arm. Several changes were made to C – her clawed leg, her tail and her sting were added, the latter very late on. The apple was added to Venus's left hand and her right hand, which originally rested on Cupid's head, was moved to its current position. The masks were originally at the bottom left-hand corner; they were moved to the right-hand side because Cupid's right foot now had to occupy the space they had been in, and the doves were added. The curtain held by Time and A was greener at first than it is now – the green (azurite) shows through the later ultramarine in places – and it had a golden lower border, most of which was lost with the bottom 5cm of the panel.[57] Where does this leave our analysis of the composition of the painting? Is it compromised by the changes in dimensions, in the posture of Venus and Cupid and in the mind of the painter? The original painting was 151.5cm high; now it is 3.3% shorter, not a sufficient difference, I suggest, to invalidate our tentative analysis of horizontal relationships in Figure 3. The panel that was added to the left-hand side is there today – so in that respect Figure 2 is valid. And the scaffold in Figure 2 still matches the initial composition revealed by the technical analysis.[58] But we can't afford to be dogmatic in our conclusions about Bronzino's whole approach to the painting – if he and his patron did start out with a physical and intellectual schema in mind it looks as though it was a partial and less erotic one, a plan which they were prepared to develop and amend as the painting progressed. Their amendments were intended to clarify the identity of some of the protagonists by adding their familiar attributes (Venus's apple, for example) and to increase the sexual charge of the work by making radical changes to Cupid's age and pose, introducing elements of homosexuality and of incest to the painting. Bronzino habitually made changes to his paintings while he was working on them,[59] but the formal (the radical repositioning of Cupid, for example) and psychological (the greatly increased emphasis on the erotic) revisions that he made to the *London Allegory* were so substantial that I wonder if they give us an important insight into Cosimo's mind? Perhaps it was only after Bronzino had got quite a long way with a relatively straightforward painting of the familiar mythological subject of Venus and Cupid that Cosimo got involved and had the idea that, with some non-trivial changes, it would make a suitable gift for Francis I? The changes made to C – the introduction of the animal's paw and of the reptilian tail neither of which was present in the initial composition – are particularly revealing in this context. I'll explain why in the next chapter, where we begin to think about what the painting means – at last, you might very well say.

V

The London Allegory: Who is who; What is what?

'The time has come,' the Walrus said,
'To talk of many things:
Of shoes – and ships – and sealing wax –
Of cabbages – and kings –
And why the sea is boiling hot –
And whether pigs have wings.'
(Louis Carol. 'The Walrus and the Carpenter')

Armed now with some understanding of the social, political and cultural environment in which the *London Allegory* was made and of how and why it was made we can start to think about what it might mean. Many before us have made the attempt and we shall look at the most coherent of the interpretations that have been proposed. The fact that there are many credible exegeses is in part a consequence of the fact that many of the figures in the painting are unique, they fall into no recognisable iconographic category, nor into any readily recognisable assemblage. This may result in no single interpretation ever being found, and it suggests that Bronzino deliberately created a multi-layered, ambiguous painting open to several valid interpretations that would challenge and thereby entertain its viewers – while legitimising their enjoyment of its eroticism.

If we are to understand the painting we shall have to take a careful look at every element in it and try to decide what each represents (Plate 1 and Figure 1). Doing this, however, runs the risk of losing sight of the wood for the trees, of turning a full blooded enjoyment of the painting into an arid intellectual exercise. This would be a terrible mistake: Bronzino has crafted a fiendishly complicated puzzle, full of pitfalls for the unwary and full of fun for those prepared to enter into its spirit. So before we start to examine the trees to decide on their species, let's spend a few moments looking at the wood. Is it deciduous or evergreen; is it temperate or tropical; primary or secondary?

What strikes us on first seeing the *London Allegory*? Surely, it's the nude figures of Venus and Cupid – they have great shock value because of their size, their nudity, their hue and their actions. The fact that this is a sexy picture is inescapable, and surprising given the straight-laced moral probity of its likely sponsor, Cosimo I, Grand Duke of Tuscany; but it is a curiously detached, unemotional work; it reports but it doesn't judge – it neither condemns nor celebrates; and the world which it reports is an enclosed, fictive one. The figures are barely human; they are like mannequins, frozen in their allusive representation of virtues and vices. Only Venus and Cupid are in the 'real world'; the other five figures are allegorical, they provide a commentary on the action – both for us and for Venus and Cupid themselves. Next to strike us perhaps is its vibrant colour. Michael Glover writes about 'the billowing of gorgeous fabrics, pink, blue, green, yellow . . . this grand, peacockish display'[1] – true enough and remember that 'peacockish', we shall return to it. But for all the undeniable beauty of the painting it's white and blue, both 'cold' hues that dominate. What do we focus on next? On its complexity, perhaps, or on figure B. Then, surely, we start to wonder what it's all about. Is this a piece, akin to a Madonna and Child, intended to aid devotional reflection? Is it a piece of propaganda? Is it meant to instruct, as a Last Judgement instructs the viewer about the ultimate consequences of behaviour on earth? At first sight, it is none of these: it is just a bit of rather naughty fun, intended to titillate, to offend, to evoke knowing winks and nudges from those who like to call themselves cognoscenti. The *London Allegory* is a reminder that Bronzino's equivalent to his painting is his burlesque poetry. Look closer, though, and it may turn out to instruct, to have a moral message, and maybe it has a sting in its tail – we shall see.

The surface is very smooth, with few traces of a brush-stroke (though there are traces of the *pentimenti*); this is Mannerism, for sure, but the scene is artificial, a claustrophobic *tableau vivant*. The space occupied by the figures is very shallow. Venus and Cupid, in the foreground, are right up against the front of the painting; A, B and Time are in the middle-ground, but still very close to Venus and Cupid; the other figures are a little bit further back. Then, closing off the back of the scene is the blue curtain. We know that something is going on behind the curtain – a laurel hedge is poking over the top of it and the bodies of Time and A are hidden behind it – are Time and A trying to hide or to reveal whatever lies behind the curtain, or are they screening the several characters from whatever might be lurking there?

The chubby *putto* (B) is full of life and he looks cheerful; Time is believable but Venus and Cupid are statuesque in their poses, marmoreal in their colour, and sharply defined. They are barely credible as living, breathing human beings and their expressions are somewhat vacant. Charles Hope[2] and Michael Levey[3] both interpret their embrace as loving, but each is covertly taking something from the other – Venus Cupid's arrow and Cupid Venus's headdress. They are up to some sexy games but there's no romantic love here. We keep coming back to sex: the picture is shockingly factual. The position of Venus's left hand in Titian's *Venus of Urbino* (c.1538, Galleria degli Uffizi, Florence) leaves little to the imagination, but where in main-stream, as opposed to frankly pornographic, Renaissance classical art except in the *London Allegory* do we see a youth fondling a woman's erect nipple, or a woman about to put her tongue into her lover's (let alone her son's) mouth? Venus's tongue and erect nipple and Cupid's bottom make one conclusion inescapable: before it is about anything else this detached, voyeuristic, seemingly cold painting is about sex, not about love.

What else might it be about? Let's try to make some sense of the characters and objects for ourselves before finally turning to think about the work as a whole, about what it meant for those who saw it in the sixteenth century and about its meaning for us today. It may prove to be impossible unequivocally to link the individual figures to Vasari's faulty description of the painting. We should accept this, take account of what others, including Vasari, have said about the figures but try to look at them afresh. Bronzino invented some of the characters himself (A, C, K) – they don't occur elsewhere at this time though some objects (e.g. masks, an apple, a cushion, two doves) do. Where might he have got his ideas from? Until the end of the sixteenth century there were no standardised iconographic dictionaries for Italian painters, or us, to consult, which is one reason why there is so much debate about what the figures connote;[4] once again, Bronzino may have intended there to be several valid interpretations for each of them.

This would fit with Bronzino's practice as a burlesque poet, which we touched on in Chapter I; his erudite but often subversive and bawdy verse is replete with humour, multiple meanings, parody, coded eroticism and hidden references to contemporary people and events.[5] We can imagine Francis and his coterie puzzling over the elusive meaning of the painting, just as they would have done over the poetry, arguing amongst themselves, enjoying drawing each other's attention to features which would support or refute their favoured interpretations of the work. Perhaps they would go off to the palace library to check on the literary allusions which they thought they had seen in the painting. Bronzino had worked hard to give them something sophisticated, a riddle that would hold their attention for more than a few minutes, which demanded repeated study and allowed them to display their erudition – just what they needed to relieve the tedium of life at court.

Lacking a standardised iconography, Renaissance painters turned for their symbols to the Bible, to folk traditions, and to Classical mythology and literature. The use of flowers and plants as symbols grew in the fifteenth and sixteenth centuries; they were used as attributes or because they had been assigned moral or philosophical connotations. Alessandro Allori began his career in Bronzino's workshop by creating flower and plant fantasies for the borders of the tapestries that his master was designing.[6] He continued to use realistic representations of flowers and shrubs as symbols throughout his subsequent career.[7] Classical, Renaissance and contemporary literature – particularly poetry because Bronzino was a poet – may also have guided Bronzino in his *London Allegory* and much thought has gone into identifying exactly what his sources might have been. Gaston, who has been particularly active in this field of research, warns against assuming that the publication of a book or the translation of a Classical work into Italian necessarily means that Bronzino or his circle would have been familiar with it.[8] He maintains that the risk is much less when we think about contemporary vernacular literature, that Bronzino's own poetry includes themes similar to those evident in the *London Allegory*, and that contributions from Bronzino's fellow Florentine poet Benedetto Varchi were also influential. Gaston has found many possible sources for parts of Bronzino's painting in the literature and poetry with which the painter could have been familiar.[9] He is sure that Bronzino would have been able to consult Mario Equicola's *Libro di natura d'amore* (1525), a comprehensive review of love prose and poetry from Classical times to the sixteenth century. It provided painters as well as writers with detailed descriptions of love scenes on which they could draw for their own work. This and the other literature which was very familiar to him would have provided descriptions, which to us are extraordinarily offensive, of women as physically disgusting, the users of feminine wiles to cause men pain and suffering, as venomous snakes, and love as inevitably accompanied by bitterness, as a spreader of disease.

We should begin our analysis by looking at Vasari's account of the painting; it is as close to contemporaneous as we have. We have already discussed Vasari's confused and incomplete description of the painting. We know that we can't depend on his analysis but let's remind ourselves of it:

> Dentro al quale era una **Venere** ignuda con **Cupido** que la baciava; ed **il Piacere** da un lato e il **Giuocco** con altre amore, e dall'altro **la Fraude, la Gelosia** ed altre passioni d'Amore.
>
> wherein was a nude Venus, with a Cupid who was kissing her, and Pleasure on one side with Play and other loves, and on the other side Fraud and Jealousy and other passions of Love.[10]

Many, perhaps most, of the art historians who have offered interpretations of the painting have felt constrained to fit their identifications of the individual figures into the straight-jacket provided by Vasari – so one figure 'has to be' *la Fraude*, another *Gelosia*, and so on – and many scholars have tried to accommodate their interpretations to his idea that the positive passions lie on one side of the painting and the negative passions on the other. This has led to some tortuous attempts to make sensible first-hand observations compatible with contradictory statements by the revered Vasari. This is a mistake – we know that Vasari's description of the painting is inaccurate and, in any case, his identifications may not be those that Bronzino intended or the same as those chosen by Cosimo, Francis and others who saw the painting in the sixteenth century. I think we should make our own interpretations of the figures; I am reluctant to assign unequivocal names to most of the figures because I believe that it was Bronzino's intention to make them (and the painting as a whole) ambiguous.

Venus

There has never been any doubt about the identity of the dominant female figure in the centre of the painting. She is holding what appears to be a golden apple in her left (*sinister*) hand, so she must be Venus. Erwin Panofsky says that the apple is 'tendered to the eager boy' (i.e. to Cupid).[11] I can't see that she is tendering it to anyone, let alone to Cupid. Does it matter? Well, if the apple represents her beauty, her love, even her psyche, then it does matter that she is offering her body but not her personality to him. The apple is an attribute of Venus (Aphrodite in Greek mythology), goddess of love and fertility: the apple was the prize – the Apple of Discord – awarded by Paris, to signify the victory of Venus in the beauty contest between her, Juno and Minerva. Paris gave the prize to Venus because she bribed him to do so, promising him the love of any woman he chose and steering him to Helen of Troy. Here, in addition to serving to identify Venus for us, it is a reminder that she won the contest by bribery as well as because of her beauty, the first of many hints of dishonesty that we shall encounter in our study of the *London Allegory* – in which Venus is using her beauty and her theft of his arrow to defeat Cupid. Drawing on other Italian literary precedents, the apple may also allude to sexual activity – subverted by the worms inside the fruit which represent the horrible diseases which lurk beneath the skin of the fruit or of the lover.[12] Indeed, Venus herself was often seen as the personification of contamination and pollution: the appellation 'venereal' referred to the route of transmission of these diseases and also to the motives of the Venus from whom they originated.

The golden 'apple' in the painting does have a dimple on the left-hand side but it is rather too spherical to look much like a real apple, prompting the suggestion that it may instead (or as well) be intended to represent one of the balls, called *palle*, on the Medici coat of arms.[13] Another idea is that the object resembles an onion, which Bronzino used in one of his burlesque poems to signify the penis (Francis is unlikely to have read the poem).[14] Alternatively, the effects of an onion had been compared to those of love – entering through the eyes and nose it causes more tears and torment than love.[12]

Venus is a beautiful young woman in her twenties, highlighted against the luxurious blue backcloth, a 'full-frontal' nude, concealing nothing, with her thighs slightly apart – signalling her availability to Cupid, perhaps. He is fondling her left breast but the position of his fingers is typical of those of a mother (or wet-nurse) offering her nipple to a suckling infant.[15] Lest we should fail to notice that Venus's pose and colouring make her look like a statue, close inspection reveals that her diadem includes the golden figurine of a nude female figure posed in almost exactly the same way as Venus herself is. It signifies her sensuality, a conceit borrowed from the High Renaissance[16] – and another allusion to the debate about the relative merits of painting and sculpture. The close inspection that the diadem demands necessarily draws us intimately, disconcertingly, close to Venus's naked body, blinding us to the other figures in the painting with whatever messages they may have about the delights and dangers of a close encounter with the goddess of love.

Hesiod, an eighth century BCE Greek poet, wrote a genealogy, the *Theogony*, of the Greek pantheon:

> Thus spoke the fluent daughters of mighty Zeus, and they gave me [Hesiod] a sceptre, a branch of flourishing laurel that they had plucked, a thing of wonder. They breathed in me an inspired voice so I might celebrate what will be and what has been, and they bid me to hymn the clan of the blessed ones who always are and to sing of them first and last.[17]

Hesiod explains that Venus was born (Botticelli: *Birth of Venus*) from the sea that foamed (aphros) round the severed testicles of Ouranos (Sky), castrated by his son Kronos (Time) as punishment for murdering his wife Gaia (Earth).[18] Alternatively, both Sappho and Homer saw Venus as a 'daughter of Zeus'.[19] Venus was often attended by her 'Erotes', winged gods of love. Sometimes portrayed as clones of Cupid (Eros), the number of Erotes grew over the years, Hesiod described two and there were at least eight in later Classical poetry. We shall meet three Erotes later: Himeros (Sexual Desire. According to Hesiod he was present with Eros at the birth of Venus), Pothos (Passionate Loving) and Hymerus (the god of the wedding ceremony).[20]

Cupid doesn't realise that Venus has grabbed one of his arrows (a phallic symbol if ever there was one) – she has seduced and disarmed (emasculated) him, either to neutralise his powers or to steal his powers for herself. Alternatively, her appropriation of the arrow could signify the disarming of Love by Beauty, a familiar trope in Renaissance literature.[21] Or it may mean that Venus has protected herself from the effects of an arrow wound – she can enjoy the pleasures of sex without psychological commitment. The arrow is pointing downwards: Venus could easily use it to wound Cupid – or herself. Perhaps this is a reminder of the wound which the myths tell us led to her infatuation with Adonis, himself the offspring of an incestuous liaison between King Cinyras of Paphos in Cyprus and his daughter Myrrha.[22] (Does the portrayal of Cupid as an adolescent rather than as a child allude to Adonis?[23]), Adonis was later killed by a wild boar despite Venus's efforts to save him. While rushing to his aid she stepped on a thorn and drops of her blood fell on a white rose (all roses were white at this time), staining the petals red – the origin of the red rose, its association with Venus and the presence of red rose petals in this painting.[24]

Venus and Cupid are kissing in an overtly sexualised way, a representation perhaps of the kiss with which Venus rewarded Cupid when he promised to arrange the downfall of Psyche, her beautiful rival.[25] The tongue itself may have a more than immediately obvious significance. In Bronzino's day the tongue was a phallic symbol, likened to the penis in its 'power of erection and retraction . . . even as movements [of the penis] beget progeny of the body, so motions of the tongue bring forth progeny of the spirit in speech. . .'[26]

Bronzino has given us a privileged vantage point: unlike Venus and Cupid themselves we have a clear view of what is going on. Gaston draws attention to a similar conceit in a 1540 woodcut by Salviati in which a half-naked woman feels in a man's purse while she distracts him with a kiss.[27] Her pose, the way the man and woman gaze rapturously at each other and the way the man's right hand fondles the deceitful woman's breast are all reminiscent of the *London Allegory*. This device of giving the spectator privileged insight into the true nature of the action was adopted later in even more familiar paintings: *The Fortune Teller* (1633-9, Metropolitan Museum of Art) and *The Cheat with the Ace of Clubs*, (c. late 1620s, Kimbell Art Museum, Fort Worth, Texas), both by George de La Tour, who allows us to see what the pickpocket and the card-sharp are doing behind their victims' backs.

Cupid

The androgynous youth kissing Venus has the attributes of Cupid (Eros in Greek mythology): he is winged and wearing a quiver (J) in which to carry his arrows; these were the source of his power: a person, or even a deity, shot by Cupid's arrow was filled with uncontrollable desire or revulsion. Cupid is winged, allegedly because lovers are flighty and likely to change their minds. The display of his buttocks is blatant – it steals the show from Venus. Gaston suggests that Cupid's pose may also be designed to conceal his likely erection.[28] Compared with the subtlety of the rest of the painting this display of Cupid's buttocks is crude. One has to ask why Bronzino chose to make this late change, apparently to the detriment of the painting. Cupid's cheeks are flushed – markedly more so than Venus's are – possibly following a poetic convention in which Cupid was said to have 'signified burning and inordinate love and desire which know no restraint'.[29]

In Classical Greek art Eros was a slender young man, later he became a chubby boy. In the Renaissance Cupid was most often portrayed as a child (more like B) rather than as someone whose body and behaviour are those of a pubertal adolescent, as they are in the *London Allegory*. His face is smooth, hairless and could be male or female; his buttocks and thighs are similarly androgynous. Cupid's splayed legs and the position and angle of the quiver add to this confusion about his sexuality; ideas about homosexuality (in the shadows of the painting as they were in Cosimo's Florence) are inescapable. He is kneeling on a cushion (I), which according to Panofsky was 'a common symbol of idleness and lechery'.[30] Levey prefers to read the cushion as a symbol of flattery, another indication that Cupid is being hoodwinked by Venus.[31]

Will Fisher has analysed the bisexual imagery in the *London Allegory*, noting in particular the late changes which substantially enhance the eroticism of the painting. He suggests that both Venus and Cupid were meant to appeal to a single viewer, rather than the heterosexual male viewer enjoying Venus and the homosexual male enjoying Cupid (and most likely it would have been a male viewer not only because that was the way the power structure worked but also because it was probably inconceivable to Bronzino and his peers that a woman could have taken the role of an appreciative bisexual voyeur.[32]) This places the painting squarely in the ambit of contemporary debates about whether women or boys provided the greater sexual pleasure. Bronzino was familiar with the voluminous classical and contemporary poetry treating this theme, for example a debate in verse between Francesco Berni (1497-1535) and Francesco Molza (1489-1544) – Berni favouring 'peaches' (i.e. boys' buttocks) and Molza 'figs' (i.e. vaginas). And with the burlesque (or pornographic, make your choice) sonnets of Aretino (1492-1556; reputed to be the model for St Bartholomew in Michelangelo's *Last Judgement*; pensioner of both Francis I and Charles V) in which he celebrates the attractions of buttocks (male and female) and discusses the relative pleasures of anal and vaginal intercourse, deciding eventually in favour of the *potta* rather than the *culo*.[33] So we have a fetishised, androgynous male posed provocatively alongside the more usual fetishised nude female. It looks as though we are being shown a deviant (in sixteenth century terms) act here between a woman and a bisexual youth.

Most interpreters of the *London Allegory* say that the couple transgress accepted norms even more blatantly than this. Venus and Cupid, they say, are mother and son – this is a scene of incestuous coupling. But the mythology is not quite so straightforward; in fact it is thoroughly confusing. Eros (Cupid) first emerges in the writings of Hesiod as one of four original deities. They were Chaos, the dark and silent abyss from which all things are born; Gaia or mother earth; Tartaros, the lowest regions of the underworld, and Eros, the god of love – 'the son of Chaos hatched from the egg of night'.

> Tell me these things, Muses who hold your halls on Olympus. From the beginning, also tell the one of them who came first. First

of all Chawos . . .came into being. But then Gaia broad-chested, always the unshakable seat of all the immortals who hold the peaks of snowy Olympus, and dark Tartaros in the recesses of the wide-wayed earth, and Eros, the most beautiful among the immortal gods, losener of limbs, who subdues the mind and prudent counsel in the chests of all gods and of all men.[34]

In Aristophanes's *The Birds*:

> There was Chaos at first, and Erebos black, and Night, and the Void profound, No Earth, no Air, no Heaven; when, lo, in the realm of the Dark without bound, In a vortex of winds the Primordial Egg was engendered by black-winged Night; And out of the Egg, as the seasons revolved, sprang Eros, the world's delight. His back soft-gleaming with feathers of gold, his heart like a whirlwind storm. And he with Chaos the winged and dark, being mixed in the Void without form, Begat the original nestlings of us, and guided them up to the sun.[35]

According to Hesiod, Cupid 'attended her [Venus's] birth' and was 'her constant companion';[36] but later Cupid was held to be Venus's son, so he couldn't have attended her birth.[37] Homer and Ovid say that Venus married Vulcan (Hephaistos) but bore no children by him. She was infatuated with Mars (Ares), took him as a lover and had several children by him – Cupid amongst them.[38] By the time of the Renaissance, the various stories about Cupid's antecedents and about his relationship with Venus had become hopelessly muddled and the myths had been adapted to accommodate Christian ethics: Cupid retained his power to seduce but he was now said to be a malicious figure who exploits desire to draw people into vice. He was portrayed naked, so that his deceit and evil were revealed. His wings came to symbolise the fickleness of lovers; his bow, symbolised trickery and his quiver his depraved mind. He had two types of arrow, one sharp and tipped with gold (as is the arrow in Venus's hand), the other blunt and tipped with lead; the golden arrow induced uncontrollable desire in its victim, the lead-tipped one induced aversion and the urge to flee.[39]

Of all the Classical accounts of the Venus and Cupid stories, that by Ovid would have been the most familiar to Bronzino's audience:

> ...while the boy that wears the quiver is giving kisses to his mother, he unconsciously grazes her breast with a protruding arrow. The Goddess, wounded, pushed away her son with her hand. The wound was inflicted more deeply than it seemed to be, and at first had deceived *even* herself.[40]

So they would have seen an incestuous relationship, though Ovid does not say that it was consummated. The taboo against incest is a particularly strong one (though not as universal as we in the West might think[41]) and our fascination with it correspondingly strong; its force and ubiquity suggest that the drive to incest is at least as powerful as the taboo which seeks to control it. If this is so, as Freud believed, the painting is activating this subconscious drive as well as the drives to voyeurism and scoptophilia.

William Keach agrees that the quotation from Ovid above is a likely literary source for Bronzino's painting.[42] Drawing on precedents in Michelangelo's treatment of the same passage he argues that Venus in the *London Allegory* is in danger of injuring herself in the arm with the arrow that she has seized from Cupid, thereby making the 'Wounding of Venus' a possible subject for the painting – Venus's foolhardy sexual encounter with Cupid leads to her own powers being turned against her with the dire consequences that are usually visited upon mortal lovers. All very well if we accept that the arrow threatens Venus – it doesn't look to me as though it is doing so.

John Moffitt draws attention to the *Metamorphosis Ovidiana moraliter explanata* (1340) of Petrus Berchorius. This widely read work, he says, dilated on the problem of a specific type of *Luxuria* that would be represented by lascivious scenes such as 'Cupid kissing and fondling his mother'. He took this to be a particularly objectionable illustration of the potentially lethal effects of incestuous couplings – which led inexorably to a taste for lechery. There are obvious parallels with the *London Allegory*.[43]

Is Cupid merely toying with Venus's self-referential headdress or trying surreptitiously to remove it, and if the latter, does this symbolise his attempt to depersonalise her – making this gesture the equivalent of Venus's seizure of his arrow? Are we being reminded of the depersonalisation, disintegration of psychic boundaries and erosion of self-control that accompany both passionate love and overpowering lust?

A

Commentators have been baffled by this strange figure, most of which is hidden behind the blue curtain (Plate 11). A has been the subject of substantially less scholarly attention then C but I believe it is more difficult to understand and of much greater importance than the superficially more challenging C.

A's gender is uncertain, though most commentators take it to be female. The face is mask-like but not necessarily a mask; it has no eyes and the back of its head appears either to be missing or to be covered by a dense black scarf. It has been identified as Truth, Night, Fraud (Vasari's *la Fraude*), Error and Oblivion. The fact that it is very difficult to see does not help: that part of the painting is dark and in the National Gallery it is quite high up on the wall and affected by glare from the overhead lights. Charles Hope and Iris Cheney think it is a face.[44] Levey and others have seen it as a hollowed-out mask, dishonestly appearing to be a human head and face; in their eyes the viewer has been tricked by Bronzino into thinking that it is a real female face,[45] leading Levey to identify A as *la Fraude* and to say it was Bronzino's intention to make the face so convincing that only close examination could reveal it to be a mask.

The copy of the *London Allegory* by a Fontainebleau-school artist, which antedates the revisions made to the painting during and after Louis XIV's reign, appears to show a less agitated figure with curled hair,[46] making it an altogether more convincing real person, not a mask. Of course, the Fontainebleau artist may have made some modifications to the original in his copy of the painting, thinking perhaps either to clarify some bits which he imagined Bronzino to have left obscure by accident or to reinforce his own interpretation of the painting.

At first Panofsky thought that she was 'Truth' and that she is helping her father 'Time' to pull the curtain back to reveal the consequences of luxury. Later he changed his mind and decided that she is 'Night' trying to prevent the unveiling.[47] Lynette Bosch also thinks that A's appearance fits ancient literary descriptions of Nyx (Night) and that Renaissance tradition gave Night a mask as her attribute. She points out that poets had described Night as a mature woman who wore a voluminous cloak and whose head was veiled, and that Empedocles wrote of 'Night, the lonely with her sightless eyes'.[48] She cites several Classical sources which describe Night in a way compatible with A and which associate the night-time with deceitful activities and sexual encounters.[49] And, as in the passage from Aristophanes above, some sources say that Cupid was Night's son, which could explain A's proximity to Cupid in the painting.[48]

The figure has no eyes (Cheney thinks that it does have eyes) but it does have part of an ear (does this indicate that she is deaf?), some hair and a neck. So if it is a mask it is an unusual one, unlike the masks at the bottom right-hand corner of the painting which, being real masks, also lack eyes. Maurice Brock believes that A's position diametrically opposite the masks on the ground suggests that A is a mask, which could be taken to show that Venus, who also lies on this diagonal, is as dishonest as the two sets of masks. But we know that the masks on the ground were moved from the left-hand corner of the painting to their final position on the right-hand side quite late in the day, and after most of A had been painted,[50] so this is not a convincing argument.

Hope thinks that the skin of A's face continues down into her neck, so she is not a mask at all; but she is blind, she has no teeth or tongue and the back of her head is missing: she has no brain, no memory and is unable to speak – so perhaps she represents 'Oblivion'?[51] Perhaps forgetfulness is being presented as the only remedy for the pain of having being deceived in love or the lack of a brain signifies the loss of reason that characterises infatuation?

Cheney, who agrees that this is a woman and not a mask, denies that the back of her head is missing and rightly points out that there is something there which blocks out the laurel hedge in this upper-left corner of the picture. Instead, she thinks that a dark head of hair and a billowing scarf obscure the back of the woman's head.[52] Levey, however, says that 'in the original . . . leaves fill the space where the back of the head should be'.[53] He is only partially correct: there are leaves in the upper left-hand corner of the painting but they do not fill the void at the back of A's head. (Plate 11) Cheney identifies the woman as 'Virtue' who on raising the curtain sees what Venus and Cupid are up to and reacts with horror; Time, who is looking at A and not elsewhere, tries to spare her blushes by dragging the curtain back into place.[52]

It is impossible to see the back of A's head, the demarcation between the visible and invisible parts of her head is very sharp and I'm not convinced that continuation of her scarf can account for the featureless obscurity behind her head – so perhaps this is a mask. But Hope also is correct – A's neck does continue downwards in a life-like way – so A is a real woman, not a mask. Yet again, Bronzino has left us with an irresolvable dilemma. He has led us mistakenly to identify A first as a mask then as a person of uncertain gender, a rationale for A A Bromham's suggestion that A is Error.[54]

The changes that Bronzino made during the progress of the painting included changes to A to accommodate Cupid's enlarged wing. A's right hand which had been supporting the left-hand edge of curtain now appears to be pulling the curtain, possibly in opposition to Time's tug in the opposite direction.[55] Whether mask or person, A is holding the blue curtain – but is she trying to move the curtain to hide the scene or to reveal it? Or, maybe, thinking only of herself, she is trying to prevent Time from pulling the curtain away, exposing her and revealing either her identity or the fact that she is a mask – that she is *la Fraude*? But if Time were trying to reveal her he should be tearing off her mask rather than trying to expose her body.[56]

We are finding it difficult to decide whether or not A's skull is complete, if she is a person or a mask and what she is doing with the curtain – we should ask ourselves if Bronzino meant us to struggle in this way. Perhaps we should accept – even delight in – the confusion of possible interpretations, which change as we move from figure to figure and as we change the vantage point from which we peer into the depths of the painting.

Hope doubts it would make sense for Time to be trying to reveal Oblivion; nor does he think that they are both trying to pull the curtain back, since Oblivion can only obliterate. Perhaps she is throwing a veil over the distasteful scene to help the viewer to ignore it or forget it? On this reading, Time and Oblivion could be working together, to cover the figures in the foreground.[56] Ross Kilpatrick, though, thinks that A is Blind Fortune, often portrayed as blind because her works cannot be foreseen; she is trying to keep the curtain closed.[57]

Time

The elderly, bearded, bald, winged figure in the upper right-hand corner has an hourglass on his shoulder, so he must be Time. Most of his body is hidden behind the blue curtain which he is holding in the hand of his powerful, outstretched right arm. Is he straining to pull the curtain down[58] or to hold it up against A's attempt to pull it away from him?[59] Panofsky wrote extensively about the history of representations of Time and about the way in which their meaning changed over the centuries. In one tradition Time assumes the role of 'Revealer': Truth revealed or rescued by Time; Virtue vindicated by Time; Innocence justified by Time; and so on.[60] Panofsky uses *L'Innocenntia del Bronzino* (Galleria degli Arazzi, Florence) a tapestry woven to a cartoon by Bronzino (and believed by Panofsky to be a companion piece to the *London Allegory*) to illustrate the theme of Time, with an hourglass on his shoulder, lifting a curtain or veil to reveal a young girl whom Panofsky identifies as Truth. Extrapolating this argument enabled him to conclude that in the *London Allegory* Time is lifting the curtain, that A is helping him to do this and that A is Truth.[61] As we have seen, Panofsky later changed his mind about the identity of A, which led him to decide that Time is trying to raise the curtain and that A (now 'Night') is trying to thwart him.[62]

Other interpretations have been offered. What is the purpose of the curtain – is it to hide the sexy encounter from an audience gathered behind it? Time is largely hidden behind the curtain – in the classic voyeur's position but he is looking at A and not at the erotic encounter being played out in front of him. Perhaps he is offended by the scene – or he's too old to be aroused by it?[63] And, if A is trying to wrench the curtain from Time's grasp what is her motive – does she want to expose the lovers to the audience's opprobrium or does she want them to enjoy the scene as we are doing? Brock says that the rich blue curtain creates a private space in which Venus and Cupid can pleasure each other but that this is not a scene fit for mortal view – the tussle between A and Time signals the privilege granted to the viewer of the painting, who is allowed to witness a proscribed scene. Levey, though, thinks that Time is trying to tear the curtain from A's grasp in order to expose her 'deceitful vacuity'.[64]

Alone among the painting's would-be interpreters, Joshua

Korenblat thinks that Time's hourglass is broken and the sand is spilling out of it.[59] I have used binoculars to look very carefully at the painting but I can see neither this break nor the sand.

Possibly because of the similarity of Chronos (Greek: time) and Kronos (the Roman Saturn),[65] Time was considered to be an alter ego of Saturn whose castration of Ouranos, led to the birth of Venus. In astrological terms Saturn was the planet that ruled when Cosimo was born;[66] it was therefore particularly relevant to his horoscope, though this would have been a mixed blessing – those born under Saturn were destined to be of a melancholy disposition even if wealthy and powerful. There is some similarity between Time's face and that of an older Cosimo.[67] Saturn is also associated with the metal lead and hence with the first stage in the alchemical process. A feast of allusions here too, then, to challenge viewers of the painting.

Time looks angry but his gaze is directed towards A, so it is she who has infuriated him, not the behaviour of Venus and Cupid. He may also, or instead, be looking at Venus's theft of Cupid's arrow – is this what he is angry about? He is directly above B, who is happy so we have an interesting juxtaposition of the angry Time, concerned with the long-term, and the happy B, whose priority is immediate gratification and who is possibly looking with delight on Cupid's theft of Venus's diadem. Margaret Healy thinks that A is looking at the honeycomb (E), and with shock and horror at C, whom she has just uncovered.[68]

Laurel hedge

A laurel hedge (*Prunus* sp.) is just visible behind A and Time, above the blue curtain. From Classical times laurel has been associated with noble deeds and with victories, be they military, athletic, political or artistic and with virtue and perseverance. It was also associated with Venus's enemy, Chastity – virtuous Daphne chose to be changed into a laurel to evade Apollo's pursuit.[69] Petrarch, whom Bronzino admired, made the laurel human as his elusive love, Laura.[59]

The laurel hedge and the blue curtain form a barrier between the fictive space of the painting and whatever lies in the void behind it. The laurel may signify the innocence, incorruptibility and nobility of the world behind the curtain, in stark contrast with the louche world conjured up by Bronzino. Bosch thinks that the blue curtain separates the principal figures in the present from the previous generation of Night (A) and Time; they in turn are separated by the laurel (symbolising regeneration) from the impenetrably dark primeval Chaos which lies behind it.[70]

Cheney likes the laurel's proximity to Time – Virtue coupled with perseverance being appropriate attributes of Time and an instructive contrast with the ephemeral character of love.[71]

Hope suggests that the laurel was placed here to remind us that poetry endures, unlike love and the passions, which are subject to Time and Oblivion.[72] He rejects two ideas which I find attractive. First, the evergreen plant may be there to counter the actions of Time. Second, is the idea that this is the laurel favoured by the Medici family and by Cosimo in particular.[73] Hope doesn't like this because Cosimo's laurel 'depended for its significance on the contrast between a flourishing and a dead or cut branch [*broncone*], an idea to which the artist nowhere alludes.' I think he may be wrong to dismiss the idea so quickly. It is true that there is no *broncone* in the *London Allegory* but if Bronzino didn't want to make the meaning of the painting too obvious he may have intended the laurel on its own to have been enough to prompt the viewer to think of the Medici and to remember that the painting was a gift from Cosimo. We applied the same reasoning to the Apple, which might be a subtle allusion to the Medicis' *palle*.

B – the *putto*

This jolly, rosy cheeked, little chap introduces the only element of frivolity in the painting – Time (immediately above him) looks angry, Venus and Cupid are self-absorbed but hardly rapturous and C is impassive. B's curly locks are very like those seen in Bronzino's other paintings in Room 8 – the dark hair of the young man (*Portrait of a Young Man*) and the golden hair of the Christ Child in *Madonna and Child with Saints* – in fact B and Cupid both look remarkably like the Christ Child. He bounces into the scene, throwing a handful of rose petals – associated with Venus, as we saw above – and wearing an anklet of bells, the attribute of a jester or fool. His smile, his carefree pose and nudity, his sweet scented rose petals and the cheerful sound of his bells must connote the immediate pleasures of sex or love. These features led Bosch to identify him as *Jocus* (Mirth), conflated with two

Erotes: Hymerus (Desire, the roses) and his twin, Pothos (Painful longing, the thorn on which he has trodden) or as Hymerus himself.[74] Red roses were also used to symbolise the sorrow of the Virgin – but it's difficult to see how this could be the case here. Much more likely they are included as attributes of Venus, to evoke a carefree atmosphere and to signify the impending sexual relationship between Venus and Cupid.

But, like everything else in this painting not all is as it first appears. Is there a hint of malice in B's smile? His right foot has trodden on a thorny branch (or possibly C's claw[75]). One thorn has drawn a drop of blood (just as happened to Venus when she created the first red rose). Christ was abused with a 'Crown of Thorns', leading to the adoption of thorns as symbols of grief and tribulation. They were also associated with sin: the Pharisees put thorns in the hems of their clothes to remind themselves to guard against sinning – they mortified their flesh, giving us the phrase 'thorn in the flesh'.[76] The thorn under B's foot is difficult to see; he is oblivious of it and to the pain we would expect it to have caused him. We would think an injury like this one to be trivial but those who saw the painting in Bronzino's day would know that it was potentially lethal, for it carried risks of tetanus, other bacterial infections and septicaemia. B's failure to react to the injury may have led them to think that his foot was anaesthetic, due to leprosy perhaps. The message is that the immediate pleasure to be gained from sex makes one ignore the immediate and long-term pain and danger that accompany it. Biondo[77] wrote of woman as a scorpion or a horned viper whose poison was injected by the tongue and through the kiss, in the sucking and licking of the tongue, her poison was hidden from her lover; she was a pricking thorn who pricks most painfully with her tongue – Bronzino appears to be making the point by giving us two thorns, Venus's tongue and the thorn in B's foot.

Do we join Hope and Panofsky in identifying B as either 'Foolish Pleasure' (*Il Piacere*) or 'Jest' (*il Giuocco*),[78] 'foolishly indifferent to the hurts which he receives in the pursuit of his desires'[79] or join Levey who says he is, 'Folly' (his translation of Vasari's *il Giuocco*),[64] or Bosch who thinks he may be Mirth or Desire?[74]

The happy B is enjoying Bronzino's scene and, being the only one in the picture who is looking at the amorous couple, he is

h

getting a voyeuristic thrill – just like us. Can we identify still further with this character, instead of (or as well as) with Venus or Cupid? If so, are we being warned about the attention that we ourselves give to immediate, short term pleasures, ignoring the dangers (thorns in the foot) on which we should be concentrating? Is he a personification of our own impetuous neglect of long-term consequences?

C

Of all the characters in the painting C is the one which has caused scholars the most trouble – and the best opportunity for research. Decades of study have failed to come up with a generally accepted explanation of whom or what her individual features represent. Nonetheless, I think a broad, initial interpretation of C is pretty uncontroversial: she is 'deceit' or 'deception', personified as a female and intended in the first instance to warn about Venus's superficial attractiveness but hidden malignancy. She may be taken more generically to warn about the perils of taking people of either sex at face value.

What was Bronzino trying to do when he came to construct C 'the most sophisticated symbol of perverted duplicity ever devised by an artist'?[61] He had a menagerie of weird, wonderful and malign mythical beasts to turn to for inspiration.[80] He would not have chosen at random, he must have had a meaning (or several meanings) in mind which he wanted C to convey and selected or invented forms which he hoped would connote the meaning. In their attempts to decide who or what C is intended to represent scholars have trawled through the forms available to Bronzino in Classical and Renaissance literature and art; most have tended to champion one interpretation or another, finding evidence to support their choice while playing down or ignoring facts which do not. Bronzino managed to create a chimera that defies unequivocal identification – and maybe he never intended it to be just one recognisable creature but instead a mixture of individual features taken from several sources, each of which could support a host of diverting connotations.

This strange, hybrid creature is made all the more difficult to understand by the fact that crucial parts of it are hidden behind B. And the lighting is strange – why is the space to the right of B so well lit while C's face, other hand (E) and lower parts are in shadow? Bronzino is adding to the ambiguity that permeates his allegory.

C has an upper body that is incontrovertibly human, and female; somehow this human torso is grafted onto a reptilian-mammalian lower body: the junction between the animal and the human parts of the creature's anatomy is hidden behind B. The animal part is obscure; it appears to comprise the rear limb of a lion or similar big cat (F), a long segmented tail (G) that terminates in a sting or fang-like structure (D). The scales of a fish or reptile (or possibly the feathers of a bird) lie between the edge of the green dress and the cat's leg.

The human part of the creature is an attractive young woman wearing a green dress, with a blue cape held in place by a jewelled clasp. She is depicted in the manner Bronzino used in his portraits of ladies in the Medici court, albeit her gaze is unconventionally intense rather than affectless.[81] There are even similarities between C's face and those of some of Cosimo's children in portraits by Bronzino.[82] Her hair is elegantly styled and adorned with a simple row of pearls. This apparently normal part of the creature is looking at us, drawing us into a situation which, to judge by her countenance, is an innocent one; only when we look more closely do we realise that she has lured us into her web of deceit. Venus is as attractive as this girl: we now know that she too leads one astray.

The girl's hands have been the subject of an intense debate which can probably never be resolved and which therefore contributes to the painting's challenge to its viewers. Panofsky said that what appears to be her right (poorly lit) hand (E) is actually a left hand, while her other (well lit) hand (D), which is presumably on the end of her left arm, is a right hand. Hope[51] says he is wrong about this, but I think it's Hope who is in error. The only alternatives are that C is facing both ways, with her back turned towards us, making her hands attached to their appropriate arm[83]– which requires her to be something of a contortionist; or that C has her arms crossed – but they would have to be unusually long for this to work – in which case Panofsky would still be partially correct, the left hand is on the right-hand side of her body and *vice versa*. Since the left (*sinister*) hand is traditionally associated with bad things, the fact that it is holding a honeycomb here, while the right ('good') hand holds the creature's sting, adds to the ambiguity and underlines the deceitfulness of the character. Simona Cohen has suggested that the odd anatomy is the result of overenthusiastic application of cautery in a misplaced attempt to treat syphilis.[84] Whatever the explanation, we can be confident that Bronzino meant to confuse us – the peculiar orientation of the hands is deliberate and not a mistake, let alone incompetence. Once again, the ambiguity is not obvious – we are seduced by the luscious painting into entering into the scene before we realise that we have been lured into a perilous web of deception.

Bronzino made substantial changes to C when his work on the painting was already well advanced. Unlike the changes to Cupid, which were substantial enough, but which comprised only changes to his posture, the changes to C entailed changes to the lion's paw and the addition of the articulated part of her tail and the sting in her hand (D).[85] Obviously, these features were significant to him; he has made her inescapably allegorical. There are several ideas about what the lower half of the creature represents; most assume that its mixture of different animal forms derives from one or more of the mythological chimerae. In Bronzino's day chimeras connoted homosexuality.[86]

Running through these ideas we can begin with Bosch who has seized on this description of the goddess Echidna by Hesiod:

> … monstrous and unmanageable thing, like neither to mortal men or immortal gods, in a hollow cave, the divine strong-hearted Echnida [sic], half glancing-eyed maiden with beautiful cheeks, and half monstrous serpent, dreadful and huge, swift eater of raw flesh[87]

She thinks that this description may have given Bronzino the idea for C and she draws our attention to the proximity of C's honeycomb (E) (another attribute of Venus) to Venus's body. She identifies C as the goddess Peitho (Persuasion), the daughter of Venus in some accounts (hence, maybe, her similar appearance to Venus in Bronzino's portrayal of her), who promised good but delivered evil. This idea is made more compelling by the story of Echidna mating with her son Orthos (another case of incest) to produce two more fearsome beasts, the Sphinx and the Nemean Lion, whose hide was impervious to weapons.[88]

Graham Smith believes her to be a lamia[89] – a mythical,

hideous, libidinous creature and avid devourer of human flesh who inhabited the Libyan desert. She had the face and breasts of a pretty girl and at first sight gave every appearance of being charming and benign but the rest of her body was covered in hard scales so that it gradually turned into a serpent, finally ending up as a horrible snake. A lamia's naked, white breasts were essential lures that enabled her to ensnare her victims, whom she then ate. So the fact that C's breasts are covered is a powerful argument against her being a lamia, as is the fact that lamias seem not to have had any feline features.[4] Smith acknowledges the problem of her covered breasts but points out that the viewer's first impression (like that of a lamia's victim) is of a beguiling young girl who is offering a honeycomb instead of bare breasts: she promises pleasure – it is only later that her horrific nether regions and sting are noticed; they will bring disaster.[89]

Brock, rather blithely says that 'once grasped, its hybridity is easy to interpret'.[90] He doesn't refer to the lamia but he does draw the same conclusion about the girl's duplicity. According to him the painting tells us that in matters of love, woman is superficially brightly lit and alluring but her real, repulsive nature lies hidden and in shadow. He and others suggest that C's leonine foot shows that she is related to the Sphinx.

Healy looks to Froda in Dante's Inferno for clues.[91] He was a savage animal with a pointed tail, a gentle face and a reptilian body; he had two paws on hairy limbs and was associated with infection.

Moffitt, who is convinced that this is Vasari's *la Fraude*, has explored the many descriptions of the Sphinx that pepper Classical, Medieval and Renaissance literature by Horace, Homer, Virgil, Dante, Ariosto, Pico della Mirandola and others.[92] He says that, like Bronzino himself, each of the *London Allegory*'s intended viewers would have been familiar with at least some of this literature; they would have recognised the deceitfully fraudulent Sphinx in C with its connotations of incest, parricide and consanguinity. For them, C would have represented an 'emblematic type' that had evolved a bit earlier in the sixteenth century and which then took on, besides the connotation of Fraud, the much more specific significance of Ignorance of Causes, a serious fault leading to potentially fatal consequences – unless it is speedily overcome and then 'banished'.[93] If Bronzino didn't already know what a Sphinx was he could very easily have found out for there were plenty in Cosimo's court who had a deep interest in, and thorough knowledge, of it. The Sphinx challenged any passing Theban with her famous riddle which asked what comprised evil and good. She ate those who failed to give the correct answer. Oedipus did answer correctly so she rewarded him by foretelling his future. She told him that he was destined to kill his father, Laius, and marry his mother. But having been told by the Sphinx that he would make a disastrous marriage, he nonetheless went ahead and innocently contracted an incestuous marriage to his mother (Jocaster) leading her to kill herself when she realised what she had done and leaving him bereft. The warning was not enough to prevent Oedipus from doing wrong and in the painting the reference to the Sphinx tells us that the actions of Venus and Cupid (entered into in full knowledge of their hazards) will have dire consequences.

If Bronzino did intend C to be a Sphinx the various descriptions of the creature would have given him plenty of scope: it was 'fantastic in some parts, yet realistic in others'; it was male, or sometimes female; it was beautiful, it was ugly; winged or wingless; it had dark fur; it was half woman and half lion; it had the feathers of a bird, the body of a dog, the voice of a human, the tail of a dragon or of a curling snake. Moffitt quotes Piccinelli who one hundred and fifty years after Bronzino painted the *London Allegory* said that the Sphinx represented a shameless, sexually dissolute wanton woman, with the face of a beautifully imposing virgin but the wings of a bird and a shameless body, 'the very image of a dog'. She stole modesty, chastity, fame and life itself. The only means of protection from her was 'foreknowledge about the wiles of lascivious woman'.[94] More generally, she was taken to be a libidinous, deceitful, evil character who stood for Ignorance or Stupidity: her feathers suggested frivolity or inconstancy; her beautiful face represented frivolous pleasure which distracted from the pursuit of Knowledge; her leonine hind-quarters were a sign of Pride, Arrogance and Cruelty. A Mythology published in 1551 described the Sphinx: 'it has the head of and hands of a virgin, the body of a dog, the voice of a human, the tail of a dragon, the talons of a lion, a bird's wing . . .its ravenous cruelty is signified by the lion's or griffon's claws, and the wings may be associated with the speed of a robber . . .Why is the face human? Because a human being is made subject to the calamities and vicissitudes of Fate. The Lion signifies that even the strongest part of the soul might be struck down in adversity . . . I would say that the myth warns us to return to wisdom and prudence.'[95]

Moffitt sets particular store by *The Theban Tablet of Cebes*, a first-century Greek text that does have impressive similarities to the painting. It was translated into Italian by Francesco Coccio, published in Venice in 1536 and widely read.[96] Coccio's edition had a frontispiece by Francesco Marcolini which would have been familiar to all readers of the book: it shows winged Time at the top lifting a naked woman – Truth – out of the grasp of another naked woman with a serpent's tail and holding a hooked implement or a sting of some sort. The resemblance with C is at least sufficient to remind those puzzling over Bronzino's hybrid girl of this book. It quickly became a popular Greek primer and while there is no evidence that Bronzino learnt Greek he may have read the book in translation; some members of Cosimo's court will have been familiar with it. It is reasonable to assume that some of the expected viewers of the painting will have been familiar with the story too (as well as with much of Classical mythology and Renaissance poetry and literature) and that they would therefore be able to spot and appreciate the multi-layered allusions built into it.

Cebes's Tablet[97] tells the story of two strangers who come across an allegorical picture in the temple of Kronos (Saturn, Time). A sage explains what the painting means – after warning them that understanding brings dangers with it. He says that the picture, which depicts three concentric walled enclosures with people scattered throughout, is an allegorical representation of the course of a human life with its various temptations and perils. Cebes tells his readers:

> Should you understand and assimilate what I should say, you shall become wise and happy; but if not, you will live badly, having become foolish, unfortunate, bitter, and ignorant.
>
> For the explanation is not unlike the Sphinx's Riddle, that he propounded to all men. Whosoever solved it was saved; but destruction by the Sphinx overtook those who could not. And this was the Sphinx's question: Within our life, What is a good? What is an evil? What is neither?

If anyone does not solve this, the Sphinx destroys him; not all at once, as in ancient times, but gradually, in his whole life, he perishes away, just like victims tortured to death. But if he understands, he is saved, and attains felicity.

Attention, therefore! And make sure you understand![98]

Both good and bad characters populate the three circles. The evil ones include Fraud (or Deceit), from whom the strangers must accept a drink of 'Ignorance and Error'; Fortune, blind, frantic, deaf, with restless wing; Opinion, Lust and Lechery; Pain, tearing her hair, weeping, brutish, emaciated and naked; Sadness, wild and skinny; Fortune, blind, deaf and raving mad; Retribution with her gaunt and ragged crew; Sorrow, Anguish, Lament and Despair; and Fierce Anguish, who stamps, and rends her shaggy hair.

The lesson the *Tablet* coveys is that readers should avoid the road of False Learning with its alluring courtesans such as Luxury and Wantonness and instead choose the path of True Learning, inhabited by figures such as Knowledge, Justice, and Self-Control: true education consists not in mere erudition, but rather in the formation of character:

Culture, not Wealth, gives Virtue…
No real Goods result from Evil means…
Wisdom alone is a Good while Foolishness is the only Evil.[99]

There are some obvious similarities between the characters in this story and those in the *London Allegory*. But the parallels are broad and C can hardly be described as a 'typical Sphinx' – she doesn't have unequivocal feathers, let alone feathers that cover her whole body, she has no wings and while her lower half does include a feline leg the rest is open to several interpretations. Moffitt claims that the 'girl-faced Sphinx was … consistently shown by all emblem-book illustrators to be quite wing-less',[100] but the illustrations he has chosen to support this contention also lack reptilian features, in fact they are, in effect, hairy human beings with leonine feet so they don't look like Bronzino's figure. Moffitt's suggestion that C's billowing blue cape might hide folded wings is not persuasive.[101] More credible, I think, is the fact that, at first glance, the more easily visible parts of the blue cape might themselves be mistaken for a wing.

Moffitt looks carefully at the part of the creature lying between the lower edge of its green gown and its left hind leg. This part of her body is covered in something with a repeating pattern. Moffitt (writing from New Mexico State University, USA) thinks that this is 'a thick coating of wide and rounded, gleaming and smoothly overlaid, bird feathers, with light brown edge and much darker centres.' He identifies 'this regularly mottled material as the plumage, body-feathers covering belly and flanks of the common, female black duck, *Anas rubripes*' and Time's wings 'are evidently those of a grey-leg [sic] goose.'[102] Neither claim is convincing. *Anas rubripes* is popularly known as the American Black Duck, which says a lot about where it is found:

> **Native:** Bermuda; Canada; Martinique; Mexico; Puerto Rico; Saint Pierre and Miquelon; United States **Vagrant:** Bahamas; Denmark; Guadeloupe; Ireland; Morocco; Norway; Portugal; Spain (Canary Is.); Sweden; Turks and Caicos Islands; United Kingdom[103]

Although we cannot be certain about the bird's distribution half a millennium ago, it is unlikely that it would have been a common sight in Florence in the sixteenth century, and highly unlikely that Bronzino would have chosen it as his pattern for part of C – if indeed he was trying to represent feathers at all. And I can find no record of a Grey-leg Goose – there is a Greylag Goose (*Anser anser*), which is found in northern Italy today; whether or not it served as a model for Time's wing is unimportant as there is no argument about the fact that in this instance Bronzino was depicting a feathered wing.

There's a circular argument here, which exemplifies one of the great dangers that confronts any effort to interpret the painting: C is a Sphinx so this pattern probably represents the feathers which form part of a Sphinx's surface / this pattern appears to represent feathers, so C is probably intended to be a Sphinx. As a further example of the danger of reading whatsoever one likes into this painting, consider this: if the laurel and the apple are intended as subtle allusions to the Medici can we find any others? How about the area which Moffitt thinks is covered in the feathers of a North American duck being instead the scales or pattern on the shell of a tortoise (Cosimo's personal symbol) (Plate 12)? Unlikely, perhaps but if I can think of this interpretation so too could Francis I, and the thought is all that is needed to trigger a chain of entertaining associations and speculation. Cohen unwittingly offers me some support by writing that C's 'body is covered with alligator scales'[104] – which do resemble tortoise scales.

The best that can be said, I think, is that while Bronzino did not mean C to be an unambiguous Sphinx he may have incorporated some features intended to trigger thoughts about the Sphinx and its several, and relevant, connotations – including Oedipus's incestuous relationship with his mother.

Gaston quotes extensively from Michelangelo Biondo (1500-c.1565) a Venetian doctor who wrote a discomfortingly misogynistic trilogy in which he likens woman to a scorpion or a horned viper:

> a wild, crazy, venomous animal with an angel's face… a deformed ugly animal who administers her sweet poison, the honeyed nectar, to her lover, with a 'flicker of her tongue', like the venomous serpent she is… the male must flee from her… as he instinctively does from the snake.[77]

C displays many of the threatening features that Biondo attributes to women but not the lethal tongue – Bronzino has given that to Venus herself. The snake-like part of C lies close to Venus's apple in the painting – snake plus apple equalling Eve, an allusion to that other misogynistic tale of temptation and The Fall.

Bromham[105] prefers to think that she is a representation of 'Whoredom', basing his opinion on Proverbs, 5: 3-5:[106]

> For though the lips of an adulteress drip honey
> And her tongue is smoother than oil,
> Yet in the end she is more bitter than wormwood,
> And sharp as a two edged sword.
> Her feet go downwards on the path to death. . .

Another biblical source, used also by Dante, could have been the 'locusts' described in Revelations 9:7-11:[106]

> On their heads were what looked like golden crowns; their faces were like human faces and their hair like women's hair; they had teeth like lions' teeth, and wore breastplates of iron… they had tails like scorpions, with stings in them, and in their tails lay their power to plague mankind for five months.

These interpretations of C have merit, some or all may be correct – after all, we do not need to assume that there is a single meaning here; in fact we probably shouldn't do so. And the fact that Bronzino made such substantial changes to the form of C so late in the day tells us that he wasn't working to a specific, predetermined plan based on a literary source, such as *The Theban Tablet of Cebes*. Instead, he was improvising, adding allusions to several sources as they occurred to him, or were suggested to him by others. The decision to give the painting to Francis I may have given him some new ideas, amongst which there could be a new explanation for the form of this hybrid creature. We know that Francis I adopted the salamander as his personal emblem, adorning his properties and furniture with representations of the animal. These representations were somewhat fanciful: they bear little relation to the appearance of a real salamander but they do strongly resemble the weird parts of our hybrid (Plate 13). The heraldic representation of the salamander is even less realistic than the crowned salamander used by Francis but in its hind limbs it is remarkably similar to C's clawed leg. Bronzino couldn't possibly have seen any of Francis's salamanders, which have feline hind limbs and reptilian tails. However, he may have been familiar with heraldic forms of the beast and he could also have come across descriptions of the salamander by Leonardo da Vinci, who says that it has a scaly skin,[107] and by Paracelsus who discussed the salamander in the context of the alchemical 'elementals', the association of four elemental categories (gnomes, undines, sylphs and salamanders) with the four classical elements (earth, water, air and fire respectively). Bronzino added the animal's paw and the reptilian tail when work on the *London Allegory* was well advanced, neither featured in the initial composition.[85] Maybe, knowing of Francis's liking for the salamander and having just been told by Cosimo that the painting was destined for Francis, he introduced references to the animal to flatter the king, to accompany the *palle*, the laurel and, just possibly, the tortoise's scales which were intended to remind Francis who had given him this generous, personalised gift.

Salamander or not, the barb or sting in C's left (or right) hand (D) is difficult to see and impossible to identify. To see exactly what this object is we have to get ever closer to the hidden 'sting in the tail'– a close encounter with this pretty, smiling girl may promise to be pleasant but it will also be dangerous. It looks as though it is on the end of the creature's tail. It was a very late addition to the painting,[85] so Bronzino must have attributed some significance to it. Whatever it is, it has a curious double form, with two curved, pointed structures diametrically opposed to each other and growing out of the central disc which C is holding (Plate 14). It might be a viper's venomous fang[4] or the tip of C's reptilian tail.[82] Petrarch's poetry, so admired and emulated by Bronzino, likened woman to a venomous serpent or to an animal that uses sex as a sweet, slow acting poison – an idea that could be the inspiration for C's serpentine tail and sting.[108]

Cohen has no doubt that it is the sting (*aculeus*) of a scorpion.[109] Setting aside the facts that C appears to be holding it, rather than it being attached to her body and that it is double, the more visible part of the object does look very like the sting at the end of a scorpion's tail, with its associations of death, torment and treachery.[110] The scorpion was sometimes used as a symbol of Envy or Hatred, either of which could be appropriate here. Cohen makes this tiny and ambiguous detail the key to the meaning of the *London Allegory*. She points out that the astrological Scorpio has control over the genitalia of both sexes and is associated with Venus and with venereal disease. People born under the astrological sign of the Scorpion 'whose innocent face veils malicious intent' are reputed to be 'amicable and pure at one moment, but inimical and malevolent the next.'[111] Cosimo, Francis and their courts took astrology very seriously: these meanings of the scorpion would not have escaped them. But Cohen seems to me to be attaching too much significance to this object; being a late addition to the painting it is unlikely that it reveals a unifying idea that had been in Bronzino's mind from the outset.

In her other hand C is holding a honeycomb (E), another of Venus's many attributes, signifying the sweetness that she offers her lover. The honeycomb is held close to Venus's body, indicating, perhaps that C is related to Venus.[112] It also serves as a reminder of the story of the infant Cupid who was stung by a bee when he stole a honeycomb, prompting Venus to quip that he is small, like the bee, but he too can sting (his arrow delivers the sting of love). The story teaches that pleasure is transitory and accompanied by pain. It was a popular story in the Renaissance, accounting for the frequent appearance of bees in association with Cupid in, for example, *Cupid Complaining to Venus* (c.1525, National Gallery, Room 4) or *Venus and Cupid With A Honeycomb* (c.1531, Borghese Gallery, Rome) both by Lucas Cranach the Elder.

If we have to stick to Vasari's interpretation it would be reasonable to conclude that C represents Fraud, Duplicity or Deceit (Vasari: *la Fraude*) though she might instead be Pleasure (*il Piacere*).[31] She is certainly not the unequivocal Pleasure that she appears to be at first sight. She deceives us with her open, attractive demeanour, offering sweet gifts while keeping her venomous, reptilian side hidden. We can't really say what she is – she fraudulently presents herself as human, as reptilian, as leonine and she mixes her left and right-hand sides with their traditional good and bad connotations. More than anyone else in the painting she is an overt representation of the male's worst nightmare: the seductive but lethal female.

Coda: The internet is a mixed blessing, a wonderful source of information, of products and of entertainment but a powerful tool for would-be subversives and a pitfall for the unwary. Simple Google searches using terms associated with my study of the *London Allegory* have thrown up tens of thousands of 'hits'. I have not looked at them all, let alone read all of them, but the many that I have read are the expected mix of the authoritative, the trivial and the misleading. A search for 'Bronzino chimera' with C in mind found an essay published on his own web-site by Ugo Bardi, a professor of Physical Chemistry in the University of Florence.[86] The very first line; '. . .the Florentine painter Angelo Allori, nicknamed Bronzino. . .' repeats the mistake about the painter's family name that was corrected decades ago;[113] the author is alone in calling the object in Venus's left hand a pomegranate; he says that Venus and Cupid are fighting each other; he implies that there is only one dove. Can anything in this essay be relied upon? Bardi's thesis is that Bronzino derived his figure C from an Etruscan statue, the *Chimaera of Arezzo* which was discovered in 1553 and placed on display in Cosimo I's collection in the Palazzo Vecchio. The duke, who took a special interest in Etruscan artefacts, cleaned it with Benvenuto Cellini's help. Hesiod tells us that the Chimaera was one:

> who breathes fire not to be resisted, a dreadful, great thing, swift of foot and powerful. She has three heads. One is that of a fierce lion, another of a goat, and the last of a mighty serpent snake.[114]

and that she was the daughter of Hydra and grand-daughter of Echidna; others say she was the daughter, or sister, or mother of the Sphinx – either way she's another candidate, should we need one, from the bestiary of mythical creatures with a few features which might match those of C.[115] The Etruscan statue was excavated and displayed in Florence in 1553, so on the face of it Bronzino could not have taken the statue as his inspiration for part of the *London Allegory* – which we think was given to Francis before the king's death in 1547. This doesn't exclude the possibility that Bronzino did use an illustration of another chimaera as his model nor that he had read about the creature, perhaps in Hesiod. The introduction of this particular Etruscan statue over-complicates the matter, there is no need to invoke it. But Bardi wants us to believe that it is specifically the *Chimaera of Arezzo* that is reflected in C. To make this idea credible he has to make us radically rethink the date and consequently the intended destiny of the painting. If its design is dependent on Bronzino having seen the *Chimaera of Arezzo*, it must have been painted after 1553 and therefore well after the death of Francis I. Henry II was on the throne of France in the 1550s so Bardi thinks that Cosimo (related to Henry by the latter's marriage to Catherine de'Medici) may have intended the painting for him. Janet Cox-Rearick (cited by Smith[116]) also thinks that Henry II may have been the recipient, on the grounds that diplomatic relations between Cosimo and Francis I were established only at the beginning of 1545 and between Florence and France only in 1547, on the accession of Henry. Neither Bardi nor I think that the painting could ever have reached Henry – and, surely, Vasari wouldn't have made such a gross error as to mis-name the king who was the recipient of the painting? But Henry died in 1559 and he was succeeded by Francis II, son of Henry and Catherine. Could Cosimo have decided to give the painting to this Francis? Is the *London Allegory* the sort of painting that Cosimo would have expected the fifteen-year-old Francis II to appreciate? Vasari published his description of the painting in 1568. He says only that the painting 'was sent to King Francis in France',[10] so he could have been referring to either king. But the physically and psychologically fragile Francis II delegated most of his authority to others and died after only seventeen months on the throne. He was an insignificant figure, making it very unlikely that Vasari would have referred to him rather than to his grandfather as 'King Francis'. And Vasari's account of the *London Allegory* is bracketed by his discussions of other paintings that can be dated confidently to the 1540s, making Bardi's thesis still less credible. It hangs on the need for Bronzino to have seen the statue in 1553, whereas he had no need to have seen it to know about chimeras, and no need to know about chimeras in order to construct his figure C. To be fair to Bardi he does acknowledge that Bronzino could have seen other representations of a chimera long before 1553 (or possibly even the *Chimaera of Arezzo* itself because it is reputed to have been first excavated much earlier than this and then kept hidden until 1553). Unfortunately, however, we cannot dismiss Bardi's thesis out of hand: Venus's hairstyle is that of the 1540s but it has been said that C's hairstyle is more like that of the 1550s.[117] On the other hand, Gaston thinks that her hairstyle is that of a young beauty 'such as one could see at the court of Cosimo I' (begging the question of when in Cosimo's long reign he is talking about); he thinks that 'stylistic comparison' dates the painting to 'in or about 1546'.[81] Yet another tangle of ambiguities. Bardi's argument is interesting but not compelling: the long-held opinion that the *London Allegory* was painted in the 1540s and that it was sent to Francis I continues to hold sway.

Masks

At first glance there are two masks, similar to those worn by actors in Classical Greek theatre to disguise themselves and to represent the persona of the characters whom they were playing. The female averts her gaze; the male looks disapprovingly at Venus and Cupid, or it would do so if it had eyes. The masks have been variously identified as a nymph and a satyr, a beautiful young woman and an ugly old man,[70] comedy and tragedy, pleasure and pain,[66] or the vices associated with the '*passione d'amore*.'[79] The two obvious masks rest on a third mask[50] which makes no contribution to the narrative – if, indeed, it is a mask at all.

The symbolism of masks was complicated. The two obvious masks, one a beautiful young woman, the other a saturnine old man, might indicate the susceptibility of young and old, male and female to the pleasures and pains of love.[70] But masks were also a symbol of death[118] and of deception or concealed identity,[119] just like the girl (C) on the same side of the painting. Panofsky said that masks indicate worldliness, insincerity and falsehood and that the two [sic] masks contrast youth with age and beauty with ugliness – echoing the contrasting two aspects of C.[120] Bronzino painted a group of masks hanging below the Cardinal Virtues in his decoration of the Chapel of Eleonora and Vasari painted masks on the frame of his *Allegory of Justice* (1543, Museo Nazionale di Capodimonte, Naples); in both cases they presumably symbolise vices.[79] And masks feature in Pontormo's *Venus and Cupid*, where they are attached to Cupid's bow. So the masks in the *London Allegory* symbolise vices associated with concupiscence, providing further evidence that the painting is all about trickery, deception, the assumption or presentation of false identity and the link between pleasure and pain. Masks were used in the theatre and socially (think of 'masked balls' or Carnival in Venice) to hide the wearer's identity and to add a frisson of mystery or danger – they could also be intended to be reminders that we all wear masks to project a persona which we hope accords with our immediate social situation, be it at work, socialising with friends, negotiating to buy a new car, or whatever.

H – object at bottom

I find this object by Venus's right great toe most peculiar – but maybe I am making a mountain out of what could, almost literally be a molehill. It could lie at the foot of an interesting diagonal in the painting's structural scaffold – but we are already alert to the danger of finding structural features of dubious validity. On the other hand, we know that the painting requires us to pay attention to its smallest details, so we should at least give H the opportunity to reveal some secrets. Its space is occupied by pale blue drapery in the Fontainebleau-school copy, which retained the lower 5cm strip of the panel that is now missing from the original. The lost strip also included a 'gold border of the drapery beneath Venus, and a rock beneath the two doves'.[121] So, H could be a remnant of the gold border. But in the restored version of the original painting H is prominent for its carefully modelled, concrete form. It does not appear to be under-painting, exposed by a tuck in the drapery; rather it resembles a rock or a miniaturised mountain peak which bears a passing similarity to the mountain peak in the background of Pontormo's *Venus and Cupid* – make of that what you will.

Doves

In Classical times the dove symbolised love and constancy, so one dove or a pair of doves became an attribute of Venus. A pair of doves facing each other represented concord, one of the minor virtues; they signalled the peaceful intentions of two parties.[122] Bosch, who says that the doves are symbolic of the caresses of Love, suggests that their position opposite the masks continues the duel which she identifies between Love (Venus) and Strife (K).[70] Moffitt offers a less benign interpretation, saying that they convey the messages of 'lasciviousness' and to a lesser degree 'amorous caresses'.[123] The dove also had a role in alchemy, as a representation of the *albedo* state in the Great Work. Cupid is almost treading on these doves – threatening to crush or even kill Love.

J

Cupid's quiver, from which Venus has drawn the arrow, is hard to see – it represents something to be kept hidden, something shameful, perhaps. Although it is hanging to Cupid's left-hand side, suspended by its belt, the angle of the quiver and its proximity to Cupid's provocatively presented bottom and splayed legs refer unmistakably to sodomy – like Cupid's pose it strikes a crude note in an otherwise subtle painting. The quiver has a phallic shape, and it is a long narrow tube, like a vagina – or, if you prefer, a rectum (the derivation of the words we use to identify the genitalia is instructive: the word 'penis' is derived from the Latin 'tail', while 'vagina' meant 'scabbard' and 'phallus' comes from the Greek for 'swell'). Cupid's arrow in Venus's grasp and the quiver thrusting towards Cupid's anus are symbols of the violence of sexual penetration. They add sadomasochism to the incest, paedophilia, bisexuality and hetero- and homo-sexual themes which we have already encountered in the painting.[124]

According to Cohen two horned heads are placed back-to-back on the jewel on the strap to the quiver (it looks to me as though they are facing each other). Horned heads traditionally identify a cuckolded husband; Cohen suggests that this might refer to the deception being revealed by Time.[125]

There are small white flowers at the lower end of the quiver. They have been identified as *Verbena officionalis*,[126] sometimes called the 'Holy Herb' or 'Herb of the Cross,' because it was reputed to have been used to curb the bleeding of the crucified Christ. It is also known as *Herba veneris*, making its association with Venus obvious and explaining its reputation as an aphrodisiac, or *vice versa*. The plant is just above the two 'kissing' doves – yet another name for the plant is *Herba columbaria* (a dove is *columba* in Latin). The leaves of a verbena plant have serrated edges, not easy to see near the quiver but obvious on the leaves at the lower edge of the cushion, between Cupid's right shin and Venus's right thigh, so presumably this is also *V. officionalis*.

Myrtle leaves – Cheney sees leaves of myrtle (*Myrtus communis*) close to the doves.[119] And myrtle leaves had been used to hide Cupid's bottom when the painting was bowdlerised in the nineteenth century.[127] This evergreen shrub with white, perfumed flowers was grown for its medicinal and magical properties; it was sacred to Venus and was yet another of her attributes. In the Renaissance the evergreen myrtle symbolised everlasting love and conjugal fidelity.[128] But it had less salubrious connotations too, which may account for its location in the painting: it had been used in an ancient purification rite dedicated to Venus Cloacina, the goddess of Rome's main sewer (the Cloaca); it was believed to be a potent aphrodisiac; it was a Roman slang term for the clitoris and it symbolised lust.[129] I can't differentiate Bronzino's representation of the 'laurel' hedge at the top of the painting from the 'myrtle' leaves that Cheney sees towards the bottom. Does it matter if both are intended to be the same plant? Yes, it probably does: both evergreen shrubs signified resistance to the ravages of time but of the two the laurel had more noble and fewer dark connotations. I believe the laurel's association with the Medici family is crucial here: if we assume that the upper hedge is of laurel and the lower leaves are of myrtle we can posit a more positive message from Time and A, and a more negative message from Cupid.

K

Here is another mysterious figure that defies definitive identification (Plate 15). As with A, there has been argument about its gender. The figure is middle-aged or older and obviously in distress, 'tearing its hair out'. Its partially edentulous mouth is open – crying out in physical or psychological pain; there is a small black pit where you would expect its tongue to be; its red-rimmed eyes are staring; its arthritic fingers clasp its sweat-soaked, tangled hair; there is a wound on its left wrist or its neck. Its dark colour may be a reference to Biondo's description of a male lover becoming 'smoked' by the stinking black vapour emitted by his lady.[26]

Perhaps K is suffering the anguish of unrequited love (Despair) or of not knowing whether love is true or false. Or maybe it represents the *tristesse* of old-age, turning its anguished gaze away from the youthful delights now denied to it but being enjoyed directly by Venus and Cupid and vicariously by B. Or is this Vasari's *la Gelosia*, Jealousy?

An epigram by Varchi, Bronzino's fellow poet, captured the commonly held belief that jealousy was a partner to love: 'That to love truly, one cannot be without jealousy (*che amare veramente non si può senza gelosia*).'[130] K is the figure which is placed closest to Cupid, which may support its identification as Jealousy[131] but according to a late sixteenth century catalogue of iconography, Jealousy is usually a female and an attractive one at that – often wearing a dress with a pattern of eyes and ears, holding a bunch of thorns and with a cockerel perched on her right shoulder.[132]

Smith believes that K is a woman with pendulous breasts; he dwells on her identification as Envy or *Invidia*, 'a naked old woman with pendulous breasts and long, unkempt hair . . . a squalid hag who feeds on the flesh of vipers, eats her own heart, and carries thorny darts dipped in her own blood',[133] finding that this fits well with the way in which Bronzino represented K before having to move it to make the space that he needed for Cupid's bottom. He says the extant K 'rends her tangled hair . . . and screams with fury' and he comments on her 'emotional turmoil, dark complexion. . .'[133] In Bronzino's time there was a lively debate, joined by Varchi and others, about the relationship between the emotions of jealousy and envy – jealousy being seen as a special form of envy, relating specifically to matters of love. Smith cites Varchi's opinion that jealousy stems from pleasure and that she transforms sweetness into bitterness. This, the lack of unambiguous attributes of Envy and the figure's position in Cupid's shadow leads him to come down in favour of K being 'Jealousy'.[130]

K's proximity to Cupid, however, led Bosch to suggest that: 'she could be Eris (Strife), Night's daughter and Cupid's sister. Classical descriptions of Strife depict an emaciated, unkempt harridan who exists to promote Jealousy, Envy and hatred. . .'[48] This idea is attractive because we could then claim to have a related trio on the left-hand side of the painting: A (Night) at the top and Night's children Cupid and K (Strife) below her. Once again that's fine if we can persuade ourselves that K is female and that A is Night. But while there may be room for some uncertainty, K has the musculature of a man and no sign of breasts or any other features which would point towards it being a female, let alone an attractive one. Conway sees the 'relative absence of subcutaneous fat. . . brawny forearm. . . bulging biceps. . . and deep muscular chest' as indications of 'mature and unequivocal masculinity'. There may be a bit of Bronzino's intentional ambiguity here but I don't think there's very much room for doubt: K is male.

These have been the traditional arguments about this figure and its meaning – they still have force. Then in 1986 Conway suggested that K is a personification of the later stages of syphilis. This idea has been taken up enthusiastically – the National Gallery guide says that the hypothesis is 'plausible'.[134] Some have read much more of the painting as a representation of the disease.[135] In order properly to test this 'syphilis hypothesis', we need to understand the disease as it was experienced and understood by Bronzino and his contemporaries in the first half of the sixteenth century. We shall do this in the next chapter before returning to the painting and to the question of whether or not it is likely to be a representation of syphilis.

VI

De Morbo Gallico

What contagion has ever extended so quickly to all the countries of Europe, Asia and Africa? What contagion does thus invade the whole body, so much resist medical art, becomes inoculated so readily, and so cruelly tortures the patient? It combines in itself all the terrible features of other contagions, pain, infection, danger of death, disagreeable and repugnant treatment and one which does not produce a complete cure.'

(Erasmus of Rotterdam – Letter written in 1520[1])

The first round of the Italian Wars which ravaged the peninsula for most of Bronzino's life was fought over Naples. The French king, Charles VIII ('a young and licentious hunchback of doubtful sanity'[2]) claimed Alfonso II's Kingdom of Naples because it had once been held by the Angevin dynasty; he also thought that Naples would be a useful jumping-off point from which to launch a Crusade. In October 1494 Charles invaded the peninsula at the head of 25-50,000 men, mainly mercenaries from all over Europe, supported by a large force of artillery and accompanied by some 800 camp followers – farriers, armourers, cooks, prostitutes and the like. He seized Naples in February 1495. Alfonso abdicated in favour of his son Ferdinand, who fled to Sicily, leaving Pope Alexander VI (Borgia) to rally the other Italian states, Spain and the Holy Roman Empire to form the League of Venice to oppose the French. King Charles was forced to retreat; he managed to avoid a pitched battle with the League at Fornova in July 1495 but withdrew from Italy and was back in France by the end of the year.[3]

The city of Naples which Charles's troops captured in 1495

had recently been beset by floods, earthquakes, famine and disease; it was filthy and prostitution was rampant. While they were in Naples Charles's troops indulged in a frantic round of debauchery and were soon afflicted by a horrible disease. Something similar had been reported from Barcelona the previous year but the scale and ferocity of the disease which struck in Naples seemed at the time to be completely new.[4] Just as we give catchy, often pejorative, names to diseases which are new to us (Hong-Kong 'flu, Montezuma's revenge, Spanish 'flu, Norwegian scabies) the new disease was quickly called 'the French disease' by the English and Germans, 'the Spanish pox' by the French, 'the Polish disease' by the Russians, and 'the Turkish disease' by the Persians. It was also known as the 'great pox' to differentiate it from smallpox. Soon given added authority by being Latinised it became widely known as '*Morbus Gallicus*'. Today, we call it syphilis.

Nowadays an infection with syphilis is easily treated with penicillin. If it is left untreated it follows three distinct phases, separated by latent periods.[5] In the first phase the infectious agent enters the body, usually by penetrating a mucous membrane, where it incubates for about three weeks. Then a small, painless lump (a chancre) forms at the point of entry. The chancres occur mainly on the external genitalia, vagina, anus, or in the rectum; they can also occur on the lips and in the mouth. A chancre is usually easy to see in the male but in the female it may be hidden away, out of sight in the vagina or on the cervix. The chancre heals spontaneously over about four weeks and all seems to be well for several weeks. In the next phase ('secondary' syphilis) a painless rash appears on the skin (and may be hidden on the internal organs as well); there are aches, fever and fatigue. The rash and malaise disappear after a few weeks but may recur in some patients. The following symptom-free latent period will usually last at least two and maybe several years, or in two-thirds of patients it may last for ever. One third of patients, however, will progress to the final, lethal and most feared stage of the disease: 'tertiary' syphilis, in which any system in the body may be attacked, particularly the skin, bones, heart and blood vessels, the liver and the nervous system. 'Gummas' are characteristic of this stage of syphilis: they are soft lumps of dead and swollen fibre-like tissue which most often develop in the liver but also in the bones, brain, heart, skin, testes and even the eyes. Destruction of the nose by gummas used to be a common sight. The disease is highly contagious, which means that it is easily passed from one infected person with primary or secondary sores to a new victim by intimate physical contact. Someone with syphilis may be intermittently contagious for years and is always contagious whenever an open sore or a syphilitic rash is present. Pregnant women with syphilis can transmit the infection to their unborn child and suckling infants can acquire the disease from their mothers or wet-nurses.

The disease that afflicted Charles VIII's troops bore little resemblance to modern-day syphilis. It was horrific and it progressed rapidly with little if any separation by latent periods during which the disease appeared to have been cured. It began with genital ulcers, progressed to fever, an itchy, weeping rash over the whole body and face (very obvious and called 'purple flowers'), with joint and muscle pains, sores (pocks) all over the body, then large, painful foul-smelling abscesses which left repulsive, thick greenish-black scabs. There were terrible pains in the bones and muscles, particularly at night, which provoked cries of anguish. Large lumps developed in muscles and bones, eating away cavities in them. To start with, these lumps were hard but they then turned into soft, viscous gummas which caused foul ulcers, most feared when they destroyed the nose, lips, palate, larynx and the genitalia. The disease could kill horribly in a matter of weeks. The stench from the victims' rotting flesh was particularly noticeable and repulsive.

Gruesome first-hand accounts of the disease were published from its first appearance; they chart its progress over the coming centuries and were complemented by illustrations of its victims.[6] The disease has continued to fascinate artists, poets and writers to the present day.[7] From the beginning all accounts of the disease, lay and professional, recognised the great variability of the skin rashes (collectively known as 'syphilides') and of the symptoms experienced by individual patients.

Francisco Lopez de Villalobos (1473-1560) provided one of the earliest and best descriptions of the disease, and the first in Spanish.[8] He preferred to call it *sarna egyptciaca*. *Tratado sobre las pestiferas Bubas* is a long poem published in 1498 while Villalobos was still a medical student. In it he reviews the arguments raging at the time about the origin of syphilis, its causes and its treatment. His descriptions of it dwell on its protean manifestations in the skin and on the joint pains which caused so much distress:

> On the whole skin and the face we observe,
> And here a vast foulness of eruption is displayed,
> And pain of joint that is felt very bad,
> And measureless siccidity in vein and nerve… [9]

He describes 'unendurable' pain in the shoulder and knee joints and in the shins[10] but does not mention joint pains or swelling in the hands. Nor does he report effects on the heart and blood vessels or on the nervous system, other than headache. Villalobos and Cellini, in his autobiography, both refer to 'ophthalmia' – pain and redness of the eyes, which has become an uncommon feature of secondary syphilis[11] and many authors make passing references to discolouration of the skin. Villalobos, for example, contrasted the new disease that he was describing (i.e. syphilis) with one called 'saphati' which had been described by Avicenna:

> As to how it first comes on he makes no remark
> About the virile sex, nor that of womankind,
> Nor tells of the complexion turning frightfully dark…[12]

Later he writes: 'And [saphati] makes one dark in feature and obscure in countenance'[13] and 'With dolour of the head, the face much clouded o're. . . Around lids and eyelids a dark rim.'[14]

Pope Julius II's physician, Giovanni de Vigo recognised that this was a contagious disease, transmitted by sexual intercourse and accurately described its lesions and symptoms in his *De Morbo Gallicus* (1514).[15]

Ulrich von Hutten (1488 -1523) was a friend of Erasmus, a knight, a humanist, a German patriot, a satirist, a supporter of Martin Luther's cause (he was condemned along with Luther in the first papal Bull denouncing reformation) and a fierce critic of Fugger for his defence of the sale of indulgences and of usury. He has left us one of the first accounts of any disease by a patient who suffered from it. He caught syphilis in about 1508 when the disease was still in its most aggressive form but nonetheless he survived – enduring the agonies of the disease itself and of its treatment for 15 years. He wrote a graphic account of his experience in *De morbo Gallico*, published in 1519.

> Boils that stood out like acorns, from whence issued such filthy stinking matter that, whosoever came within the scent believed himself infected. The colour of these was of a dark green, and the very aspect as shocking as the pain itself[16]

> Strangely altering the complexion of the sick[17]

> after this there will appear small holes and sores which will turn cankerous and fistulous, which the more putrid they grow, the more they will eat into the bones… the sick grows lean, his flesh wasting away… some have sores in their bladder, and oftentimes the stomach and liver is quite spoiled by the sickness…[18]

> …my body was always dropping away in the most filthy matter to my unspeakable torment… and besides so filthy to look upon, that all were offended at the sight of me, and many fled from me… I had no use of my left foot, for there had this disease lurked for more than eight years, and upon my skin were putrid ulcers, with great pain and inflammation, so soon as one part healed another breaking out… under these was a knob, so hard, that a man would have taken it for a bone, exceeding full of ache or pain, beating and throbbing continually… the calf of my leg and the whole joint of my knee seemed cold as if dead… [19]

And so on for four heart-rending pages.

He knew about the venereal origin of the disease, knew that chancres may be hidden and warned against touching women in:

> their secret places, having in those places little pretty sores full of venom poison[18]

Some disorders of the nervous system were quite quickly attributed to the new disease – headache, 'madness' and paralysis in the sixteenth century, convulsions, loss of vision, vertigo and paralysis in the seventeenth. Von Hutten said that his *morbus Gallicus* 'sometimes transforms itself . . . into a palsy and apoplexy'[18] and he talks of his leg and knee seeming cold as if dead – did he mean that he had lost the sensations of touch, pain, temperature and so on in his limb; would he have been able to feel pain caused by a thorn in his foot? Despite his, and other, vivid descriptions of epidemic syphilis it took centuries and much argument to identify all the features of its tertiary phase, many of which are very similar to those of other diseases – syphilis is a great mimic. Tabes dorsalis and General Paralysis of the Insane (GPI) were not conclusively shown to be due to syphilis until the very end of the nineteenth century. GPI does not respond to treatment with mercury, which threw investigators off the scent for years.[20] Max Adrian vividly portrayed many of the nervous system manifestations of terminal syphilis in *Song of Summer*, Ken Russell's TV dramatisation of Eric Fenby's time as Frederick Delius's amanuensis.[21]

When it left Italy Charles's polyglot army disbanded and dispersed throughout Europe, taking the new disease with it. By the end of 1495 it was epidemic in France, Switzerland and the Empire, which was particularly badly affected; it reached England and Scotland in 1497, Calcutta in 1498, Africa and China by 1520. Up to 5% of the population may have been affected.[22] It quickly claimed prominent victims in addition to the numberless soldiers, prostitutes and common folk, including the governor of Naples, Cesare Borgia (Pope Alexander VI's son), Pope Julius II and probably Charles VIII himself. It was soon realised that it was spread by sexual contact and steps were taken throughout Europe to close brothels and bathhouses. Awareness of the new disease spread rapidly – how could it not. Graphic descriptions of *morbus Gallicus* soon began to appear in the medical and lay literature. When the disease hit Nuremburg in 1496, subsiding in 1498, Dürer was commissioned to illustrate a broadsheet detailing the public health measures which the civic authorities were taking to control it.[23] His illustration (Plate 16) shows the palmer syphilides, and lumps on the limbs trunk and face but apparently no darkening of the skin. Dürer knew 'of nothing of which I am more badly afraid. Nearly everybody has it, and many people are quite eaten up by it so that they die'[24] and a German victim wrote 'nothing more terrible and disgusting has [never] been known on this earth. . . the wound on my priapic glans became so swollen, that both hands could scarcely encircle it'[25] – obviously not the same as the unobtrusive chancre that is usual today.

In 1527 the association of the disease with sex, the province of Venus, led to the suggestion that it be called venereal disease.

And then in 1530, Girolamo Fracastoro published a three-volume, epic poem in Latin, *Syphilis sive morbus Gallicus* [Syphilis, or the French disease] first published in English in 1686, which tells the story of a shepherd called Syphilus who was struck down by a new, foul-smelling disease because he had insulted the Sun-God, Apollo. Fracastoro was a distinguished Veronese physician who proposed a prescient germ-theory of disease.[26] He famously suggested (*De contagione et contagiosis morbis*, 1546) that each disease is caused by a different type of rapidly multiplying minute body which can be transferred from one person to another in three ways: by direct contact; by carriers such as soiled clothing and linen (fomites); and through the air. He persuaded Pope Paul III to relocate the Council of Trent to the papal state of Bologna to avoid the risk of plague in the town of Trent.

Fracastoro used his poem and other works to give a detailed account of the symptoms, signs and treatment of *morbus Gallicus* which he attributes to astrological misalignments. He coined the word 'gumma' for one of the late features of the disease: 'pus that escapes from the body and hardens to scabs like resin'.[27] Erasmus called the disease 'syphilis' and some other authors did so as well, but the name was not in widespread use until the nineteenth century; before then the disease was *morbus Gallicus*, 'French pox' or just 'the pox'. We shall call it syphilis from now on and by doing so we acknowledge our inability to avoid imposing our medical and cultural ideas about microbiology, antibiotics and sexual mores onto a sixteenth century episteme.[28]

Fracastoro published *Syphilis sive morbus Gallicus* some 35 years after the disease first struck. In it he described the course of syphilis as it was first encountered at the end of the fifteenth century: a relatively short illness with severe symptoms, profound debility and, often, an early death. He emphasised the discharge of stinking pus, the erosion of the lips, nose and genitalia, the gummae (often the size of an egg or a small loaf), the frequent loss of hair and beard and the agonising nocturnal pain. This has been called 'malignant' or 'galloping' syphilis Fracastoro noted that syphilis became less terrible during the sixteenth century. The florid, foul-smelling ulceration, ghastly pain, debilitation and early death were less pronounced; they were replaced by a more prolonged and less fulminant course. Genital sores or 'pocks' (only later were they called 'chancres') appeared very soon after contact with an infected partner. These healed, to be followed several weeks later by a widespread rash, fever, aches and pains – particularly nocturnal bone pain – and a warty rash in the genital area. All this cleared up and a relatively symptom-free interval of months would ensue before the dreaded, final phase of the disease began (as time progressed this latent period grew longer and longer, so that today it may extend to several years). It was characterised by abscesses and ulcers (gummas) which caused severe debility; large red sores on the scalp and on the shins; loss of hair (which prompted the fashion for wearing wigs); madness, disfigurement (signifying sin and causing social exclusion) and death.[29].

Fracastoro wrote about syphilis again in 1546 (*De contagione et contagiosis morbis*) – about the time that Bronzino was painting the *London Allegory*:[30]

> although this pestilential sickness is at present [1546] still fully active it is no longer the same as it was at first. For twenty years or so the 'pustulae' have been less numerous, on the other hand, the gummas . . . are more common. Nearly six years ago the sickness once more changed dramatically. 'Pustulae' are now only to be found on a very small number of patients, and the pains are negligible or very slight. The gummas are very common, however, and everyone is struck by the loss of the hair, and body hair in general, which turns the patients into laughing stocks: some have no beards, others no eyebrows, others have bald heads.[31]

By the end of the century 'malignant' syphilis was uncommon in Europe (but it recurred wherever a new population was exposed to the disease – Japan, Malaysia, Polynesia[32]), so Bronzino, living in the first half of the sixteenth century, would have been uncomfortably familiar with the sights – and smells – of the severe form of syphilis; he would have been aware that the disease was becoming a bit less ghastly as time went on and that its progression through the three relatively distinct phases that are characteristic of the disease today was beginning to become apparent.

Dürer's representation of the disease was by no means the only one which was circulating in the first half of the sixteenth century.[33] So in the very unlikely event that Bronzino had not seen its victims himself he would have seen illustrations of it. Two features of these illustrations are germane to our study of the *London Allegory*. First is the prominence given to the syphilitic rash and disfiguring lesions all over the face and limbs. Second, many include references to the supposed astrological origins of the disease, attributing particular importance to the sign of Scorpio.

The dramatic appearance of such a devastating new disease shook conventional, established medical thinking to its foundations. Like all diseases at the time its cause and origin were a mystery. Was it a punishment for lust, perhaps, or for blasphemy – a portent of the imminent arrival of the Last Days? Maybe it was the consequence of a malign conjunction of the planets Mars, Jupiter and Saturn in Scorpio; of bad air; of a poor life-style; of an excess of phlegm; of a pestilent germ caused by the mixture of the reproductive seeds of the two sexes or of the male seed and a menstrual discharge; or was it perhaps due to the action of harmful vapours rising from the floods which beset Italy in 1498?[34] The fact that the epidemic broke out in Naples led some to note that there were sailors in the city who had returned in 1493 from Christopher Columbus's first expedition to the New World – perhaps they had brought the disease back with them, passed it to the Neapolitan prostitutes and thence to the soldiers? This – the Columbian hypothesis – became the dominant one in the coming centuries and it has still not been conclusively confirmed or refuted.

Was syphilis really a new disease or only a pre-existing disease that had previously been lumped in with several other diseases? Clinical observation was poor in those days and many doctors viewed genital diseases with particular distaste so they were reluctant to pay close attention to them. In addition diseases which have superficial similarities but which microbiology has now shown to be distinct were often lumped together – so the venereal diseases now recognised as chancroid, lymphogranuloma venereum and syphilis may have been conflated; and skin conditions such as psoriasis, dermatitis, syphilitic rash and leprosy itself could all have been diagnosed as 'leprosy' which before 1500 was considered highly contagious, was associated with sexual contact, and was said to respond to treatment with mercury.[35] The new disease was devastating and dramatically different from anything encountered before, making it highly unlikely that it would not have been described as a distinct entity if it had existed in Europe before the epidemic at the end of the fifteenth century. Contemporary observers were in no doubt that it was novel. They scoured ancient European, Byzantine and Islamic texts and the Bible hoping to find precedents that would help them to understand and treat the condition – all in vain.[36] But they couldn't exclude the possibility that it was a very much more severe form of a pre-existing milder disease subsumed under the diagnosis of 'leprosy' (the Unitarian hypothesis).[37]

The Columbian hypothesis depends first on showing that a disease similar to syphilis existed in the pre-Columbian New World and second on showing that such a disease did not exist in Europe before 1495 (i.e. on trying to prove a negative). We now know that syphilis is due to *Treponema pallidum*, a spiral-shaped microorganism (a spirochaete) and that very similar sub-species of *T. pallidum* cause other debilitating diseases called yaws, pinta and bejel (other sub-species cause similar diseases in primates). These, which are not sexually transmitted diseases, are childhood illnesses characterised by skin ulcers, craters in the skull and swelling and pitting of shin bones. Bejel has existed for centuries in the Middle East and North Africa and it was common in parts of Europe in the eighteenth and nineteenth centuries; pinta is endemic in Central and South America, and yaws in the tropics. Conceivably Columbus's sailors caught yaws or pinta, which behaved in an uncharacteristically vicious way in these men who had not been exposed to these diseases in the past and who therefore had no immunity to them. Alternatively, the Unitarian hypothesis posits that *T. pallidum* behaves in radically different ways depending upon the environment in which it finds itself; so already endemic in Eurasia as the cause of *bejel*, it could have changed to become more aggressive when it came into contact with the devastated southern Italian environment, just as Charles VIII's soldiers were mingling with Columbus's sailors in Naples – quite a coincidence. There is hotly disputed evidence both for and against the presence of treponemal damage to the bones of Europeans who died long before the discovery of the New World. Recently, genomic analysis of the sub-species of *T. pallidum* suggests that the organism that causes syphilis today is most closely related to non-sexually transmitted yaws-causing strains which are endemic in Guyana. The skeletal, clinical and genomic data are limited and ambiguous so we still don't know where *morbus Gallicus* came from or why it behaved in the way that it did[38] but the current consensus favours the Columbian hypothesis[39] which has the added attraction of assuaging European guilt for having introduced smallpox, measles and other Old World diseases to the naïve populations of the Americas to dire effect.[40]

Lacking any clear ideas about the cause of syphilis, the sixteenth century doctors were stumped about how to treat its victims. They fell back on their usual remedies: diet, bleeding, purging and sweating; not surprisingly they had little success – though the later development of the milder form of the disease with latent periods often misled them into thinking that they were getting something right. Ancient authorities such as Galen, Avicenna and Hippocrates were looked at sceptically. Led by Paracelsus, Galenic (humoural) approaches to the treatment of syphilis were compared with chemical treatments – and found to be wanting. After a formal medical training Paracelsus worked as a barber-surgeon while he immersed himself in the ideas of the herbalists, gypsies and magicians, about which he wrote extensively; similarly he abandoned his Catholic upbringing in favour of radical Protestant sects, including the Anabaptists. He insisted that medical knowledge was to be gained not from ancient texts but by observation of afflicted patients and by study of natural philosophy, astrology, alchemy and of the power inherent in nature. He introduced effective new approaches to treatment, antisepsis and surgery despite his continued adherence to medieval ideas about astrological influences on physiology and disease.[41] He failed to distinguish between gonorrhoea and syphilis – but he was the first to describe congenital syphilis.

The old ideas about the cause of syphilis which we find preposterous were equally unappealing to Jean Fernel (1506-88), medical attendant to Francis I. He rejected the Galenic system based on the four humours and taught instead that syphilis was caused by a 'virus' and suggested that syphilis and gonorrhoea are separate diseases.[42] He knew that syphilis had become less aggressive as the sixteenth century progressed, that it was usually acquired through intercourse and that the mouth and the anus could be infectious. He likened the disease to the poison of a scorpion, which spreads throughout the body from its point of entry.[43]

Von Hutten again:

> Whilst the physicians were thus confounded like men amazed, the surgeons as wretchedly lent a hand to the same error, and first began to burn the sores with hot irons. But for as much as there seemed no end to this cruelty, they endeavoured not to avoid the same with their ointments, but all in vain unless they added Quicksilver thereto.[44]

One traditional remedy for chronic skin complaints was mercury (Quicksilver), so it was logical to give this a go. One of the toxic effects of mercury is salivation – which came to be regarded as beneficial, prompting the development of 'salivation cures' of various sorts. Mercury was applied as an ointment either just to the skin lesions or more widely, then the patient was wrapped in sheets or blankets and left in a heated room to sweat for hours. The treatment was repeated for up to four times a day for three or four weeks. Alternatively, the patient could be left in a chamber heated by a charcoal brazier, onto which mercury or mercury compounds were thrown so that the patient was bathed in, and inhaling, the mercury vapour. Poisoning was common, and probably often fatal – survivors experienced profuse salivation, loss of teeth and hair, ulceration of the throat and swelling of the gums. All-in-all patients dreaded treatment with mercury and many doctors (including Fernel) doubted its efficacy, while having no doubts about its toxicity. Paracelsus, however, was an enthusiastic supporter of mercury, advocating its oral administration and warning about the dangers of overdosage. He favoured 'blue mass' – metallic mercury; others preferred to give the metal as one of its salts. All stimulated the secretion of copious quantities of saliva, believed to be an excellent way to wash the syphilitic poison away. Profuse sweating was also thought to help eliminate the poison so patients given oral preparations of mercury were also treated in rooms heated with dry air or steam.

Von Hutten had eleven courses of treatment with mercury:

> the ointment caused such profuse salivation that the patients were in danger of losing their teeth unless care was taken. . . most of them lost their teeth, their mouths being all in a sore, and through the coldness of their stomachs and the filthy stench their appetites

> were destroyed. . . many. . . could not stand. . . some ran mad. Many I have seen die in the midst of their curations.[45]

Mercury remained the favoured treatment for syphilis until well into the nineteenth century, though there was intense debate about the need for copious salivation, about how best to give the drug and when in the course of the disease to resort to it. Mercury really is an effective treatment (though not for GPI, which wasn't described until much later anyway) but only in doses that are very close to, or even above, those which are poisonous – making its use a pretty hit-or-miss affair. Bismuth salts were introduced as alternative treatments in 1884. These were less toxic than mercury and better at killing *T. pallidum*. Iodides were then added to the armamentarium shortly before all were rendered obsolete by the advent of penicillin – which was needed to treat the roughly 45.4 million people infected with syphilis in 2015, including 6 million new cases that year. During 2015 syphilis caused about 107,000 deaths.[46]

Was there an effective, safe alternative in the sixteenth century to the unpleasant and dangerous treatment with mercury? The short answer is 'No', though plenty were tried and many had their champions.

Cautery, particularly of the top of the head, was favoured by some – like bleeding and purging, it was a treatment with a long history.[47] Many herbal medicines were tried, two finding particular favour – though in the event neither proved to be effective. These were sarsaparilla and guaiacum ('holy wood' or *lignum vitae*). Both came from plants native to the New World (though at first most sarsaparilla was imported from the Far East as 'China Root') and so they benefitted from the belief that God provides a cure for a disease in its place of origin.[48] Guaiacum is an evergreen plant with extremely hard wood, unrelated to laurel or to myrtle although the leaves of all three shrubs look very similar[49]; the wood was imported so it is unlikely that Bronzino had ever seen the leaves. The preparation of the medicine was arduous. About 1580 Jan van der Straet (Johannes Stradanus) painted *Preparation and Use of Guayaco for Treating Syphilis* (Plate 17), a scene in which a wealthy syphilitic man with no obvious syphilides or gummas but with his head bandaged, drinks an infusion prepared from the gum of the guaiacum wood while four servants are shaving the wood and heating the shavings to release the gum. Patients were treated in hot, confined chambers and were purged as well as being given guaiacum, in most cases for about a month. The treatment caused profuse sweating – and probably little else so it was eventually, and reluctantly, abandoned in favour of mercury. After eleven experiences like that described above it is not surprising that von Hutten, who gave detailed descriptions of the complicated preparation and use of guaiacum, became one of the most ardent of its many fans. Unfortunately he was misled by his disease which entered a latent phase while he was using guaiacum, making him believe that the relief of his symptoms was due to the effects of the drug rather than to the natural history of the disease – from which he died in 1523. The idea that the Fugger family may have promoted the Columbian hypothesis in order to increase the popularity of guaiacum – having been granted a monopoly on the import of the wood, by Charles V in return for a generous loan[50] has now been disproved.[51] They do seem to have had a finger in every pie, though – they also held the contract to supply the mercury needed to refine the vast quantities of silver that had been found in Mexico[52] – and incidentally needed also to treat the vast numbers of syphilitics now suffering in Europe.

Paracelsus was scathing about guaiacum and about von Hutten's confidence in it:

> …the first clamour about the wood was raised by an inexperienced and worldly man with no other ascendant in him than having his mouth resound with the latest craze. This man has been the schoolteacher and professor of the doctors and masters. What good he taught them, can daily be heard from the sick.[53]

He particularly objected to the foreign origin of guaiacum, believing that local plants would be best for treating a disease that was caught locally. By 1546 even Fracastoro had lost confidence in its efficacy.

Von Hutten and his fellow sufferers endured miserable, sweaty hours of treatment lying in heated chambers and wrapped in blankets. It's unlikely that this regimen would have caused their body temperatures to rise significantly – thermoregulatory mechanisms (including profuse sweating) would have kicked-in to prevent that. Ironically, much later the symptoms of neurosyphilis were found to improve if the patient had a high fever. In 1917, the Austrian physician Julius Wagner-Jauregg (1857-1940) gave his patients malaria (which he could later cure by treating them with quinine) to induce a high temperature. He succeeded in curing neurosyphilis, which led to his being awarded a Nobel Prize in 1927. This treatment remained in use until it was displaced by penicillin in the 1950s.[54]

Despite its initial devastating impact, syphilis soon settled down to become a constant background threat which had only a minor demographic effect and caused little social upheaval. In some places bathhouses were closed, prostitutes expelled from cities or those with signs of the disease were ostracised or denied access to public places – inns, for example. On the other hand, syphilis was a key reason for the establishment of hospitals dedicated to the care of the chronically ill – earlier there had been hospitals only for those with injuries or acute illnesses, such as the plague. The new hospitals enabled the authorities to sequester the poor, syphilitic beggars who were unable to work and who became an embarrassing nuisance as they wandered around importuning their fellow citizens for alms.[55] European populations grew throughout the sixteenth century as less virulent strains of *T. pallidum* displaced those which had killed so rapidly and as herd resistance increased. The disease may have killed members of the royal households or the aristocracy of Europe, or affected their fertility, but if so it only contributed to a reshuffling of the players at the top of society, which was not necessarily a bad thing.[56]

At first syphilis wasn't linked in the popular mind to sexual behaviour so no blame was attached to having the disease, even though it was thought to be contagious. Syphilitics had their own patron saints (St Job, St Méen and St Denis were favourites) and discussed or recorded their symptoms openly. But once its venereal origin was widely recognised it became socially unacceptable; attempts were made to hide its stigmata, and its distressing treatment with mercury was encouraged as an appropriate punishment for the patient's sins.[57]

The realisation that syphilis could be transmitted by kissing led to the development of hand-shaking in place of kissing as the accepted form of social greeting. Other changes in public behaviour were also attributable to the disease. At first syphilides signified that the victim moved in the best social circles – until they became so florid as to be disfiguring, and until they afflicted so many of the less affluent that they lost their social cachet. Then wigs, and for women forehead pendants, to hide hair loss and ulcers on the scalp became fashionable, they were often scented to counter the vile odour emanating from the ulcers; masks, copper noses, heavy make-up and velvet patches were worn in public to hide facial disfigurement.[58] In time, wigs became essential fashion accessories, even for those who did not have the disease.[59] Syphilis was also a fashionable trope for art in the 1540s, particularly art intended for elite courtly audiences.[60] The xenophobic names given to it ('the French disease' and so on) extended in the case of England, for example, to equating French fashions with syphilis – to dress like the French was to be like the French: diseased.[61]

We can now return to the painting and focus on figure K (Plate 15). It used to be thought that K is female, but the figure's muscular physique and relative lack of subcutaneous fat led Conway to identify K as a male; in this he is correct, I think, making it unlikely that Bronzino intended K to represent Jealousy or Envy, who were usually portrayed as female. Conway's suggestion that the male K was intended to be a representation of the effects of syphilis was published in 1986; it has been enthusiastically taken up by most commentators since.

K is clutching his head, 'tearing his hair out', the muscles in his neck are contracted, and his mouth is open as if crying out in anguish. Conway believes that this is a representation of the terrible headache and bone pain that were such prominent features of the disease. But while K is undoubtedly in pain we cannot tell whether this is physical or psychological pain. Then Conway considers the reddening of K's eyes, which he attributes to syphilitic inflammation. Certainly, syphilis can affect the eyes, but K's eyes do not look particularly red to me – no redder than might be due to weeping.

Next there is the issue of the colour of K's skin – described by Conway and others[62] as 'darkened', leading him to identify this as syphilitic *rupia* (Ancient Greek ῥύπος, 'dirt, filth'). He is misusing the term *rupia*, which in this context signifies a syphilitic rash comprising thick dark crusts on the skin that resemble oyster shells[63] – obviously K does not have *rupia*. Once syphilis had passed through its malignant stage the discolouration seen in the skin tended to occur where the original rash had been, forming dark patches or small pale patches with fuzzy borders especially on the neck in bands (called Venus's Collar). Nonetheless, darkening of the skin was described by Villalobos, von Hutten[64] and others who were writing about the disease they experienced soon after its first appearance, so the dark skin does deserve discussion (but it is not mentioned by de Vigo nor by Morton in his survey of visual representations of the disease). We can't exclude the possibility that it is due to syphilis but is it really unnaturally dark? The figure is in shadow, tucked behind Cupid's body and under his wing; he is not as dark as the lower part of the girl's hybrid body (F and G). Smith argued that the purpose of K's intense emotion and dark colour is to point a contrast with the white heat of Cupid's passion and the dazzling whiteness of Venus's skin.[66]

The joints in K's claw-like fingers are swollen. Conway suggests that this is evidence of syphilitic arthritis, an idea that has been challenged by doctors, who think that the deformities are of a type that would have been unusual in patients with syphilis and more like those of osteoarthritis.[67]

It is much more likely, I believe, that Bronzino is simply using K's hands to convey emotion. There is a long and continuing history of the use of extremely distorted hands in this way: tormented souls being dragged into hell in endless '*Last Judgements*'; Christ in Grünewald's *Isenheim Altarpiece* (c.1512-5; Musée d'Unterlinden, Colmar, France) or in Hans Holbein the Younger's *The Body of the Dead Christ* (1521; Öffentliche Kunstsammlung, Basel) and Schiele's numerous self-portraits are but a few examples. Hands in Bronzino's paintings are usually limply elegant but one or two examples of slightly more expressive hands can be found in the frescos in Eleonora's Chapel.[68] K's hands are expressive, not diseased: there is no need to attribute their appearance to syphilis or to any other type of arthritis.

Conway can't see a nail on K's right index finger – this, he says, is syphilitic anonchia. K's finger, though, is partially buried in his hair, making it very difficult to tell whether he has a fingernail or not. He has lost most of his teeth – could this be due to mercury poisoning? Maybe, but many people lost their teeth despite diligent efforts to look after them. Some teeth were lost in fights or accidents; attempts to keep the teeth clean and the breath fresh by rubbing them with a mixture of powdered pumice stone, brick and coral often did more harm than good. Tooth decay was becoming more common – particularly amongst those rich enough to indulge in the new fashion for refined sugar; Queen Elizabeth I lost so many teeth that her speech was difficult to understand and she used to stuff rags in her mouth to hide the collapse of her cheeks. Charles V was almost toothless by the time he retired to the monastery of Yuste at the age of 56,[69] and Francis I had lost many of his teeth by the time he died – but in his case this could have been due to mercury poisoning.[70] The state of dental surgery was such that there was little alternative to extraction by a barber surgeon, a blacksmith or the tooth drawer.

If Bronzino intended K to represent syphilis he chose uncommon manifestations of the disease with which to achieve his objective – is he being subtle and ambiguous as he was with the other signs and symbols that he used throughout the rest of the painting? But the signs in this case are very subtle indeed – where are the syphilides, where the destruction of the nasal bones that were such common and easily seen features of syphilis? Where are the bald patches – K is tearing at his hair but, contrary to what Conway says, it is not falling out in clumps; he doesn't have the moth-eaten alopecia that is characteristic of secondary syphilis today[71] there is no suggestion that he needs to think about buying a wig. Gummas are certainly not as prominent as we might expect – Fracastoro said they could be the size of eggs or bread rolls – though perhaps there is a gumma inside his mouth,[72] and there is a curious and indecipherable mark on K's neck, behind his left wrist. Or, if K is representing mercury poisoning, where is the profuse salivation that invariably accompanied it – and that was believed to be part of its effectiveness as a treatment for syphilis – and where are the swollen jaws, the sores in the mouth and the stinking matter that von Hutten complains of?

Conway makes some interesting suggestions and has opened a productive debate – but his case is far from proven. Can Margaret Healy come to his aid? Healy expanded on Conway's arguments, seeing representations of syphilis throughout the *London Allegory*. She begins with the prominence of Venus's nipple, being clasped between the fore- and middle-fingers of Cupid's right hand. Is this just a Mannerist conceit or does it signify something important? And why, she asks, does the arrow so assertively direct our gaze to K? She thinks the answers to these and many other questions about the painting are relatively straightforward. There is no 'difficult riddle' here – the *London Allegory* is all about syphilis. Cupid's grip on his mother's nipple resembles that of a woman offering her lactating breast to a suckling infant, suggesting to Healy that this is a reminder that syphilis can be transmitted through breast milk. And there are references throughout the painting to each of the other routes of infection that were known at the time: kissing, homosexual and heterosexual intercourse. She also says that the masks which could symbolise Vice or Deceit were a reminder of the use of masks to disguise the facial disfigurement caused by syphilis; that the blue curtain represents a polluted 'River of Love' and that Time is trying to cover up, or drown, the disease and its associations. Time has a duplicitous role in the natural history of the disease which appears in time to be cured spontaneously or as a result of treatment, only to flare up again as it progresses through its primary, secondary and tertiary phases, separated by misleading latent periods. A in Healy's reading of the *London Allegory* is Night, positioned above the syphilitic K, who suffers the worst agonies of the disease at night. The laurel hedge alludes to poetry in which the joys and pains of love, beguiling women, truth and falsehood are recurring tropes – as they are in the painting.

This may all be correct but the argument is very thin; most credible is the idea that the routes of infection are represented in the painting – true and perhaps, taken with Conway's analysis of K, that's enough to conclude that the *London Allegory* is indeed about syphilis.

Christopher Cook contributes the idea that A may be showing some other effects of syphilis: she is blind (optic nerve damage) and mindless (demented – GPI). He suggests that B, the *putto*, is also showing signs of syphilitic nerve damage: he is not disturbed by the thorn in his foot – maybe he can't feel it because his foot is numb?

Finally, recalling the various descriptions of sphinxes, lamias and so on – in particular some elements of Hesiod's description of the Echidna:

> … monstrous and unmanageable thing … in a hollow cave … dreadful and huge, swift eater of raw flesh[73]

we might go so far as to suggest that C's lower half is a representation of syphilis hidden away either in the vaginal 'cave' or in its latent phases, dreadful in its impact, huge in its scale, and a destroyer of healthy flesh in a peculiarly disgusting way.

Is the *London Allegory* a representation of syphilis or not? Like everything else about the painting most of us are left feeling ambivalent about this. Barolsky has no doubts. He thinks that the idea that the painting is a representation of syphilis is 'highly improbable, indeed fabulous' and that it has more to do with our 'unamused preoccupation with venereal sexual disease' than it has with Bronzino's real intentions.[74] So, Bronzino has, at best, hinted at the disease – but maybe that's all he needed to do. Taken together Conway, Healy and Cook have adduced some evidence to say that K has syphilis but their evidence is suggestive rather than compelling. The appeal of the hypothesis lies in its simplicity, to which may be added a touch of prurience.

When I first started to think about this idea it seemed to me highly improbable that a diplomatic, even sycophantic, gift for a dissolute king, widely believed to be suffering from advanced syphilis, would have alluded to the disease – let alone portrayed it in a horrific way and attributed it to past sexual indiscretions. Andrew Graham-Dixon, who found Conway's thesis 'plausible' has come up with an appealing way round this conundrum. He suggests that Bronzino and Cosimo designed the painting (or at least the parts alluding to syphilis) as a 'mischievous in-joke.' Had Francis I asked them to explain what the painting meant they could have talked about sphinxes, love leading to jealousy and so on. All the while they would have been smiling quietly to themselves, knowing that they had produced a 'subtle dig at the famously lascivious foreign king. . . A little sting in the tail of its meaning, just like that concealed by the sweetly smiling girl.'[75]

VII

Conclusion

The London Allegory

What does it mean?

Th' expense of spirit in a waste of shame
Is lust in action; and till action, lust
Is perjured, murd'rous, bloody, full of blame,
Savage, extreme, rude, cruel, not to trust,
Enjoyed no sooner but despisèd straight,
Past reason hunted; and, no sooner had
Past reason hated as a swallowed bait
On purpose laid to make the taker mad;
Mad in pursuit and in possession so,
Had, having, and in quest to have, extreme;
A bliss in proof and proved, a very woe;
Before, a joy proposed; behind, a dream.
All this the world well knows; yet none knows well
To shun the heaven that leads men to this hell.
Shakespeare: Sonnet 129

Bronzino was a poet, a master of the art of conveying inchoate, multiple, elusive meanings and emotions through the use of elliptical, elegantly arranged written language, of using words for their connotive as much as for their dennotive value, of demanding close attention and careful reflection from his readers. He applied the same skills to his painted language: the *London Allegory* is a poem in paint,[1] and –

A poem should not mean but be. (MacLeish, *Ars Poetica*)

Much as we want to break the painting's code, subject it to rational analysis and work out what it means we must remember that it was designed to be a visual experience; it was not necessarily intended to convey a single meaning. Instead the painting has multiple meanings – almost as many meanings as it has viewers. We are now in a position to decide for ourselves what these meanings might be. It is likely that our ideas about the painting will change over time, making repeated visits to see it endlessly rewarding. We can begin by asking what solutions others have offered to the riddle of its meaning.

Our predecessors' scholarly contributions to our appreciation of the *London Allegory* have been concerned as much with the identity of the individual characters in the painting and about their sources in art and literature as they have been with the overall meaning of the work. Many have focussed their research on one or a couple of the characters within it, unearthing likely precedents in literature and art which they believe would have influenced Bronzino's composition. As we saw in Chapter V there is no shortage of material that Bronzino could have consulted. Some scholars, though, have looked for a single meaning for the work, one which ties together every element in it – standing in front of the painting they have looked for a 'Eureka moment' that would solve the riddle once and for all. But some of the conclusions that have been reached about its meaning have been rather superficial and reached at the expense of ignoring one or more features of the painting; herein lie their weakness and their diversity. To some degree the 'syphilis hypothesis', seized upon with often prurient enthusiasm, does provide the sought after single, all-embracing interpretation. But it too fails to account for all the characters and objects, their actions and their location relative one to another. And something of the spirit of a work produced in the episteme of mid-sixteenth century Florence is bound to be lost in our post-modern approach to it, let alone in a rationalist, reductive, post-Enlightenment search for the answer.

Virtually all the scholars whose work we have been considering have been working, consciously or unconsciously, in the shadow of Vasari. For all the deficiencies in his description of the painting, and therefore in his interpretation of it, many of his successors have felt obliged to align their own interpretations of the characters with Vasari's – or to justify themselves when they disagree with Vasari. Unfortunately, these attempts to fit the straight-jacket bequeathed to us by Vasari constrain thinking and limit options

Panofsky, one of the most highly regarded art historians, published his analysis of the painting in 1939,[2] before the 1958 restoration removed the bowdlerising Victorian and earlier additions, which inevitably influenced his identification of the various characters; the painting that he saw is illustrated in his book and in Jaynie Anderson's paper.[3] He came up with a moralistic interpretation. We can take account of his identification of the various characters but he did not see the painting that we are discussing so we should be reticent about accepting his overall interpretation.

Panofsky read the *London Allegory* as 'Luxury surrounded by personifications and symbols of treacherous pleasures and manifest evils of love'; the pleasures are futile and the dangers and tortures are great and real evils. The true subject is the 'Exposure of Luxury by Time and Truth': Character A joins feminine disgust with Time's masculine wrath to pull back the curtain and expose vice. Panofsky said that Bronzino chose to illustrate 'alluring sexual voluptuousness' rather than any other type of evil, because that was 'in perfect harmony with the spirit of the Counter-Reformation'. Maybe so, there was growing religious disapproval of Mannerism, and Cosimo might also have welcomed a condemnation of sexual excess – but the Council of Trent didn't formalise its approach to religious art until 1563 and throughout the 1540s Cosimo was patronising both those who supported reform of the Church and also subversive works by Pontormo.[4] Quite apart from any wish on Bronzino's part to avoid giving offence to the religious authorities, the Venus and Cupid story gave him an excuse to paint nude bodies engaged in sexual games, a more immediately engaging exemplar of vice than, for example, nepotism, sloth or gluttony.

Most other interpretations of the *London Allegory* follow Panofsky's idea that the painting conveys a moral about the pleasures and pains of love being inseparable, but with greater emphasis on the sexual nature of the encounter between Venus and Cupid – understandably so because they are based on the extant version of the painting. The homoerotic elements of

Cupid's pose and quiver are rarely discussed or incorporated in these accounts.

Brock offers a comprehensive analysis which, like the painting itself, is discursive and at times contradictory. He says Bronzino's single image includes representations of beauty and ugliness, attraction and repulsion, pleasure and pain, present and future, thereby revealing the several components of a loving (or sexual) relationship and the ways in which these mutate over time.[6]

Like Panofsky, Levey detected Michelangelo's influence but he broke with his predecessors by interpreting B as Folly rather than Jest (Panofsky) and C as *la Fraude*, the 'double aspect of Pleasure', which led him to read the painting as a 'Triumph of Venus'. The late addition of the arrow, mentioned in Gould's discussion of the painting, which was cited by Levey, implies that this could not have been its original subject. Be that as it may, in Levey's interpretation of the final version of the *London Allegory*, Venus is seducing Cupid in order that she might control his powers; when she has achieved this she will have nothing else to fear – she will retain her beauty while disarming love.[7] Time is trying to rip the curtain away to expose *la Fraude*'s 'deceitful vacuity'. C's honeycomb and sting connote the immediate pleasure and long-term pain that Cupid will experience in Time.[8] Levey identified K as Jealousy, one of the pains of love that will torment Cupid; he did not comment on Cupid's pose nor did he discuss the masks, doves, laurel or peculiar lower half of C. Smith was also convinced that K is Jealousy. He found echoes of Petrarch and Bembo in Varchi's poetry and lectures about love and identified the latter's *Sulla Gelosia* as Bronzino's likely inspiration for the idea of sweetness and bitterness being inseparable components of love and for 'the pleasures of love [being] matched in intensity only by their accompanying torments'.[9] The *Sulla Gelosia* associated 'in a single text a number of visual abstractions given visual form by Bronzino, and it [offered] an explanation for their being gathered together'. The honeycomb and sting were identified as the sweet and bitter double aspects of pleasure; C is a lamia; B is happy but wounded in his foot – the double aspect of love again. Jealousy, deliberately portrayed to resemble *Invidia* (Envy) and positioned close to Cupid, provided a visual restatement of Varchi's distinction between Envy, the generic sentiment and Jealousy, the specific related to love. Like Levey, he concluded that the painting is a 'Triumph of Venus'.[10]

In 1978, Keach drew on Ovid for his interpretation: Venus, deceived by the power of the wound she accidentally inflicted on herself with Cupid's arrow, is surrounded by the figures of Time – the Revealer – and Deceit (C).[11] The 'precarious' position of Cupid's arrow in the Michelangelo/Pontormo *Venus and Cupid* is like the threat posed by the arrow seized by Venus in the *London Allegory* where it is 'perilously close to the inside of her arm'.[12] The central subject of both paintings is therefore 'The Wounding of Venus'. This is not credible: Venus does not appear to be in any danger from the arrow in the *London Allegory*. In any case, Smith interprets Ovid to mean that Venus did not wound herself, on the contrary she duplicitously turned the arrow back onto Cupid.[13] A, B, C and K are all ignored in Keach's analysis.

To Cheney the foreground scene is a warning about the perils of Love, with overtones of Luxury (or Lechery) and of Eve as temptress. This left her to account for Time, A and K. She linked the laurel (perseverance and virtue) with Time to oppose the ephemeral nature of love. Alternatively, or also, the laurel's association with chastity opposes it to Venus. A is a representation of Virtue who, lifting the curtain, is horrified to see Lust in action; Time hastens to lower the curtain to shield her from the ghastly sight. Virtue and Time, therefore, are opposed to Lust. Time's power over Venus's affairs is revealed by the different stages in the loss of innocence displayed by the foreground figures. B is innocent, unaware of the pain – symbolised by the thorn – which he is about to experience; C is a manipulative seductress; Cupid represents unbridled sexuality; Venus, well aware of her sexual allure is now more interested in power and K represents the despair that comes with age, decay and jealousy. Time takes its toll, sexual pleasure is transitory, Virtue is an enduring quality. She interprets the work as an example of a *Psychomachia* – an artistic work expressing conflict within the soul between the forces of good and evil.[27]

Unlike most of her fellow scholars Bosch offered a comprehensive interpretation of the *London Allegory*, in which she identified all the characters and objects within it and discussed their interrelationships and their positions relative to one another. She said that the painting is a representation of the

Classical *magno anno* – the endless cycle of destruction and renewal of the world – in which all the figures are deities associated with Venus and Cupid. The gods of Love are assembled beneath Time's arm, locked in the battle waged eternally between Love and Time: the Universe emerged from Chaos under the power of Love; Time will return creation to Chaos. In the painting Venus and her allies temporarily resist Time's force, A (Night) struggles against Time, grimacing as she fights for control of the curtain which Time tries to pull away. K is Strife, whose opposition to Cupid provides the motive power needed to maintain the cycle of creation, destruction and re-birth. Such a balance of opposites recurs throughout the painting: the doves, symbolising the caresses of Love are opposite the masks that represent Love's deceit; arrow and apple; honeycomb and viper; beautiful figures and ugly ones. In Classical literature the destruction of the Universe was predicted to be accompanied by a reversal of the positive and negative conventions – so evil would become good and *vice versa* – a cataclysm which would be followed by a new cycle of creation and destruction. Bosch detected a representation of this cycle in the structure of the *London Allegory*: movement from foreground to background retraces the path from the present (Venus, Cupid, B, C and K) to the past (Night and Time), the two generations being separated by the curtain. The laurel hedge (regeneration) separates Night and Time from the primeval Chaos. Reversing the movement from background to foreground follows the cycle of creation from the Void to the Triumph of Love. Bronzino temporarily arrests the cycle, putting Venus, Cupid and their court in the ascendant; but Time's power will prove to be inexorable.

Hope[14] broke with Vasari by identifying A as Oblivion who, together with Time obscures Love and the disagreeable passions that it engenders. It is Cupid rather than Venus who is about to experience the *passioni d'amore* because Venus has covertly removed his arrow to make sure she will not be wounded. The central group does not represent love in general but the incompletely reciprocated love of a man for a woman. The laurel is there as a symbol of poetic fame: the poet sings of Love and its passions, which are subject to Time and Oblivion – only poetry endures.

In Conway's ground-breaking contribution K is male and a

representation of syphilis; Time frustrates Oblivion's (A) efforts to use the curtain to veil K; the lascivious kiss exchanged by Venus and Cupid symbolises illicit love. The cushion of lechery and the masks of vice drive the message home, while C (*la Fraude*) offers a sweet honeycomb with her left (at first glance the expected right) hand and a venomous sting with her right (left) hand. B (*il Giuocco*), deceived by C, rushes towards love, heedless of the pain it will bring him. The result of the rash union will be K – syphilis, which will enter a latent phase (be covered by Oblivion's veil) but Time will ensure that the terrible disease re-emerges to claim its victim. Healy surpassed Conway by finding allusions to syphilis throughout the painting. She saw an educative purpose in it – it is a piece of health education made palatable by its beauty. Its message is not only about the dangers of syphilis, its horrors and its routes of transmission but also about the need to be distrustful of sensory experience and to be aware of the painful ruin that can follow dalliance with a voluptuous but tainted woman. Cook agreed with her: Bronzino has used Classical mythology and stylised imagery to make a topical public health message palatable.

Cohen focused attention on the object in C's hand (D) and hung an astrological interpretation of the whole painting on this small detail, which she assumes to be a scorpion's sting.[15] She accepted the idea that the painting is a representation of syphilis and noted the association of the constellation Scorpio with all things venereal – and symbols of Scorpio do appear in many illustrations of the disease (e.g. Plate 16).[16] She also pointed to the conjunction of Saturn and Jupiter in Scorpio in 1544 – roughly the time when Bronzino was working on his painting. Fernel's analogy of syphilis to the scorpion's sting which spreads throughout the body from the first infected part, and the scorpion's reputed mixing of its venom with honey led her to read the *London Allegory* as a learned social satire which represents the horrible consequences of deceit, pretension and transgression. Her interpretation relies quite heavily on the assumption that the *London Allegory* is, or includes, a depiction of syphilis.

Bromham set the painting in the context of the Renaissance practice of taking the potentially subversive pre-Christian Classical myths and allegorising them to draw moralising lessons which combat the sexual licence sanctioned by the myths. By this account, Bronzino mixes nude Classical figures in the foreground with clothed background figures which represent contemporary morality. So, alternative perspectives are shown in the painting: erotic and moral, Classical and Christian. The painting gives a grim warning about the consequences of behaviour like that of Venus and Cupid. Oblivion tries to draw a curtain across the scene, Time, the father of truth, will reveal all.[17]

Having rejected Vasari's description of the *London Allegory* because of its widely acknowledged flaws, Gaston did adopt Hope's identification of A as Oblivion and Conway's designation of K as male.[18] He saw three spatial layers: Venus, Cupid and B, strongly lit in the foreground; C in the middle-ground with K and the curtain behind her; Time and A in the background, behind the curtain. The appearance and clothing of C are those of a young girl likely to be encountered at Cosimo's court – and like those seen in Bronzino's portraits, except for the intensity of her gaze which is directed at the (male) viewer whom she alerts to the delight and suffering which will follow surrender to her allure. Like Parker, Gaston focussed on understanding Bronzino's poetry (which may explain his decision intentionally to overlook 'the questions raised by X-ray examination of the picture'[19] – by which, I assume, he means the *pentimenti*), in the expectation that the poetry would help to unlock the complexities of his paintings. Gaston believed that the *London Allegory* is about representation, specifically about the representation of Love[20] and that it is 'naturally expressive of Florentine culture'.[21] He mined a morass of Renaissance Italian literature, 'long-winded works in verse' (his words)[22] and in some cases their representation in woodcuts, finding a plethora of descriptions and themes which could have informed either the overall concept or the details of the painting. Bronzino's hero Petrarch and his successors were much taken with their ability to describe landscape, architecture, beautiful women and even works of art in their literature and the superiority, they thought, of these poetic descriptions to the attempts to represent the same subjects in painting or sculpture. As both a poet and a painter, and as a self-proclaimed 'servant' of Michelangelo, Bronzino believed the two disciplines to be inseparable. Varchi, a poet but not a painter, recognised the illusionistic power of painting but maintained that only poetry could represent the inner experience of the 'concepts and passions of the soul'. In his own poetry Bronzino dilates on the impossibility of knowing whether love is true or false, whether there is 'bitterness in the breast and sweetness in the hand'. Simple souls, he said, are betrayed or deceived; appearance is deceptive; one cannot distinguish 'thieves and assassins from sodomites, the sad from the fools'. One of his sonnets begins 'If my eyes don't deceive me, and tell me the truth' but disillusionment sets in, Amor plays and smiles and suffering begins.[23]

Gaston, like Smith a decade before him, was particularly impressed by the influence that Varchi's work and ideas had on Bronzino; he suggested that the painting may have been Bronzino's attempt to show Varchi and the Accademia Fiorentina that he could surpass his illustrious predecessors – Michelangelo and Pontormo in particular – in the representation of poetic tropes and sensibility. The meaning of the painting then 'hovers between the personal, the poetic, and the pictorial'. The poetry that he strove to surpass was full of images of women as ugly animals whose poison was hidden behind their beauty, spreading love – 'a bitter fruit' – and syphilis.[24] The *London Allegory* was Bronzino's response to the poets' challenge, its objective was to represent erotic love and its consequences more truthfully than poetry could do. While Venus and Cupid enjoy their sexual dalliance, urged on by the *putto*, C engages with the viewer of the painting; her gaze and honeycomb seduce him; her serpent's sting will wound him; Venus's flickering, honeyed tongue is similarly deceitful; her lover will experience such a mixture of pleasure and pain that he will rend his hair and beg Time and Forgetfulness to deliver him; they will respond to his cries with such agonising slowness that his suffering will seem eternal. But such a beautiful creature is irresistible despite her dangers – perhaps, we might add, because of them.

The didactic, moralising tone that has been assigned to the *London Allegory* was rejected by Oard. On the contrary, he said, the blatantly erotic painting which 'combines incest, pedophilia, bisexuality, hetero- and homo-sexual acts and S-M [sadomasochism]... is a vision of astounding perversity, as transgressive and multifaceted as desire itself'. It is about the many faces of desire in all its complexity, unveiled and unmasked (drapery in background, discarded masks). Pleasure (B) accompanies Love but Deceit (C) is always there too,

k

symbolising the deception, including self-deception that haunts our most carefree moments. Time looms over Love as it does over all our activities.

Apuleius, a Roman novelist (probably 3rd century CE) wrote *The Metamorphoses of Lucius* (St. Augustine called it *The Golden Ass*), which became well known in the original Latin and in translation during the Renaissance; Machiavelli began a version of it; Raphael used it as the inspiration for some frescoes. The book is about the long journey undertaken by Lucius in search of opportunities to see and practise magic, during which he is turned into an ass. In Books Four to Six of the novel there is an account of the Classical story of Venus, Cupid and Psyche which Kilpatrick thought provided a comprehensive account of the meaning of the characters in the *London Allegory*.[25]

Psyche, the most beautiful woman in the world, is envied for her beauty by her family and by Venus, who sends Cupid to shoot Psyche with one of his arrows to make her fall in love with a monster. Anticipating Cupid's success, Venus rewards him with lascivious kisses. Cupid however falls in love with Psyche himself and doesn't shoot her. Fearing his mother's anger, he makes himself invisible, marries Psyche and makes love to her. Psyche's envious and duplicitous sisters persuade her to find out who her invisible husband is but when she sneaks a look at him she accidentally pricks one of her fingers on his arrow (so, unlike Venus, she does injure herself) and spills hot lamp oil over him. He wakes up, is furious and leaves her. Venus is as angry as expected; she has Cupid beaten, blunts his arrows, cuts his hair, clips his wings and takes his quiver – a pretty comprehensive attempt to emasculate him. While Psyche hunts for Cupid, Venus hunts for Psyche, offering a reward of 'Seven luscious kisses, plus another honeyed by a thrust of her seductive tongue' for news of her whereabouts. Kilpatrick sees Venus's kisses as a 'key to the dramatic motivation of Bronzino's kiss'; he reads K as a representation of the Envy that motivates Venus and Psyche's sisters and C as the Deceit practised by the sisters. Elsewhere in the novel, Lucius is returned to human form by the magical power of roses; the thorn in B's foot may allude to the sufferings of Lucius and of Psyche in their searches. B himself therefore represents the joys and pains of true love and also, perhaps foretells the joyful and amusing dénouement to the story where, after various trials, Cupid rescues Psyche and the two are forever united, fulfilling Psyche's prediction that Time will mitigate Venus's rage. What about A in this account? She is Blind Fortune, nemesis of Lucius and Psyche, struggling against Time to keep the blue curtain closed. And where is Psyche? Kilpatrick thinks she is hidden behind the curtain because to have included her in the painting would have been to give the game away – it would have made Bronzino's riddle too easy to solve.

To paraphrase these interpretations, the influence of Ovid's and Apuleius's stories[26] is, surely, inescapable – they must have been the starting point for any Renaissance viewer of the painting, and probably were so for Bronzino and his patron also. But to read the *London Allegory* as a straightforward 'Triumph of Venus' leaves a lot unexplained. The several studies summarised above have identified many other literary sources that appear to have contributed to the work – and more may remain to be found. Bronzino, poet and *artifice* was indebted to his fellow poets past and present; he anticipates Shakespeare, poet and playwright by half a century or so – Sonnet 129 could be a commentary on the painting, though Shakespeare never saw it and probably had never heard of it. The sonnet delivers much the same message as the *London Allegory*: lustful activity is irresistible, it may be fun in the short-term but we all know that it will bring pain, anguish and possibly disease, in the future. Time will be the final arbiter of human fortune: short-term hubris will always eventually be followed by nemesis.

The scholarly interpretations are often as concerned with identifying Bronzino's sources as they are with the meaning of the painting; each has merit, none can or should be ignored and each contributes to our appreciation of the painting and our understanding of it. But it is a mistake to try to assign a single meaning or purpose to the painting. It has several meanings, or if seen as a group of marks on a piece of wood, no meaning – Magritte: '*Ceci n'est pas une pipe*'. It is dream-like; in Freudian terms its deceitful surface (its 'manifest content') hides its truth (its 'latent thought') which we are trying to discover. Bronzino designed the *London Allegory* to convey multiple, multi-layered, interacting and cross-referring meanings, to be susceptible to several valid interpretations, to be elusive, to be a riddle. Some commentators do recognise this complexity and Cheney expresses it very well:

> [this]...is a painting about unveiling. The conception of allegorical personification here is synthetic, allusive, unstable rather than concrete, and static... Figures, even attributes, are continually shown to have new meanings as they are read in new configurations. And interpretations of the Allegory do not so much displace each other as convey a cumulative meaning... Its dense layering of overlapping meanings is certainly typical of major works produced in [Cosimo's] court during the 1540s... It is also possible to imagine why Cosimo may have finally felt uncomfortable with the painting and chose to use it as a diplomatic gift. Even when the erotic theme is presented in a partially negative light, it places the spectator in the position of voyeur.[27]

This is akin to Parker's analysis of Bronzino's poetry: the numerous interpretative viewpoints associated with the work contribute to a greater appreciation of its allusiveness – its 'evasive representation'. She finds Bronzino's poetry (and by extension his painting) to mix ordered elegance with disordered subversion. Bronzino intended the *London Allegory* to be more than a set of independent characters with no relationship one to another; he wanted it to be a coherent, albeit ambiguous, infuriatingly elusive work. He succeeded; it is allusive, multi-dimensional and expressed in the elusive visual language of late Renaissance Florence – making it very difficult to present a coherent, written exegesis. When we look at the *London Allegory* our thoughts meander from foreground to background, from Venus to C, then to the masks. We chase fugitive ideas about the Medicean *palle* and life in Medicean Florence and about how time and penicillin have changed our experience of syphilis. We draw comparisons between the personal and social impact of syphilis in sixteenth century Europe and the HIV-AIDS epidemic in the twentieth. As our attention elides from one aspect of the painting to another, rarely following the same path twice, we encounter ambiguities and polarities: Venus is both mother and lover; Cupid is bisexual; Time reveals but ends with oblivion; A and K may be male or female; C has good and bad features. Is the curtain being moved, and if it is in which direction, and by whom? If we decide that K is male, we then have a balance of sexes: three males, three females and A, who could be either – or both. And on the left we have characters of disputed gender (Cupid, A and K) and on the right those whose gender assignment is indisputable (Venus, Time, B and C). So the painting is also about identity and its loss – we are unsure about the identity of many of the figures; A may have lost the back of her head – her Self, perhaps; Venus and Cupid have taken the symbols of each other's identity; masks were intended to hide the wearer's identity. Blindness is another recurrent theme – the masks are blind; A and B are blind to pain; we are initially blind to C's duplicity; Venus and Cupid are blind to the consequences of their actions; the curtain hides something, we are blind to whatever lies behind it.

Rather than trying to capture such a stream-of-consciousness I'll present my ideas about the meanings of the painting in a series of falsely differentiated tranches, some of which are mutually contradictory – and were probably intended to be so. This does make some repetition unavoidable. And if the true source of our interest in the *London Allegory* lies in the process of deciphering and not in the final result, the confusion doesn't really matter. Most obvious but never to be forgotten, viewing the painting is a pleasurable experience – even being offended, like being frightened, can be pleasurable in the right circumstances. The *London Allegory* is a gorgeous explosion of beautiful colour and form – the marks do have meaning in themselves. Here is Fry's 'significant form' writ large. We can appreciate the painter's skilful arrangement of his marks on the scaffold which gives the forms coherence and stability, his masterful balance of light and shade, his choice and arrangement of colours and his preparation and application of his materials to create a work which has survived for almost five hundred years. This does matter: if a painting becomes only a riddle to intrigue its viewers it becomes 'not an immortal Muse but a Sphinx who dies as soon as her riddles are answered'; it will bore once the riddle has been solved.[28] This is not the case with Bronzino's painting – it is a delight now even though the riddle within it has yet to be solved and it will continue to delight even if all its secrets are revealed. We might even go so far as to say that it is 'Shakespearian' in its complexity, subtlety and psychological insight.

The *London Allegory* contains many references to Classical and Renaissance poetry and literature and to Renaissance painting – in particular to Florentine poetry and literature. Many of these references would have been recognised by those who saw the painting in the sixteenth century but they are inaccessible to most of us today. Our ignorance no doubt does detract from our understanding and enjoyment of the painting but scholars such as Gaston have done a lot to help us compensate for our ignorance. There is still plenty to be gained from a close look at the *London Allegory*, to which we bring perceptions and concepts which would have been incomprehensible to those who first saw it. Because we can't avoid bringing a twenty-first century eye to the picture it's not unreasonable to apply a twenty-first century mind and vocabulary to our interpretation of it: anachronisms far from being egregious mistakes, are reminders that we are enjoying the painting for ourselves, not as proxies for a French king who died some four hundred and seventy years ago.

The allusions to the painting's donor, presumed to be Cosimo de'Medici (*palle*, laurel leaves, possibly the scales of a tortoise), remind the French king whom he should thank for his wonderful painting. And to flatter Francis I, Bronzino, encouraged or instructed by Cosimo, has incorporated the salamander, Francis's personal emblem into character C. Yes, Francis I, it's unnecessarily complicated and at odds with every other opinion to assume that the painting went to Francis II; though we might worry about what Francis I would have thought about the incorporation of his emblem in the negative half of a deceitful character, just as we have to be concerned about his reaction to reminders about the cause and effects of syphilis.

The *London Allegory* is a representation of a voluptuous nude woman and a nude youth caressing each other, watched by a nude young *putto* (B). It plays to our scoptophilia, heterosexual and homosexual desires and fantasies (overt or covert, accepted or repressed) and to our feelings about incest, whatever they may be.[29] The forms are beautiful and if we enjoy looking at naked bodies of one or other gender, or both, (as most people do) we will enjoy looking at these and, perhaps, projecting ourselves into one role or another. We readily identify Venus and Cupid by their attributes and recognise that their encounter is overtly sexual – the pleasure we derive from looking at them is voyeuristic. And if we delight in assuming the roles of Venus or Cupid we can also share in B's joy and K's suffering. The attributes of Venus (apple, rose petals, doves and honeycomb) and of Cupid (quiver and arrow) are fundamental to understanding the painting – they signify their owner's personality or ego, which may be read as being given, withheld or violated depending upon which interpretation is being advocated.

B is joyful, he is showering Venus and Cupid with rose petals. This part of the scene is brightly lit, there are no shadows – he is telling us that the encounter between Venus and Cupid is rapturous, something which should delight us – sex is fun: 'Go for it!' Bronzino has used the Classical myth as an excuse for his very frank display of nudity; he did not need to be faithful to the details of any particular version of the stories about Venus and Cupid. So, we don't have to assume that Venus and Cupid are mother and son, maybe they are simply representations of romantic love. The trivial pain from the thorn in B's foot is rightly ignored, it represents the minor upsets that beset any relationship between two people; it doesn't devalue the relationship. Perhaps C is intended to convey a similar meaning: she is pretty and she offers a sweet honeycomb – both signifying the delights of a sexual relationship; her nether regions are less pleasant – reminding us of the pains that accompany any relationship of this sort.

If we were content with this comforting, romantic view we could say that Venus and Cupid represent a sexual relationship which is built on mutual understanding and love. We would read Venus's hold on Cupid's arrow and his grasp of Venus's diadem as metaphors for the mutual breakdown of ego boundaries that defines such a relationship. But this bland reading is unsustainable. It fails to account for most of the characters in the more obscure parts of the painting. They represent less pleasing emotions – fear of the predatory woman; fear of venereal disease; the difference between sex and love (there is no sign here of an emotional attachment between Venus and Cupid); recognition of the transitory nature of sexual gratification; acknowledgement of the role of deception in a relationship, particularly a sexual one. The naïve reading wilfully ignores the incestuous relationship which is central to most of the relevant stories and it is contradicted by Venus's retention of her apple, by Cupid's seizure of her diadem, by Cupid's bisexuality and by his stamping on Venus's doves. The style of the painting also runs counter to the bland reading of it as a representation of romantic love: this is hard-edged Mannerism, not a Rococo *Fête champêtre* by Fragonard; nor is it courtly love as might be found in a medieval Book of Hours.

Eschewing the superficial and optimistic reading, we have to acknowledge that there is a moralising tone to the painting – identified by scholars from Panofsky onwards: sexual encounters are great fun at the time but they are supposed to conform to society's norms, they entail responsibilities and they cause problems which Time will reveal. And this particular relationship does indeed offend society's norms even while it satiates deep cravings. Venus and Cupid may be mother and son, making their liaison incestuous, a violation of one of the most powerful of mankind's taboos. If we choose to ignore that element in their relationship (the foundation myths are contradictory about this after all) the *London Allegory* remains a representation of a lustful sexual encounter between a youth and a mature woman – plenty here to cause offence – and there's more to come. Cupid may be offering himself for a homosexual liaison, which would offend against one of Renaissance Italy's social mores. Recalling the convenience of a Classical story as an excuse for a *risqué* nude painting we should look on this possibly incestuous coupling as a surrogate for paraphilias, adultery and other transgressive behaviours that break important taboos and offend conventional morality. And we can add blasphemy to this impressive list of offences – Venus's pose is modelled on that of Christ's dead body in Michelangelo's *Pieta* and Time resembles both the Sistine God himself and Joseph in the *Doni Tondo*.[30] An incestuous relationship may also have reminded Francis and Cosimo of the tribulations of the Habsburg family, though the really bad effects of their interbreeding didn't become apparent for another couple of generations so the family's rivals may not have realised what was going on at the time the painting was created.

But, is the relationship incestuous? If we accept Ovid's or Apuleius's accounts, it is: Cupid has failed to break away from the all enveloping love for his mother that he enjoyed in his infancy – he has failed to differentiate himself from her – he envies and wants to kill his father, with whom he should be identifying. Conversely, his father is furiously jealous of the relationship between his partner and their child – all very Oedipal. There are clues to this in the *London Allegory* – Healy pointed out that Cupid's grasp of his mother's left nipple is like that of a mother offering her breast to her baby[31] – Cupid wants Venus to suckle him. And Time, who resembles a stern father (God the Father; Old Father Time) lies on a crucial diagonal line (Fig. 5) which passes from his face, through Venus's diadem, through the infamous kiss and on to K, who is male because he represents the Father's complex mixture of emotions – jealousy, anger, frustration and despair – triggered by his son's (Cupid/ Oedipus) bond with Venus and his patricidal urges. It is striking how many important features are captured by this diagonal. Not only the mouths of Time, Cupid, Venus and K – their ability to articulate, express themselves and use language but also the eyes of Time and of Venus: they can see what's going on, they are in control. And, confirming the significance of the line, proving that it is not coincidental, is its definition of the boundary between two tones in the colour of the curtain – darker (in shadow) above the line, lighter below it.

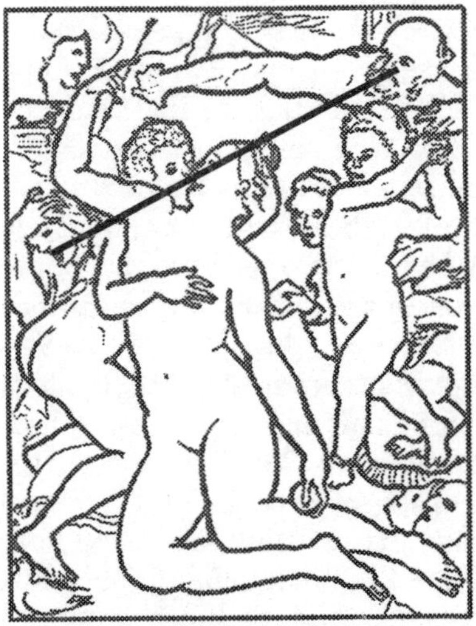

Figure 5

The *London Allegory*: key diagonal defining the upper and lower portions of the painting.

Venus's and Cupid's feelings for each other are not unreserved, each holds something back and each may reject the other in favour of a rival – Venus withholds her apple and despite the precedents it doesn't look as though our Venus is in any danger of a self-inflicted arrow wound; Cupid is bi-sexual – he may take other lovers in addition to Venus. By extension, loving relationships between two humans are also unlikely to be unreserved; each party will hold something back. Sartre reminded us that we want the person we love to give themself to us freely – but that if we have been freely chosen we might as readily be rejected in favour of another. Such inconstancy and the incestuous, lascivious and homosexual acts alluded to in the *London Allegory* would have been particularly offensive to Cosimo, who was trying to improve public morality in Florence.

C carries a vicious barb in her hand (D) and the whole of her nether region is open to various interpretations (sphinx, lamia and so on) all of which can be taken to signify hidden danger, predation and envenomation. Quite what danger she is intended to signify is open to speculation. Is she telling us that the illicit relationship between Venus and Cupid will cause them to be ostracised? Is she warning about the risk of venereal disease? Is she a representation of the deceitfulness of woman – seductive but devouring of her prey? She is all of these things – and through being all of them she personifies the male's deepest fears – fears which lust, infatuation or romantic love cause him to ignore.

Does K represent syphilis? His features bear only a passing similarity to those of syphilis, and wouldn't Francis I have been deeply upset and offended by a painting that confronted him with a graphic illustration of the ghastly disease and its treatment that many would have said was a just punishment for his sins?[32] And if the king himself was not immediately offended, wouldn't there be plenty of malicious courtiers ready to tell him that he should be angered by Cosimo's double-edged and far from 'diplomatic' gift? Some of them might even incite the king to interpret the painting as evidence that Cosimo was delighted to learn of his affliction? Certainly, K and much of the rest of the *London Allegory* could represent syphilis but it is more likely that K is meant to drop veiled, deniable hints about the treatment of the disease and thereby about syphilis itself. If syphilis or the side-effects of mercury are represented in the painting they are included in order to point up the dangers of unwary sexual encounters and to amplify C's message about the duplicity of women – the painting is not intended only to be a representation of the disease nor is the disease meant to take centre stage in it: this is not a health education poster. In fact the suggestion that this is an educational work at all – the ideas for example that C is intended to be an ominous warning to Cupid of the 'double aspect of pleasure' or that it contains 'admonitions . . . directed at the king'[33]– are facile. No one in Cosimo's sophisticated circle, let alone Francis I, was unaware of the physical and psychological perils attendant on transgressive sexual relationships – they didn't need to be told about them by Bronzino. I believe that C and the other figures and details tucked away in the shadows of the *London Allegory* are personifications of the thoughts and fears that Venus and Cupid repress as, out of control, they satiate their lust for each other. All that matters to them is their desire: passion makes them oblivious to the world and to their responsibilities; the sense of danger is an important component of the erotic thrill they are experiencing.[34]

Pursuing these ideas we can explore this relationship between Venus and Cupid. There is no doubt that it is sexual – Cupid's hands and Venus's tongue make that clear enough. But even if we allow for the conventions of the Mannerist style, the affectless facial expressions (compare them with B's expression) of both Venus and Cupid tell us that we are not looking at a mature physical and psychological relationship. This is lust or infatuation – engaging their bodies but not their minds. Venus doesn't offer her apple to her lover: she is reluctant to engage psychologically with him. If the idea that the relationship of Venus and Cupid is one of lust is valid, we can say that through their thefts of the arrow and the diadem each has neutralised the other's ability to control their actions.

Now the division of the *London Allegory* into two parts becomes very significant. Our line (Fig. 5) represents the boundary between the conscious and the unconscious – Bronzino might have said it was the boundary between thought and instinct. Above the line lies the realm of the unconscious; it provides a solution to the riddle of the painting – we shall return to it. Below the line the behaviour of Venus and Cupid is ego-centric. To understand what Bronzino is telling us we have to pay close attention to the details and to peer into the shadows, most of which lie at the sides of the painting – a visual allusion to the psychological process of 'side-lining', repressing or wilfully ignoring disconcerting facts. Unlike Venus and Cupid we are able to peer into the shadows; we can take perverse pleasure from our recognition of the unwelcome facts hidden there: they ignore them. And while getting really close to the painting in order studiously to examine details like the honeycomb or the verbena flowers, we may be covertly relishing the finer points of Bronzino's portrayal of Venus's erect nipple or B's penis – justifying this to ourselves and to any censorious observer of our behaviour as a dispassionate exercise in Art Appreciation. Our enjoyment of the painting is increased by the knowledge that it will meet with some disapproval on the grounds that it is obscene – pleasure is enhanced if it is transgressive. The details buried in the shadows at the sides of the painting are portentous – they contradict our first impressions of this as a carefree, joyful painting that celebrates the pleasures of a sexual dalliance. Bronzino forces the viewer to get very close to the painting in order to see even the attractive details, mimicking of the experience of lovers, particularly those consumed by lust, who lose perspective as they become more and more closely engaged with each other. They see only the engaging persona of their partner, not the whole personality; unable to see the whole picture they cannot appreciate the dangers to which they are exposing themselves.

C appears at first to be human – but she has deceived us, she is only partially so, at least in her physical form – psychologically things may be rather different. What's more, her hidden part is mysterious, we can't understand it but it is definitely dangerous. She is the personification of Deceit. Her beauty, luxurious, colourful clothing and sweet gift distract attention from her bestial underbelly, she is the Terrible Mother, the *femme fatale*, an elaborate representation of the dreaded *vagina dentata*.[35] She is a seductress but she is also a sphinx, lamia, snake, lion, scorpion, salamander – all of these and none of these: exactly as in *Nineteen Eighty-four* when Winston Smith had to confront his own most feared 'Worst thing in the world' in Room 101, so she is whatever our worst fears drive us to make of her. Bronzino made her up as he went along, cobbling together bits and pieces from several sources with the intention of creating a unique figure to intrigue, challenge and entertain, hoping that one part or another would resonate with everyone who saw her and evoke deep emotions within each of them. He would be delighted to know that regiments of scholars and enthusiasts are still trawling through arcane literature and the by-ways of art history in their efforts to identify the sources that informed his creation – that's exactly what he hoped Cosimo, Francis and their circle would do. No doubt many of these scholars have been correct, at least in part; his sources were not chosen at random.

Where did Bronzino get his ideas from? He probably did intend C to display some features reminiscent of, for example, a sphinx. But he did not intend her be to a sphinx and nothing but a sphinx. He wanted her to trigger thoughts about scorpions, about lots of mythological beasts, about Classical and contemporary poetry and about a pretty girl who offers something sweet, each with its mixed positive and negative connotations. What he may not have realised, and what he certainly could not articulate, was the psychological significance of the figure that he had created. Bronzino has revealed Venus's Shadow; her persona as a charming, loving, nurturing woman has been cast aside – her mask lies discarded at her feet – leaving her seductive, vicious Shadow there for all to see: a reminder to her (male) audience that woman is deceitful – she presents herself as attractive but like all of us she has a hidden less attractive side to her personality.[36]

She is an extreme manifestation of the insecure male's fears about the predatory female who offers sweet delights while underneath being vengeful, poisonous, an enigma intent on controlling his personality and emasculating him. She is looking directly at the viewer, commanding his attention. She is directing her warning at the viewer at least as much as to Venus and Cupid. Where do these fears come from and what drove Bronzino to paint such a disconcerting figure? Apparently he was influenced by the misogynistic poetry of Biondo and others, but why was such stuff written and why was Bronzino drawn to it? In part, no doubt, female promiscuity was feared and demonised because it threatened the family and the established social order. An adulterous wife undermined the public credit of her husband and challenged the legitimacy of his progeny, property and legacy. Several popular beliefs developed about the sexuality of women and were incorporated in the prevailing episteme because they served to instil a dread of female promiscuity, helping thereby to maintain social stability. Biondo and others expressed some of these beliefs – albeit in an extreme way. So, female sexuality was associated with filth and disease; women were looked upon as inherently polluting; menstruation was thought to be a form of excretion; sex with a menstruating woman was thought either to cause leprosy in the man or to produce a child with birth defects; promiscuous women were believed to spread disease despite the fact that at the time there was no germ theory of disease on which to base this belief.[37]

C is also a compelling depiction of one of the most important archetypes which, according to Jung, are components of a person's psyche. C is an *anima* the archetype which shapes a man's response to women and his relationship to feminine values 'An inherited collective image of woman exists in a man's unconscious with the help of which he apprehends the nature of woman'.[38] Although archetypal and heavily dependent on elements of the collective unconscious, a man's *anima* is powerfully influenced by the introjection of his experience of the first woman he encounters – his mother. Some men never succeed in freeing themselves from their overpowering identification with this figure, or at least from their idea of this figure. The *anima* is always two-sided: light where the Self dominates – pure, good, a goddess, Cinderella; dark, where the ego has usurped the archetype – prostitute, seductress, witch, Gorgon. C represents Cupid's idea of womanhood, she is his *anima* – but Bronzino has also, unknowingly, given us an insight into the nature of his own *anima* and probably also that of the poets to whose work he looked for inspiration. Cupid (Bronzino) is projecting his *anima* onto Venus, and it is not a pretty sight. In his heart he knows that she is deceitful, that she will cause him pain. But she is irresistible: she is his mother, either in reality or in his *anima* – it matters not which. More discomforting: who is C looking at? She is looking at you or at me – the (male) viewers of the painting. She represents my *anima* – and yours. We must come to terms with her if we are to achieve complete individuation. I hope Bronzino has got the balance of light and dark wrong here – but he has certainly given us pause for thought.

The key to the *London Allegory*, if single key there be, lies above the line in Figure 5, along the painting's enigmatic upper border – in the realm of the unconscious, the repository of the archetypes and of the Law of the Father. Here we encounter A and Time, who rule over the action taking place below them; they control the curtain which, together with the laurel hedge, isolates them from the action and from us. Behind them lies – who knows what?

Bronzino made A carry several layers of meaning, which explains why it is so contentious. Most likely A is real but let's acknowledge that the dispute between those who think it is real and those who think it is a mask with the back of its head missing is irresolvable. There is no agreement about what sex A is – this is not an accident: A is both male and female. It represents the ambivalence of both Venus and Cupid, who are struggling ineffectually to resist their mutual attraction despite being fully aware both of its physical dangers and of the fact that by consummating their passion they are breaking the Father's laws. They know the risks – B, C and K personify them; they know that sex is fun but that it carries a sting in its tail; Cupid knows that women can be deceitful; Venus knows that men can be unfaithful; they both know that they are likely to be ostracised by their peers; they know that they are likely to despair, to be wracked by jealousy and that disease may rot the bodies which promise them such transports of delight. But, 'No! Let's have fun while we can. If that means breaking some rules – so much the more exciting! After all, we may never be found out; we may escape the Law of the Father; the worst may never happen and our world is full of more immediate perils – war, famine or plague might carry us off tomorrow, so let's enjoy ourselves while we can.' So, as Cheney suggested, this is a *Psychomachia* – a representation of the ambivalence that accompanies an internal conflict between forces for good and for evil.

Bronzino, like the rest of us, will have experienced such ambivalence for himself and, Italian translations of the Bible having been available since 1471, he will most likely have known St Paul's description of such internal turmoil and of the anguish it causes:

> . . .except through the law I should never have become acquainted with sin. For example, I should never have known what it was to covet, if the law had not said, 'Thou shalt not covet'. In the

> absence of law, sin is a dead thing. . . sin found its opportunity in the commandment, seduced me, and through the commandment killed me.
>
> . . .what I do is not what I want to do, but what I detest. But if what I do is against my will, it means that I agree with the law and hold it to be admirable. But as things are, it is no longer I who perform the action, but sin that lodges in me. . . nothing good lodges in me. . . though the will to do good is there, the deed is not. . . when I want to do the right, only the wrong is within my reach. In my inmost self I delight in the law of God, but I perceive that there is in my bodily members a different law, fighting against the law that my reason approves and making me a prisoner under the law that is in my members, the law of sin. Romans 7, vv.7-24[39]

Human nature has not changed in the last 450 years – despite knowing the risks that we are running we are still sexually adventurous, we smoke, we drink and drive, we allow ourselves to become morbidly obese. We are conflicted about our behaviour, as is A, but the drives to instant gratification often prove irresistible, as they do for Venus and Cupid. And breaking the law adds to the excitement – in fact, as St Paul recognised, the law creates the desire to violate it: 'I should never have known what it was to covet, if the law had not said, 'Thou shalt not covet', or 'Even when my desires are transgressive, even when they violate social norms, this very transgression relies on what it transgresses.'[40]

The void at the back of A's head does not signify the lack of a brain – quite the opposite – it is Bronzino's solution to the problem of representing that very important part of the mind which is inaccessible to consciousness ('invisible') but extraordinarily potent in the scenario he was trying to depict. A is the unconscious, the Psyche, the Self, the site of the psychological conflict experienced by Venus and Cupid each of whom, knowing the dangers that their liaison exposes them to, is powerless to resist the lure of sex. Similarly, being unable to articulate its 'thoughts' and not dependent on the faculties of hearing or sight to know and understand what's going on, A is powerless directly to intervene to prevent the inevitable disaster. A may also be 'lack', that inner sense of loss that is initiated when the infant's own separate identity is established following its break with its mother.[40]

K straddles the line, he is in both worlds and able to express the anguish that accompanies Venus's and Cupid's internal conflict – do they respond to the Siren's call or tie themselves to the mast until she is out of earshot? Time knows that the consequences of the scene being played out before our eyes will be revealed eventually – 'in the fullness of time'.

Bronzino has portrayed the patriarchal figure of Time as god-like (Sistine Chapel) and powerful. His intense gaze shows him to be in full command of his faculties; he disapproves of what's going on and is determined to prevail in the end. He is the great moralising force: Authority, the Law-giver, tradition, the super-ego, the Keeper of Language, the Father. He is the guardian of the virtues connoted by the laurel. Not only will all be revealed by Time either now or in the future, it will also be judged by him. It is he who ruptures an infant's bond with its mother to constitute its separate identity – its sense of the other – and institutes its sense of loss, its continuous inner sense of lack. He is the rival whom the individuating infant wants to kill so that it can remain attached to its mother. As super-ego he protects the ego from the id's instinctual urges, in this instance the pleasure principle. In Bronzino's painting Cupid is breaking all the rules; his relationship with Venus is deeply offensive to Time, the personification of moral values – it both breaks his law and activates the Oedipus complex, frustrating Time's plans, throwing the world-order out of kilter. No wonder Time looks cross.

There are two possible positions for the curtain and two characters who are trying to control it – four permutations: both want it up, both want it down, one wants it up and the other down, and *vice versa*. Bronzino has made it impossible for us to decide which of these permutations he intended, leaving it up to us to find explanations to account for or exclude them. As we try to do this we discover that Bronzino has confronted us with a metaphor for the ambivalence experienced by Venus and Cupid.

To pull back the curtain would be to make the unconscious accessible to consciousness; it would reconcile the Self with the ego, fully individuating the person. A wants this to happen now, to resolve the conflict in favour of morality, prudence, the Law. Time may also be trying to pull the curtain back – he wants to bring the risks of the relationship between Venus and Cupid to consciousness now, hoping thereby to end the encounter and restore the rule of law, represented by the laurel hedge which will be fully exposed when the curtain is pulled down. Or perhaps not, we too are allowed to be ambivalent. A is trying to keep the curtain in place – it doesn't want the enjoyable encounter curtailed (different etymology but an entertaining congruence in this context) by the internal censor nor by the authority of the Father. This is the other side of the ambivalence – the side that wants the instant gratification and accepts the deferred risks.

Another plausible interpretation takes account of the fact that individuation – the reconciliation of the Self and the ego – is a prolonged process, often not achieved until middle-age. Time knows that the young lovers must be allowed to run their risks, to take their chances and to learn by experience. Being stronger than A, Time will prevail. Eventually he will pull the curtain back to reveal the nobility and rejuvenative potential of the laurel hedge along with the profound knowledge and understanding that lie in the depths behind it. In the short-term, however, Time is keeping the curtain in place, he is blocking A's attempts to rush the process. In his role as law-enforcer he demands that moral hazard be fully worked through.

Time's hourglass will run out eventually and the consequences of Venus's and Cupid's actions will be revealed. The aging K, on the straight line linking him to Time and the kiss, is anguished in the full consciousness of his past actions, which he now regrets, jealous of the young lovers who are enjoying pleasures now denied to him, and tormented by his foreknowledge of the pain to which those selfsame pleasures have condemned them. He represents decay, the end result of a lifetime of hard work and hard play, with a dash of despair: a *Picture of Dorian Grey*. The figure is reminiscent of Francis Bacon's paintings of popes screaming (*Studies after Velazquez's Portrait of Pope Innocent X*). Is he similarly expressing existential agony and desolation at the state of the world, at the seemingly endless round of wars, disease and famine and at the threats to the Church, as well as at the consequences of the scene being played out before him? Remorseful at the end of life he realises that he has left undone those things which he ought to have done and has done those things which he ought not to have done. He regrets missed opportunities, lost loves, rash carnal adventures, foolish exploits, time wasted. He knows that his current lamentable situation is a consequence of his past lack of self-control:

> Lack of Self-control
> Seeing glitt'ring visions in succession rise,
> He laughs at Socrates the chaste and wise.
> Till, sobered by distress, awake, confused,
> Amazed, he knows himself a wretch abused.
>
> *The Theban Tablet of Cebes*[41]

A surrogate for the viewer, for whom he is suffering, K personifies the havoc that Time will eventually wreak. Time tells us 'this is what I have in store for you; your sins will find you out'.

Bronzino has managed to use symbols and characters to give objective form to our subjective inner conflicts and compulsions although he lacked an articulated belief in the unconscious as we understand it – the mixed Freudian and Jungian jargon used above would have mystified him. He would have seen himself and his viewers as humans endowed with reason and with the ability to resist animal lusts. Recalling St Paul's 'it is no longer I who perform the action, but sin that lodges in me' he would have interpreted failure to resist as a descent into madness, the result of humanity having been overwhelmed either by animal passion or by divine madness. Had Bronzino been able to read Kant he would have come to believe that the drive to transgress is immanent, that it lies at the core of our subjectivity and that madness comes from within. Jung taught that we project on to others those parts of our personality that drive us to transgress, and which we deny; our interpretations of Venus and Cupid are therefore projections of aspects of ourselves. Freud disagreed – rather than being a projection of ourselves he said that we view others as impenetrable. He talked about *das Ding* (the Thing) – the ultimate object of our desires in its unbearable intensity and impenetrability. Pursuing these insights returns us to the back of A's head, which isn't missing, it's hidden: an impenetrable void. We just can't make out what's going on in there – and the effort of trying to is frustrating in itself. In fact, the ambiguities and contradictions throughout the painting (and consequently throughout this book) evoke emotions – frustration, annoyance, bewilderment, even despair – that are themselves part of its meaning. We can't read A's mind – its personality is inaccessible. Bronzino has found a way brilliantly to represent the unknowability of the other – the 'abyssal dimension of another human being – the abyss of the depth of another personality, the abyss of the radical otherness of one about whom I finally know nothing'.[40]

Bronzino couldn't have known what he was doing – could he? Classical mythology provided many informative precedents for him (and for both Freud and Jung as they developed their ideas 350 years later). Bronzino was familiar with many of the Classical myths and with the inspiration that Renaissance poets and writers derived from them. If he was also familiar with some of the tenets of Judaism, he would have been aware of the tradition which saw the neighbour as an inert, impenetrable, enigmatic presence and which invoked divine Law to regulate interpersonal relationships, to keep the neighbour at a safe distance. A is telling us, and Venus and Cupid, who are the 'real' as opposed to allegorical, figures in the *London Allegory*, that although we relate to other persons as though we understand them, deep down we are aware that they are not just a mystery to us but an unsolvable mystery. Our relation to them is unavoidably mediated by that knowledge, made socially acceptable by adherence to the Law. Venus and Cupid give us a glimpse of life dominated by an unconstrained super-ego, the rule of the Law has been temporarily suspended, though were the Law not to exist in the background to be transgressed their pleasure would be much reduced.

The whole image is a detached, non-judgemental unmasking of desire, the motive force of human activity and the root cause of anxiety – now every bit as much as in the sixteenth century. The desire is for sex in whatever guise, money, power, love, celebrity – whatever. The *London Allegory* is an image of us, our motivations and the perils they bring with them. 'It is an anxious mirror in which viewers must try desperately not [sic] to see themselves'.[42]

Before closing this exegesis we must return to Time, because we and others have failed to consider one of the vital roles traditionally assigned to him. He is Death[43] whom both Freud and Klein identified as Thanatos (the death instinct, aggression) which counters Eros [Cupid] (the life instinct, preservation of the species), the sustaining and uniting principle of life. Time's hourglass measures the passing of a life; after him comes oblivion, perhaps A is Oblivion after all. Freud linked desire and the death wish, saying that Death stalks transgressive passion – and the French do call orgasm *le petit mort*, acknowledging the collapse of psychical, and sometimes societal and legal boundaries that accompany it. In the *London Allegory* Time/Death is telling us about the futility of our passions, the transience of the pleasures and pains that they cause us. He reminds us of the brevity of our life on earth compared with the endless rapture or torment which will follow it. In due course – and it could be tomorrow – Death will lower the curtain, justice will be done, the void behind the curtain will be revealed, the characters in the painting, and we ourselves, will tumble into it, our mundane loves, hates, triumphs and disasters will be as naught.

Given free rein to ruminate about the *London Allegory* it is all too easy to go up a blind alley or two. What is the sting (D) intended to represent – a scorpion's sting, the venomous fangs of a serpent, perhaps? Or is it just intended to be frightening? Both the Medici and the Valois took a more than casual interest in astrology and in alchemy. Maybe the painting would have flattered Cosimo and Francis by incorporating references to both subjects? The alchemist's *albedo* state was immediately preceded by the vivid colours of the Peacock's Tail which would overcome the blackness of the first state (Saturn) – Glover described the colours in the *London Allegory* as 'peacockish'. Are there any other alchemical allusions in the painting? Yes, there are tenuous links to alchemy – in Paracelsus's work the salamander represented the element fire; Venus and doves were associated with the *albedo* stage and many of the ambiguous components of C could find a place in alchemical lore. However, none of these possible references to alchemy is convincing. Similarly, Cohen builds an entire analysis of the painting on the astrological allusions that she is able to find in it, but it's all a bit insubstantial, particularly as much of her argument needs the painting also to refer to syphilis. H, the object now at the lower edge of the painting, bears a tantalising but probably spurious resemblance to Pontormo's mountain; more likely it is simply a remnant of the gold border on the curtain.

Having disposed of a couple of possible red-herrings let me recapitulate my ideas about the core meaning of the *London Allegory*. The key to the painting lies, I believe, in its division by the line shown in Figure 5. Below the line we are in the conscious world. Venus and Cupid know several things: they know that sex is fun, an overwhelmingly powerful emotion; they know too that society disapproves of several types of sexual encounter: incest, homosexuality, adultery to name but a few, and that society can punish offenders severely; they know that sexual encounters can cause pain as well as pleasure – jealousy, insecurity, remorse and sometimes disease. They also know that sexual partners can be promiscuous, deceitful and vengeful. Obviously, Venus and Cupid are conflicted: they are being tempted to indulge in a sexual adventure which they know to be dangerous and, in many ways, against their best interest. Above the line, we are in the world of the unconscious, where our protagonists attempt to resolve the conflict which confronts them. By definition, the unconscious processes are invisible to us as they are to them – hence the impenetrable space behind A's face. The unconscious working-out of their dilemma takes place in the context of their personal history and of rules (norms, mores, laws, religious injunctions) represented in the painting by the laurel hedge and space behind the curtain and personified by Time (the Father), who will determine the ultimate fate of the protagonists, whatever decision they make about their behaviour in the short-term. And the decision 'to sin or not to sin' is not an easy one to make, particularly when sexual gratification is on offer. A's face shows us just how difficult it is. So, to generalise: the painting is about choices and how we make them – Venus and Cupid are ourselves, their sexual encounter represents in a particularly vivid way any of the moral dilemmas or temptations which confront us, and the characters 'above the line' remind us of how opaque many of our decision-making processes are. Needless to say Bronzino doesn't tell us how Venus and Cupid should resolve their dilemma – though it does look as though they have gone too far to turn back now.

Many of these conclusions about the *London Allegory* are rather negative – as are those of most commentators – loss of ego boundaries, ambivalence, *vagina dentata*, disease, death and so on. It is about exciting but damaging behaviour and why we are unable to resist it. But remember that Rodin told us that immorality cannot exist in art; and Camille Paglia believes that 'Art has nothing to do with morality. Moral themes may be present, but they are incidental'.[44] Is the *London Allegory* really a miserable, po-faced moralising work – the last thing that Francis needed: he knew perfectly well that he was leading a life filled with risks?

Step back; resist for the moment the urge to dissect the painting's delightful complexity in minute and fanciful detail. Now it becomes obvious that Bronzino has maintained a studious neutrality in his presentation of the moral issues; he does not tell Venus and Cupid how they should resolve the ambivalence that torments them. Instead, after giving us acres of beautifully crafted but intrinsically boring portraits Bronzino has let his hair down. He wants us to smile at the trials and tribulations of love; to laugh at the self-indulgent, over-the-top emotion displayed by B and by K; to chuckle over the absurd polymorphism of C; to relish the eroticism he has thrust in front of our eyes. He wants us to be infuriated by the many possible, often mutually contradictory, meanings we can assign to his masterpiece and to join in spirited arguments about it. The *London Allegory* was the aristocrat's equivalent to the plebeian pageant or festival; they loved complicated works of art, replete with double meanings[45] – it was their equivalent to the modern 'QI programme' or to a Sudoku or crossword puzzle. And just as one of Shakespeare's tragedies is as entertaining and psychologically penetrating as one of his comedies, so the fact that the *London Allegory* treats moral dilemmas does not make it a depressing work. It was a gift meant to enthral the king of France and all those with whom he chose to share it, discuss it and try to decipher it; we are extraordinarily lucky that it is still here to delight us. Barolsky and Ladis are almost alone in their emphasis on the playful nature of the painting and in their dislike of the intense academic interest in it, which has 'devolved into a joyless academic parlor game. . . inappropriately foreign' to its playful irony.[46] They see the painting in the context of Renaissance burlesque: teasing, ironic, deceptive, full of ambiguities and double meanings which defy definitive interpretation, 'highly contrived – *artificioso*. . . [it is] exquisitely self-conscious and playful. . . ludicrous transformations of allegory into farce'.

Barolsky and Ladis are right. Let's look at the *putto* for the last time – he is so prominent in the painting and his smile so knowing that he must, surely, be intended to convey a significant message? I think that Bronzino – author of scurrilous, burlesque poems and painter of risqué, allegorical portraits – is using the *putto* to tell us that his *London Allegory*, and life itself, is a bagatelle, a riddle and not to be taken too seriously. After all: 'All flesh is as grass. . . '

The *London Allegory* is a masterful demonstration of Bronzino's skill as a painter – beautifully proportioned, lusciously coloured, impeccably composed, brilliantly executed: a feast for the eyes as well as for the mind. It is knowingly ironic, tongue-in-cheek, glorious, escapist fun: an entertaining distraction from the horrors and vicissitudes of day-to-day life in the middle of the sixteenth century. That is an appropriate note on which to end our attempt to solve the riddle Bronzino set for us in his painting. Many others have made the attempt and no doubt many will follow; some will be content with solutions which would have made sense in the sixteenth century, others, myself included, will try to find solutions which will resonate with twenty-first century viewers. Now, however, it's over to you to find a solution – or more realistically a set of solutions – which satisfy you and which may also convince others. Whatever that solution is, you – and I – will always be left wondering what Bronzino would have made of our ideas.

I beseech you, in the bowels of Christ,
think it possible that you may be mistaken.
(Oliver Cromwell [1599-1668] Letter to the General Assembly
of the Church of Scotland, 3 August 1650.)

Time Line

1493	Columbus's sailors return from the Americas.
1494	Pisa rebels and secedes from Florence.
	Piero de'Medici and Cardinal Giovanni exiled.
	Republican regime in Florence until 1512.
	Birth of Pontormo.
1495	Charles VIII's troops in Naples.
1498	Villalobos *Sumario de la medicina en romance trovado con un tratado sobre las pestiferas Bubas por el lecenciado Francisco Lopez de Villalobos.*
1503	Julius II (della Rovere) elected Pope.
	Leonardo da Vinci *Mona Lisa.*
	Birth of Bronzino.
1504	Michelangelo *David.*
1506	Julius II retakes Perugia and Bologna.
1508	Michelangelo begins painting the ceiling of the Sistine Chapel.
	League of Cambrai.
1510	Martin Luther visits Rome.
1511	Birth of Vasari.
1512	End of the republican period in Florence.
	Giovanni di Lorenzo de'Medici takes power in Florence.
	5th Lateran Council.
	Parma and Piacenza become papal cities.
	Pope beaten by the French at River Ronco.
1513	Lorenzo rules in Florence (to 1519).
	Pope Julius II dies.
	Giovanni de'Medici elected Pope Leo X.
	Machiavelli *The Prince.*
	Balboa discovers the Pacific Ocean.
1514	Copernicus *Commentariolus* postulates heliocentricity.
1515	Francis I crowned King of France; takes Milan.
1516	Giuliano de'Medici dies.
	Concordat between Francis I and Leo X.
1517	Luther 95 *Theses.*
1518	Pontormo *Joseph in Egypt.*

1519	Giulio di Giuliano de'Medici rules in Florence (to 1523). Birth of Cosimo de'Medici. Charles V (Habsberg) elected Holy Roman Emperor. French expelled from Milan. Ulrich von Hutten *De guaiaci medicina et morbo gallico.* Herán Cortéz lands in Vera Cruz.
1520	Luther excommunicated.
1521	Pope Leo X dies. Ottoman forces take Belgrade. Cortéz defeats the Aztecs. Fracastoro *Syphilis.* Ferdinando Ponzetti *Handbook of poisons.*
1522	Adriaan Floriszoon Boeyens elected Pope Adrian VI. Magellan circumnavigates the globe – 18 survivors reach Lisbon.
1523	Ippollito and Alessandro de'Medici rule Florence (to 1527). Pope Adrian VI dies. Giulio de'Medici elected Pope Clement VII. Clement VII attends lectures in Rome on *Commentariolus.* Holbein *Erasmus.*
1524-25	Peasants' War in central Europe.
1525	Battle of Pavia. Francis I hostage in Madrid.
1526	Fall of Buda, Battle of Mohács. Durer *Four apostles.*
1527	Republican regime restored in Florence (to 1530). Sack of Rome.
1530	Medici rule re-established in Florence by Pope and Emperor. Alessandro rules Florence. Treaty of Bologna (Clement VII and Charles V) partitions Italy.
c.1532	Correggio *Danae.*
1533	Francisco Pizarro sacks Cuzco – end of the Inca.
1534	Henry VIII Head of the Church in England. Pope Clement VII dies. *L'affaire des placards* in France.
1535	Defeat of Anabaptists at Münster.
1537	Alessandro de'Medici murdered by his cousin Lorenzino. Cosimo de'Medici rules Florence, created Duke of Tuscany. Informal alliance between French and Ottomans for projected invasion of Italy.

1538	Truce between France and the Holy Roman Empire.
1541	Colloquy of Regensburg between Melanchton, Eck *et al.*
1543	Copernicus *De revolutionibus orbium caelestium.* Versalius *De humani corporis fabrica.* Titian *Pope Paul III.*
1545	Council of Trent begins (ends 1563). The Mary Rose sinks in Portsmouth harbour.
1545-50	**Bronzino paints The *London Allegory.***
1547	Death of Francis I, King of France, succeeded by his son Henri II.
1548	Italian translation of Thomas More's *Utopia* (*Eutopia*).
1549	Prayer Book Rebellion in England.
1550	Vasari *Lives of the Most Excellent Architects, Painters and Sculptors* (1st Edition).
1551	Siege of Magdeburg.
1552	French assault Holy Roman Empire in Italy, Germany and Netherlands.
1556	Charles V abdicates Spanish throne in favour of his son Felipe.
1557	Death of Pontormo.
1558	Elizabeth I becomes Queen of England. France renounces its claims in Italy. Death of Charles V, remains of the Empire pass to his brother Ferdinand.
1559	Henri II dies, Francis II becomes King of France.
1560	Francis II dies.
1563	Church of England established.
1565	Tintoretto *Crucifixion.* Bruegel *Harvesters.*
1566	Unrest in Spanish Netherlands.
1568	Vasari *Lives of the Most Excellent Architects, Painters and Sculptors* (2nd Edition).
1571	Battle of Lepanto.
1572	St Bartholomew's Day massacre of Protestants in Paris.
1572	**Death of Bronzino.**
1574	Death of Grand Duke Cosimo I.

Notes

Introduction

Background: Bell; Benjamin; Berger; Gould; Kandel; Langmuir; Panofsky; Vasari

Citations

1 Anon.(a)
2. Anon. (b)
3. Wind p. 15
4. Langmuir pp. 106-7.
5. Hartley
6. Mantel
7. Morris
8. Foucault p.18
9. Fox
10. Langmuir pp.123-4
North
11. Savage
12. Gould, C, p.41-4.
13. Sallay, Tátrai & Vécsey
14. Anderson, p.22
15. Monk
16. Eaude
17. Eiland
18. Benjamin.
19. Benjamin p.3
20. Seward p. 207
21. Frankel
22. Cecil & Cecil
23. Anon (c)
24. Anon (d)
25. Biernoff
26. Haycock
27. Barker
28. Anon. (e)
29. Anon.(f)
30. Kandel p. 393

I. Bronzino's Life and Times

Background: Brock; Burckhardt; Cohen & Cohen; Cole; Cronin; Davies; Dickens; Greengrass; Hibbert; MacCulloch (2004); Martinelli; Moffat; Norwich (2011 and 2016); Richard; Strathern; Wheatcroft; Wilson; Winder (2010 & 2013); Williams; Vasari

Citations

1. Jones, Chapter 11
2. Vasari, Vol. 7, pp.167-71;
Vol.10, pp.3 ff.
Cronin, p.126-9
3. Pilliod
4. Gould C, p.41
5. Ruskin (a), p.99
6. Brock, p.14
7. Anon.(g)
8. Vasari, Vol 7 p.164; Vol10, p.4
9. Falletti & Scudieri, pp. 74-90
10. Burckhardt, pp.279 ff.
Cole, pp. 19-21
Cohen & Cohen, Chap. 4
Martinelli, pp. 91-2
11. Siena, p.567
12. Pilliod, p.94
13. Anon (h)
14. Greengrass, p.152
15. Shiner, p.40
Cole, p.28
16. Cole, pp. 32-3

17. Norwich (2016), p.3
18. Moffat
Strathern
Cronin
Hibbert
19. Martinelli, pp.214-23
Strathern
20. Kohn
21. Morrison, Kirshner & Molho
22. Strathern, p.266
Cronin, p. 56
23. Greenblatt
24. Stanford, p.160
25. MacCulloch (2004), p. 214
MacCulloch (2010), pp. 664-5
26. MacCulloch (2016), Chapter 6
27. Strathern, p.293
28. Rabin
Copernicus
29. Greengrass, pp. 56, 98
30. Anon.(i)
31. Martin
Morrison, Kirshner & Molho
Youngs
32. McManus, Carrieri & Serraino
33. MacCulloch (2004), p.94 & Chap.13
34. MacCulloch (2016), pp.6, 16
35. Stanford, pp.138-9
36. MacCulloch (2004), pp.76-105
37. Hibbert, p.153
Oriel, p.11
38. Richard
Greengrass, pp.272-7
39. Cronin, pp.32-55
40. Hibbert, p.165
41. Strathern, p.261
42. Strathern, p.262
43. Hibbert, p.169
Cronin, p.57
44. Strathern, pp 244, 267-8,
45. Cronin, p.57
46. Cronin, p.58
Seward, pp. 63, 73
47. Strathern, p. 243
48. Cohen & Cohen, Chap. 3
49. Greengrass, pp.288, 403-4
Seward, pp. 180-2
50. Goldstone, p.16
51. Carroll
52. Gordetsky, Rabinowitz & O'Brien
53. Oriel, p.16
54. Anon. (j)
Granit
55. Fletcher
Strathern, p.308
56. Strathern, p.290-2, 297
57. Hibbert, p.171
Cronin, pp.93-5
58. Harris, p.143
59. Lipscomb
60. Strathern, p.314
61. Fletcher
Srathern, pp.326-7
62. Burckhardt, p.286
63. Norwich (2011)
64. MacCulloch (2016), Chap. 5
65. Greengrass, p. 13
Winder (2013), pp.45-50
66. Wheatcroft
67. Greengrass, pp.277-85
68. Williams, p. 102
69. Blendinger
Winder (2013), pp.70-76
70. Winder (2010), p.140
71. Greengrass, pp. 505-6
72. Greengrass, p.124
73. *The Local*, 11 February 2008. Cited by Murray D, p.156
74. Rachman, p.203
75. Williams, p.109
Norwich (2016), pp.26-7, 226-9
76. Alvarez, Ceballos & Quinteiro
Álvarez & Ceballos

77. Sheridan, Wright, Small *et al*
78. Greengrass, p.32
79. Pogge
80. Houtz
81. Greengrass, pp. 216-22
82. Cronin, pp.59 ff.
83. Greengrass, p.241
84. Villalobos
85. Oriel, p.12
86. Greengrass, pp.250-3
87. Crone
    Greengrass, pp.202 ff.

II. Bronzino's Art

Background: Brock; Burckhardt; Cole; Cox-Rearick; Falletti & Scudieri; Gould C; Murray; Paglia; Parker (1997 and 2004); Pilliod; Ruskin; Shearman; Vasari

Citations

1. Elsen p.131
2. Smith, p.256
3. Gaston
   Smith, p.256
4. Gaston, p.261
5. Shearman, p.194
6. Goodchild
7. Vasari, Vol.7, p.182
8. Wainwright, Chapter 5
9. Shearman, p.190
10. Broeck
11. Berti
    Cronin, p.297-301.
    Shearman
12. Cronin, p.126
13. Honor & Fleming
14. Baxandall (1988), pp.139-41
    Shearman, pp. 172-3
15. Shearman, p. 19
16. Honor & Fleming p. 497
17. Ruskin, Vol. II. Ch. VI, Para.8
18. Ruskin, Vol. III. Ch. VIII, Para.8
19. Langmuir pp.146-7
    Murray, p.151
20. Vasari, Vol.7 p.160
21. Giovannoni in: Falletti
    & Scudieri pp. 77-8
22. Murray, L, p.159
23. Marsolek
24. Hockney, p.39
25. Berger, p.97
26. Hall (2016)
27. Parsons
    MacClennan
28. Acton, pp.123-127
29. Landow (2015 and 2016)
30. Gould SJ (1992), pp.98-100
31. Landow (2015 and 2016)
    Anon (k)
32. MacCulloch (2010), pp.838-46
    Strachey, Chapter 1
33. Brock, p.14
34. Plazzotta & Keith
35. Burkhardt, p.112
    Ravenscroft
36. O'Brien
37. Anon (l)
38. Wiesner
39. Pagé
40. Strathern, pp.13, 48
41. Marsolek, p.22
42. Moore

III. The *London Allegory*: Why did Bronzino paint it?

Background: Burckhardt; Cohen & Cohen; Cronin; Hibbert; Knecht (1982 and 2004); Greengrass; Martinelli; Norwich (2016); Seward; Strathern

Citations

1. Vasari, Vol. 10, p. 7
2. Levey
3. Gaston
   Smith
4. Plazzotta & Keith
5. Gould C, p.43
6. Strathern, Chapter 25
7. Brackett, p.291
   Cohen & Cohen, pp.116-7, 281-2
   Strathern, pp.108
8. Brackett, p.291
9. Rocke, pp.228-9
   Varnell
10. Rocke, p. 233
11. Rocke, p.235
12. Antonio da Sangallo
    quoted by Rocke, p. 233
13. Norwich (2011)
14. MacCulloch (2004) p. 231
15. Hibbert, p.185
16. Knecht (2004), p.147
17. Cronin, p. 58
    Seward, pp. 63; 73
18. Norwich (2016), p. 131
19. Norwich (2016), p.133
20. Norwich (2016), p.165
21. Hall (2010)
22. Cox-Rearick, pp.85-8
    Hibbert, pp.184-5
    Strathern, pp.336-7
23. Cronin, p.103
24. Healy
25. Hibbert, p.182
26. Burckhardt, p.233
29. Cox-Rearick, p.75
    Vasari, Vol.10, p.6
30. Mansfield
31. Seward, p. 32
32. Knecht (1982), pp.426-31
    Seward, pp.68-70
33. Greengrass, pp.286-91
    Knecht (2004), Chapter 10
    Knecht (1982), pp. 89-99
34. Knecht (2004), p.155
    Knecht (1982), p. 97
35. Greengrass, p.289
36. Seward, p.70
37. Beitchman
    Hilde
38. Mansfield, Note 5
39. Knecht (2004), p.158
40. Seward, p.33
41. Knecht (1982), p.86 Note 16
42. Seward, p.138
43. Knecht (1982), pp.187-8
44. Knecht (1982), p.408
45. Seward, p.202
46. Seward, p.244
47. Oriel, pp.165
48. Cohen & Cohen pp.114, 159
49. Gordetsky, Rabinowitz & O'Brien
50. Knecht (1982), p.427
51. Gonzalez–Crussi
52. Anderson, p.20

IV. The *London Allegory*: How did Bronzino paint it?

Background: Acton; Baxandall (1985 and 1998); Bouleau; Broeck; Cole; Corbalán; Doerner; Lucie-Smith; Thompson; Wind; Woodford

Citations

1. Perlman
2. Moffitt (1996)
3. Wind, p.164
4. Lucie-Smith
5. Oard
6. Graham-Dixon (1999), p.149
   Lucie-Smith, pp.47-8
7. Anon (m)
   Cox-Rearick, Plate 21; pp.279-80
8. Gaston, p.259
9. Smith, p.256
10. Plazzotta & Keith, Note 20
11. Cole, pp.31-2
12. Levey, p.30
13. Johnson
14. Clark, p.128
15. Brock, p.230
    Johnson, p.3
    Levey, p.33
16. Cohen, p.287
17. Levey, p.32
18. Compton
    Nelson, pp.146-7
19. Anon (n)
20. Anderson
21. Cole
    Doerner
22. Bomford pp.13-22
    Savage
23. Plazzotta & Keith, p.91
24. Moore
25. Alberge
26. Cole
    Fisk
27. Plazzotta & Keith, p.92
28. Doerner
29. Greengrass, pp.202ff
    Thompson, Chapter III
30. McLean
31. Hedesan
    McLean
32. Anon. (o)
33. Beitchman
    Knecht (2004), p.179
34. Fordham, pp.139-40
    Jung (1993), pp. 1-46
35. Baxandall (1988), pp.81-5
    Cooper, p.39
36. St Clair
37. Maglaty
38. Baxandall (1988), p. 81
39. Baxandall (1985), p.132
40. Vasari, Vol. 10, p.7
41. Ladwein, pp.61-2
42. Langmuir pp.81-3
    North, pp.95-102
43. Woodford, p.10
44. Fisher , p.155
46. Bouleau
    Osborne & Farr
47. Corbalán
48. Johnston
    Russell PA
49. Corbalán
    Knott
50. Berger, Chapter 3
51. Healy
52. Cohen & Cohen
    Martinelli
    Vandermassen
53. Attributed to Jennifer Preston
    in: Plazzotta & Keith, Note 24
54. Gould C, p.42
    Plazzotta & Keith
55. Anderson, p.19
    Gaston, p.19
56. Gould C, p.42
    Plazzotta & Keith, Note 23
57. Plazzotta & Keith, p.91
58. Plazzotta & Keith, Fig 26
59. Plazzotta & Keith, p.90

V. The *London Allegory*: Who is who and what is what?

Background: Cooper; Giovanni; Hall; Hesiod; Langmuir; March; Neumann; Ovid; Paglia; Panofsky; Wind

Citations

1. Glover
2. Hope
3. Levey
4. Moffitt (1993)
5. Fisher
   Gaston, Note 89
   Parker, 1997
6. Giovanni
   Hall (1992)
7. Ciuffi, di Fazio & Luzzi
8. Gaston
   Moffitt (1996)
9. Gaston, p.273
10. Vasari, Vol.10 p.7
11. Panofsky, p.87
12. Cohen, p.289
13. Cheney
    Mackworth-Young
    Strathern, pp.13, 48
14. Brock, p.220
    Gaston, p.279 Note 89
15. Healy, p.4
16. Johnson
17. Hesiod, Lines 29 ff.
18. Hesiod, Lines 190-5
19. March, p.69
20. Anon.(p)
21. Levey, p.32
22. Perlman
23. Perlman, p.236
24. Smith, p.254
25. Kilpatrick, p.269
26. Gaston, p.278
27. Gaston, p.283
28. Gaston, p.280
29. Gaston, p.284
30. Panofsky, p.88
31. Levey p.33
32. Fisher, p.161
33. Fisher, p.160
34. Hesiod, Lines 114-22
35. Aristophanes, lines 693-9
36. Hesiod, Line 201
37. March, p.53
38. March, pp.53, 71
39. Ovid, Book I, Fable XII
40. Ovid, Book X, Fable IX
41. Fox
42. Keach
43. Moffitt (1993), p.282-3
44. Cheney, p.14
    Hope, p.240
45. Bosch, p.32
    Brock, p.222
    Levey, p.32
46. Anderson, Fig. 4
47. Panofsky, p.vii
48. Bosch, p.32
49. Hesiod, Line 223
50. Plazzotta & Keith, p.96
51. Hope, p.241
52. Cheney, p.14
53. Levey p. 32
54. Bromham, p.148
55. Plazzotta & Keith, p.93
56. Hope, p.240
57. Kilpatrick, p.271
58. Levey, p.33
    Moffitt (1993)
59. Korenblat
60. Panofsky, p.83
61. Panofsky, p.90
62. Panofsky, p.vii
63. Fisher, p 155
64. Levey, p.33
65. Panofsky, p.73
66. Cheney, p.13
67. Cheney, p.16

68. Healey, p.3
69. Hall (1992)
70. Bosch, p.33
71. Cheney, p.14
72. Hope, p.243
73. Marsolek, p. 22
    Smith, p.256
    Vasari, Vol. 7, p.151
74. Bosch, p.30
75. Johnson, p.5
76. Morton, p.115
77. Gaston, p.277-8
78. Panofsky, p.86
79. Hope, p.242
80. Anon(p)
81. Gaston, p.258
82. Brock, p.222
83. Barolsky & Ladis, p.33
84. Cohen, p. 283
85. Plazzotta & Keith, p.97
86. Bardi
87. Hesiod, Line 295
88. March, p.39
89. Smith, p.253
90. Brock, p. 221
91. Healy, p.8
92. Moffitt (1993 & 1996)
93. Moffitt (1993), p.280
94. Moffitt (1993), p.290
95. Moffitt (1993), p.289
96. Moffitt (1993), p.292
97. MacClennan
    Guthrie
98. Guthrie, p 13
99. Guthrie, pp. 53-5
100. Moffitt (1993), pp. 288, 297
101. Moffitt (1993), p.288
102. Moffitt (1993), p.286
103. IUCN Red List (a)
104. Cohen, p.266
105. Bromham, p.147
106. The New English Bible
    Moffitt (1996)
107. Richter
108. Gaston, p.274
109. Cohen, Chapter 10
110. Hall (1992)
    Giovanni
111. Cohen, pp.268, 271, 273
112. Bosch, p.32
    Hall (1992), p.87
113. Gould C, p.41
114. Anon.(p)
    Hesiod, Lines 319-22
115. Hesiod, Lines 305-26
116. Smith, p.258, Note 48
117. Gould C, p.43
118. Wind, p.165
119. Cheney, p.12
120. Panofsky, p.89
121. Plazzotta & Keith, p.91
    and Fig.26
122. Hall (1992), p.73
123. Moffitt (1993), p.279
124. Oard
125. Cohen, p.287
126. Plazzotta & Keith, Note 24
127. Anderson, Fig.1
128. Hall (1992), p.219
129. Anon (q)
130. Smith, p.252
131. Hope, p.241
    Smith, p.251
132. Smith, p.250
133. Smith, p.251
134. Langmuir p.106-7
135. Cook
    Healy

VI. De Morbo Gallico

Background: Davies; Frith; Gould SJ (2003, 2011); McNeill; Morton; Munger; Oriel; Quétel; Richard; Schöfer; Stein; Villalobos; Von Hutten

Citations

1. Rolleston p.155
2. Oriel, p.11
3. Richard
4. Cronin, pp.141-3
   McNeill, p.512
   Quétel, p.43
5. Schöfer
6. Morton
   Tampa, Sarbu, Matei et al
7. Morton
   Rolleston
8. Oriel, p.12
9. Villalobos, Chapter XXVIII
10. Villalobos, Chapter XXXIX
11. Doyne
12. Villalobos, Chapter XXII
13. Villalobos, Chapter III
14. Villalobos, Chapter XXXVIII
15. Frith, p.51
16. Von Hutten, p.3
17. Von Hutten, p.5
18. Von Hutten, p.7-8
19. Von Hutten, pp.88-9
20. Oriel, pp.53-4
21. Russell K
22. Oriel, p.11
23. Morton, p.38
24. Morton, p.35
25. Dunant
    Quétel, p.17
26. Anon. (h)
    Iommi Echeverria
    Gould SJ (2003), pp.194ff.
27. Frith
    Oriel, p.14
28. Siena, p.12
29. Frith
30. Quétel, p.285 Note 9
31. Quétel, p.50
32. McNeill, p.54
33. Morton, Parts 1 & 2
34. Oriel, p.20
    Villalobos
35. Oriel, pp.21-3
36 Oriel, pp.2-3, 9
37. Tampa, Sarbu, Matei *et al*
38. Beck, pp.111, 115
    Harper, Zuckerman & Armelagos
    McNeill, Chapter 5
    Oriel
39. Harrison, pp.33-39
    Rothschild
40. Beck, p.112
    McNeill, Chap. 5
41. Davies, p.489
42. Anon (j) and (r)
43. Cohen, p.284
44. Von Hutten, p.9
45. Von Hutten, p.11
46. Anon. (s)
47. Cohen, p.281
    Von Hutten, p.87
48. Beck, p.113
    Munger
49. IUCN Red List (b)
50. Gould SJ (2011) p.201
    Varey, Chabrán & Weiner, p.114
51. Stein
52. Bledinger
53. Crone, p.113
54. Karamanou, Liappas, Antoniou, Androutsos & Lykouras
55. Harrison, p.123
56. McNeill, p.194
57. Beck, pp.112-3

58. Gonzalez-Crussi
59. Ajanki, p.149
60. Healy, p.6
61. Siena, p.16
62. Conway, p.253
    Smith, p.251
63. Barnett, pp.192,199
    Schöfer, Fig. 13.9
64. Villalobos, Chapters III, XXII, XXXVIII
    Von Hutten, p.5
66. Smith, p.252
67. Lazzeri, Albury, Lippi & Weisz
68. Cox-Rearick, Plate 10; Fig.180
69. Williams, p.109
70. Seward, p.244
71. Schöfer, Fig 13.11
72. Cook, p.459
73. Hesiod, Line 295
74. Barolsky, p.24
75. Graham-Dixon (2002)

VII. Conclusion: The *London Allegory: What does it mean?*

Citations:

1. Gaston, p.262
2. Panofsky, pp.86-91
3. Anderson, Plate 1
   Panofsky, Plate XXXVIII
4. Council of Trent
   MacCulloch (2010), p.665
   Panofsky, p.91
   Shearman, pp.167-70, 177-8
5. Merryman & Urice, pp.623-4
6. Brock, p.229
7. Levey, p.32
8. Levey, p.33
9. Cronin, p.102
   Smith p.253
10. Smith, pp.255-7
11. Keach, p.331
12. Keach, p.327
13. Smith, p. 257, Note 4
14. Hope, p.243
15. Cohen, Chapter 10
16. Morton, p.39
17. Bosch, p.32
    Bromham, pp.147-9
18. Gaston, p.257
19. Gaston, p.250
20. Gaston, p.287
21. Gaston, p.273
22. Gaston, p.282
23. Gaston, pp.260, 266, 269
24. Gaston, p.276
25. Kilpatrick, pp.268ff
26. Kilpatrick
    Ovid, X, Line 525
27. Cheney, pp.15-7
28. Wind, p.235
29. Berger
30. Clark, p.128
    Cohen, p.287
31. Healy, p.4
32. Beck, p.113
    Morton, p.39
33. Brock, p.228
34. Appignanesi, p.48
35. Neumann, pp.168-70
    Paglia, pp.13-4; 47
36. Jung (1972,a), Ch.III Para 243ff
    Jung (1972,b), Ch.II, Para 296ff
    Sharp, p.84
37. Siena, pp.567-8
38. Jung, (1972, b), Para 301
39. The New English Bible
40. Žižek, p.41-2
41. MacClennan, p.26
42. Oard
43. Panofsky, Chapter III
44. Paglia, p.29
45. Cox-Rearick, p.250
46. Barolsky & Ladis, p.32

Bibliography

Acton, M. *Learning to Look at Paintings,* Routledge, Abingdon, UK, 1997. ISBN: 0-415-14890-1

Ajanki, T. *Medicinal Reading: Of genius, pure chance and dedicated hard work* Swedish Pharmaceutical Press, 1st Edn, 1995. ISBN-13: 978-9186274610

Alberge, D. 'Man lashes out at £25m painting.' *The Times*, London, 8 Nov. 2003, p.13. The Times Digital Archive. Web: http://find.galegroup.com/ttda/infomark.do?&source=gale&prodId =TTDA&userGroupName=echeslib&tabID=T003&docPage= article&searchType=BasicSearchForm&docId=IF502523214&type =multipage&contentSet=LTO&version=1.0 Accessed 19 Nov. 2016.

Alvarez, G. Ceballos, FC, Quinteiro C. 'The Role of Inbreeding in the Extinction of a European Royal Dynasty' In: Bauchet M, ed. PLoS ONE. 2009;4(4):e5174. doi:10.1371/journal.pone.0005174. https://www.ncbi.nlm.nih.gov/pmc/articles/PMC2664480/ Accessed 9 May 2017

Álvarez. G. Ceballos, FC. 'Royal Inbreeding and the Extinction of Lineages of the Habsburg Dynasty'
. *Human Heredity*, 80(2), 62-8; 2015. doi: 10.1159/000440765. Epub 2015 Oct 9. https://www.ncbi.nlm.nih.gov/pubmed/26448057 Accessed 9 May 2017

Anderson, J. 'A 'most improper picture' Transformations of Bronzino's erotic allegory.' *Apollo*, 384, 19-28; 1994

Anon.(a) The meaning and origin of the expression: Ring a ring o'roses, a pocketful of posies, atishoo, atishoo, all fall down. http://www.phrases.org.uk/meanings/ring-a-ring-of-roses.html Accessed 13 June 2017

Anon.(b) 'O Come All Ye Faithful' - Bonnie Prince Charlie and the Christmas Carol: https://www.dur.ac.uk/news/newsitem/?itemno= 7328was-a-Catholic-rallying-call.html Accessed 13 June 2017

Anon.(c) 'Henry Tonks (1862-1937) Artist biography': http://www. tate.org.uk/art/artists/henry-tonks-2055 Accessed 9 May 2017

Anon.(d) 'Rex Whistler The Expedition in Pursuit of Rare Meats 1926–7': http://www.tate.org.uk/about/our-work/collection/about-the-collection/works-in-the-fabric-of-tate-buildings/rex-whistler-expedition-in-pursuit-of-rare-meats Accessed 9 May 2017

Anon.(e) 'Rex Whistler an English virtuoso.' http://www.rexwhistler.com/ Accessed 9 May 2017

Anon.(f) 'Artificial leg of the Earl of Uxbridge' http://waterloo200.org /200-object/artificial-leg-of-earl-of-uxbridge/ Accessed 9 May 2017

Anon.(g) '12 Famous Artists Known by their Nicknames' http://arthistoryblogger.blogspot.co.uk/2016/05/12-famous-artists-known-by-their.html Accessed 9 May 2017

Anon.(h) 'Girolamo Fracastoro Facts'. http://biography.yourdictionary .com/girolamo-fracastoro Accessed 9 May 2017

Anon.(i) 'St Bartholomew's Day' http://www.newadvent.org/cathen/ 13333b.htm Accessed 9 May 2017

Anon.(j) 'Jean Francois Fernel (1497-1558)' http://www.faqs.org/health /bios/21/Jean-Francois-Fernel.html Accessed 9 May 2017

Anon.(k) 'The Hireling Shepherd' http://manchesterartgallery.org/art-collections/search/collection/?id=1896.29 Accessed 9 May 2017

Anon.(l) 'Mediceae Familiae Rerum Feliciter Gestarum Victoriae et Triumphi' http://www.britishmuseum.org/research/collection_ online/collection_object_details.aspx?assetId=1298915& objectId=1596562&partId=1 Accessed 13 October 2017

Anon.(m) Bonzino's fresco on the ceiling of Eleonora's chapel in the Palazzo Vecchio, 1540-5 Detail: http://www.gettyimages.co.uk/detail /news-photo/st-michael-the-archangel-by-bronzino-1540-1545-16th-century-news-photo/494731640?esource=SEO_GIS_CDN_Redirect #st-michael-the-archangel-by-bronzino-15401545-16th-century-fresco-picture-id494731640 Accessed 26 June 2017

Anon.(n) 'Michelangelo's hidden drawings.' http://www.atlasobscura. com/places/michelangelos-hidden-drawings Accessed 1 August 2017

Anon.(o) 'The Alchemical Great Work' *Occult Advances:* http://www. occult-advances.org/greatwork.shtml Accessed 5 June 2017

Anon.(p) *Erotes* Theoi Project http://www.theoi.com/ Accessed 9 May 2017

Anon.(q) Venus. https://en.wikipedia.org/wiki/Venus_(mythology) #cite_note-17 Accessed 30 October 2017

Anon.(r) 'Fernel': http://www.encyclopedia.com/people/history/historians -miscellaneous-biographies/jean-fernel Accessed 1 August 2017

Anon.(s) Syphilis. https://en.wikipedia.org/wiki/Syphilis Accessed 9 May 2017

Appignanesi L. *All about love: Anatomy of an unruly emotion* Virago 2011 ASIN: B0068GZ9HE

Aristophanes. *The Birds*, Translated by Gilbert Murray, George Allen & Unwin, London, 1950: https://www.gutenberg.ca/ebooks/murray aristophanes-birds/murrayaristophanes-birds-00-h.html Accessed 9 May 2017

Bardi, U. 'Bronzino's chimera', *Chimeara*, Hosted by The University of Florence, Italy, 2001. http://www.surfchem.unifi.it/solid/bardi/chimera/ and 2014. http://chimeramyth.blogspot.co.uk/2014/12/bronzinos-chimera.html Accessed 9 May 2017

Barker, P. *Life* Class Hamish Hamilton, London, 2007. ISBN 13: 978-0241142974 *Toby's Room,* Hamish Hamilton, London, 2012. ISBN: 9780241144572

Barnett R. *The Sick Rose. Or Disease and the Art of Medical Illustration* Thames & Hudson, London, 2014 ISBN: 97805000517345

Barolsky, P. 'Bronzino's fictions'. *Source: Notes in the History of Art,* 25 (2), 23-25; 2006

Barolsky, P & Ladis, A. 'The "Pleasurable Deceits" of Bronzino's so-called *London Allegory*' *Source: Notes in the History of Art,* 10(3), 32-6; 1991

Baxandall, M. *Patterns of Intention: on the Historical Explanation of Pictures* Yale University Press, New Haven and London. 1985. ISBN: 0-300-034565-2

Baxandall, M. *Painting and Experience in Fifteenth Century Italy* Oxford University Press, 2nd Edn, 1988. ISBN: 978-0-19-282144-7

Beck, SV. *Syphilis: The Great Pox* In: Kiple, KF. (Ed.) *Plague, Pestilence and Pox* Weidenfeld & Nicolson, London, 1997. ISBN 0 297 82254 3 Chapter 17, pp. 110-5

Beitchman, P. *Alchemy of the Word: Cabala of the Renaissance* State University of New York Press, 1998. ISBN-13: 978-0791437377

Bell J. *What is painting?* Thames & Hudson, London, Revised Edn. 2017 ISBN: 978-0-500-23973-5

Benjamin, W. *The Work of Art in the Age of Mechanical Reproduction* In: Arendt, H ed. *Illuminations* Fontana, London, 1968. ISBN: 978-1407085500. Available at: http://web.mit.edu/allanmc /www/benjamin.pdf Accessed 24 October 2017

Berger, J. *Ways of Seeing* Penguin Modern Classics, London, 2008. ISBN: 978-0141035796

Berti L. 'Michelangelo and the Florentine Painting of the Sixteenth Century' In: Falletti, F, Scudieri, M (Eds.). *Around the David: The Great Art of Michelangelo's Century* Guinti, Florence, 2003. ISBN:88-09-03316-7 pp.29-73

Bierce, A. *The Devil's Dictionary* http://www.gutenberg.org/files/ 972/972-h/972-h.htm Accessed 19 July 2017

Biernoff, S. 'Flesh Poems: Henry Tonks and the Art of Surgery', *Visual Culture in Britain.* 11(1), 25–47; 2010 http://www.ncbi.nlm,. nih.gov/pmc/articles/PMC3158130/ Accessed 9 May 2017

Blendinger, F. 'The Fugger Family', Encyclopædia Britannica https:// www.britannica.com/topic/Fugger-family Accessed 2 November 2017

Bomford, D. (Ed.) *A Closer Look: Conservation of Paintings* Yale University Press, 2009. ISBN-13: 978-1857094411

Bosch, LMF. 'Bronzino's *London Allegory*: Love versus Time', *Source: Notes in the History of Art*, 9(2), 30-5; 1990

Bouleau, C. *The Painter's Secret Geometry: A Study of Composition in Art* Dover Publications Inc., 2014. ISBN-13: 978-0486780405

Brackett, JK. 'The Florentine Onesta and the Control of Prostitution, 1403-1680', *Sixteenth Century Journal*, 24(2), 273-300; 1993

Brock, M. *Bronzino* Translated from the French by Poole Radzinowicz D & Schultz-Touge C. Flammarion, 2002. ISBN: 2-0801-0877-8

Broeck, L. *Cennino Cennini's Il Libro Dell'arte: A New English Translation and Commentary with Italian Transcription* Archetype Publications Ltd, Bilingual edition, 2015. ISBN 13: 978-1909492288

Bromham, AA. "A plague will come:" Art, Rape, and Venereal Disease in Middleton's *Women Beware Women*. EnterText 3.1, 45-60; 2003

Burckhardt, J. *The Civilisation of the Renaissance in Italy.* Penguin Classics, London, 1990. ISBN 13: 978-0-140-44534-3

Carrieri, MP, Serraino D. 'Longevity of popes and artists between the 13th and the 19th century'. *International Journal of Epidemiology.* (December) 34 (6); 2005, 1435-1436. http://ije.oxfordjournals.org /content/34/6/1435.full#aff-2 Accessed 9 May 2017

Carroll, L. 'The secret sex life of Catherine de Medici' http://www.passagestothepast.com/2010/01/guest-post-from-leslie-carroll.html Accessed 9 May 2017

Cecil, M, Cecil H. *In search of Rex Whistler his Life and his Work* Frances Lincoln, London, 2012. ISBN-13: 978-0711232303

Cheney, I. 'Bronzino's *London Allegory*: Venus, Cupid, Virtue, and Time', *Source: Notes in the History of Art*, 6(2), 12-18; 1987

Ciuffi GC. di Fazio L, Luzzi P. Allori's Flowers In: Falletti F, Scudieri M (Eds.). *Around the David: The Great Art of Michelangelo's Century* Guinti, Florence, 2003. ISBN:88-09-03316-791-119

Clark, K. *The Nude: A Study in Ideal Art* John Murray, London. 1936.

Cohen, S. *Animals disguised as Symbols in Renaissance Art*, Brill Academic Publishers, Leiden, 2008. ISBN 13: 978-9004171015

Cohen, TV, Cohen, ES. *Daily Life in Renaissance Italy* Greenwood Publishing Group, Connecticut, USA, 2008. ISBN-13: 978-0313361142

Cole, B. *The Renaissance Artist at Work: From Pisano to Titian*, Westview Press, Boulder, Colorado, USA, Revised edn.,1990. ISBN-13: 978-0064301299

Compton, R. '*Omnia Vincit Amor* The Sovereignty of Love in Tuscan Poetry and Michelangelo's *Venus and Cupid*', *Mediaevalia*, 33, 229-260; 2012. https://muse.jhu.edu/article/505544/pdf Accessed 9 May 2017

Conway, JF. 'Syphilis and Bronzino's *London Allegory*,' *Journal of the Warburg and Courtauld Institutes*, 49, 250–5; 1986

Cook, C. 'An Allegory with Venus and Cupid: a Story of Syphilis' *Journal of the Royal Society of Medicine*, 1, 458-60; 2010 Available at: https://www.ncbi.nlm.nih.gov/pmc/articles/PMC2966887/ Accessed 27 June 2017

Cooper, JC. *An Illustrated Encyclopaedia of Traditional Symbols* Thames & Hudson, London, 1978. ISBN: 0-500-27125-9

Copernicus, N. *The Commentariolus* http://dbanach.com/copernicus-commentarilous.htm Accessed 9 May 2017

Corbalán, F. *The Golden Ratio: the Mathematical Language of Beauty* RBA Coleccionables, S.A. ISBN: 978-84-473-8764-9

Council of Trent 25th session, Second Decree: 'On the Invocation, Veneration, and Relics, of Saints, and on Sacred Images', Available at http://www.thecounciloftrent.com/ch25.htm and at http://www.documentacatholicaomnia.eu/03d/1545-1545,_Concilium_Tridentinum,_Canons_And_Decrees,_EN.pdf Both accessed 3 November 2017

Cox-Rearick, J. *Bronzino's Chapel of Eleonora in the Palazzo Vecchio* University of California Press, Berkeley & Los Angeles, USA,1993. ISBN: 0-520-07480-7

Crone HD. Paracelsus: *The Man who Defied Medicine: His Real Contribution to Medicine and Science*, Albarello Press, Melbourne, Australia, 2004. ISBN: 064643327X

Cronin V. *The Flowering of the Renaissance* Pimlico, London, 1992. ISBN: 0-7126-9884-1

Davies N. *Europe: a History* Pimlico, London, 1997. ISBN: 0-7126-6633-8

Dickens AG. *The Age of Humanism and Reformation* Prentice-Hall International, Inc, London, 1977. ISBN: 0-13-018507-8

Doerner M. *The Materials of the Artist* Hart-Davis, MacGibbon, London, 2nd revised edn.,1976. ISBN: 0-246-63877

Doyne PG. 'Syphilitic diseases of the eye': https://www.ncbi.nlm.nih.gov/pmc/articles/PMC1046666/pdf/brjvendis00241-0041.pdf Accessed 27 June 2017

Dunant S. 'Syphilis, sex and fear: How the French disease conquered the world'. *The Guardian*, 13 May 2013: https://www.theguardian.com/books/2013/may/17/syphilis-sex-fear-borgias Accessed 9 May 2017

Dupre S. *Laboratories of Art: Alchemy and Art Technology from Antiquity to the 18th Century (Archimedes)* Springer, 2014. ISBN 13: 978-3319050645

Eaude M. *Catalonia: A cultural history,* Oxford University Press, 2008. ISBN: 978 0 19 532797 7

Eiland H. *Walter Benjamin: A Critical Life,* Harvard University Press, 2014. ISBN: 978-0674051867

Elsen AE. *The Gates of Hell by Rodin* Stanford University Press, 1985. ISBN-13: 978-0804712811 and https://www.quotescosmos.com/people/Auguste-Rodin.html Accessed 28 August 2018

Erotes *Theoi Project:* http://www.theoi.com/ Accessed 9 May 2017
Falletti F, Scudieri M (Eds.). *Around the David: The Great Art of Michelangelo's Century,* Guinti, Florence, 2003. ISBN:88-09-03316-7
Fisk A. *Cupid and the Silent Goddess*, Twenty First Century Publishers Ltd, 2003. ISBN: 1-904433-08-1
Fisher W. 'Peaches and Figs: bisexual eroticism in the paintings and burlesque poetry of Bronzino.' In:Levy A. (Ed.) *Sex Acts in Early Modern Italy*, Routledge, London, 2010, pp. 151-64. ISBN-13: 9780754667483
Fletcher C. *The Black Prince of Florence: The Spectacular Life and Treacherous World of Alessandro de'Medici,* The Bodley Head, London, 2016. ISBN: 9781847922694
Fordham F. *An introduction to Jung's psychology*, Penguin, London, 1966. ISBN: 0140202730
Foucault M. *The Order of Things,* Routledge, London, 2001 ISBN: 978-0415267373 Available at: http://www.naturalthinker.net/trl/texts/Foucault,Michel/Foucault,%20Michel%20-%20The%20Order%20of%20Things%20-%20An%20Archaeology%20of%20the%20Human%20Sciences.pdf Accessed 4 August 2017
Fox R. *The Red Lamp of Incest,* Hutchinson, London 1981 ISBN: 9780091440800
Frankel N. *On the Whistler-Ruskin Trial*, 1878: http://www.branchcollective.org/?ps_articles=nicholas-frankel-on-the-whistler-ruskin-trial-1878 Accessed 28 July 2017
Frith J. 'Syphilis – Its early history and Treatment until Penicillin and the Debate on its Origins' *Journal of Military and Veterans' Health* 20(4), 49-58; 2012: http://jmvh.org/article/syphilis-its-early-history-and-treatment-until-penicillin-and-the-debate-on-its-origins/ Accessed 9 May 2017
Gaston RW. 'Love's sweet poison: a new reading of Bronzino's *London Allegory*.' *I Tatti Studies in the Italian Renaissance*, 4, 249-88; 1991.
Giovanni SL. 'In the House of the Saints' In: Falletti F, Scudieri M (Eds.). *Around the David: The Great Art of Michelangelo's Century,* Guinti, Florence, 2003. ISBN:88-09-03316-7 77-81
Glover M. 'Great Works: An Allegory with Venus and Cupid, by Bronzino' *The Independent* http://www.independent.co.uk/arts-entertainment/art/great-works/great-works-an-allegory-with-venus-and-cupid-by-bronzino-8096389.html Accessed 9 May 2017
Goldstone N. *The Rival Queens*, Weidenfeld & Nicolson, London, 2015. ISBN: 9780297868637.
Goodchild CH. 'Vasari contra Bronzino'. *Notes in the History of Art*, 28, (2, Winter), 28-32; 2009.
Gonzalez-Crussi F. 'Bronzino and the wages of sin,' *Hektoen International Journal: A Journal of Medical Humanities*, Summer 2012. Available at http://hekint.org/bronzino-and-the-wages-of-sin/ Accessed 23 June 2017

Gordetsky J, Rabinowitz R, O'Brien J. 'The "infertility" of Catherine de'Medici and its influence on 16th century France'. *Canadian Journal* of Urology 16(2), 4584-8; 2009

Gould C. *National Gallery Catalogues. The Sixteenth-century Italian Schools*, Publications Department, The National Gallery, London, 1975.

Gould SJ. 'A biological homage to Mickey Mouse'. In: Gould SJ. *The Panda's Thumb: More Reflections in Natural History,* WW Norton, New York, 1992. ISBN 0-393-30819-7 Available at: http://www.s-f-walker.org.uk/pubsebooks/pdfs/Gould_Stephen_Jay_The_Panda's_Thumb.pdf

Gould SJ. 'Syphilis and the Shepherd of Atlantis' In: Gould SJ. *I Have Landed*, Vintage, Random House, London, 2003. pp.192-207 ISBN: 0 09 974971 8

Graham-Dixon A. *Renaissance* BBC Worldwide Ltd., London, 1999. ISBN: 0 563 38396 8

Graham-Dixon A. In the Picture 95: 'Allegory of Venus and Cupid, by Bronzino' *The Sunday Telegraph*, 10 February 2002. Available at: http://www.andrewgrahamdixon.com/archive/itp-95-allegory-of-venus-and-cupid-by-bronzino.html Accessed 27 June 2017

Granit R. 'Fernel, Jean François': http://www.encyclopedia.com/people/history/historians-miscellaneous-biographies/jean-fernel Accessed 3 August 2017

Greenblatt S. *The Swerve* Vintage Books, London, 2012. ISBN: 9780099572442

Greengrass M. *Christendom Destroyed: Europe 1517-1648,* Allen Lane, London, 2014. ISBN: 9780713990867

Guthrie KS. *The Greek Pilgrim's Progress* Luzac & Co., London, 1910. Available at: https://archive.org/details/greekpilgrimspro00cebeuoft Accessed 20 August 2018

Haberlein M. *The Fuggers of Augsburg: Pursuing Wealth and Honor in Renaissance Germany* University of Virginia Press, Charlottesville, VA, USA, 2012. ISBN: 9780813932446

Hall J. *Dictionary of Subjects and Symbols in Art*, John Murray, London, 1992. ISBN: 0 7195 4147 6

Hall J. 'Bronzino's Medici portraits: Review' *The Guardian*, London, 23 October 2010: https://www.theguardian.com/artanddesign/2010/oct/23/bronzino-medici-portraits-art-review Accessed 9 May 2017

Hall J. 'The artist as spider: Signs and symbolism in the Armada Portrait of Elizabeth I'. *Art Quarterly*, Summer 2016, 38-43

Harper KN, Zuckerman MK, Armelagos GJ. 'Syphilis: Then and Now' *The Scientist*, February 1, 2014. http://www.the-scientist.com/?articles.view/articleNo/38985/title/Syphilis--Then-and-Now/ Accessed 9 May 2017

Harris R. *Pompeii* Hutchinson, London, 2003. ISBN: 0 09 177925 1
Harrison M. *Disease and the Modern World: 1500 to the Present Day,* John Wiley & Sons, London, 2013. ISBN: 978 074563 8010
Hartley LP. *The Go-between,* Penguin Classics; New edition, 2004. ISBN: 9780141187785
Haycock D. *A Crisis of Brilliance,* Old Street Publishing, London, 2009. ISBN: 9781905847846
Healy M. 'Bronzino's *London Allegory* and the Art of Syphilis', *Oxford Art Journal*, 20(1),3-11; 1997
Hedesan J. The Four Stages of Alchemical Work, Published in *Esoteric Coffeehouse* on 26 Jan 2009. https://www.scribd.com/doc/11441835/The-Four-Stages-of-Alchemical-Work Accessed 9 May 2017
Hesiod, *Theogony*, https://msu.edu/~tyrrell/theogon.pdf Accessed 9 May 2017
Hibbert C. *Florence: the biography of a city,* Penguin, 1993. ISBN 0-670-842974
Hilde. 'Francis I – the Salamander King': https://hemmahoshilde.wordpress.com/2015/05/21/francis-i-with-his-salamander/ Accessed 1 August 2017
Hockney D. *Secret Knowledge* Thames & Hudson, 2001. ISBN: 0-500-23785-9
Honor H, Fleming J. *A World History of Art*, Laurence King Publishing, London, Revised 7th Edn. 2009. ISBN: 9781856695848
Hope C. 'Bronzino's allegory in the National Gallery', *Journal of the Warburg and Courtauld Institutes*, 45, 239-43; 1982
Houtz W. 'John Calvin on Nicolaus Copernicus and Heliocentrism' http://biologos.org/blogs/archive/john-calvin-on-nicolaus-copernicus-and-heliocentrism Accessed 27 October 2017
Iommi Echeverria V. 'Girolamo Fracastoro and the invention of syphilis.' 17, (4), 877-884; 2010: http://www.scielo.br/scielo.php?script=sci_arttext&pid=S0104-59702010000400002&lng=en&nrm=iso Accessed 15 Dec. 2016.
IUCN Red List of Threatened Species 2016 (a) 'Anas rubripes': http://dx.doi.org/10.2305/IUCN.UK.2016-3.RLTS.T22680174A92848173.en Accessed 1 March 2017.
IUCN Red List of Threatened Species 2016 (b) 'Guaiacum officinale' http://dx.doi.org/10.2305/IUCN.UK.1998.RLTS.T33701A9802341.en Accessed 2 November 2017
Johnson A. 'Bronzino', Child of the High Renaissance: Emulazio in Bronzino's "An Allegory with Venus and Cupid", *Journal of Undergraduate Research*, 10, 1-11; 2008

Johnston I. 'Mathematicians dispute claims that the 'golden ratio' is a natural blueprint for beauty' *Independent*, April 25, 2015 http://www.independent.co.uk/news/science/mathematicians-dispute-claims-that-the-golden-ratio-is-a-natural-blueprint-for-beauty-10204354.html Accessed 9 May 2017

Jones J. The Loves of the Artists. Art and Passion in the Renaissance, Simon & Schuster, UK, Ltd, London, 2013. ISBN: 9780857203205

Jung CG. *Man and his symbols,* Arkana, Penguin Group, London, 1964. ISBN: 0-14-019316-2

Jung CG. 'The persona as segment of the collective psyche' In: Jung CG (Author), Adler G, Hull RFC. (Eds.) *Collected Works of C. G. Jung, Vol. 7. Two essays on Analytical Psychology*. Part 1. 'The effects of the unconscious upon consciousness', Princeton University Press, USA. 1972(a) ISBN: 978 0691017822. https://archive.org/stream/C.G.JungCollectedWorksVol7Part1TheEffectsOfTheUnconsciousUponConsciousness/C.g.Jung-CollectedWorksVol7-Part1TheEffectsOfTheUnconsciousUponConsciousness#page/n15/mode/2up Accessed 3 August 2017

Jung CG. 'Anima and animus'. In: Jung CG (Author), Adler G, Hull RFC. (Eds.) *Collected Works of C. G. Jung, Vol. 7. Two essays on Analytical Psychology*. Part 2. 'Individuation'. Princeton University Press, USA. 1972(b). ISBN: 978 0691017822 https://archive.org/stream/C.G.JungCollectedWorksVol7Part2Individuation/C.g.Jung-CollectedWorksVol7-Part2-Individuation#page/n7/mode/2up Accessed 3 August 2017

Jung CG. 'Psychology and Alchemy' In: Adler G, Hull RFC. (Eds.) In: *Collected Works of C. G. Jung, Vol. 12*. Routledge, London, 1993. ISBN: 9780415034524

Kandel ER. *The Age of Insight: The quest to understand the unconscious in art, mind, and brain, from Vienna 1900 to the present* Random House, New York, 2012. ISBN: 9781400068715

Karamanou M. Liappas I, Antoniou Ch, Androutsos G, Lykouras E. 'Julius Wagner-Jauregg (1857-1940): Introducing fever therapy in the treatment of neurosyphilis'. *Psychiatriki*, 24(3),208-12; 2013 and: https://www.ncbi.nlm.nih.gov/pubmed/24185088 Accessed 9 May 2017

Keach W. 'Cupid Disarmed or Venus Wounded? An Ovidian Source for Michelangelo and Bronzino' *Journal of the Warburg Institute*, 41, 327-31; 1978

Kilpatrick RS. 'Bronzino and Apuleius: An Allegory with Venus and Cupid London, National Gallery NG651', *Memoirs of the American Academy in Rome*, 55, 265-78; 2010.

Knecht RJ. *Francis I* Cambridge University Press, Cambridge, UK, 1982 ISBN: 0-521-24344-0

Knecht RJ. *The Valois: Kings of France 1328-1589*, Hambledon & London, London, 2004. ISBN: 1-85285-420-0

Knott R. 'Fibonacci Numbers and The Golden Section in Art, Architecture and Music' http://www.maths.surrey.ac.uk/hosted-sites/R.Knott/Fibonacci/fibInArt.html Accessed 9 May 2017

Kohn GC. *Encyclopedia of Plague and Pestilence: From Ancient Times to the Present* Facts on File, New York; 3rd Revised edition, 2007 ISBN: 9780816069354

Korenblat J. https://static1.squarespace.com/static/50aefb40e4b0e23b1e8c4d45/t/50c385b3e4b09caa63d5a01f/1354991027559/Bronzino.pdf Accessed 9 May 2017

Landow GP. *William Holman Hunt and typological symbolism* Routledge Revivals, 2015 ISBN: 9781138842809

Landow GP. 'Replete with meaning: William Holman Hunt and Typological Symbolism'. http://www.victorianweb.org/painting/whh/replete/hireling.html Accessed 7 September 2016

Ladwein M. *Leonado da Vinci The Last Supper: A Cosmic Drama and an Act of Redemption,* Temple Lodge, Forest Row, UK, 2006. ISBN: 1-902636-75-9

Langmuir E. *The National Gallery Companion Guide,* National Gallery Company, London, 2016. ISBN: 978-1857095968

Lazzeri D, Albury WR, Lippi D, Weisz GM. 'The Hand in Art: Bronzino's Allegory of Venus and Cupid' *The Journal of Hand Surgery*, 40(8),1664-5; 2015

Levey M. 'Sacred and Profane Significance of Two paintings by Bronzino' In: *Studies in Renaissance and Baroque Art presented to Sir Antony Blunt on his 60th Birthday,* Phaidon, London, 1967

Lipscomb S. 'Face to face with history'. *History Today*, June 2016, 45

Lucie-Smith E. *Sexuality in Western Art*, Thames & Hudson, London, 1991. ISBN:0-500-20252-4

MacLennan B. *The Tablet of Cebes* https://studylib.net/doc/11909781/the-tablet-of-cebes-bruce-maclennan Accessed 18 February 2019

MacCulloch D. *Reformation: Europe's House Divided*, Penguin Books, 2004. ISBN-13: 978-0-140-28534-5

MacCulloch D. *A History of Christianity: The First Three Thousand Years,* Penguin Books, 2010. ISBN: 9780141021898

MacCulloch D. 'The Council of Trent'. In: *All things made new. Writings on the Reformation,* Penguin, UK, 2016. ISBN: 978-0-241-25400-4

McLean A. 'Animal Symbolism in the Alchemical Tradition', *The Alchemical Web-site*, http://www.levity.com/alchemy/animal.html Accessed 9 May 2017

MacLean R. 'Pox, pustules and pestilence – A history of syphilis treatment.' September 7, 2015. https://universityofglasgowlibrary.wordpress.com/2015/09/07/pox-pustules-and-pestilence-a-history-of-syphilis-treatment/ Accessed 9 May 2017

McManus IC. 'Life expectation of Italian renaissance artists'. *Lancet* 1975 (1), 266–7.

McNeill WH. *Plagues and Peoples,* Doubleday, London, 1976. ISBN: 0-385-12122-9

Mackworth-Young R. 'The Medici balls: Origins of the family's coat of arms' *The Florentine*, Issue 160, March 29, 2012. http://www.theflorentine.net/lifestyle/2012/03/the-medici-balls/ Accessed 9 May 2017

Maglaty J. 'When did girls start wearing pink?' Smithsonian.com April 7, 2011 http://www.smithsonianmag.com/arts-culture/when-did-girls-start-wearing-pink1370097/#b2Z6OV0JeQLZVZ75.99 Accessed 9 May 2017

Mandel C. 'Review: L'Alchemie A La Cour De Come I[er] De Medicis: Savoirs, Culture Et Politique. By Alfredo Perifano' *Sixteenth Century Journal*, 29 (3), 826-9; 1998.

Mansfield L. 'The most charismatic king: nascent celebrity in the French Renaissance' *Refractory: a Journal of Entertainment Media*, June 26, 2003. http://refractory.unimelb.edu.au/2003/06/26/the-most-charismatic-king-nascent-celebrity-in-the-french-renaissance-lisa-mansfield/ Accessed 9 May 2017

Mantel H. 'The Iron Maiden' Reith Lecture BBC Radio 4, 20 June 2017 Available at: http://www.bbc.co.uk/programmes/b08v08m5 Accessed 26 October 2017

March J. *The Penguin Book of Classical Myths*, Allen Lane, London, 2008. ISBN: 978-1-846-14130-0

Marsolek L. 'The Jewelry of Eleonora di Toledo in the Official 1545 Portrait by Bronzino' *Syracuse University Honors Program Capstone Projects*. Paper 24, (2013). http://surface.syr.edu/cgi/viewcontent.cgi?article=1023&context=honors_capstone Accessed 2 August 2017

Martin JJ. (Ed.) *The Renaissance World,* Routledge, Abingdon, UK, 2007. ISBN-13: 978-0415332590

Martinelli G (Ed.). *The World of Renaissance Florence* Macdonald, London, 1968. ISBN: 356 02439 7

Moffat A. *Tuscany: A History,* Birlinn Ltd, London, 2011. ISBN: 9781841588605

Moffitt JF. 'A Hidden Sphinx by Agnolo Bronzino, 'ex tabula Cebetis Thebani." *Renaissance Quarterly*, 46, 277-307; 1993

Moffitt JF. 'An exemplary humanist hybrid: Vasari's 'Fraude' with reference to Bronzino's "Sphinx" *Renaissance Quarterly*, 49 (2), 303-333; 1996

Monk R. *Walter Benjamin, the first pop philosopher*. New Statesman 19 October 2015. Available at: http://www.newstatesman.com/culture/books/2015/10/walter-benjamin-first-pop-philosopher Accessed 28 July 2016

Moore S. 'The Bronzino code' *Financial Times*, London. November 12, 2010. https://www.ft.com/content/69998870-ede9-11df-8616-00144feab49a Accessed 5 September 2017

Morris W. On Ruskin: 'The Nature of Gothic' in The Stones of Venice. In: *The Revival of Architecture* (1888) (Para 7) Available at: https://www.marxists.org/archive/morris/works/1888/revival.htm Accessed 28 October 2017

Morrison AS, Kirshner J, Molho A. 'Epidemics in Renaissance Florence' *American Journal of Public Health* 75,528-35; 1985 Available at: https://www.ncbi.nlm.nih.gov/pmc/articles/PMC1646284/pdf/amjph00281-0082.pdf Accessed 2 June 2017

Morton RS. 'Syphilis in art: and entertainment in four parts'. *Genitourinary Medicine*, 66, Part 1: 33-40; Part 2: 112-23; Part 3 208-21; Part 4: 280-94; 1990.

Munger RS. 'Guaiacum, the Holy Wood from the New World', *Journal of the History of Medicine*, Spring 1949, pp.195-229

Murray D. *The Strange Death of Europe: Immigration, Identity, Islam,* Bloomsbury, London, 2017. ISBN: 978-1-4729-4224-1

Murray L. *The High Renaissance and Mannerism*, Thames & Hudson, London 1993. ISBN: 0-500-20162-3

Nelson JK. 'Jacopo Carruci, Known as Il Pontormo: Venus and Cupid' In: Falletti F, Scudieri M (Eds.). *Around the David: The Great Art of Michelangelo's Century* Guinti, Florence, 2003. ISBN:88-09-03316-7

Neumann E. *The Great Mother,* Tr. R Manheim, Routledge, London, 1996. ISBN 0-415-13673-3

North JD. *The Ambassadors' Secret* – Revised Edition, Phoenix, London, 2004 ISBN: 1-84212-661 X

Norwich JJ. *The Popes: A History*, Chatto & Windus, London, 2011 ISBN: 978 070 1182908

Norwich JJ. *Four Princes: Henry VIII, Francis I, CharlesV, Suleiman the Magnificent and the Obsessions that Forged Modern Europe*, John Murray, London, 2016. ISBN: 978-1-47363-295-0

O'Brien R. 'Grotesque Bodies, Princely Delight: Dwarfs in Italian Renaissance Court Imagery' Yale University Library 2012 Available at: https://www.academia.edu/2096511/_Grotesque_Bodies_Princely_Delight_Dwarfs_in_Italian_Renaissance_Court_Imagery_ Accessed 13 October 2017

Oard BA. 'The Mirror of Mannerism: Angelo Bronzino, an Allegory with Venus and Cupid, 1540-50' https://sites.google.com/site/beautyandterror/Home/mannerist-desires Accessed 9 May 2017

Oriel JD. *The Scars of Venus. A History of Venerology*. Springer-Verlag, London, 1994. ISBN: 3-540-19844-X

Osborne H, Farr D (Eds.). *The Oxford Dictionary of Art,* The Softback Preview for Oxford University Press, 1993. ISBN: 978-0198600848

Ovid. *Metamorphoses*, Tr. Riley TH.1893 Available at: http://www.gutenberg.org/ebooks/21765 and http://www.gutenberg.org/ebooks/26073 Accessed 20 August 2018

Pagé M. 'Nano Morgante: Court dwarf of the Medici' https://extraneusart.wordpress.com/2014/01/28/nano-morgante-court-dwarf-of-the-medici/ Accessed 29 June 2017

Paglia C. *Sexual Personae: Art and Decadence from Nefertiti to Emily Dickinson*, Vintage, New York 1991 ISBN: 9780679735793.

Panofsky E. *Studies in Iconology: Humanistic Themes in the Art of the Renaissance*, (First Published 1939) Icon Edition, Harper & Row, London, 1972. ISBN: 06-430025-0

Parker D. 'Towards a Reading of Bronzino's Burlesque Poetry,' *Renaissance Quarterly*, 50 (4),1011-44; 1997

Parker D. 'Bronzino and the Diligence of Art' *Artibus et Historiae*, 25 (49),161-74; 2004

Parsons R. *Cebes' tablet, with introduction, notes, vocabulary, and grammatical questions*. 1904 https://archive.org/details/cebestablet withi00cebeiala Accessed 9 May 2017

Perlman JB. Venus, *Myrrha, Cupid and/as Adonis: Metampophoses 10 and the Artistry of Incest*. In: Keith A, James K (Eds) Rupp KJ (Eds.) *Metamorphosis: The Changing Face of Ovid in Medieval and Early Modern Europe (Essays and Studies, Volume 13)* pp. 223-38 Centre for Reformation and Renaissance Studies, Toronto, Ontario, Canada, 2007. ISBN-13: 978-0772720351

Pilliod E. Bronzino's Household, *Burlington Magazine*, 134,(1067), 92-100;1992

Plazzotta C, Keith L. 'Bronzino's 'Allegory': new evidence of the artist's revisions', *Burlington Magazine*, 141, 89-99;1999

Pogge R. 'A Brief Note on Religious Objections to Copernicus' http://www.astronomy.ohio-state.edu/~pogge/Ast161/Unit3/response.html Accessed 29 October 2017

Quétel C. *History of Syphilis*. Translated by Braddock J & Pike B. Polity Press, Cambridge, UK, 1992. ISBN: 0-7456-1030-7

Rabin S. 'Nicolaus Copernicus', in: Edward N Zalta (ed.).*The Stanford Encyclopedia of Philosophy,* Fall 2015 Edition. http://plato.stanford.edu/entries/copernicus/ Accessed 9 May 2017

Rachman G. *Easternisation*, The Bodley Head, London, 2016. ISBN: 9781847923332

Rau AF, Rastrelli M. *Degli uomini illustri nella pintura, scultura, e architetura con I loro elogi, e ritratti*, Florence 1763-76 Vol. 6, p114 https://archive.org/stream/seriedegliuomini06paci#page/n157 Accessed 19 August 2018

Ravenscroft J. 'Past Imperfect' *History Today*, 62 (12); 2012 Available at: http://www.historytoday.com/janet-ravenscroft/past-imperfect Accessed 13 October 2017

Richard J. 'The Italian Wars, 1494-1559', (3 October 2014) http://www.historyofwar.org/articles/wars_italian_wars.html Accessed 9 May 2017

Richter P. (ed.) *Notebooks of Leonado da Vinci XX: Humorous Writings*, 1236; 1880 http://www.fromoldbooks.org/Richter-NotebooksOfLeonardo/section-20/item-1236.html Accessed 1 May 2017

Rocke M. *Forbidden Friendships: Homosexuality and Male Culture in Renaissance Florence (Studies in the History of Sexuality)*, Oxford University Press USA, 1996. ISBN-13: 978-0195122923

Rolleston JD. 'Venereal disease in literature' *British Journal of Venereal Disease*, 10 (3),147-74; 1934 Available at: https://www.ncbi.nlm.nih.gov/pmc/articles/PMC1046803/pdf/brjvendis00225-0003.pdf Accessed 20 June 2017

Rothschild BM. 'History of Syphilis,' *Clinical Infectious Disease* 40(10), 1454-63; 2005. https://academic.oup.com/cid/article/40/10/1454/308400/History-of-Syphilis Accessed 22 June 2017

Ruskin J. (a) *Modern Painters* The Project Gutenberg EBook of Modern Painters Vol. II. Chapter VI, Para.8 http://www.gutenberg.org/files/29906/29906-h/29906-h.htm#s1c6p8 Accessed 3 August 2017

Ruskin J. (b) *Modern Painters* The Project Gutenberg EBook of Modern Painters Vol. III. Chapter VIII, Para.8. https://www.gutenberg.org/files/38923/38923-h/38923-h.htm#CHAPTER_VIII Accessed 9 May 2017

Russell K. (Director) *Song of Summer* (1968) ASIN: B00005N9FK https://www.youtube.com/watch?v=Vyy2SagDwcY Accessed 31 July 2017

Russell PA. 'Testing the aesthetic significance of the golden-section rectangle'. *Perception*, 29(12),1413-22; 2000.

Sallay D, Tátrai V, Vécsey A. (Eds). *Botticelli to Titian. Two Centuries of Italian Masterpieces*. Budapest, Szépművészeti Múzeum, 28 October 2009 – 14 February 2010. pp.396-7. Budapest: Szépművészeti Múzeum, 2009. http://www.academia.edu/3091564/Botticelli_to_Titian._Two_Centuries_of_Italian_Masterpieces._Exhibition_catalogue_edited_by_D%C3%B3ra_Sallay_Vilmos_T%C3%A1trai_and_Axel_V%C3%A9csey._Budapest_Sz%C3%A9pm%C5%B1v%C3%A9szeti_M%C3%BAzeum_28_October_2009_14_February_2010._Budapest_Sz%C3%A9pm%C5%B1v%C3%A9szeti_M%C3%BAzeum_2009 Accessed 26 July 2016

Savage D. 'A guide to the works of the major Italian Renaissance Painters' http://cavallinitoveronese.co.uk/general/view_artist/76 Accessed 9 May 2017

Schöfer H. *Early and late syphilis* In: Gross G, Tyring SK. (Eds) *Sexually Transmitted Infections and Sexually Transmitted Diseases*, Springer, New York, 2011. Chapter 13 ISBN 13: 978-3642146626

Seward D. *Prince of the Renaissance: The Life of François I*, Cardinal, Sphere Books Ltd, London, 1974. ISBN: 0-351-18234-9

Sharp D. *The Survival Papers: Applied Jungian Psychology*, Quantum, London, 1990. ISBN: 0-572-01585-2

Shearman J. *Mannerism* Penguin Books, London, 1990. ISBN:0-14-013759-9

Sheridan E, Wright J, Small N, Corry PC, Oddie S, Whibley C, Petherick ES, Malikm T, Pawson N, McKinney PA, Parslow RC. 'Risk factors for congenital anomaly in a multiethnic birth cohort: an analysis of the Born in Bradford study'. *Lancet*, 382 (9901), 1350-9; 2013. http://dx.doi.org/10.1016/S0140-6736(13)61132-0 Accessed 1 August 2017

Shiner L. *The Invention of Art*, The University of Chicago Press, London, 2001. ISBN: 0-226-75342-5

Siena K P. 'Pollution, Promiscuity, and the Pox: English Venereology and the Early Modern Medical Discourse on Social and Sexual Danger', *Journal of the History of Sexuality*, 8 (4), 553-74; 1998 Available at: http://www.jstor.org/stable/3840410 Accessed: 26 July 2017

Siena KP. (Ed.) *Sins of the Flesh: Responding to Sexual Disease in Early Modern Europe*, Centre for Reformation and Renaissance Studies, Victoria University of Toronto, Ontario, Canada, Vol. 7, 2005. ISBN: 9780772720290

Smith G. 'Jealousy, Pleasure and Pain in Angelo Bronzino's 'Allegory of Venus and Cupid', *Pantheon*, 39, 250-8;1981

St Clair K. *The Secret Lives of Colour*, Penguin Books, London, 2007. ISBN-13: 978-0143131144

Stanford P. *Martin Luther: Catholic Dissident*, Hodder & Stoughton London, 2017. ISBN: 9781473 62166 4

Stein C. 'Excursus: Dispelling a Myth' In: *Negotiating the French Pox in Early Modern Germany,* Routledge, London, 2016. ISBN: 9781351915465

Strachey L. *Eminent Victorians*, Oxford University Press, Oxford, Reissue edition, 2009. ISBN-13: 978-0199555017

Strathern P. *The Medici: Godfathers of the Renaissance,* Vintage, Random House, London, 2007 ISBN: 9780099522973

Tampa M, Sarbu I, Matei C, Benea V, Georgescu SR. 'Brief History of Syphilis' *Journal of Medicine and Life* 7(1),4–10; 2014 https://www.ncbi.nlm.nih.gov/pmc/articles/PMC3956094/ Accessed 9 May 2017

The New English Bible Oxford and Cambridge University Presses, 1961 (Old Testament) and 1970 (New Testament)

Thompson DV. *The Materials and Techniques of Medieval Painting* (1936) Reissued by Dover Publications Inc., New York, 1956 ISBN: 0-486-20327-1

Vandermassen G. 'Woman as Erotic Object: A Darwinian Inquiry into the Male Gaze' Exploring The Erotic, 3rd Global Conference, Salzburg, Austria, 2007. http://www.inter-disciplinary.net/ci/erotic /er3/Vandermassen%20paper.pdf Accessed 9 May 2017

Varey S, Chabrán R, Weiner D. (Eds.) *Searching for the Secrets of Nature: The Life and Works of Dr Francisco Hernandez*, Stanford University Press, Redwood City, CA, USA, 2002. ISBN: 9780804739641

Varnell P. 'Homosexuality in Renaissance Florence', *Windy City Times,* May 28, 1998 Available at: https://igfculturewatch.com/1998/05/28/ homosexuality-in-renaissance-florence/ Accessed 3 July 2017

Vasari G. *Lives of the Most Excellent Architects, Painters and Sculptors*. Published in 10 Volumes, Florence, 1550 and 1568, Volume 7: https://www.gutenberg.org/files/31845/31845-h/31845-h.htm Volume 10: http://www.gutenberg.org/files/33203/33203-h/33203-h.htm Both accessed 9 May 2017

Villalobos FL. de *Tratado sobre las pestiferas Bubas*, 1498. In: Gascoin G. *The Medical Works of Francisco Lopez de Villalobos,Translated with Commentary and Biography,* John Churchill & Sons, London, 1870. Available in translation at: https://archive.org/stream/ b21782052#page/n105/mode/2up Accessed 9 May 2017 and in the original Spanish at: http://bdh.bne.es/bnesearch/biblioteca/Sumario %20de%20la%20medicina%20;%20%20%20Tratado%20sobre %20las%20pestiferas%20bubas%20%20%20%20%20/qls/L%C3 %B3pez%20de%20Villalobos,%20Francisco%20(1473%201549)/ qls/bdh0000176839;jsessionid=E59A9633476EBB0B817074 D66855DB79 and http://bdh-rd.bne.es/viewer.vm?id=0000176839 &page=1 Accessed 26 June 2017

Von Hutten U. *De Morbo Gallico*, https://archive.org/stream/demorbo gallicotr00hutt#page/2/mode/2up Accessed 9 May 2017

Wainwright J. 'Telling Times: Revisiting *The Greeting*' In: Townsend C (Ed.) *The Art of Bill Viola*. Thames & Hudson Ltd, London, 2004. ISBN: 0-500-28472-5

Wiesner ME. *The Marvelous Hairy Girls: The Gonzales Sisters and Their Worlds,* Yale University Press, 2009. ISBN: 9780300127331

Wheatcroft A. *The Habsburgs. Embodying Empire*, Penguin, 1996. ISBN: 0-14-023634-1

Williams M. *The Story of Spain*, Santana Books, Málaga, Spain, 2000. ISBN: 84-89954-13-5

Wilson PH. *The Holy Roman Empire: a Thousand Years of Europe's History,* Penguin, Random House, London, 2016. ISBN: 9781846143182

Wind E. *Pagan Mysteries of the Renaissance,* Oxford University Press, Revised Edn. 1980. ISBN: 0-19-281295-5

Winder S. *Germania*, Farrar, Straus and Giroux, New York, 2010. ISBN: 9780374254001

Winder S. *Danubia,* Picador, Pan Macmillan, London, 2013. ISBN: 9780330522793

Woodford S. *The Cambridge Introduction to Art: Looking at Pictures,* Cambridge University Press,1983. ISBN: 0-521-28647-6

Youngs D. *The Life-cycle in Western Europe*, c.1300–c.1500 (Manchester Medieval Studies) Manchester University Press. 2006. ISBN: 9780719059155

Žižek S. *How to Read Lacan,* Granta Books, London, 2006. ISBN: 9781862078949

Index

Accademia Fiorentina 72-3, 103, 217
Adonis 158
affectless, in Mannerism 43, 79, 103, 171, 227
Agnadello, Battle of 40-1
Aigues-Mortes, Treaty of 99–100
Alberti, Leon Battista 134,
On Painting 74
alchemy 47, 69, 108, 129, 131-2, 185, 199, 237
Alfonso II, King of Naples 189
allegiance 42, 57, 100
allegory 18, 81–4, 171, 239
Allori 25, 181
Alessandro (1535-1607) 27–8, 74, 123, 154
Cristofano (died 1541) 27
Cristofano (1577-1621) 27
altarpiece 106, 114, 205
Alvarez di Toledo, Don Pedro di 79
Ambassadors, The, Hans Holbein 17, 110
Ambassador's Secret, The, John North 17
anguish 12, 176, 187, 191, 204, 219, 231, 233–4
Angoulême 97,111
anima, Jung 230
antibiotics 195
anus 26, 185, 190, 199
aphrodisiac 186
apple 82–3, 140, 142, 144, 147, 149–50, 154, 156–7, 168, 177–8, 214, 223–4, 226–7
apprenticeship, *artifice* of 74
Apuleius 218-9, 224
The Metamorphoses of Lucius 218
Machiavelli, version of 218
Raphael, frescos after 218
Aragon 51, 59–61
archetype, Jung 230–1
Arena Chapel 21
aristocracy 21, 203
Aristophanes, *The Birds* 161, 164
armature, in composition 138
arrogance 55, 81, 174
artifice 29–30, 36, 40, 50, 75–6, 79, 89, 93, 104, 107, 119, 129, 219
artist(s) 17, 19, 22–6, 29, 64, 72, 77, 83, 125, 163, 168, 170
arrow(s) 15, 88, 121, 144, 147–9, 153, 156, 158–9, 161–2, 167, 180, 185, 207, 212–4, 218, 223, 226–7
arthritis of hands127, 205
assassination in Renaissance Italy 30, 54–5, 87, 92, 94
astrology 16, 48, 69, 129, 132, 180, 199, 237
attributes 84, 150, 154, 159, 168–9, 178 180, 186, 188, 195, 204, 220, 222–3
aura, loss of 20–3, 142
Augsburg, Peace of 57, 61, 64

background 14, 25, 42, 59, 78, 81–4, 88, 122, 134–5, 185, 203, 214, 216–7, 220, 236
Bacon, Francis
Studies after Velazquez's Portrait of Pope Innocent X 234
balance of power 55, 59, 100
bald patches in syphilis 206
Balkans 42, 58, 62–3
barb 179, 226
Barbarossa 62
Bardi, U 181–3
Barolsky, P 208, 239–40
Basilica, Assisi, 21
St Peter's, Rome 45
Basso, Fortezza de 92, 95, 100
bathhouses 109, 194, 203
Beaucousin, Edouard 115
bee 180
bells 168
Bembo, Pietro 104, 212

Benjamin, W 19–20, 22, 139
The work of art in the age of mechanical reproduction 19
Berger, J
Ways of Seeing 19–20
bestiary 182
Bettini, Bartolomeo 90, 121
Bible 11, 32, 56, 67, 154, 198, 231
binder 127
Biondo, Michelangelo 169, 178, 187, 229–30
bisexuality 185, 217, 224
bismuth 201
bitterness 155, 188, 212, 217
Black Death 13, 26, 31
blasphemy 94, 197, 224
blindness 16, 221
Blind Fortune 165, 219
bone pain 196, 204
Bonfire of the Vanities 73
Bosch, L 163, 167–9, 172, 185, 188, 213–4
Botticelli 26, 87
Birth of Venus 117, 123, 157
Venus and Mars 117
bottom, Cupid's 141, 153, 185–7
Bouleau, C 137–9
The Painter's Secret Geometry 137
Boulogne 101, 111
Bradford 26, 65
breast(s) 14, 81, 117, 157, 159, 162, 173, 187–8, 207, 217, 225
Brock, M 164, 166, 173, 212
Bromham, AA 165, 178, 215
broncone 87, 168
Bronzino, Angelo (1503-71)
Accademia Fiorentina, and the 73, 103, 217
archival documents 25
background 12, 72–88
birth 25
court of Cosimo I, in 79
family, Allori 27, 74
insecurity detectable in works by 238
literature, knowledge of 84, 154–5, 170, 173, 175, 222, 229
name 11, 25–6
nickname 26, 181
paintings by:
Admiral Doria as Neptune 84, 123
Budapest Allegory 18, 88, 91, 124–5
Chapel of Eleonora 103, 184
Cosimo I de' Medici as Orpheus 85, 88, 118, 122
Eleonora of Toledo with her Son Giovanni 79, 87
Madonna and Child with Saints 18, 168
Nano Morgante 87, 123
Portrait of a Young Man 18, 78, 168
Venus, Cupid and Jealousy – ('The Budapest Allegory') 18
poetry 12, 26, 43, 72–3, 75, 85, 103–4, 107, 118–20, 152, 154–5, 216–7, 220
La padella 84
portraits by/of 12, 66, 75, 78, 105, 121, 171
Pisa, in 26, 103
support to Allori family 27, 74
training 73–78
Vasari on 25–6, 75–8, 89–91
workshop of 78, 123, 134, 154
brothel(s) 40, 113, 194
buttocks 14, 84, 122, 140, 144, 148–9, 159–60

Cambrai, League and Treaty of (*Paix des Dames*) 40, 99
camera lucida 81
Campana, Francesco 92
Caravaggio 84, 120
Boy bitten by a lizard 84
Cartoon 82, 90, 119, 125
L'Innocenntia del Bronzino 166
Castile 33, 59–60, 63, 65
Catalan language 68–70
catamite, Bronzino's imagined 119
Caterina de'Medici 182
Catherine of Aragon, Queen of England 51, 60–1
Caucasus 63
cautery 172, 201
Cebes, Theban Tablet of 82, 175, 179, 235
Cellini, Benvenuto 81, 102, 105, 111, 182, 192

Cennini, Cennino d'Andrea 74, 126, 129
Il libro dell'arte 74, 135
centrifugal forces 144–5, 148
centripetal forces 148
Ceresole, Battle of 101
Cervantes 63
Chaos 160–1, 168, 214
chancre, syphilitic 190, 193–5
chancroid 112, 197
Charles II, King of Spain 65
Charles V, Emperor (Charles of Ghent) 29, 552–3, 57–65, 68. 80, 95, 97–101, 160, 202, 206
abdicates 64
appearance 64–5
coronation 51
divides territories 40, 44, 58
elected Holy Roman Emperor 44, 51, 59–61
expels French from Milan 59
life in Retirement 64, 206
inheritance 58–9
invests Florence 52–3
marriage 61, 98
Ottomans, battles with 62–3
progeny 52–3, 57, 61–2, 80, 95–6
Plus Oultre 29, 62
sister, Eleanor of Portugal 99
Charles VIII, King of France 38, 189, 191, 194, 198
invades Italy 38
occupies Naples (1495) 189
occupies Rome 39
deposes Piero and Giovanni de' Medici 39
Chastity 108, 167, 174, 213
Chateaubriant, Francoise de 97
Chaucer 69
chemistry 131–2, 181
Cheney, I 163–4, 168, 186, 213, 220, 231
Chimaera of Arezzo 181–3
chimera 170, 173, 181, 183
Church, Roman Catholic 32–3, 37, 41, 45–6, 49, 51, 55–7, 61, 67–8, 83, 101, 133, 211, 234
Cibó, Cardinal 92
cities 30, 40, 42, 57, 65, 92, 101, 203
Claude, Queen of France 97, 99, 113, 122
clitoris 186
Cloaca 186
Cloth of Gold, The Field of the 98
coda 181
code(s) 11, 13, 16, 26, 133, 154, 210
Cohen, S 172, 178, 180, 186, 215, 237
Collective Unconscious 132, 230
Collège de France
colours
adulteration 126
alchemy, in 129–33
chemistry 125–9
manufacture 125–30, 134
preparation 125–30, 134
sources 125–29
symbolism 126, 132–3
Columbian Exchange 34
Columbian hypothesis 197–9, 202
Columbus, Christopher 33–4, 197–8
comedy 69, 183
commissions for paintings 23, 29, 36, 43, 79–80, 85–6, 89–91, 103, 105, 108, 116, 119, 126, 129, 145
Conciliar Movement 33
conclave 32, 49
Concordat 44, 98
consanguinity 65, 173
construction lines 137, 139
contado, the Florentine 30, 53, 93
context, importance of 16, 20, 22, 75, 83, 90, 146, 150, 179, 204, 215, 234, 238–9
Converterite, Convent of the 93
Conway, J F 188, 204–8, 214–6
Copernicus 67
De revolutionibus orbium coelestium 34–5
Commentariolus 34
Cook, C 207–8, 215
corruption 35, 91, 93
Council of Trent 33, 56, 195, 211
Counter-Reformation 33, 56–7, 73, 78, 211
Cox-Rearick, J 182
craftsmanship 29, 116

Cranach, Lucas the Elder
Cupid complaining to Venus 181
Venus and Cupid With A Honeycomb 181
creation 119, 130–1, 214, 229
Crépy, Peace of 101
crime 54, 63
critics, influence of 22, 72, 76–7
crossword puzzle 11, 239
Crown Lands 58–9, 61–2, 64
Cruelty 174
culture 14, 16, 33, 93, 133, 146, 176, 216
Cupid 159–62
androgyny 122, 159–62
arrows 15, 88, 121. 144, 148, 153, 156, 158–62
attributes 15, 88, 121–2, 135–7, 140–1, 143–45, 149–50, 153, 159–62
Christian ethics, interpretation in 161
disarmed 158
mythology 15, 119, 135, 157–62
quiver q.v.
sexuality 15, 90, 115, 120, 145–7, 150, 152–3, 158, 159–62
symbolism 157–9
curtain 115, 134, 149, 153, 163–8, 207, 211–6, 219, 221, 225, 231, 233–4, 237–8
cushion 142, 149, 154, 159, 186, 215

Dante 69, 104, 119, 121, 173, 178
das Ding, Freud 235
Dauphin 98–9
Death 13, 26, 31, 236–7
deceit 11–2, 161, 170–1, 176, 181, 207, 213–5, 217–8, 228
deception 170, 172, 184, 186, 218, 223
deciphering 133, 221
Delius, Frederick 194
desire 72, 158–9, 161, 169, 217, 222, 227, 232, 235–7
despair 19, 176, 187, 213, 225, 231, 234, 236
destruction 35, 52, 175, 191, 206, 214
diadem, Venus's 157, 167, 223–5, 227
diagonal, painting structure in 140, 144, 164, 184, 225
Diet 57, 61
diplomacy 37, 40, 61
disegno 76, 117
Disney, eyes infantilised in 82
DNA 47
Don Juan of Austria 61, 63
doves 14, 140–1, 144, 146, 149, 154, 185,–6, 212, 214, 223–4, 237
drapery, paintings in 85, 117, 121, 184–5, 217
duck, American and Greylag 177
duplicity 170, 173, 181, 221, 227
Dürer, Albrecht 194, 196
dwarfs in European courts 85–6

Eastlake, Charles 115, 148
Echidna 172, 182, 207
economy 52, 68
Ego 167, 223, 227, 230, 233–4, 238
Eleanor of Portugal 99
Eleonora, Chapel of 79, 103, 105–6, 114, 118, 184, 205
Eleonora de Toledo 79–81, 85, 87, 96, 100, 103, 131
Elizabeth I, Queen of England 81, 206
England 13–4, 31, 33, 35, 42, 47, 59, 61, 65, 69, 81, 83, 98, 101, 114, 194, 204
Envy 18, 88, 180, 187–8, 204, 212, 218
epidemic 31, 68, 194, 197–8, 220
Erasmus of Rotterdam 38, 68, 107, 117, 189, 192, 195
Eros 158–61, 237
Erotes 157–8, 169
erotic art 117
Error 163, 165, 176
Etampes, Duchess of (Anne de Pisseleu) 97, 101
ethnographic dazzle 16
Etruscan(s), Cosimo's interest in 104, 181–2
European Parliament 107
European Union (EU) 45, 70
Eve 178, 213
excavation of Chimaera of Arezzo 181–2
exile of Medici 39–40, 53
existential threats 36–7
eyes, in paintings 77, 82, 143, 163–4, 183, 187, 204, 225

famine 30, 31, 35, 190, 231, 234
Farnese 56, 101, 106
Fear 43, 223, 226, 229
feathers 161, 171, 174, 176–7
Ferdinand of Aragon 39, 58–60
Ferdinand, Emperor 57–8, 61, 64
femme fatale 228
Fernel, Jean Francois (1497-1558)
  attends Caterina de'Medici 47–8
  life 48, 199, 215
  rejects mercury 113, 200
  treats Francis I 113
Ferronière, La Belle 113
Festivals 28, 30, 74
finger-nail 205
Fisher, W 140, 160
flag 29
fleur(s)-de-lis 86–7, 102
Florence
  in sixteenth century 11, 25–36, 39, 70, 73, 91–6, 99, 100–1, 103–8, 118, 120–2, 159, 177, 182, 210, 220, 226
  crime 54, 92
  diet during siege 52
  disease 31–2, 35
  economy 30–1
  extent of its territory 30
  marriage, age at 93
  mortality 31, 36
  plague, outbreaks of 26, 31
  population 30–1
  Reformation, the in 33, 38, 56
  siege of 30, 52
  succession crisis 48
  threats of war 35
flowers 13, 88, 132, 146, 154, 186, 191, 228
Folly 169, 212
Fontainebleau, Palace of 105, 108–9, 111, 114, 163, 184
foot (in painting) 140–1, 149, 169–70, 173, 193, 207, 212, 218, 223
foreground 134, 153, 165, 213–4, 216, 220
Foucault, M 15–6
Fracastoro, Giorlamo 28, 195–6, 202, 206
  Syphilis sive morbus Gallicus 195
  De contagione et contagiosis morbis 195–6
  Plus Oultre 29
France 18–9, 38–9, 41–2, 44, 46–7, 49, 54–5, 59–61, 70, 80, 86, 91–1, 95, 97–9, 101, 105, 107–9, 112, 114, 116, 132, 182–3, 189, 194, 205, 239
Francis I, King of France (1494-1547)
  abscesses 110–11
  alchemy, interest in 108, 132, 237
  ambition v. Habsburgs 49, 59, 95, 97–8, 100, 108, 224
  appearance 106
  astrology, interest in 132, 137
  bids for imperial crown 49, 59, 98
  captured at Pavia 59, 98
  character 97, 102–6
  chateaux building 107
  children 62, 98
  court of 102–7, 112, 180
  death 111–2
  education 97
  health 98
  hedonistic life-style 103,106
  hostage in Milan 49, 59, 98
  illnesses 98, 109–14, 199, 206
  London Allegory, and
    Chateaubriant, Francoise de 97
    Etampes, Duchess of (Anne de Pisseleu) 101
    marriage to Claude 97, 99, 113
    marriage to Eleanor of Portugal 99
    mistresses 97, 106, 113
    mother, Louise de Valois 99, 110
    patronage of the arts 102
    philandering 97, 106, 113
    respect for Catherine de'Medici 102
    Royal progresses 106–7
    salamander 107–8, 179, 222
    signs Treaty of Madrid 98–9
    sister, Marguerite de Valois 97
    sons held hostage in Milan 98
  syphilis 104, 110–2, 226
  venereal disease 112
Francis II, King of France (1544-60) 57
  London Allegory, and 182–3, 222
Fraud 90, 135, 155, 163, 173, 176, 181

Fraude, la 155, 163, 165, 173, 181, 212, 215
Freud, Sigmund 162, 235–7
Froda 173
Fugger 59, 192, 202
Fun 152, 219, 223–4, 231, 238, 240

Galen(ic) 69, 199
Gama, Vasco da 34
Garbo, Raffaellino del 25
Gaston, R 118–9, 154–5, 158–9, 178, 183, 216–7, 222
Gelosia, la 155, 187
gender 163, 165, 187, 221–2
General Paralysis of the Insane (GPI) 194, 201, 207
genes
- dominant 65
- recessive 64

genitalia 87, 117, 180, 185, 190–1, 195
geometry 137–8
gesso 125, 135
gifts 79, 181
girl 22, 82–3, 133, 166, 171, 173, 175–6, 180, 184, 205, 208, 216, 229
Giuocco, *il* 155, 169, 215
Glover, M 152, 237
God 32–3, 36, 38, 40, 43, 77–8, 94, 98, 102 102, 108, 121, 142, 201, 224–5. 232–3
- Greek 84, 157–8, 160–1, 172, 195, 214
- Pagan 109

Goddess 130, 156–7, 162, 172, 186, 230
God the Father 225
Golden Section 142–4
gonorrhoea 111–2, 199
Gonzales sisters 86
goose, Greylag 177
gossip 66, 112–3
Gould, SJ 212
Graham-Dixon, A 208
Granvelle, Nicolas Perrenot de 106
Great Work 130–2, 185
ground 125, 128, 135, 138
guaiacum 201–2
Grünewald, M
- *Isenheim Altarpiece, The* 205

Guicciardini, Francesco 92
guild 27
gumma 190–1, 195–6, 201, 206

Habsburg 29, 47, 55, 58–66, 98, 100–1, 224
- Dynasty 39
- Crown Lands 58, 61, 64
- genes 47
- jaw 64–5

hair 26, 62, 86, 88, 96, 111, 117, 122, 163–4, 168, 171, 176, 178, 183, 187, 195–6, 200, 204–6, 217–8, 239
hands (painted) 77, 122, 171–2, 174, 205, 227
headache 192–3, 204
health education 215, 227
Healy, M 167, 173, 206–8, 215, 225
heliocentricity 17, 35, 67
Henri II, King of France (1519-59) 47, 62, 80, 98–100
- consummation of marriage 47,112
- death 47
- hostage in Milan 98
- hypospadias and chordee 47–8
- marriage to Caterina de' Medici 47
- mistresses 47
- slogan 62

Henry VIII, King of England 18, 49, 51, 59–61, 81, 98, 101, 111–2
Hesiod 157–8, 160–1, 172, 182, 207
HIV-AIDS 31, 220
Hockney, David 81
Holbein, Hans the Younger
- *The Ambassadors* 17–8
- *The Body of the Dead Christ in the Tomb* 205
- *Portraits of Henry VIII* 81

Holy Roman Empire
- constituents of 37, 57
- Diets 57
- Electors 57
- end of 37
- French resistance to 61, 95, 101–2
- governance 57, 61

homoerotic(ism) 14, 73, 140, 211
homosexuality 26, 93, 150, 159, 172, 238
honeycomb 167, 171–3, 180–1, 212, 214–5, 217, 223, 228

horoscope 167
hospitals 203
hourglass 15, 135, 146, 166–7, 234, 237
hubris 219
humanism 17, 44, 107
Hungary 42, 58, 62
Hunt, William Holman
  The Hireling Shepherd 82–3
Hutten, U Von 192–3, 200, 202, 205–6
Hope, C 153, 163–5, 168–9, 171, 214, 216
Hus, Jan van 33
hybrid(s) 86, 170, 173, 175, 179, 205

iconograph(ic)y 151, 154, 187
identity 50, 117, 137, 150, 156, 165–6, 184, 210, 221, 232–3
imperial crown 64, 98
inbreeding 65
incest(uous) 15, 147, 150, 158, 160, 162, 172–4, 178, 185, 217, 222–4, 226, 238
individuation 132, 230, 234
indulgences 32, 45, 56, 192
infatuation 158, 164, 226–7
injury 169
innocence 88, 166–7, 213
instinct 146, 227, 236–7
internet 66, 181
interpretation of texts 14, 36, 110
invenzione 120
Isabella, Queen of Castile 33, 39, 59–60, 96
Italian Wars, the 39, 189

Jarman, Derek
  Sebastiane 70
Jealousy 18, 88, 90, 135, 155, 187–8, 204, 208, 212–3, 225, 231, 238
Jest 169, 212
Joanna the Mad, Queen of Castile 58
Judaism 236
Jung, Carl 132, 230, 235–6
Jupiter 106, 197, 215

Keach, W 162, 213
Keeper of Language 233
Kilpatrick, RS 165, 218–9
kiss 121, 141, 145, 158, 169, 218, 225, 234
Klein, M 236
Knowledge 174, 176

laboratory, alchemical of Medici 131–2
l'affaire des placards 101, 107
Lamia(s) 172–3, 207, 212, 226, 228
language 13–4, 29, 37, 68–70, 104, 118, 134, 209, 220, 225
lapis lazuli 116, 126–7
Last Days 36, 197
latent period, syphilitic 190–1, 196, 199, 207
Latent thought, Freud 219
Lateran Council, 5th 36, 46
Latin language 28, 68–70, 97, 118, 185–6, 190, 195, 218
laudanum 69
laugh, about *London Allegory 239*
laurel 87, 153, 157, 164, 167–8, 177, 179, 186, 201, 207, 212–4, 222, 231, 233–4, 238
Law 231, 233, 236
Law of the Father 231
Leagues
  Cambrai 40
  Cognac 49, 99
  Holy 39, 41–2
  Venice 39, 189
lechery 159, 162, 176, 213, 215
Lepanto, Battle of 36, 42, 61, 63
leprosy 113, 169, 197–8, 230
Lives of the most excellent Italian Architects, Painters and Sculptors (Lives of the Artists)
    First Edition (1550) 28–9
    Second Edition (1568) 25, 29
Levey, M 153, 159,163–4, 166, 169, 212–3
life expectancy 36
lion 84, 130, 171–2, 174–5, 178, 182, 228
lips 14, 178, 190–1, 195
literature 18, 44, 75, 84,106, 130, 154–5, 158, 170, 173, 175, 194, 210, 214, 216, 222, 229
locusts 178

London Allegory, The
ambiguity 171–2, 188
armature 138
border 121, 139, 149, 185, 231, 237
cartoon119, 125
changes to 90, 119, 150, 165, 172, 179
colours 22, 134, 139, 221, 237
commission 90–1, 105, 114, 116, 119
construction lines 139
copy 22, 163, 184
depersonalisation in 162
description of
by others 153, 155, 172–88
by Vasari 90–1, 135, 153, 155, 181, 183, 210, 216
details 91, 146–8, 184, 216, 223, 227–8
diagonals 140, 144, 164, 184, 225
dimensions 15, 22, 138, 150
drapery 184–5, 217
eroticism 14, 114, 119, 148, 151, 160, 239
geometry 138, 150
iconography 187
interpretation 16, 84, 91, 110, 114, 119, 133, 1365–7, 151, 154–6, 163, 165–6, 170, 176, 178–9, 181, 185, 210–3, 215, 21–20, 222–3, 226, 234, 235, 239
pentimenti 88, 124, 148, 152, 216
planks of wood, construction from 124–5
precedents 156, 162, 210, 226, 236
preparation 123, 125, 221
provenance 114
reproductions of, deficiencies in 19, 139
restorations 115, 148–9, 211
revisions by Bronzino 88, 114, 118, 150
sources in literature 18
support 15, 116, 123–5, 136–7, 149
Los Reyes Catholicos 59
Louise de Valois 97
Louis XI, King of France 86, 102
Louis XII, King of France 97
Louis XIV, King of France 148, 163
Low Countries 64, 101
Lucca 38
lust 12, 42, 84, 162, 176, 186, 197, 209, 213, 219, 224, 226–8, 235
Luther, Martin 32–3, 37, 45–6, 56–7, 61, 67, 192
Luxury 163, 176, 211, 213
lymphogranuloma venereum 112, 197
lyric poetry 12

Machiavelli 43, 60, 218
Madrid, Treaty of 98–9
madrigals, in Cosimo's court 104
magno anno 214
malaria 31, 50, 64, 80, 96, 110, 203
maniera 75, 117, 122
Manifest content, Freud 219
Mannerism 73, 76, 79, 81, 103, 108–9, 120, 134, 152, ,211, 224
Mantel, H 15
Marignano, Battle of 98
Marguerite de Valois 47, 97, 110
marriage 27, 41, 46–7, 56, 60, 64–6, 79, 96, 102, 112, 174, 182
Mary Rose, sinking of 101
Mary Tudor 61
masks 14, 121, 141–2, 145–6, 149, 154, 164, 183–5, 204, 207, 212, 214–5, 217, 220–1
Maximilian I, Emperor 39,58, 64, 98
Medici
heraldic arms and symbols of
broncone 87, 168
fleur-de-lys 87, 102
laurel 87, 168, 177, 179, 186, 222
palle 86, 157, 168, 179, 220, 222
Alessandro de' (1512-37)
assassination 28, 54–5, 87, 91–2
parentage 48
rules Florence 49, 51, 53
Caterina de', Queen of France (1519-89)
infertility 47, 112
progeny 47–8, 96, 182
Regency 47, 102
religious wars in France and 51
St Bartholomew's Day Massacre and 35

Cosimo de', Grand Duke of Tuscany (1519-74)
alchemy, interest in 69, 131, 237
archaeology, interest in 104
asserts his authority in Florence 54–5
Cellini goes to France 102
character 55, 91–5, 104–5, 150
children 80, 96, 103, 171
their deaths 80
choice of Bronzino for *London Allegory* 118–9
chosen to rule Florence 28, 54, 91
Etruscans, interest in 104, 182
excavations of Etruscan artefacts 182
foreign policy 94
gifts of paintings 79
horoscope 167
marriages 79, 96
modernises civil service in Florence 103
mother's influence, his 91–2
moves to Palazzo Pitti 103
patronage of arts in Florence 103–5
targets immorality 93–4
unpopularity 94
Eleanora de' (Eleanora of Toledo) (1522-62) 79–81, 85, 87, 96, 100, 103, 131
Francesco de', Grand Duke of Tuscany (1541-87) 80, 96, 103, 131
Giovanni de', Pope Leo X (1475-1521) see under 'Popes'
Giuliano de', Duke of Nemours (1479-1516) 43
Giulio de', Pope Clement VII (1478-1534) see under 'Popes'
Ippolito de' (1511-35) 48–9, 51, 53
death of 53
Lorenzo de' (The Magnificent), (1449-92) 41, 80, 87, 91, 93
Lorenzo de', Duke of Urbino (1492-1519) 43, 46–8, 102
Lorenzino de' (1514-47) 54, 91–2
Piero de', 'The Unfortunate' (1471-1503) 39, 43, 80
medicine 32, 48, 69, 109, 124, 131–2, 201
mercury
Fernel on 113, 200
in treatment of syphilis
and other skin complaints 113, 194, 197–8, 200–3
poisoning 113, 127, 205–6, 226
source of 127, 202
toxicity 113, 127, 200
Michelangelo 28–9, 40, 52, 72, 75–7, 93, 105, 119–22, 160, 162, 212–3, 216–7, 224
Doni Tondo 120, 224
drawings in Chapel of San Lorenzo, Florence 122
Pieta 120, 224
Sistine Chapel frescos 121–2, 124
Middle East 34, 63, 198
Milan 38–41, 44, 49, 59, 95, 97, 100, 102
Mirandola, Battle of (1511) 41
misogyny 178, 229
Moffitt, J 162, 173–7, 185
Mohács, Battle of (1526) 42, 49, 58, 62
moral hazard 234
morality 72, 94, 216, 224, 226, 233, 239
Morgante (Braccio di Bartolommeo) 85–7, 104, 123
motto 29, 44, 86, 117
mouth(s) 64–6, 127, 143, 153, 187, 190, 199–200, 202, 204, 206, 225
Mühlberg, Battle of 61
murder in Renaissance Italy 44, 50, 54–5
music in Cosimo's court 102–4
myrtle 114, 148, 186, 201
mythology 15, 28, 84, 133, 154, 156, 159–60, 174–5, 215, 236

Naples 37–40, 48–9, 51, 54, 59, 80, 96, 184, 189–90, 194, 197–8
Naples, Viceroy of 80, 96
National Gallery, London 11–2, 18–9, 21, 77–8, 84, 115, 117, 125, 138–9, 148, 163, 181, 188
nemesis 62, 219
nervous system 48, 190, 192–4
networks 66
neurosyphilis 203
news 19, 55, 66, 112, 218

nicknames of artists 26
Night 161, 163–4, 166, 168, 188, 207, 214
Nineteen Eighty-four 228
Ninety-five Theses, The 32
nipple 115, 140, 144, 148, 153, 157, 206–7, 225, 228
nocturnal pain 195
non plus ultra 28
nude 14, 77, 79, 84, 87, 90, 109, 117, 121, 135, 145, 147, 152, 155, 157, 160, 211, 216, 222, 224

Oblivion 163–5, 168, 214–6, 220, 237
Oedipus 174, 178, 225, 233
offensive
  to clergymen and others 115, 211, 226
  to Francis 226
Old Father Time 225
Onestà, (Office of Decency) 93
ophthalmia 192
orgasm 237
Orpheus 85, 88, 118, 122
Orvieto 50–1
Ottomans 36, 38, 42, 49, 53, 58, 61–4, 84, 100–2
Ovid 118–9, 161–2, 213, 219, 224
  Metamorphoses 117
Oxford Movement 83

paedophilia 185
Paget, Lord Uxbridge 23
pain 32, 69, 110, 121, 136, 146, 155, 164, 169, 192–3, 196, 204, 212–3, 215, 217, 223, 234, 238
paint, preparation of 125–31
Paix des Dames (Treaty of Cambrai) 99
Palazzo
  della Signoria 94, 103
  Medici 103
  Pitti 103
  Vecchio 79, 86, 103–4, 118, 131, 181
  Studiolo 131
palle 86, 157, 168, 179, 220, 222
Panciatichi, Bartolomeo 105, 113
Panofsky, E 156, 159, 163, 166, 169, 171, 184, 211–2, 224
papacy 37, 39–41, 43, 45–6, 49, 51, 55, 80, 95
Papal States 37, 46, 49, 63
Paracelsus 69, 129, 132, 179, 199–200, 202, 237
paraphilia 224
Paris 101–2, 105, 107–8, 111, 115, 122, 156
Parker, D 216, 220
passioni de amore 135, 155, 214
patricide 225
patron 28, 73, 89, 103, 105, 107, 118–9, 123, 126, 150, 203, 219
Pavia, Battle of 49, 59, 98
Peace of Augsburg 57, 61
peacock 130, 152, 237
Peacock's Tail 130–1, 237
Peasants' War 35, 59
penicillin, in treatment of syphilis 190, 201, 203, 220
penis 84, 117, 157–8, 185, 228
pentimenti 85, 88, 124, 148, 152, 216
periphery 134, 140, 146
Perry, Grayson 26
personification 78, 156, 170, 188, 211, 220, 227–8, 233
Persuasion 172
perversity 217
pestilence 35
Peter the Great 86
Petrarch 72–3, 103–4, 119, 121, 167, 180, 212, 216
phallic symbol 84, 158, 185
Phillip of Burgundy 60
Philip the Handsome 58
Philosopher's Stone, the 70, 129, 131
Piero della Francesca 138, 142–3
  Baptism of Christ 138, 143
pigeon loft, Francis's escape from 41
pigments
  properties 74, 116, 126–8, 134
  sources 126–8
Pilgrim's Progress 81
Pillars of Hercules 28–9
Pisa 26, 30, 38–9, 41, 100, 103, 132
plague 13, 26, 31–2, 50–2, 74, 97, 108, 111, 178, 195, 203, 231
plants 76, 124, 126, 143, 154, 201–2
Plas Newydd 23
Pleasure 90, 135, 155, 169, 181, 212, 217

Plus Oultre 29
Plus Ultra 28, 62
Poitiers, Diane de' 47–8
Pontormo, Jacopo 25–7, 73–4, 77–9, 90, 93, 105, 108, 120–2, 211, 217, 237
  Deposition 122
  drawing of Hermaphrodite 122
  Joseph with Jacob in Egypt 77–8, 137
  Venus and Cupid (after Michelangelo) 121, 184–5, 213
  Visitation, The 74
Popes
  Alexander VI (Borgia) 38, 40, 189, 194
  Clement VII (Medici) 49–51, 53, 55, 99, 102–3
    arranges marriage of Caterina de' Medici 47, 102
    attends lecture on Commentariolus 34
    character 49
    crowns Charles V 51
    flees Rome for Orvieto 50
    Leo's Viceroy in Florence 48–9
  Gregory XIII
    reacts to St Bartholomew's Day Massacre 35
  Leo X (Medici) 80, 102
    character 43–6
    commissions painting from Raphael for Claude 98, 108, 122
    finances 45
    installs Lorenzo de'Medici as Duke of Urbino 46
    Latin language 63
    life style 46–7
    poisoning 55
    strategic challenges 45
  Paul III (Farnese) 56, 96, 99, 101, 195
  Paul IV 56
  Pius IV (Medici) 55, 95
  Pius V 55, 57
  Julius II (della Rovere) 32, 40, 44–6, 192, 194
pornography 153, 160
pose 84, 120, 141, 149, 157, 159, 168, 185, 212, 224
Prato 42, 92
Prayer Book Rebellion (1549) 35
precedents for elements of *London Allegory* 120, 156, 162, 226, 236
Pre-Raphaelite Brotherhood 22
Pride 85, 174
printmakers 109
privacy, lack of in 16th C. society 112
promiscuity 229–30
propaganda 29, 43, 78–81, 106, 152
prostitution 93, 190
Protestantism 17, 33, 55–7, 61, 95, 100, 102
Providence 17
Psyche 158, 218–9, 232
psychology 69, 129, 132
Psychomachia 213, 231
public health 31, 194, 215
punishment 40, 42–3, 45, 56, 94, 157, 197, 203, 226
pus, syphilitic 111, 195
putto 14–5, 118, 122, 153, 168, 207, 217, 222, 240

quality 76, 89, 109–10, 117, 123, 126–7, 213
quicksilver 200
quiver 15, 121, 140, 147, 149, 159, 161–2, 185–6, 212, 218, 223

Raphael 28, 30, 45, 75, 218
  Holy Family of Francis I 108, 122
  Madonna 98
rash, skin 190–1, 196–7, 204–5
Ravenna, Battle of (1512) 41
Reconquista 59
rectum 185, 190
Reformation 33, 37, 42, 46, 56–7, 73, 78, 192, 211
Regensburg, Colloquy at (1541) 33, 95
relationship 26–7, 75, 81, 83, 86, 95–7, 101–2, 116, 120, 137, 140–1, 143, 146, 150, 161–2, 169, 178, 187, 212, 220, 223–7, 230, 233, 236
religion 32–3, 36–7, 52, 57, 67, 101

Renaissance 14, 26–30, 36–8, 48, 70, 74–6, 78, 84–6, 93, 106, 117, 120, 126, 128–9, 132, 134, 136, 138, 142, 146, 153–4, 157–9, 161, 163, 170, 173, 175, 181, 186, 215–6, 218–20, 222, 224, 236, 239
reprisals 35, 53
reproductions, deficiencies of 19–23, 139–40, 146
reptile 171
Republic of Christ 51
Revealer 166, 213
revulsion 91, 159
Reynolds, Sir Joshua 128
riddle 11–2, 89, 114, 117–8, 120, 147, 154, 174–5, 207, 210, 219, 221, 227, 240
River of Love 207
Rome 21, 26, 28, 30, 32, 34–7, 39–40, 44–6, 48, 50–2, 61, 80, 83, 92, 95, 99, 101, 107–8, 121–2, 181, 186
Room 101 228
rose petals 140, 143, 158, 168, 223
Royal Progresses 106–7
Rudolf II, Emperor 85
rupia 204
Ruskin, John 15, 22, 77, 82

Sack of Rome 35, 51, 95, 99
sadomasochism 185, 217
salamander 107–8, 179, 222, 228, 237
salivation 200–1, 206
salvation 17, 56
sarsaparilla 201
Sarto, Andrea del 28, 73, 108
Saturn 167. 175, 197, 215, 237
Savonarola 38–9, 51, 73
Saxony 35
  Elector of 57, 61
scaffold 138, 140–2, 144–5, 148, 150, 184, 221
scale 139–40, 190, 208
scales, tortoise 171, 173, 177–9, 222
Schiele, E 205
School of Fontainebleau 109
scoptophilia 145, 162, 222
Scorpio 180, 197, 215
scorpion 169, 178, 180, 200, 215, 228–9, 237
sculpture(s) 29, 76, 78, 85–7, 99, 106, 108, 117, 119, 122, 147, 157, 216
seductive 83, 181, 218, 226, 229
seductress 213, 228, 230
Self, the 230, 232–4
self-control 162, 176, 235
selfish gene 47
Selve, Georges, Bishop of Lavaur 17–8, 110
serpent 172–3, 175, 178, 180, 182, 217, 237
sex 26, 82, 146, 153, 158, 168–70, 180, 192, 194, 223, 230–2, 236, 238
Sforza, Caterina 131
Sforza, Duke 97–8
sieges
  Florence 42, 52–3
  Magdeburg 35
  Rome 35, 39–40, 50–1, 95, 99
  Siena 100
shadowed areas in the *London Allegory* 134, 140, 146, 159, 171, 173, 188, 205, 225, 227–8
Shadow, Venus's 229
Shakespeare 11, 82, 209, 219, 239
sin 196, 232, 235, 238
sinister 156, 171
skin 112–3, 125, 127, 156, 164, 179, 190–4, 197–8, 200, 204–5
Smith, G 172–3, 182, 187–8, 205, 212–3, 217, 228
snake(s) 52, 88, 155, 173–4, 178, 182, 228
sodomy 26, 40, 73, 84, 93–4, 185
sonnet(s) 72, 74, 103, 160, 209, 217, 219
sources available to Bronzino 77, 119, 154–5, 164, 170, 179,210, 219, 229
Spain 19, 29, 34, 38–9, 41–2, 47, 57–64, 68, 80, 98, 101, 129, 177, 189
sphinx(es) 11, 172–8, 182, 207–8, 221, 226, 228–9
Spirituali 33, 95
St Bartholomew's Day Massacre 35

St Denis 61, 203
St Paul 231–2, 235
starvation 52
status of *artifice* 29–30, 36, 76
sting 149, 152, 171–3, 175, 178–81, 208, 212, 215, 217, 231, 237
Strife 185, 188, 214
Strozzi, Filippo 92, 100
Strozzi, Piero 100
succession crisis 48
suckling 157, 191, 207
Sudoku 11, 239
Suleiman 'The Magnificent' 62, 100–1
sumptuary laws 51, 93
Super-ego 233, 236
supernatural 17
support for painting 15, 116, 123–5, 136–7, 149
sweating 199–200, 202
sweating sickness, The 31
sweetness 103, 180, 188, 212, 217
symbols 82, 86, 130, 132, 148, 154, 169, 185, 206, 211, 215, 221, 235
syphilis 32, 46, 110, 112–3, 188, 191, 196–8, 203–8, 210, 215, 217, 220, 222, 226, 237
  astrology and 195
  illustrations of 194, 201
  malignant 196
  modern, symptoms and signs 190–1, 198, 201, 206
  names for 112, 189–90, 192, 195
  origins of 189–90, 192
  16th C., symptoms and signs 104, 110–1, 113, 194–5, 198–9, 201, 206
  treatment of 68, 111, 113, 172, 190
syphilides 191, 194, 201, 203, 206

tail(s) 130–1, 149–50, 152, 171–5, 178–80, 208, 231, 237
teeth 111. 127, 146, 164, 178, 200, 205–6
text 13–4, 18, 68, 75, 78, 118, 135, 175, 198, 212
Thanatos 236
theology 17, 37, 133
thorn 146, 158, 169–70, 187, 193, 207, 213, 218, 223
Time 15, 91, 115, 120–1, 135, 139–41, 145, 147–9, 153, 157, 163–8, 175, 177, 186–7, 207, 211–21, 224–5, 231, 233–8
Titian 40, 105, 120, 123
  Venus of Urbino 153
toe 122, 140, 149, 184
Toledo, Eleonora de (see Eleonora)
tongue 64–5, 115, 148, 153, 158, 164, 169, 178, 187, 217–8, 227
Tonks, Henry 23
tortoise 86–7, 177–9, 222
toxicity 113, 200
tragedy 54, 183
transgression 215, 217, 224, 227–8, 232, 235–7
Tratado sobre las pestiferas Bubas 68, 191
Trent, Council of (1545-63) 33, 56, 195, 211
Treponema pallidum 198
Triumph of Venus 212–3, 219
Truth 163, 166, 175, 211
tuberculosis 31, 98, 111
Tunis 53, 62, 99
Turkey 63
Tuscan language 104

Uffizi 28, 79, 103, 117, 120, 122, 153
ulceration 195, 200
Unconscious, the 132, 148, 227, 230–3, 235, 238
Unitarian hypothesis 198

Vagina 160, 185, 190, 208, 228, 238
vagina dentata 228, 238
Valois dynasty 47, 59, 97, 102
  friendly links with Medici 47, 102, 237
Valois, Elizabeth 47, 61, 80
Varchi, Benedetto 72, 103, 118–9, 155, 187–8, 212, 216–7
  Sulla Gelosia 212

Vasari, Giorgio (1511-74) 25–6, 28–30, 36, 73–6, 78–9, 89–90, 103, 105–6, 114, 116, 121, 131, 135, 153, 1556, 163, 169, 173, 181–4, 187, 210–1, 214–6
  alchemical scenes in Studiolo 131
  Allegory of Justice 184
  career 28
  describes the *London Allegory* 90–1, 135, 155, 183
  designs Uffizi 28, 103
  Frescos in Sala Regina, Vatican 36, 63
  Lives of the Artists 25, 28–9
  Opinion of Bronzino 75–6, 89–90
venereal disease/infection 112–3, 156, 180, 193–4, 197, 203, 208, 215, 223, 226
Venice 30, 37, 39–41, 49, 54, 63, 81, 92, 105, 123, 175, 184, 189
Venus 15, 18, 88, 90, 114–5, 117, 120–3, 130, 135–7, 140–50, 152–3, 155–62, 164, 166–72, 174, 178, 180–81, 183–7, 194, 205–6, 211–39
Verbena 146, 186, 228
Verdi, Giuseppe
  Don Carlos 80
  Rigoletto 54
vernacular 68–9, 118, 155
Vettori, Francesco 92
vice 121, 152, 161, 183–4, 207, 211, 215
Vienna 42, 62–4
Viceroy 48, 80, 96
Villalobos, Francisco de 68, 192, 205
  Tratado sobre las pestiferas Bubas 191
Vinci, Leonardo da 28, 75, 108, 134, 142–3, 179
  The Battle of Anghiari 122
  Mona Lisa 108
Viola, Bill
  The Greeting 74
viper 169, 178, 180, 187, 214
Virtue 121, 164, 166, 168, 176, 184, 213
Vitelli, Alessandro 92
void 77, 122, 140, 144, 161, 164, 167, 214, 232, 235, 237
voyeurism 145, 147, 153, 160, 162, 166, 170, 220, 222

Wagner-Jauregg, J 203
Wellington, Duke of 23
Whistler, James Abbott MacNeill
  Nocturne in Black and Gold 22
Whistler, Rex 23
whoredom 178
wigs 196, 204
wings 15, 157, 161, 174, 176–7, 218
Wolsey, Cardinal 49, 110
wooden panels/planks 14–5, 123, 125, 149
words 13, 185, 209, 216
Worms, Diet of 57, 61
Wounding of Venus 162, 213
Wycliffe, John 33